Group Counseling and Psychotherapy With Children and Adolescents

Theory, Research, and Practice

Group Counseling and Psychotherapy With Children and Adolescents

Theory, Research, and Practice

Zipora Shechtman

Routledge
Taylor & Francis Group
New York   London

Routledge is an imprint of the
Taylor & Francis Group, an informa business

Routledge
Taylor & Francis Group
270 Madison Avenue
New York, NY 10016

Published in Great Britain by
Routledge
Taylor & Francis Group
2 Park Square
Milton Park, Abingdon
Oxon OX14 4RN

© 2007 by Taylor & Francis Group, LLC
Originally published by Lawrence Erlbaum Associates
Routledge is an imprint of Taylor & Francis Group

Printed in the United States of America on acid-free paper
10 9 8 7 6 5 4 3 2
International Standard Book Number-13: 978-0-8058-5686-6 (Softcover)
Library of Congress catalog number: 2006013779
Cover Design by Tomai Maridou

Library of Congress Cataloging-in-Publication Data

Catalog record is available from the Library of Congress

Visit the Taylor & Francis Web site at
http://www.taylorandfrancis.com

and the Routledge Web site at
http://www.routledge.com

Dedicated with love to my family:
My husband Dan, for setting standards of excellence.
My children, Tamar, Ruth, Ella and Yoav,
for their constant support.

Contents

**PART III: ACCOUNTABILITY AND PROCESSES
WITH VARIOUS GROUPS**

Preface

The aim of this book is to promote the psychological wellness of children and adolescents. The three arenas where children live most of their meaningful experiences—home, school, and community—have become unsafe places for them. Emotional support is often missing in these arenas, and children often suffer from criticism, rejection, and emotional and social abuse. Children and adolescents are alone in coping with their developmental or situational difficulties. In contrast to adults, who may look for professional support and assistance when facing a difficulty, children and most adolescents would not initiate such a move, and they often resist it when offered. Although they expect significant adults in their lives to support them, for various objective or subjective reasons they are often let down. This is not necessarily true only of children and adolescents with identified problems. Many normative children remain alone in their struggle with life events and stressors.

My personal experience as a child was no different. Although I did not suffer any identified psychological problem and I was a very successful student and well accepted by my peers, I often felt lonely and helpless. Growing up in an immigrant family, I could not turn to my parents for much support. I could not even share with them my joy in academic achievement, because I thought that it might hurt their feelings because they were uneducated. So I developed a kind of exaggerated modesty, which made me hide any success. School was a place in which bullies reigned quite freely, and I was the victim of my next-door neighbor each time I received a higher grade and she was punished by her mother. A teacher who would not accept my shyness decided to fight it rather than encourage me, making public comments about it. There was no grownup to comfort, advise, or assist me. Only recently, in a therapy group, did I become aware of my fear of success. I could certainly have used this wisdom at an earlier stage and felt less lonely.

I believe that this is a normal situation for many normative children. But there are children who, in addition, suffer developmental difficulties, school failure, social rejection, or family breakdown; they need even more support. Many of these difficulties cannot be avoided, but they need to be addressed if psychological wellness of children is important to people.

There is more than one way to assist children and adolescents. In this book, I offer group counseling and psychotherapy as a viable means of addressing many of these issues. School seems to be a natural place to offer children effective assistance without labeling them, although there are other settings in which group counseling and therapy may be viable as well, such as community centers, corrective institutions, and in private practice. What is important is to bring counseling to clients who are not capable of seeking it for themselves, thus reducing their sense of distress.

Although groups, in general, are highly recommended for counseling children and adolescents, in schools and elsewhere, they are infrequently used. When they are used, particularly in the school setting, they are preventive psycho-educational groups with a cognitive behavioral orientation and a problem-solving and skills-training focus (Barlow, Burlingame, & Fuhriman, 2000). In contrast, in my practice I offer counseling groups within an integrative approach, including a strong focus on affect. In keeping with Roger's (1980) criticism of schools that invite the child's mind and allow the body to tag along, but reject feelings, I invite feelings to come along with the mind and body.

The premise of this book is that all children, normative children and children with special needs alike, are more likely to grow in process-oriented groups in which emotional experiencing is allowed and encouraged, interpersonal support is constantly present, and instrumental assistance with practical issues is offered. I suggest that change in behavior and skills acquisition will be more efficiently achieved through reexperiencing positive relationships than through training. In our long experience in working with children in group counseling and psychotherapy, my colleagues, students, and I have witnessed many exciting moments in which the children set new goals for their lives and ask for assistance in modifying their maladaptive behavior. These acts, however, are always preceded by self-disclosure and by the experience of being accepted, supported, and empowered.

Group counseling and psychotherapy are psychological and social processes operating simultaneously on personal and interpersonal levels. On the personal level, my colleagues and I employ an integrative model in which psychodynamic, humanistic, and cognitive orientations are used, as suggested in the literature on child group psychotherapy (Cramer-Azima, 2002) and in accordance with the developmental change process (Hill, 2005). On the interpersonal level, we employ a transtheoretical model in which interpersonal interaction is the main mechanism of change (Yalom & Leszcz, 2005). The focus of treatment can best be characterized as expressive–supportive (Spiegel & Classen, 2000). It emphasizes release of emotions, self-disclosure, and catharsis in an all-accepting and supportive group climate where support is emotional, as well as instrumental.

Despite the unique focus on emotions, these groups operate successfully in schools. Like other groups commonly conducted in the school setting, they are short-term and are attended by normative children referred by teachers and other school personnel for various social, emotional, and behavioral difficulties. The focus on affect prior to coaching and training reflects our strong belief that children must be heard, accepted, recognized, and empowered before they can be expected to change their behavior. Such process-oriented groups require an educated and skillful leader, a goal I hope to achieve, at least partly, through this book.

The uniqueness of this book—beyond its focus on affect—lies in its research base. It is extremely important to demonstrate accountability of counseling and psychotherapy. Evidence-based treatments for children have only been recently published, and these are mostly cognitive–behavioral individual treatments (Kazdin & Weisz, 2003). Group counseling with children and adolescents has hardly been investigated (Barlow et al., 2000). This book presents information regarding the accountability of our model of group treatment for a variety of difficulties. Moreover, it presents research on the processes of child group therapy, which hardly exists in the professional literature. Such information may help practitioners, who are usually undertrained in methods of child group treatment, conduct effective groups. Moreover, it may expand the scope of treatment—in terms of population and issues to focus on. It may also convince policy makers to consider and allow the practice of such groups. Finally, I hope to encourage researchers to join us in our research efforts.

The book may be of interest to counseling psychology students and practitioners working with young people. It may be an important source of information to school counseling students and professionals, who are encouraged to work with children in groups but often are not well prepared for it. Social workers who work with deviant populations may find creative tips for their practice. Teachers devoted to the promotion of wellness may want to use methods and techniques offered in this book to help their students feel safer in school. This book may also appeal to parents of children with socioemotional needs and enhance their awareness of their child's difficulties. Finally, researchers in counseling and psychotherapy are invited to join my colleagues and I in advancing knowledge in child group counseling and psychotherapy.

ACKNOWLEDGMENTS

To my students, whose work is mentioned in this book, and to the many others who helped me learn about group counseling;
To my dear friend, Dr. Adina Flesher, for supervising my students and for teaching me creative group work with children;
To my dedicated and exceptionally capable editor, Ms. Helene Hogri;
I repectfully acknowledge the valuable contribution of all of you.

I

The Rationale for Child and Adolescent Group Counseling and Psychotherapy

Introduction to Part I

Group counseling and psychotherapy has been practiced with children and adolescents since the turn of the 19th Century, and yet it is still considered an underdeveloped field that needs "additional nurturing and time to fully mature" (Hoag & Burlingame, 1997b, p. 65). It lags behind individual therapy, as well as group psychotherapy with adults, in respect to both theory and research (Barlow et al., 2000). Therefore, in this book I borrow the knowledge accumulated on individual and group therapy with adults and apply some of it to child and adolescent group counseling, in accordance with my clinical experience and research.

Child group psychotherapy was first suggested by Slavson (1943) and Redle (1944), who labeled it *activity group therapy*, stressing the expression of feelings and fantasies through action, activities, and play. Ginnott (1961) and Schiffer (1969), among others, extended this psychoanalytical model, and Cramer-Azima (1989) expanded it to include adolescent group therapy. Axline (1947) developed a play group model built on a nondirective humanistic approach, which was followed by others (see review by Page, Weiss & Lietaer, 2001). More recently, cognitive-behavioral orientations (therapies) have taken over and are currently dominant in the field of group counseling and psychotherapy with children and adolescents (Kazdin & Weisz, 2003).

All these orientations are embedded in a single theoretical approach and focus on working with the individual within a group context. However, the current literature on individual therapy with adults has suggested that integrative interventions are more appropriate than any single theory (Hill, 2005; Prochaska, 1999). I believe that even the best single theory cannot explain group work. Therefore, I have adopted an integrative approach to help individuals progress toward their goals within the group context. Furthermore, in group counseling and psychotherapy, it is the dynamics of the group and its therapeutic properties that help individuals in their process of change (Yalom & Leszcz, 2005). Thus, group work functions on two interconnected levels—the individual and the group—and both must be recognized (Burlingame, MacKenzie, & Strauss, 2004). For the individual level of work, I have borrowed from literature on the change process; for the group level, I apply the principles of therapeutic factors in groups (Yalom & Leszcz, 2005).

Yalom (2005) argued that it is acceptable to borrow from the literature on individual and group therapy with adults and apply it to children. He suggested that, to specialize in a specific type of group, one first needs to know basic group therapy principles, which can then be applied to the unique population or setting in which they are practiced (Yalom & Leszcz, 2005). Indeed, child group counselors and therapists have agreed that "the basic principles of group counseling and psychotherapy apply to working with children in groups, although additional essential considerations are needed regarding the structuring of sessions" (Berg, Landreth, & Fall, 1998, p. 313). Similarly, I believe that the same principles that work with children apply also to adolescents in group counseling, but at the same time the intervention must be adjusted to the developmental level. For this reason, I do not make a sharp distinction between child and adolescent group counseling principles, although I do provide unique illustrations for each age group. I also go a step further and study these applications in children's groups.

The chapters in this book are structured in such a way as to reflect both the shared elements and the uniqueness of group work with different age groups. I therefore begin each chapter with general principles of group counseling and psychotherapy, followed by a discussion of the unique characteristics of group counseling with children and adolescents, as my colleagues and I have observed and studied them.

1
Who Needs Group Counseling and Psychotherapy?

Children's dysfunctions are grouped into three categories: social, emotional, and behavioral problems. Included are major disorders that are first evident in infancy, childhood, and adolescence, such as mental retardation, learning disorders, motor skill disorders, speech disorders, and attention-deficit disorders. Included as well are disorders that may become evident at any point over the life span, such as depression disorders, posttraumatic stress disorder, eating disorders, and adjustment disorders. Most of the clinical problems that are brought to counseling and psychotherapy are labeled *externalizing disorders* or *internalizing disorders*. The former are problems directed toward the environment and others (oppositional, hyperactive, aggressive, and antisocial); the latter are problems directed toward inner experience (anxiety, withdrawal, and depression). Externalizing behavior dominates as the primary basis for referring children and adolescents to inpatient and outpatient treatment (Kazdin & Weisz, 2003) because of their disturbing nature to the social environment. Yet, internalizing behavior may be more dangerous to the individual child and certainly requires similar attention.

Between 17% and 22% of children and adolescents suffer significant developmental, emotional, or behavioral problems (Tolan & Dodge, 2005; World Health Organization, 2001). Yet, even this high prevalence rate is likely to underestimate the range of mental disorders and impairment. Children who fail to meet the cutoff for a diagnosis can nevertheless suffer significant impairment (Lewinsohn, Solomon, Seeley, & Zeiss, 2000), and thus need assistance. Such is true, for instance, in the case of children engaged in at-risk behavior such as substance abuse, unprotected sexual activity, teenage pregnancy, delinquency, violent behavior, dropping out of school, or running away from home (DiClemente, Hansen, & Ponton, 1996). There are even more children and adolescents who experience extreme stressful life events that have a detrimental impact on their emotional well-being, social life, and school performance. Family break-up, parental neglect and abuse, death, war, and world disasters are all stressors that affect how children function (American Psychiatric Association, 2000; MacLeanan, 2000). Finally, there are many children and adolescents who experience problems that emerge from their developmental tasks. For instance, the transition from one country, neighborhood, or school to another may be a normal transition for some, yet might present a greater emotional and social challenge to others. Moreover, many children experience test anxiety, school failure, social isolation, and rejection.

Recently, a compelling article by Tolan and Dodge (2005) argued that children's mental health services are in crisis and suggested a more active and proactive approach to address the situation. Clinicians and researchers alike see group counseling as a viable and efficient means to respond to this crisis in respect to a wide range of problems (Dagley, Gazda, Eppinger, & Stewart, 1994). Following is a detailed description of some of the more frequent difficulties that children and adolescents present, illustrating how group counseling and psychotherapy can be helpful.

CHILDREN WITH LEARNING DISABILITIES (LD)

About 25% of all children and adolescents worldwide have LD (Kazdin & Johnson, 1994). Some are diagnosed as LD students, but most are just considered low achievers. A great portion of them suffer from social deficits, affect disorder, low self-esteem, loneliness, and rejection (Elbaum & Vaughn, 2001; Margalit & Al-Yagon, 2002; Wiener, 2002). When they do get assistance, it is of an academic type (Price, Johnson, & Evelo, 1994), and the many other difficulties that bother them remain mostly unaddressed. From my conversations with these children and adolescents, I have learned that school performance is an issue that is least disturbing to them. They are bothered much more by social rejection and loneliness, relationship with authority figures, and family matters. These issues can be effectively addressed in group counseling, as evidenced in the following case.

Dan is a seventh grader diagnosed with learning disabilities. He lives with his mother and younger sister; his father left home a few years ago. His mother, a schoolteacher, is still struggling with her own loss. She is well aware of his difficulties and has been quite desperate to find assistance. School personnel complain about his behavior problems, lack of motivation, and low academic achievements. He is accused of being lazy and undisciplined, but is not offered help. For his part, Dan complains of loneliness and rejection by his peer group, particularly since entering middle school. Usually, he does not like to share his frustrations with his mother, but one evening, in a therapeutic conversation she initiated, he confessed that his despair is so great that it "blocks his stomach;" he feels physical pain, and often does not attend school as a consequence. He recently started to associate with youngsters who are on the verge of breaking the law just to avoid the sense of loneliness.

His mother feels that she must save him before it is too late, yet all her attempts to get help from school have been turned down. They do not have the trained personnel available to work with him on an individual or group basis, beyond the academic assistance he is already getting, which he dislikes, as it labels him "disabled" and focuses his thoughts on his dysfunction. She cannot afford to pay for private therapy and, besides, Dan refuses to see a "shrink."

Finally, a new school counselor trained to work with children with LD in groups established a group of five children and invited Dan to join. Three were children with LD and two were average students who were invited to join the group. Soon, Dan realized that he was not alone with his learning disability; that other peers experience similar frustrations and disappointments, and that they, too, are anxious about peer rejection. Moreover, he discovered that children without LD have their own problems, too. Dan had a hard time sharing with the group his major difficulty—his relationship with his father, who has never accepted his disabilities. Following the group session in which he disclosed his secret, he confronted his father, and the relationship between them improved. In the small group, he became friends with another boy, from a parallel classroom, who did not have LD, and they started meeting after school.

Having a friend who is not a problem child was a big step in Dan's social, emotional, and academic progress. But perhaps Dan's greatest achievement was his newly acquired ability to express his feelings directly rather than through psychosomatic behavior. This helped him release tension, identify and articulate his problems, and even solve some of them. All of this could be achieved only in an accepting and supportive group climate.

CHILDREN OF DIVORCE

Children of divorce usually feel abandoned, anxious, depressed, isolated, and rejected (Leon, 2003; Wallerstein & Lewis, 1998). They fear being left behind and carry a great deal of unexpressed anger and resentment (Guttman & Rosenberg, 2003). They are sad and confused and often feel guilty, blaming themselves for their parents' separation (Goodman & Pickens, 2001). Parental divorce is often related to a decrease in socioeconomic status and a general change in lifestyle (Ozawa & Yoom, 2003). As a result, children of divorce have a poorer rate of school attendance, higher dropout rates, more difficulties in social interaction, more discipline problems in the classroom, and a greater number of learning disorders than other children (Ham, 2003). They often also exhibit high levels of aggression, violence, and delinquency (Hilton & Desrochers, 2002).

The stressors of parental divorce block progress in all areas of the child's functioning, and require a supportive long-term intervention (Baker, 2000). Although school counselors seem to consider this population as one at risk, requiring their attention (Bauman et al., 2002), in reality the typical policy of intervention with these children involves crisis interventions only. With the high rates of divorce common today, it is unrealistic to expect psychologists or school counselors to work with all children of divorce who need help on an individual basis. At the same time, parents are often unavailable to the children because of their own struggle with separation. Group counseling is a necessary response. Such groups are quite rare, and when practiced they are mostly of an educational type of group treatment (Rose, 1998), which does not fully address the needs of these children. What such children need is a place in which loving and caring peers help them to reduce stress and gain trust in their shaky world.

Take the example of Maggie, a fourth grader who lived with her grandparents following her parents' divorce. She was extremely unhappy there and furious with her mother, who so easily gave up on her. Maggie even hesitated to visit her mother, because she felt unwanted: "She does not like me around because I get in the way with her boyfriend." Her father was rather helpless: "He looks for a place for us to live, but I often need to remind him to take care of it; sometimes he is too drunk, and then I need to take care of him." Maggie felt lonely and helpless; she was extremely withdrawn, detached from peers and adults, and a poor student.

Maggie was lucky enough to be offered group counseling in school, together with other girls her age from divorced families. For a long while, she was the silent patient in the group. She was so fearful of expressing her own emotions that she would hide in a corner when she heard emotions voiced in the group. Gradually, she relaxed; influenced by the modeling of other group members, she began to share her story. The group responded with strong emotional support. The girls expressed acceptance and understanding of her difficulties and even offered instrumental assistance. The universality of the problems made it easier to cope with them, and although little had actually changed in her life circumstances, Maggie's sense of being attended to and supported had been a significant gift. At termination, a group member provided her with the following feedback: "I am impressed by the progress you made. I remember you hiding in the corner when we discussed 'hot stuff,' and now you are a leading force in this group." Our process research on this particular group (Shechtman, Vurembrand, & Malajek, 1993) indicated that a turning point in Maggie's behavior did not occur until the middle of her second year of treatment, but by the end of that year she had the highest rate of self-disclosure. She became less withdrawn, less depressed, more social, and a better student.

A related issue is the more frequent emergence of nontraditional family structures in recent years. Take the case of Jane, an only child in a single-parent household who never knew her father. At the age of 12, she became obsessed with the question of who her father was, but could not find a way to even open it up for discussion with her mother, who seemed to her too fragile, sad, and depressed to be burdened with additional stress. Jane admitted that in that year she was so occupied with this issue, she could not concentrate on anything else. She would wander the streets, wondering if each man she saw could be him. She was also preoccupied with the fear that her mother would commit suicide: "I was sitting in class thinking of my mother, whether I would find her alive when I came back. ... My fantasy was to find my father so he could stop her from committing suicide." This is an extremely heavy burden for a 12-year-old child to carry alone. Even though Jane may not be diagnosed as having a distinct disorder, she certainly needed help.

In the group counseling sessions she attended, Jane was extremely withdrawn for a long time. After another group member shared his concern about his mother abandoning him, Jane responded: "At least, you know who your mother is." This reaction led to the disclosure of her story. At this point, she became open and hopeful that the group may be of help. Group members encouraged her to approach her mother, which she did. Contrary to her expectations, her mother cooperated and disclosed to her who her father was (it was someone she knew as her "uncle"). This was a tremendous relief for Jane, which also led to the development of a relationship with her father. At group termination, she admitted that this was the critical incident for her in the group, and she also expressed her appreciation of the other children's mature reactions to her story.

IMMIGRANT CHILDREN

Immigration to a new country may be a neutral or even a positive change for some children, yet a difficult transition for others, often depending on their age, economic situation, degree of family support, and social climate. Adolescence appears to be the most difficult stage for immigration (Aronowitz, 1992), because the psychological distress is related to self-identity development and social belonging—the two major tasks in adolescence (Erikson, 1974; Goodenow & Epsin, 1993). When immigrant children are, in addition, somewhat exceptional, they become easily scapegoated, which complicates their adjustment efforts even more.

Consider, for example, Miriam, a 14-year-old immigrant from Ethiopia to Israel. She is the oldest of four children, and both her parents are physically disabled. In an early group session, a book describing different kinds of fish was read to the children, and each was asked to select the fish that best represents him or her. Miriam described herself as a lonely fish who would like to swim along with the other fish, but they would not let her. "They call me names (Negro), bully me, and insult my disabled parents; I feel really helpless." At another session, she stated:

> There is so much for me to do. I clean, cook, take care of my brother. We are moving now, and I packed 40 or 50 boxes all by myself. I know I have to help, because what would I do without my parents? But, sometimes, at night, I talk to God and say to him: "I know you are very busy taking care of so many problems and people, but would you once please pay attention to me, too? You will find that I am a good daughter and a hard-working student. Can't you make it a bit easier for me?"

Miriam seemed to present more than one problem, as often happens. The group helped her mainly by listening to and understanding her, but also by providing her with security and support inside and outside the group sessions. One group member who tended to give her a hard time became her protector in class and at recess. Such an attitudinal change toward a rejected child could not occur through training in empathic skills only. The children had to listen empathetically to her pain, which was so authentically expressed, before they could change their feelings toward her.

THE IMPACT OF TERROR

Traumatic events have a strong impact on people's well being. Reactions to traumatic experiences include loss of emotional control (e.g., panic, anxiety, depression), psychosomatic reactions (e.g., sleep disorder, illness), and social dysfunction (e.g., loss of trust and intimacy, withdrawal). In repetitive traumas, such reactions tend to increase (NcNally, 2003). Moreover, in childhood and adolescence, traumatic experiences tend to also affect identity issues, particularly beliefs (Roth, 2002).

The ability to cope with trauma is related to one's degree of social support, and low support is associated with high levels of anxiety and depression (Galea et al., 2002). Peer support is particularly needed in adolescence (Vernberg, 1999). A group whose members have had similar experiences of trauma are particularly helpful, as they provide a sense of support and cohesion (Nuttman-Schwartz, Karniel-Lauer, & Offir, 2000). Such a group buffers the sense of loneliness and is sometimes a replacement for a family that does not cope. Group members help each other to express themselves—by direct invitation, modeling, or feedback, as this case illustrates. They provide legitimization to deal with beliefs and values, immanent to issues of identity.

Not surprisingly, since September 11, groups for children and adolescents coping with trauma following terror are flourishing. The *International Journal of Group Psychotherapy* has published an entire volume on such groups. For example, Scheidlinger and Kahn (2005) offered a comprehensive prevention and intervention program including small support groups, in which children derive their power from the shared sense of "being in the same boat." Several other clinicians have suggested support groups for traumatized children. Webb (2005) argued that children may be so overwhelmed by the intensity of the trauma that they can hardly speak or show emotions. Peer support and modeling may help children verbalize their emotions. Aronson (2005) suggested that the group helps to "take a constructivist approach" (p. 386) to the trauma; that is, it helps develop a revised perception of the event, and provides a sense of power to go on after the tragedy.

Whereas traumatized people tend to deny traumatic experiences, because these experiences are sometimes too difficult to face, expressing emotions and coping with the traumatic event are necessary for a person's well-being (Pennebaker & Seagal, 1999; Spiegel & Classen, 2000). In a culture that restricts the expression of such feelings, these needs cannot be met. Consider, for example, the case of Sara, who was 16 when a terrorist attacked the bus she took to school. Seated near two classmates who were killed, she herself was badly wounded. She never spoke about the traumatic event, because this was not accepted in her social environment. Belonging to a conservative culture, she was expected to accept her fate and thank God for remaining alive.

A year later, Sara was invited to attend a psychotherapy group offered to the children involved in that attack. She was quite reserved initially, but reacted strongly to a poem introduced to the group called "It is OK to be Weak." She could not accept the message and suggested changing the title to "It is Not OK to be Weak." She also refused to empathize with a literary character who suffered from a serious illness, blaming the character for taking advantage of the situation. It seemed that Sara's emotional world was blocked, and that she took great effort to stay in control for fear of breaking down. It was obvious that she repressed her pain, fears, and anger.

At one point in the group process, she received feedback saying that she only pretended to be strong and always in control. "Let yourself feel; say it is difficult," said the girl. This made Sara cry for a while; then she shared with the group the difficulty of always being in control, explaining that "Everything frightens me so much, it destroys me. I break down so easily; my shield is so fragile." She later also shared her difficulties coping with her physical disability, her fears of a repeat attack, and her guilt about staying alive. She even admitted that she raised questions about God, and could not accept her conservative environment's explanation of punishment. "I could not see why I was punished so badly, as my sins do not justify it," she said. She was confused and terrified by such disturbing thoughts, but had to cope with them all alone, as such questioning is not accepted in her social milieu. At termination, she selected a card with a picture of a lamp, explaining that she now feels more courageous in facing her fears, and more faithful in her belief in God, who saved her during the terrorist attack.

It appears that Sara went through the whole cycle of the individual change process. She started from a point of total denial, went through cognitive and affective exploration, developed some insight, and ended with an increased sense of strength and hope towards the future. All these achievements were made possible mainly through group interactions. Group members were extremely attentive to Sara's story and reacted with empathy to her feelings. However, it was not until she was challenged by one of the group members about wearing a mask that she could admit to her great fears and talk openly about her true feelings. In a group of mature adolescents, such processes are quite common.

CHILDREN WITH VARIOUS PROBLEMS

Dan, Maggie, Jane, Miriam, and Sara are only a few examples of children who may not meet the criteria for emotional dysfunction, yet are in great need of psychological support. They all experienced unusual stressful life events that have had a detrimental impact on their emotional well being, social life, and school performance. Such events have been reflected in deviant behavior of an internalized or externalized nature: withdrawal, depression, suicidal behavior, eating disorders, aggression, violence, and delinquency.

Many other children, who have not necessarily experienced unusually stressful events, but face developmental difficulties that negatively impact their normal functioning, can also benefit from work in a group. For example, Jim, an only child, was brought up in an extremely protective and anxious family. Although he had an average IQ, his parents devoted many hours a day helping him with his schoolwork. As a result, he had developed a low sense of self-efficacy and total dependence on his parents. He never had time to make friends, was totally disarmed of social skills, and remained isolated and scapegoated in school. He was extremely unhappy and lonely, but could not share this problem with his overly protective parents "because it will make them cry, they will be so upset." He was trapped in unhealthy relationships and felt he was about to explode. He decided to distance himself, refusing to talk to his parents and shutting himself in his room to listen to music. School personnel never recognized his problems, as he was a quiet and polite student from a functioning family. In an individual therapy session, he confessed that he would like to start his life over; if he could do it all again, he would devote less time to academic achievement and more time to friends that he never had. He also felt that he needed to learn to cope with peer rejection, to be less sensitive and defensive. Such goals are typical of group counseling, but he had never been offered such an opportunity.

Dawn was 12 when she tried to commit suicide, together with her best friend. She was shy and withdrawn. Although she did not recall any particular trauma in her life, she described it as lonely and empty. She was an only child; her parents were both busy physicians who worked late and she felt that "they will not miss me at all." At an intake interview, she talked about her loneliness quite openly. In a counseling or psychotherapy group she might gain a sense of belonging and cohesion, which would also prevent her from depending on a poor relationship with her single destructive friend.

Finally, Joshua was occupied with issues of power. He was a gifted student, but a disturbance to teachers and students. He manipulated the class and always needed to be the best. Peers and adults were often subjected to his put downs and rejected him for that. He was not invited to birthday parties or other out-of-school social activities. He did not quite understand the reasons for his rejection, because they were always brought to his attention in a destructive form, which made him even more defensive. He needed to receive constructive feedback in a supportive context, such as is usually established in counseling and therapy groups.

PROVIDING SUPPORT TO ALL CHILDREN

So far, I have cited examples of children whose problems were overt and recognizable. Yet, there are many more children who could benefit from emotional and social support. Actually, every child is entitled to be happy, satisfied, hopeful, and optimistic; this is what well being is about according to positive psychology (Seligman & Csikszentmihalyi, 2000), the new trend in the science of psychology. Counseling and therapy, therefore, focuses on systematically building competency and resilience, not correcting weaknesses. Moreover, positive psychology works at both an individual and a group level. The individual level involves enhancement of such traits as the capacity for love, forgiveness, courage, and meaningful relationships. The group level develops responsibility, responsiveness, altruism, and tolerance. The type of group counseling and psychotherapy that I offer in my practice and recommend in this book works at both levels. These are not groups for skill training, but rather for emotional growth within a setting that provides the social and emotional conditions needed for such growth.

Whether their problems are merely developmental or anchored in mildly or severely stressful life events, children need help, but their chances of getting it are limited unless society brings counseling to them. The most convenient place to offer such assistance to young clients is the school, in which students are a captive audience. Indeed, the trend among mental health professionals in the school is to move from a reactive approach to a proactive one, to help children and adolescents with the many challenges they face in emotional, social, and behavior arenas. School counselors, for instance, have expanded their role from promoting career development to promoting child development, with a focus on life skills training (Gazda, Ginter, & Horne, 2001; Gysber & Henderson, 2000).

New trends in psychology have extended therapeutic help beyond the clinics to other normative settings, such as schools and communities. The current emphasis on positive psychology has further moved the focus of psychological interventions to improving the well being of all children. One of the greatest obstacles to happiness is a lack of intimacy among people, loneliness, and alienation (Buss, 2000; Myers, 2000). For children and adolescents, positive peer relationships have been found to be the strongest protective factor and the most significant predictor of antisocial behavior (Wiener, 2002). These factors were clearly presented across all the case illustrations previously cited. This approach naturally goes beyond responding only to children diagnosed with some problem or deficit. Gradually, counseling psychologists are encouraged to move away from total dependence on the DSM (see Tolan & Dodge, 2005)—the most important source of psychological diagnosis—and treatment manuals (Goodheart, 2004) to more process-oriented, less structured treatments that are suited to a variety of difficulties and applicable to basic human needs.

THE TYPE OF GROUP OFFERED

The definition of child group psychotherapy itself has expanded to include any intervention that is designed to alleviate distress, reduce maladaptive behavior, or enhance adaptive functioning and that uses means that include counseling, as well as planned, structured, and unstructured interventions (Dagley et al., 1994). Such a comprehensive definition encompasses all types of group intervention: guidance/educational, counseling/interpersonal problem solving, and psychotherapy/personality reconstruction (Gazda et al., 2001). Psychoeducational groups are the most frequently used with children, particularly in the school setting; counseling groups are next; and only 10% of the groups with children and adolescents are psychotherapy groups, although they tend to be the most effective ones (Hoag & Burlingame, 1997b; Kulic, Dagley, & Horne, 2001). Moreover, both psychoeducational and counseling groups are most often cognitive behavioral oriented, structured around specific content, and focused on skills training. Even though they may address the same difficulties illustrated previously (e.g., children of divorce; learning disabilities), the process in these groups is very different. For example, Margarett Smead (Morganet, 1990; Smead-Morganet, 1994) has offered structured programs for children of divorce, friendship difficulties, and anger management, among others. All these programs have an outlined content based on the common difficulties expected of these children, and the sessions are highly structured to achieve predefined goals. Although feelings are discussed, most of the therapeutic work takes place on a cognitive level, with the purpose of teaching the children how to cope with common difficulties.

Consider the children discussed earlier. In a structured group for students with LD, Dan would probably be guided to identify his LD and be taught problem-solving skills. Although he would probably gain a sense of universality, realizing that he is not alone with his problems, would he get a chance to deal with his greatest source of stress—his relationship with his abandoning father? Would he have the chance to express his strong feelings of social rejection in a group that deals with learning improvement? Similarly, would Maggie be able to come out of her shell and express her emotions in an eight-session group process? My observation of the group in which she participated suggested that it took her longer than that. Without an extremely intimate and supportive group climate, would Jane be able to discuss her obsession with her unknown father, would Miriam disclose her vulnerability, and would Sara be capable of recognizing and expressing her fragile emotional state? These children and adolescents have learned a lot about their own problems and those of others, but their learning process was a result of their group experiences. It was the positive reexperiencing of relationships that made the greatest difference in their lives.

It appears that the life of these children and adolescents can be extremely complicated, difficult to handle, and sometimes unbearable. These children are confused, frustrated, anxious, painful, and lonely, with little attention given to their problems. They are expected to perform well in class, to adjust to school and home requirements, to get along with peers and authority figures—all this while ignoring the strong emotions boiling inside their young bodies, blocking their ability to concentrate on their formal obligations, limiting their empathy to the pain of others, and minimizing their energy to cope with their own problems.

The premise of this book is that children who experience one or more of these emotional difficulties are not ready to be taught or trained in areas of skills deficit; rather, their major needs are to experience emotional release, to be accepted, cared for, understood, and loved. These needs can be met successfully in counseling or psychotherapy groups in which the expression of emotions is highly encouraged and the response to such intimate sharing of feeling and experiences is empathic support.

It is important to consider that, before society starts offering groups to large school populations, counselors need to be clearer on what the needs of these children are, how the process should work, and what outcomes can be expected. Too much of what is known about group work with children is based on adult groups. This is not surprising, as there is not enough research on child and adolescent group psychotherapy (Barlow et al., 2000). Yet, it is clear that the dynamics in children's groups—as well as children's needs—are very different from those of adults (Riva & Haub, 2004). Age, cognitive developmental level, social cognitions, empathy skills, attribution processes in social situations, and prosocial behavior are developmental tasks that may influence the process in counseling.

SUMMARY

This chapter presented some of the children who were lucky enough to receive assistance in a counseling group. Most are children and adolescents from regular school settings who are coping with difficult life events or developmental deficits. Social and emotional support seems to be the key to reducing their stress level, followed by instrumental assistance in coping with their difficulties. This is very different from psychoeducational groups commonly employed in schools. My colleagues and I offer counseling and psychotherapy groups that involve relationships, bonding, emotional expressiveness, insight, and motivation. These groups do not exclude education and training children in coping skills; it is only that such processes precede the training in coping skills.

Children and adolescents appear to need a unique theory of change, special methods of intervention, and leaders with specific skills. The following chapters discuss the type of group I recommend and its theoretical orientation, largely based on the clinical experience and process research of my colleagues and myself. Although I draw from knowledge on adult groups—a legitimate approach, as the basic principles of group therapy are similar (Berg et al., 1998; Thompson & Rudolph, 2000)—I offer a unique theory adjusted to the developmental needs of children and adolescents.

2 The Theory of Group Counseling With Children

A theory of counseling or psychotherapy should guide practitioners in the way they treat their clients. The philosophy on life of my colleagues, my students, and myself; our familiarity with the most current principles of individual and group change; our observations of the process of growth among children and adolescents in groups; and our research results have all led to the following basic assumptions:

1. The group should be an intimate place where children and adolescents can gain a sense of well being and grow personally. This implies that group participants are expected to talk freely about their disturbing thoughts and feelings, release tension, and, if possible, develop insight and make some behavioral change. To meet these expectations, children and adolescents should engage in cognitive and affective exploration of their most disturbing difficulties, those that they choose to discuss with the group, when they feel motivated to do so. Hopefully, these client behaviors will lead to self-understanding and to change of behavior.

2. To achieve such personal goals, the group should be a caring and supportive place in which members are accepted and understood. Only through such relationships can a child develop a sense of trust in self and others. This means that the child should feel close to the counselor and the group members, be involved in interpersonal interaction among group members, help others, and accept the help provided by others.

These two assumptions refer to the interplay between the psychological and social processes that characterize group counseling and psychotherapy. Although they are distinct levels of performance, they cannot be separated. Too much emphasis on the individual level of therapy will result in a mere extension of individual therapy to the group context; too much emphasis on group dynamics may ignore an individual child's distress (Burlingame et al., 2004). The counselor walks a fine line between these two processes, encouraging both emotional experiencing of personal issues brought into the group and here-and-now group interactions that provide emotional and social support. Therefore, what best describes the modality of group counseling and psychotherapy with children and adolescent used by my colleagues and myself is expressive-supportive therapy. To help explain the way we travel both roads, I review the literature from which we drew our theory, illustrate the processes with case examples, and support our premise with research results. I begin by reviewing research on expressive–supportive therapy, followed by literature on the individual's process of change. This is complemented by a review of studies on the group process of change in the next chapter.

EXPRESSIVE–SUPPORTIVE THERAPY

Piper and colleagues (2002) introduced the distinction between interpretive–expressive and supportive therapy for inpatients and outpatients in individual and group formats. Successful interpretive therapy depends on the patient's willingness to self-disclose, to experience unpleasant feelings, to think about puzzling and frightening interpretations, and to deal with the unconscious. The therapist takes a passive–receptive approach; it is a talker–listener relationship with a focus on transferences. The intention of the therapist is to enhance insight, which will eventually lead to change in behavior. In contrast, supportive therapy focuses on reflection and adaptation. Its goals are to resolve present life concerns and improve the patient's reality testing and coping capacity. The emphasis is on conscious problems, using supportive advisory, informative, clarifying, and confronting interventions, without ignoring the importance of ventilation of feelings. The therapist engages in active listening, conveys concern and understanding, and thereby creates a *holding environment* through the establishment of a secure relationship. Stress is kept to a minimum, and universality and hope are promoted. At the same time, therapy is problem-focused and based on logical and rational processes. As the general goal is to promote ego strength, interventions include supportive collaboration, permissiveness, advising, informing (educating), and managing (setting limits).

Both interpretive therapies and supportive therapies are considered to be dynamically oriented, but the use of interpretive intervention is encouraged in the former and discouraged in the latter. In their extensive research, Piper and colleagues (2002) found that certain patient qualities are conducive to short-term interpretive therapies. Two of the major ones are Quality of Object Relations (QOR) and Psychological Mindedness (PM). In several studies, these characteristics were linked to the therapist–patient working alliance and to outcomes, both in individual and group therapy. A high level of QOR is believed to assist patients in tolerating the interpersonal demands of interpretive therapy, and a high level of PM is believed to provide the ability to work productively in examining intrapsychic conflicts in interpretive therapy. Their conclusion, therefore, was that patients low in both characteristics will do better in supportive therapy. In supportive therapy, there were also fewer dropouts (6% vs. 23%; Piper et al., 2002).

Interpretive interventions are considered to be among the most rigorous helping skills for adults in both individual counseling (Hill, 2005; Ivey & Ivey, 1999) and group counseling (M. S. Corey & Corey, 2006; Cramer-Azima, 1989; Yalom & Leszcz, 2005). However, taking into consideration the low QOR and PM of children and young adolescents—their developmental ability, restricted ego strength, dependency on adults, and sense of helplessness—supportive counseling and therapy seems to be the treatment of choice for them.

SUPPORT FROM RESEARCH

In our long practice of group counseling with children, my colleagues, my students, and myself have observed children's difficulty in handling interpretive interactions in groups. These observations led us to conduct a study designed to specifically investigate the effect of such interventions (feedback, confrontation, and interpretation) on elementary-school children (Shechtman & Yanuv, 2001). Based on transcripts of recorded sessions, we analyzed children's use of these interventions and their responses to them in the group process. Results indicated that the most frequent child intervention was confrontation (57%), followed by feedback (38%); interpretation was rare (5%). Overall, the children used more low-quality interpretive interventions than high-quality ones (54% vs. 46%), mostly owing to differences in confrontations. Feedback was almost equally divided into high- and low-quality categories; interpretations, when used, were usually of high quality. Feedback produced mostly productive behavior; not only was high-quality feedback usually followed by productive behavior (70%), but even low-quality feedback was followed by a relatively high percentage of productive behavior (40%). In contrast, confrontations were mostly followed by nonproductive client behavior, particularly when they were low quality (80%). Interpretations, too, particularly low-quality ones, were followed by nonproductive behavior. In general, the conclusion of this study was that children are not skilled in using constructive interpretative interventions; confrontations, in particular, seem to be quite destructive and should be kept to a minimum in children's groups, unless children are trained to use them constructively.

This study, carried out in a school in which children's groups are often used and led by an experienced counselor, confirms our observations that children are intolerant of criticism and intimidated by negative interactions. It supports the preference of supportive counseling and therapy over interpretive therapy for children. Nonetheless, it is impossible to ignore the vast literature on the importance of experiencing in adult counseling and therapy, which is less common in supportive therapy, as described by Piper and colleagues (2002). Although ventilation of feelings is part of the supportive modality and the counselor or therapist is an effective listener, emotional experiencing is not an actual part of this type of therapy. In fact, it is the main feature of interpretive therapy (hence the name *interpretive–expressive*).

In my attempt to reserve a central place for expressiveness, I raised the question of whether expressiveness is necessarily provoked by interpretive interventions. Could it be part of supportive counseling and psychotherapy evoked through alternative methods and techniques? In my clinical work with children, I noted a strong need to express emotions and disclose private information, and I found that emotional experiencing was a precondition for positive outcomes. One study (Leichtentritt & Shechtman, 1998) investigated children's verbal responses in groups, as well as the counselor's interventions that affected children's responses. All 160 sessions were audiotaped, transcribed, and analyzed based on the Client Verbal Response Mode System (Hill, 1986) for both the counselor and the children, as the latter assume some of the leader's responses. The most frequent child response was self-disclosure; boys and girls alike used it at least once in more than 90% of the sessions, whereas feedback was used in about 50% of the sessions and questions were used in 35%. Moreover, analysis of responses by stage of group development indicated that frequency of self-disclosure was already high at the first stage of the group (first four sessions), with both boys and girls giving an average of 10–14 self-disclosure responses per session, a level that was maintained throughout the group process. For comparison's sake, consider that the next frequent response at the initial stage was feedback (0.95 and 0.49 average responses per session, for boys and girls, respectively), and all other types of responses were quite rare. Thus, the most impressive finding regarding children's behavior was their high level of self-disclosure, which was often self-initiated, from the beginning of the group process through termination. It appears that self-expressiveness is a central need for children in group counseling, which should be allowed and encouraged. This prepares the groundwork for affective exploration and experiencing, which is so treasured in individual counseling and psychotherapy.

How was this high level of self-disclosure possible in these groups? When counselor responses were investigated for their impact on children's self-disclosure, it appeared that the counselor, in contrast to the children, used a variety of responses. Although she also disclosed quite a lot, she asked even more questions, provided feedback, and used encouragement, directives, and paraphrases. For example, the counselor voiced encouragement in 80% of the sessions at least once; the children used this response in less than 10% of the sessions. Interestingly, the two counselor behaviors that stood out in their impact on children's self-disclosure were structured activities and questions, leading to self-disclosure in about 90% of the sessions in both cases. The conclusion of this study was that interpretive interventions are not necessarily the counselor behaviors needed to promote experiencing in children's groups. In fact, other behaviors (questions) and techniques (therapeutic activities) appear to work very well.

Other researchers have also combined expressive and supportive therapies, without necessarily relying on interpretive interventions. Spiegel and Classen (2000), for example, proposed such a model in work with cancer patients, arguing that the two components of expressiveness and support are interrelated. Intimate social relationships both allow and encourage the expression of strong emotions, which, in turn, stimulate the development of social support. Social support is an important mediating factor in dealing with stressful life events. In a group of cancer patients, such support reduced the feeling of isolation and provided new important social connections. But the expression of strong emotion is no less important. In fact, Spiegel and Classen concluded that the central task of the therapist is to follow the affect more than the content (p. 33). This conveys to the patients that the group is a place where their distress can be expressed and addressed. Positive, as well as negative, feelings are invited because hiding them, denying, or pretending consume considerable energy, which is needed to deal with so many other issues that these patients face. The clinicians encourage open expression of feelings relating to the worst of all—the threat of death, arguing that by facing one's own worst fears openly and directly, patients realize that they can tolerate it, which further lessens the level of anxiety. Indeed, there is vast research that supports this. Not only do the patients feel more empowered, but they also live longer (Spiegel & Classen, 2000). Similar to the support groups described by Piper and colleagues (2002), the emphasis of Spiegel and Classen's expressive–supportive model is on cultivating a realistic optimism, by finding those aspects of life that can be controlled, and making the most out of them. Redefining life priorities, increasing support of friends and family, and improving coping skills are all issues that can be handled on a conscious level. Often instrumental and practical advice coming from people who have been in a similar situation is of imminent importance.

How is support and emotional expression developed in such groups? Because patients have a similar problem and are all in a needy situation, supportive behavior develops quite naturally. The group setting is often the only place where patients feel understood, accepted, and a little less alone. Thus, the need to share similar emotions and experiences stems from intrinsic motivation for many of these patients. However, these emotions are not necessarily evoked through interpretive interventions or the discussion of transference issues. They become present because the atmosphere is of a shared experience of common emotions, a pool of feelings in which the group immerses itself. When these feelings are acknowledged, explored, identified, openly discussed, and understood, therapeutic progress is made. Thus, expressive therapy need not be synonymous with interpretive therapy, and support can be both instrumental and emotional.

A CASE ILLUSTRATION

In illustrating how counseling groups for children can incorporate an expressive–supportive model, I cite the example of counseling offered to children of divorce. Because such children usually feel embarrassed talking about their families with children of intact families, they are often placed in special groups, as is the case described here.

This particular group included six sixth-grade boys and girls. Over the course of several sessions, the group developed a supportive climate and many of the children shared common experiences and difficulties, disclosing that they feel puzzled, insecure, and often lonely. However, it was not until two-thirds of the sessions had passed that Jack whispered at the end of a session, "I hate her, I never want to see her again." The children barely heard his comment, but Margo, the counselor, saw the tears in his eyes and said, "I can see you are very upset. Let's remember to bring this up next time."

Jack had been very quiet to this point, slow in keeping up with the group's progress. Margo was moved by his expression of emotion; understanding how risky it must have been for him and how vulnerable he must have felt, she immediately acknowledged his affect. The next session opened with her turning to Jack, repeating his earlier comment, and suggesting, "You probably mean your mom." She invited him to tell the group more about his feelings. Jack revealed that his birthday was coming up and his mother had not even called. She had called a while ago, asking what present he would like for his birthday, but he responded angrily that he did not need her presents and hung up. The group helped him explore his emotions in various ways. Some children shared similar feelings of neglect and rejection. Others asked questions, helping Jack to understand that he actually needed his mother's attention. In the Echo Game that they played that session, other children expressed the emotions that Jack had not yet able to express: anger, frustration, and disappointment, but also a sense of longing. Sarah, playing Jack's echo, said, "I feel that you gave up on me, you are not interested in me, and this is very painful because I miss you, I want my mom." At this point Jack started crying. When he calmed down, Francine explained, "You do not hate your mother; you love her, but you are disappointed."

The group identified the real emotion and shared mutual feelings that provided Jack with some sense of power. Then they role-played the phone conversation in which he rejected his mother. Jasmine, who played his mother, explained that she felt rejected and confused about future contact with her son. Jack did not know what to do with this information at this point. There were suggestions to call her and explain to her his true feelings, but he was not ready for this yet. The group then decided to write a collective letter to his mother expressing his real feelings, which they then read to Jack. This helped him understand his emotions, but he was not ready to send the letter. However, the next session Jack said he felt much better, and that, although he was still uncertain about sending the letter, he was not so angry anymore. He expressed his love and appreciation for the group; this was the first time that he expressed any feelings so spontaneously.

Mobilizing the expression of emotion is a crucial part of the counselor's role. In this case, the counselor noticed and acknowledged the child's distress; she also led group members to be involved with each other and to learn from mutual experiences. Feelings were explored, identified, and understood, and instrumental steps were taken to resolve the problem. The power of the expressive–supportive model clearly emerges from this case: when emotions are expressed rather than suppressed, the client's emotional health improves. Moreover, this was achieved through therapeutic activities such as the Echo Game and the collective letter, rather than via the discussion of deep interpretations or transference issues.

Emotional experiencing appears to be the heart of counseling and psychotherapy in the current literature (Bohart et al., 1997; L. S. Greenberg, 2002; Wiser & Goldfried, 1998). L. S. Greenberg (2002) stipulated that "the greatest complexity of being human is that, in essence, we are two 'selves' that do not necessarily get along" (p. ix). One self drives the rational stream of consciousness, and the other drives the experiential, sensory stream of consciousness. The resolution to the two selves dilemma lies not in favoring one stream of consciousness over the other, but in integrating the two: allowing emotional experience, attending to it, and reflecting on it. L. S. Greenberg thus offered emotion-focused therapy, which is basically emotion coaching. This involves being attuned to clients' feelings, offering suggestions to help them process their experience more deeply, and using cognition to make sense of emotion.

L. S. Greenberg (2002) suggested that working with emotion is applicable across orientations. Although most approaches to therapy, to some degree or another, involve coaching people in emotions, L. S. Greenberg's (2002) model suggested using emotions as a guide for change. Research has supported the notion that experiencing emotion is the core of many emotional change processes. In many situations in counseling and therapy, arousing emotions seems to be an important precondition for changing them. Mounting evidence that emotional arousal and depth of experience relate to therapy outcomes supports the importance of access to emotion in counseling and therapy (L. S. Greenberg, 2002). However, venting alone is insufficient to promote change. Further processing is needed, in which reflection on emotional experience or the development of awareness is needed. "It is the integration of emotion and reason that results in a whole that is greater than the sum of its parts," he argued (L. S. Greenberg, 2002, p. 10).

Hill (2005) claimed that it is how people make sense of and use their emotional experiences that makes the difference. In her three-stage model and her vast research, she helps one understand and practice the process that leads to emotional experiencing. From her model of change, as well as that of Prochaska (1999), I draw the principles of the change process on the individual level of group work.

INDIVIDUAL PROCESSES OF CHANGE

Hill (2005) and Prochaska (1999) both offered an integrative model of counseling and psychotherapy that I have adopted in my work with groups of children and adolescents, as have many other child and adolescent clinicians (see review in Cramer-Azima, 2002). Both of these stage models of change have enhanced the expressive half of the expressive–supportive model that I apply. Accordingly, I discuss their theoretical principles in this chapter. The supportive part of my model is discussed in the next chapter.

Despite the prevalence of cognitive behavioral orientations in counseling and psychotherapy for children and adolescents (Kazdin & Weisz, 2003), I prefer the more recent trend in psychology that suggests an integrative approach—the use of several theories within a developmental perception of change. Accordingly, the children are first encouraged to express their concerns, explore their difficulties, and understand the reasons for and consequences of their behavior. Only when motivation to make a change in behavior is observed are they assisted in changing their perceptions and trained in areas of skills deficit.

The purposes of this counseling are to release tension, to make life a bit easier for the children, and to empower them. In this respect, the goals resemble those of humanistic therapies, as defined by Kirschenbaum (1979): "The aim of humanistic therapy is not to solve a particular problem, but to assist the individual to grow, so he can cope with the present problem" (p. 113). However, the model goes further in an effort to have the children reflect on their behavior and understand what causes their stress. Other aims include increasing the children's motivation to take charge of their behavior, and, of course, to offer help to achieve such change.

This theory suits not only my philosophy of work, but also the needs of the children that my colleagues and I work with (see the first chapter). These children need to talk to someone who will listen to them in a caring way, someone who will accept their feelings and understand their chaotic emotions. They also need to feel that they are liked and appreciated by adults and peers, and that they will be supported with their difficulties. In addition, they usually need guidance and training in areas of social deficit, but will probably reject this if their basic needs for acceptance and understanding are not met first. Motivation becomes a key factor in such a process of change. I believe that children, like adults, must make choices based on free will. Any attempt to set goals for them or impose skills training on them is doomed to failure because the intrinsic motivation is missing. Even young children resent any type of coercion and prefer making decisions on their own. Motivated children are more likely not only to produce change, but also to put effort into maintaining that change. However, they are liable to need considerable assistance in increasing their motivation. This entails more than just raising awareness, as children do not easily make the connection between understanding a problem and making actual change. If child counseling and therapy is to be adjusted to children's developmental needs, it should not be based on a change in theoretical principles, but rather on changing the methods of work, which will be discussed in a later chapter.

I now explore, in greater depth, the two theoretical models that underlie the expressive part of the expressive–supportive model that my colleagues and I apply to child and adolescent counseling groups. In particular, I focus on how each of the influencing theories helped us develop our theory of change for group counseling with children and adolescents.

HILL'S (2005) THREE-STAGE MODEL OF COUNSELING

Hill's (2005) three-stage model begins with exploration, is followed by insight, and ends with action. This model serves as a framework for using helping skills to lead clients through the process of exploring concerns, coming to greater understanding of problems, and making change in their lives. It is based on extensive research (Hill, 2001), suggesting that it is a transtheoretical model. The three-stage model is influenced by client-centered, psychoanalytic, and cognitive-behavioral theories. Each of these theories is the primary influence for one of the model's three stages.

The exploration stage is influenced by client-centered theory. It is intended to help clients explore their thoughts, feelings, and actions. The helpers at this stage develop a therapeutic relationship with the clients, encourage the clients to tell their story, and facilitate arousal of emotions. The insight stage is influenced by psychoanalytic theory. It aims to help clients understand their thoughts, feelings, and action. Helpers work with clients to construct new insight and understanding, to determine their role in their thoughts, feelings, and action, and to work with clients on issues in the therapeutic relationship. Finally, in the action stage, helpers encourage clients to explore possible new behaviors, facilitate the development of skills, and assist clients in evaluating changes and modifying action plans.

The usefulness of this model, beyond its three stages, lies in its inclusion of sets of client behaviors and counselor helping skills, which aid in defining the effective performance of client and helper. Effective client functioning in counseling means reduction of resistance to counseling, as well as fewer simple responses, such as recounting or simple request. In contrast, cognitive and affective exploration, developing insight, and making a commitment and a plan to change should increase. The counselor guides the client through the three stages using a set of helping skills appropriate for each stage. Questions and encouragement are used primarily during the exploration stage; challenges, interpretations, and self-disclosure are used mostly at the insight stage; and information provision and guidance are the main counselor skills during the action stage. Hence, similar to L. S. Greenberg's (2002) model, Hill (2005) considered experiencing as a major mechanism of change, along with the development of insight; but she also added the action stage, emphasizing the need to guide clients to achieve actual change.

A CASE ILLUSTRATION OF THE THREE-STAGE MODEL

This case illustrates the three-stage model, emphasizing the importance of the action stage, which is an important addition where child counseling is concerned. Owing to their weak ego, lack of skills, and dependence on others, children, in particular, need extra help at this stage to guide them to make a change.

Rita had been anxious about her relationship with her father, whom she perceived as highly old-fashioned, with a tendency to restrict her social relationships. Every Friday night was a new battle. For instance, she wanted to return from a party together with all her friends, but he insisted that she come home earlier. They both got angry, and then she gave up and did not go. This made her very angry with her father, and she perceived him as being bossy and inconsiderate of her feelings. She thought that he must not love her if he did not want her to have a good time. So, she told the group she had decided to run away to resolve the issue once and for all. When other girls in the group shared similar family battles, it became clearer to Rita that it was not just her father who acted this way. In exploring their relationship more in depth, she realized that she loved him dearly, and that she tended to give up because she could not bear to see him in pain. It became clear to her that running away was not the right solution, because it would make him suffer even more and she would not be able to stand that. The alternative was to talk to him and try to convince him to give her more freedom. She agreed to try, but was not sure she could do it. Role-playing helped her practice the necessary skills to talk to him convincingly. When she argued that coming home earlier means walking alone, which is less safe, he agreed.

In this case, the action stage was needed to resolve the problem. Although Hill's three-stage model was developed on the basis of individual counseling with adults, I find it useful for group counseling with children as well.

APPLICATION OF THE THREE-STAGE MODEL: SUPPORT FROM RESEARCH

Research by colleagues and I has indicated that the patterns of both client and counselor responses are quite similar in individual and group counseling for children, and they are also similar to adult counseling processes. We found simple response to be the most frequent client response, followed by experiencing and insight; other responses (asking for help, future goals, and counselor-client alliance) were quite rare, in keeping with the literature on individual adult counseling (Hill, 2001). Experiencing was more frequent in group counseling (Shechtman, 2004a; Shechtman & Ben-David, 1999). The higher rate of experiencing in group counseling is not a trivial finding, as it is the heart and soul of psychotherapy (Bohart et al., 1997; L. S. Greenberg, 2002). There were no differences in outcomes between individual and group treatment children. As clients in individual counseling undoubtedly receive more therapeutic attention, we attributed the equal gains to the higher rate of experiencing in group counseling, hence underlining the importance of emotional experiencing in counseling.

In regard to counselor responses, we found that group counselors used mostly questions, followed by paraphrases, encourages, and interpretives, regardless of the treatment format. Other differences were minimal. The conclusion drawn from these two studies is that the client behavior system and the helping skills system can be safely applied to group treatment research and practice with children.

An interesting finding in these two studies (along with an earlier one; Leichtentritt & Shechtman, 1998) is that the most frequent counselor response is asking questions and not providing challenges or interpretations, which were extremely rare. In other words, interpretive interventions are not needed to generate emotional experiencing in children's groups. Rather, there are alternative methods, which I discuss further.

PROCHASKA'S (1999) TRANSTHEORETICAL MODEL OF CHANGE

Prochaska (1999) has suggested a more extended transtheoretical model, in which change involves progression through a series of stages, and, at any given stage, people apply specific processes to progress to the next one. The change process entails six stages: (a) precontemplation, (b) contemplation, (c) preparation, (d) action, (e) maintenance, and (f) termination. Precontemplation is the stage in which people do not intend to change, because they are unaware of their problem, demoralized about the ability to change, defensive about their behavior, or denying that there is a problem. At the contemplation stage, people intend to change and weigh the pros and cons of doing so. The balance between costs and benefits can provoke profound ambivalence, which can keep people immobilized in this stage for a long period. In the preparation stage, people intend to take action in the immediate future and usually have a plan for action. These are the people best recruited for brief counseling. Action is the stage in which people have made specific modifications in their life or changes in their behavior. In maintenance, people work to prevent relapse, and are increasingly more confident that they can continue their changes. Finally, at termination, individuals experience no temptation to return to their previous behavior and are confident about their ability to maintain the change, no matter what the temptation will be.

As in the Hill (2005) model, Prochaska's (1999) recommendation was to match particular processes of change to specific stages of change. In the beginning stages of change, the intention is to raise awareness and increase information about the causes, consequences, and cures for a particular problem; to help with emotional relief; and to lead to environmental reevaluation. To progress from the contemplation stage to the preparation stage, self-reevaluation and self-liberation are needed. Self-reevaluation combines cognitive and affective assessments of one's self-image. People at this stage reevaluate how they have been as troubled individuals and how their life will be once they are free of the problem. Self-liberation encompasses both the belief that one can change and a commitment to act on that belief. Finally, at the action and maintenance stages, a cognitive–behavioral orientation is in order. These stages require counter conditioning (learning healthier behaviors to replace problem behaviors), contingency management (particularly reinforcement), stimulus control (modifying the environment to minimize temptation), and helping relationships.

Prochaska (1999) offered an integrative model in which therapeutic processes originating from competing theories can be compatible when they are matched to the client's stage of change. With patients in earlier stages of change, counselors or psychotherapists can enhance progress through more experiential processes that produce healthier cognitions, emotions, evaluations, decisions, and commitments. In later stages, the therapist should seek to build on such solid preparation and motivation by emphasizing more behavioral processes that can help condition healthier habits, reinforce these habits, and provide physical and social environments supportive of healthier lifestyles. Techniques are also adjusted to the stage of change. At the first stages, people have low expectations and poor therapeutic alliance, and these problems must be addressed first. A safe and caring relationship and environment can be established through careful listening and accepting; allowing release of emotions; and developing awareness, understanding, and empathy (through direct interactions, such as clarifying processes, and through indirect methods, such as art therapy). Only afterwards is it helpful to confront clients, but this, too, should be done in a sensitive and caring manner.

Perhaps Prochaska's (1999) most meaningful contribution was his emphasis on motivation or the will to make a change, which receives little emphasis in cognitive–behavioral theory. According to his model, only after a person has shown some intention to change and has developed some ideas about possible ways to reach his goal can the therapist work on mastery of skills. I, too, believe that the motivation and intention to change is the key to success, even with young children and certainly with adolescents.

A CASE ILLUSTRATION
OF THE TRANSTHEORETICAL MODEL OF CHANGE

My colleagues and I have applied Prochaska's (1999) model in our group treatment, particularly with aggressive children. The following case illustrates the change processes for one boy over the course of a short-term group counseling treatment (10 sessions).

Joe was a 10-year-old boy in the fourth grade who was identified by teachers and peers as highly aggressive. His family history was difficult: his parents were divorced; he had no relationship with his father; his mother, who worked hard to make a living, was seldom around; and he was "bossed around" by his only (older) sister. Joe had a history of physical abuse by both parents; he also witnessed his father abusing his mother. Joe was being treated in a group that included two additional aggressive boys and two nonaggressive classmates. The group was introduced to him as a storytelling group, which he liked. The first session was aimed at breaking the ice, getting to know each other, and introducing the language of feelings. The group plays The Legacy of My Name game. Joe indicated that he did not like his name, because it reminded him of his father's family ties. Next, in a game in which several objects were selected, he chose a rock, explaining that he was strong as a rock and that he liked being in power; he wanted children to know who was boss, to respect his strength, and to fear him. "This way they will never bug me," he explained. At this session, Joe was clearly in the precontemplation stage. Any attempt to probe, confront, or teach him about his behavior was useless. There was no point in showing him the negative side of such behavior before rapport had been established with the counselor and other group members. Realizing the stage he was in, Marie, the counselor, only reflected on what he said, refraining from criticism and exhibiting acceptance. She also acknowledged the positive feeling of being in power. At this point, Joe may have been surprised, even puzzled, at her calm reaction, but it was also a sign for him that the group was safe and that real feelings could be expressed.

In the next session, Marie used the book *The Soul Bird* (Snunit, 1999), which describes a variety of feelings (e.g., happiness, frustration, anger), each living in a drawer that may be opened by a certain behavior (e.g., a hug opens the happiness drawer). Joe opened the anger drawer, explaining, "When someone bugs me or is angry with me, the drawer of anger immediately opens up, and I have no control over it." It was only the second session, and Joe had already moved to the contemplation stage. Marie asked how he felt when he lost control, and he admitted that sometimes it was disturbing. He gave an example of an incident with his mother, because he felt sorry for her. Marie acknowledged his empathy for his mother and his good intentions, suggesting that perhaps one day they would discuss ways to increase self-control. There was no rush to change behavior—although Joe had exhibited a rising motivation to change, there was still too much to risk.

In the following session, Marie presented a picture of an adult abusing a boy quite brutally and asked the children to make up a story about it. Joe's story told of a frustrated father who left his family, but not before taking out his anger on his innocent son, who was trying to protect his mother. It was clear that Joe was going through a cathartic experience; he was highly emotionally aroused when telling the story and then withdrew. The group reacted enthusiastically to his story, acknowledging the son's efforts to help his mother.

The fourth session focused on a poem in which a frustrated boy destroyed his own drawing. In the process of identification with the literary figure, group members described their own experiences of loss of control. Joe shared with the group an incident in which his father smashed his computer, and others related similar instances. Quickly, the children moved to describing their own angry reactions. Joe said, "I can't think straight when I'm angry, my hands move automatically." When asked if he wants to change that, he responded with a "maybe."

Marie introduced a story about an abusive father in the next session. Joe left the room in tears, but came back after a while and shared with the group his experiences of being abused by his father. "I felt really helpless when it happened, because my mom could not protect me. I could not hit back because he was so strong, but I wanted to hit someone, so I chose a younger child and hit him." He continued, "I know it's not right, but I'm not thinking at such moments." This seemed to indicate the development of insight and perhaps the beginnings of motivation to take some action.

In the sixth session, the children drew their own monsters, on the basis of the poem "My Own Monster." Discussion focused on the extent to which they wanted to control their monster. Joe, like the others, said he wanted to control his monster, which looked very ugly and threatening to the children. This was the time for a clarifying process, in which the children investigated the pros and cons of their behavior and were confronted about the consequences of their aggression. Each child placed himself on a continuum of aggression from 1 (*no self-control*) to 10 (*always in control*). Joe considered himself a 4, explaining that he lost control more often than not, but said he used to be a 1, with no control at all. Asked what he would like to become, he chose 7, i.e., usually with control. Probed about the price he paid for his lack of control, he offered a whole list of things: "Kids won't become friends with me, I'm not invited to parties, teachers are angry, my mother suffers." He was also able to foresee the positive consequences of his possible change in behavior: "I will not be that stressed, I will have things to do, I will not be that isolated." It appeared that Joe (like the others) had reached the action stage and it was time to work on change.

The next session featured the film *Madi* (Keymeulen, 1987) in which a child is badly injured as a result of aggressive behavior. This made a strong impression on the boys because of the dramatic consequences of anger and aggression. The struggle for self-control came up again, and more alternatives to aggressive reaction were found. Joe continued informing the group about changes he had already noticed: "We lost the game because the other group was cheating. Normally, I would have been really angry, but I just left." He shared with his mom the fact that he attended the group and she, too, reinforced his progress.

Finally, the group read the poem "I Am My Own Commander," which focuses on taking responsibility and controlling oneself. At this stage, Joe was quite ready to take charge of his behavior. He felt he was moving in the right direction. At termination, in his feedback on the group experience, he said that he liked the way he had been treated in the group, how the counselor listened to him and was nonjudgmental, and that this made him cooperative. "When they yell at me, I do not listen, but when people talk quietly, I can understand." Maintenance and termination were not possible to follow in this course of treatment.

APPLICATION OF THE TRANSTHEORETICAL MODEL: SUPPORT FROM RESEARCH

Prochaska's (1999) theory was further examined in terms of the process of change undergone by various aggressive children receiving individual and group treatment.

The first study (Shechtman & Ben-David, 1999) analyzed the change process for 15 children in individual treatment and 15 children in group treatment. Results indicated that about 60% of the children in both formats reached the action stage. Moreover, a correlation between stage of change and session number was revealed, suggesting progress in stages as the treatment evolved. The second study (Shechtman, 2003) analyzed the process of change for 25 aggressive boys in individual treatment and 25 in group treatment. Here, too, a pattern of growth was revealed; as treatment progressed, children moved to higher stages of change. At the onset of counseling, only a few of the boys (about 10%) in both formats had reached the preparation or action stage. In contrast, at termination most of the boys had reached one of these two advanced stages (83% and 79% for individual and group treatment, respectively). Furthermore, a hierarchical analysis confirmed that the probability of reaching a higher stage of change increases significantly as a function of the treatment session.

SUMMARY

In sum, I offer a unique theory of child group counseling and psychotherapy using an expressive–supportive modality. Although we acknowledge the importance of self-expressiveness noticed by Piper and his colleagues (2002), my colleagues and I refrain from interpretive interventions due to the deficit in children's abilities to cope with such interactions. To enhance self-expressiveness, we employ an integrative theory of change based on stages of progress, as suggested by Hill (2005) and Prochaska (1999). This multistage theory is also conducive to the supportive aspect of our model, as the action stage employs numerous techniques that provide instrumental assistance. These three sources of influence are reflected in our long and intensive clinical experience, as well as on a vast body of research. However, they are not the whole process of change; in fact, they only explain the individual process of change in the group and help practitioners work with the individual within the group.

Despite some similarities in both client and counselor behaviors in individual and group treatment formats (M. S. Corey & Corey, 2006; Hill, 1990), there are also unique characteristics of group work (Fuhriman & Burlingame, 1990). Although some (e.g., insight, catharsis, reality testing, hope, self-disclosure) exist at both individual and group levels, owing to the similar goals in counseling there are also factors unique to group counseling situations (such as vicarious learning, role flexibility, universality, altruism, family reenactment, and interpersonal learning). More recently, Burlingame and colleagues (2004) concluded that the best predictors of outcomes in group are the interpersonal (e.g., feedback, positive climate). Others indicated important differences in therapeutic factors between individual and group treatment. In his work with cancer patients, Spiegel and Classen (2000) argued that it is the exchange of self-disclosure and mutual support that affects outcomes. Thus, the second part of the expressive–supportive equation is drawn mostly from group dynamics. As therapeutic factors are an important aspect of process analysis in group counseling and psychotherapy, they are discussed in depth in the next chapter, which addresses the social aspects of the group process.

3 Therapeutic Factors in Children's Groups

This chapter focuses on the interpersonal level of group functioning, examining how children and adolescents are helped through the group process. It complements the previous chapter, which discussed the therapeutic processes of the individual client in the group. This individual process of change is made possible by the therapeutic forces in the group. Yet, little is known about such processes in groups with children and adolescents. Therefore, here, too, I borrow from the knowledge accumulated on groups with adults, followed by a review of the limited information existing on therapeutic factors in children's groups.

THERAPEUTIC FACTORS IN ADULT GROUPS

The literature on group treatments offers the common description of the therapeutic factor, "an element of group therapy that contributes to improvement in a patients' condition and is a function of the action of the group therapist, the other group member, and the patient himself" (Bloch & Crouch, 1985, p. 4). Indeed, empirical research has found a direct link between therapeutic factors and outcomes (Cheung & Sun, 2001; Johnson, Burlingame, Davies, & Olsen, 2002; Ogrodniczuk & Piper, 2003; Robbins, 2003; Yalom & Leszcz, 2005).

The professional community has generally accepted Yalom's (Yalom & Leszcz, 2005) list of 11 therapeutic factors as the basic elements essential to group-promoted change—instillation of hope, universality, imparting information, altruism, family recapitulation, developing of socializing techniques, interpersonal learning, cohesiveness, catharsis, existential factors, and imitative behavior. A consensus has been established regarding the factors that clients perceive to be most helpful: group cohesiveness, catharsis, and interpersonal learning (Fuhriman, Burlingame, Seaman, & Barlow, 1999; Yalom & Leszcz, 2005). Recently, Cheung and Sun (2001) reported support and catharsis as the strongest correlates of patients' benefits. Similarly, Lieberman and Golant (2002) found that support and self-disclosure were the two most helpful experiences related to outcomes. Differences have been found between reports by clients and by therapists (Crouch, Bloch, & Wanlass, 1994; Shechtman & Pearl-Dekel, 2000; Yalom & Leszcz, 2005), as well as between inpatients and outpatients (Crouch et al., 1994; Yalom & Leszcz, 2005).

Some researchers have attempted to combine some of the therapeutic factors into a few broad categories. MacKenzie (1990) suggested a division into support, self-disclosure, interpersonal learning, and personal growth. Similarly, Kivlighan, Multon, and Brossat (1996) suggested four components: emotional awareness–insight (strong affective experiences connected to gaining awareness and insight), relationship–climate (formation and maintenance of relationships in the group), other-versus self-focus (interaction with others, e.g., altruism), and problem definition–change (the problem aspect of treatment, encompassing both understanding of the problem and behavioral change).

In a study comparing therapeutic factors in individual and group treatment, Holmes and Kivlighan (2000) found relationship–climate to be the most frequent factor in both frameworks. However, as expected, participants in individual treatment identified emotional awareness–insight and problem definition–change more frequently than group participants, whereas relationship–climate and other- versus self-focus were more frequent in the group treatment sessions.

THERAPEUTIC FACTORS IN CHILDREN'S GROUPS

Therapeutic factors in children and adolescent groups have rarely been investigated. An exception is the study of Corder, Whiteside, and Haizlip (1981), who asked treated adolescents to reflect on what helped them in the group process. They mentioned factors similar to those presented in the literature on adult groups, including self-disclosure/catharsis ("learning to express feelings"), interpersonal learning ("learning from group members' feedback"), group cohesiveness and support ("being like in an accepting family," "belonging to a group that accepted me"), hope ("seeing I was just as well off as others"), and helping others ("being important in others' lives").

Shechtman, Bar-El, and Hadar (1997) also investigated therapeutic factors in groups of adolescents who exhibited social and emotional difficulties. Using the 11 therapeutic factors suggested by Yalom and Leszcz (2005), Shectman et al. (1997) found that the three most significant factors were group cohesiveness, catharsis, and developing socializing skills. Whereas the first two factors are congruent with the literature of adult groups, the third is typical of adolescents, for whom the building of social relationships is a central developmental task (Erikson, 1974). Results of the study suggested that therapy with children may be different than that for adults, that developmental issues must be taken into account, and that much more research is needed on group processes in children's groups (Barlow et al., 2000).

Another study used the classification offered by Holmes and Kivlighan (2000) to investigate therapeutic factors in groups of aggressive children (Shechtman, 2003). Emotional awareness–insight was present most frequently of all factors, in contrast to Holmes and Kivlighan's findings. This difference can be attributed to the different type of measurement: Shechtman (2003) used observational data whereas Holmes and Kivlighan used self-report data. Asking participants what seems to have helped them in the treatment process may generate responses that are more directly relevant to the question of interest (Hill & Kellems, 2002). Differences in the research findings might therefore be explained by differences between client and observer evaluations of therapeutic factors that have been shown in the literature (e.g., Shechtman & Pearl-Dekel, 2000). The second possible explanation for the difference between the two studies was the type of population. Group processes with children participating in Shechtman's (2003) study may be very different from those occurring in the groups of adults investigated in the Holmes and Kivlighan study. Children have different developmental needs, which may affect the presence of therapeutic factors. Moreover, the participants in Shechtman's (2003) study were aggressive boys, and their evaluation of therapeutic factors may be different than those that work for other types of children.

These results led to an investigation of therapeutic factors in children's groups based on children's perceptions of the critical incidents in the group process (Shechtman & Gluk, 2005). The study population in this study comprised 64 children in 10 groups that were conducted in elementary school. All these children were referred to the counseling center because of social, emotional, or behavioral difficulties. In the counseling center they were assigned to small psychotherapy groups based on age. Each group contained six to eight children and lasted 8 months (about 16 weekly 1-hr sessions). Groups were led by several leaders, all trained in the expressive—supportive modality (see Chapter 2). Counselors' intentions were to establish a positive, secure group climate and to promote emotional experiencing. They used a variety of methods and techniques adjusted to work with children in the group setting (these methods will be discussed in later chapters). To measure the therapeutic factors, the researchers used the Group Counseling Helpful Impact Scale (GCHIS) developed by Kivlighan and colleagues (1996), also used in the Holmes and Kivlighan (2000) study.

Results showed that relationship–climate was the most common factor (47%) in all groups, followed by other- versus self-focus (25%). Emotional awareness–insight accounted for only 19%, and problem definition–change was 9%. These results are very different from a previous study (Shechtman, 2003) in which relationship–climate was the least frequent, other- versus self-focus was the most frequent, and problem definition–change was more frequent than emotional awareness–insight. As both studies were conducted with children and used the same type of expressive–supportive modality, the only logical explanation remains the different sources of information: observation (ratings of transcripts) compared to self-report (participants' evaluations). The results of the Shechtman and Gluk (2005) study are similar to those of the Holmes and Kivlighan (2000) study, which was also based on critical incidents: there, too, relationship–climate was the most frequent factor.

Support for the importance of relationship and climate in groups with children and adolescents was received in a recent study of students with LD (Shechtman & Sender, 2006). This study found bonding with group members to be positively associated with outcomes in social competence.

THE MEANING OF RELATIONSHIP–CLIMATE
IN CHILDREN'S GROUPS

Even if we assume that the factor of relationship–climate—also known as group cohesiveness—is highly important, it is not clear what that entails. This is a complicated construct with multiple meanings, whose definition seems to vary from one investigator to another. Yalom (1995) defined group cohesiveness as "the condition of members feeling warmth and comfort in the group, feeling they belong, valuing the group and feeling, in turn, that they are valued and unconditionally accepted and supported by other members" (p. 48), focusing on feelings and on the humanistic conditions necessary for personal growth (see Cain, 2001). Braaten (1991) identified five dimensions of group cohesiveness: attraction and engagement, support and care, listening and empathy, self-disclosure and feedback, and action process and goal achievement. Most of these were found to be related to outcomes among group members (Johnson et al., 2002). A different classification—and one of the most frequently researched—was suggested by MacKenzie (1987), who identified three major components: engagement, avoidance, and conflict. However, for adolescents, a factor analysis by Kivlighan and Tarrant (2001) yielded only two factors: active engagement and conflict–distance.

The lack of clarity of the construct and the limited scope of research call for a qualitative investigation of cohesiveness in groups with children. Therapists need to discover what group cohesion or climate means to the children, based on interviews with them. What emerged from the interviews in the Shechtman and Gluk (2005) study is that peer and counselor support is a major component: "In our group the girls encouraged each other; we helped each other, and kept our secrets." In another case, bonding with the counselor was a major aspect of cohesiveness: "When Amy [the counselor] was gone for two weeks, I was really worried about her. I prayed every night for her to come back safely, because I missed her a lot." But most of the time it was the support of peers that was best recalled, as expressed in the following critical incident:

Shelly:	The most important event for me was when they celebrated my birthday; no one ever loved me, they always made fun of me, but on that birthday everyone said some good things about me. They said that I am pretty and that I am very sensitive, and I liked that. I suddenly felt that everyone loves me and wants my company, and I felt happy.
Interviewer:	Why was it so important to you?
Shelly:	Because deep in my heart I feel that people do not like me, that they kind of reject me. But here they said different things, I feel different here, I believed them when they say they love me.

Birthdays are celebrated in a special way in our children's groups, via an activity called *Birthday for Our Soul*. This is not the usual party, but rather an occasion to encourage and empower the birthday child. It is a session in which that child gets only positive feedback, compliments, and imaginary presents. This concentrated amount of attention and positive regard is a corrective interpersonal experience for many of these children, and a key to progress (Malekoff, 2004). Out of 54 children who had birthdays celebrated in the group, nine boys and girls labeled this event as their critical incident.

Another aspect of climate is the sense of being listened to and understood, as is evident in the following statement: "The most important time for me was when I shared my secret with the group. I felt as if I am in a sealed room full of love, with children who care, listen, and keep my secret. This is what I felt." Similarly, 12-year-old Jane said,

> For me, the most important time was when I shared with the group that I do not know who my father is. The children listened to me seriously, and encouraged me to talk to my mom. With their support, I got brave enough to talk to her one night, and now I know who he is. I feel very relieved. Never before was I able to talk about it.

Related to the sense of being supported and understood is self-disclosure, which is often referred to in the literature as the two factors of experiencing and insight. The two are interrelated, as they enhance each other. Accepting conditions provide group members with the courage to talk about their feelings and experiences, and such self-disclosure serves to increase feelings of warmth and love. Self-disclosure is needed for personal growth and development; emotional experiencing and catharsis would not occur without it, and these are major therapeutic processes, as is evident in the following critical incident report.

> The most important thing is that I revealed my secret about being adopted. I feel much better now, as if my stomach is emptier, and I thank Amy [the counselor] for helping me with this.... When I talked I felt confident in the group and knew that they would accept me. Unlike other places where children bug me, in this group they asked questions and seemed to be interested in me. They really understood my problem.

A supportive climate and self-disclosure also promote interpersonal interaction, learning from others, and trying to help others. In the next verbal exchange, this interaction was clear: "You at least know who your mother is. I do not know who my father is, so I cannot be mad at anyone, only sad." Jane had wanted to solve this issue for a while, but was not courageous enough to even discuss it in the group. It was the process of identification and sense of universality that evoked this disclosure, and, as a result, the group discussed her issue, as well, and helped her bring it to complete resolution.

Elements of affect and support were clearly of greatest importance to the interviewed children. Even when a critical incident fell into the category of problem definition–change, the emphasis seemed to be on emotions:

> I had a fight with a friend who is not in this group. It was very important for me to resolve the conflict with her. I shared the incident with the group and even though I was the cause of the conflict, the group helped me resolve the issue. They did not blame me, they tried to understand and showed me how to do it. I am thankful to the group for this.

Responses that fall in the category of problem definition–change were quite rare, which is disappointing. It is not clear whether the children did not expect, and therefore did not respect, change in behavior or whether change in behavior was actually limited. The answer to this question requires further exploration, although my research shows gains on most of the variables investigated. In any event, I value their happiness, their relief of stress, and their improved feelings about themselves for its own sake. This is what positive psychology is all about. However, I do strive for more.

In accordance with the stages of change underlying the suggested treatment model (see Chapter 2), it is important to complete the cycle and achieve actual change in behavior. The effectiveness of these groups will be further discussed in future chapters. In an era of accountability, it is important to demonstrate that such groups are efficient. This may convince authorities to allow such experiences in the school. However, to fully understand the type of group I offer in my practice, it is important to first expand on the leader's role, techniques and methods, and the clinical process with its practical considerations. All these are discussed and illustrated in the second part of the book.

Kivlighan and Holmes (2004) recently provided a unique perspective on therapeutic factors. They did not accept the argument that therapeutic factors are affected by individual differences (e.g., inpatients and outpatients). Rather, they suggested that the therapeutic factors that work for clients are related to the type of group or group orientation. Based on cluster analyses, they identified four clusters of groups: affective insight, affective supportive, cognitive supportive, and cognitive insight. The factors with the highest endorsement in affective insight groups were acceptance and catharsis, followed by interpersonal learning and self-understanding; in contrast, guidance and vicarious learning were relatively unimportant. Affective supportive groups ranked acceptance as the most important therapeutic factor, followed by instillation of hope and universality. This combination of factors suggests a pattern of seeking hope and acceptance, as well as the need to know that one is not alone in one's experiences. The groups in cluster 3 (cognitive supportive) ranked vicarious learning and guidance relatively highly, and attributed low importance to self-understanding. Finally, cognitive insight groups ranked interpersonal learning, self-understanding, and vicarious learning as the most valued therapeutic factors. In general, the taxonomy derived from this study distinguished between groups with a cognitive versus affective focus, and between groups focusing on insight versus support.

Following this distinction, and based on the theory that underlies the group therapy for children presented in this book, I classify the therapy groups run by my colleagues and I as affective supportive; they focus on emotional expressiveness within a highly supportive climate. As described earlier, this does not mean that insight and cognition are not important components, but rather that they are less present than affect and support.

SUMMARY

This chapter focuses on the social level of group functioning in an attempt to answer the question, "Which group mechanisms are responsible for the growth and change of the individual in the group?" My research of the therapeutic factors in groups with children and adolescents point to group cohesiveness as the main mechanism of change. Group cohesiveness is a complicated social construct that includes several components, including group climate, group prestige, a sense of togetherness, intimacy, and relationships. My research leads to the conclusion that interpersonal support and bonding with group members are key factors. These results strengthen the expressive–supportive model that I suggest. The two halves of the model are interrelated: Self-expressiveness elicits supportive reactions, and interpersonal support encourages self-expressiveness.

It is the counselor's role to enhance both individual and group processes of change, guided by the theories discussed earlier. Forthcoming chapters are intended to enhance counselors' understanding of their roles, tasks, skills, and techniques, as they navigate the various stages of the group process.

II

The Practice of Child and Adolescent Group Psychotherapy

Introduction to Part II

The group process in children's groups progresses through several stages, similar to that in groups with adults. Tuckman (1965) was the first to identify stages of group development. He suggested the terms *forming*, *storming*, and *performing*, to which others have added *adjourning*. Since then, a consensus has been pretty much established regarding the existence of four stages. The initial stage—of orientation and exploration—is for getting acquainted, determining the structure of the group, and exploring members' expectations. Because members are somewhat tentative and reserved at this point, the leader should focus on making sure that all members are included and feel safe. Then, as involvement in the therapeutic process increases and demands for self-disclosure are made, group members go through a transition stage in which anxiety and resistance increase. The members test the leader and the group, to determine if they can be trusted, and decide whether to get involved. The third stage, characterized by cohesion and productivity, is the working stage. Members focus on identified goals and concerns and are willing to work in and outside the group to address these concerns. In the final stage of termination, group members deal with the loss of the group, clear up unfinished business, and learn to transfer what they have learned to situations outside the group (M. S. Corey & Corey, 2006; Gladding, 2003; Yalom & Leszcz, 2005).

Similar stages, although labeled somewhat differently, have been suggested for child and adolescent group psychotherapy. Berkovitz (1989) referred to the primitive stage, the developing stage, the mature stage, and termination. At the primitive stage, group members are highly dependent on the leader, subgrouping is common, and silence occurs frequently. At the developing stage, children seek to reach out to group members, not without a struggle to gain autonomy, but with greater confidence to handle conflict based on respect for others. At the mature stage, children discover a sense of solidarity that permits each individual to feel valued by others and

39

trusting enough to share personal concerns and learn from others. At termination, the children deal with the anxiety of remaining without the group and accumulate the gains from the group process.

Some studies in the child group literature add a fifth, pregroup stage (K. G. Dies, 2000; Riva & Haub, 2004; Smead, 1995). During this stage, the group leader must prepare a place for the meeting, arrange procedures for selecting participants, prepare materials and activities, and prepare the children for their role in the group.

Along these same lines, Part II of this book contains five stages: the pregroup stage, the initial stage, the resistance stage, the working stage, and the termination stage. The counselor navigates the transition from one stage to another through strategies, direct communication, and modeling of appropriate behavior. The leader's roles and techniques are discussed in general terms first, followed by descriptions of the processes in each stage of the group.

4

Leadership in Counseling Groups With Children

The effectiveness of group counseling and psychotherapy is largely dependent on the leader's personality, interventions, and skills. M. S. Corey and Corey (2006) have argued that personality has the strongest impact on group members, and have referred to such personal traits as presence (being there for the client), personal power (self-confidence), courage (ability to take risks and be vulnerable), self-awareness, sincerity, authenticity, sense of identity, creativity, and belief in the group process. Research supports many of these characteristics. Group leaders who are warm, supportive, and genuinely interested in individual members, as well as in the group as a whole, have a positive impact on the gains of group members (R. R. Dies, 1994), whereas a leader's negative behavior tends to have a destructive impact on group members (McCallum, Piper, Ogrodniczuk, & Joyce, 2002; Smokowski, Rose, & Bacallo, 2001).

Leader interventions are defined as "purposeful actions of the leader to ensure safety and/or initiate, energize, or enhance the therapeutic factors operating within the group setting" (Morran, Stockton, & Whittingham, 2004, p. 92). Group interventions range from relatively spontaneous leader actions, such as blocking behavior or drawing out group members, to more formal planned exercises, such as structured feedback exchange. They may focus on individual members, a subgroup of members, or the entire group. Some of the most important leader interventions are directing communication traffic, facilitating the group process, blocking harmful group behavior, protecting group members, supporting, linking, moderating discussions, summarizing, and giving feedback (M. S. Corey & Corey, 2006; Morran et al., 2004).

In contrast to individual counseling, the group counselor has a number of tasks, some starting even before the group actually meets (Riva & Haub, 2004). The leader is responsible for selecting group members and pregroup preparation. After the group meets, one of the counselor's most important tasks is to establish and maintain a positive group climate. As in individual therapy, where the client–therapist relationship has been recognized as the single most important variable for therapy success (Bachelor & Horvath, 1999), therapeutic alliance is extremely important for the group's success. However, in groups this relationship is more complicated, as other significant people are involved in the therapy process. Positive relationships must be maintained among all members of the group, and the group must be attractive to its members to increase involvement and group cohesion. Group cohesion is considered the equivalent to therapeutic alliance in individual therapy, and of equal importance. Indeed, a relationship between group cohesion and therapeutic outcomes is frequently mentioned in group research (Hoag & Burlingame, 1997; Marziali, Munroe-Blum, & McCleary, 1997; Tschuschkle & Dies, 1994).

Another important role of the group leader is responsibility for giving structure to the group. Structure is provided in many ways, such as by establishing group norms, by suggesting topics, and by initiating activities. This is particularly necessary in the early stages of the group (R. R. Dies, 1994; Stockton, Rohde, & Haughey, 1992). Research suggests that structure has been associated with increased self-disclosure, cohesion and risk-taking in the group (Gazda et al., 2001).

The professional skills needed by group leaders are similar to those required in individual therapy. They include active listening, restating, clarifying, summarizing, questioning, interpreting, confronting, reflecting feelings, supporting, self-disclosure, and guidance (M. S. Corey & Corey, 2006; Hill, 2005; Ivey & Ivey, 1999).

How is all this information relevant to group work with children? The following sections explore this question. Because groups with children are conducted mostly by counselors or therapists, I will refer interchangeably to the group counselor or therapist, rather than the group leader.

COUNSELOR ROLES IN GROUPS WITH CHILDREN

There are many similarities between the leader of adult groups and the child group counselor. The latter largely needs similar personality traits, has similar tasks to perform, applies similar interventions, and requires similar skills. As goals of group counseling and psychotherapy at all age levels are similar—to encourage expression of thoughts and feelings, develop insight, and change behavior in a group interaction process—it is understandable where these similarities come from. Counselors in children's groups, as leaders in adult groups, are responsible for establishing and maintaining a positive climate, helping group members work on their personal issues, promoting the therapeutic factors that enhance individual and group progress, and helping each member apply the knowledge acquired in the group to real-life situations. To achieve these goals, therapists in children's groups have to perform similar roles, use appropriate interventions, and effectively apply helping skills.

Nonetheless, the role of group therapist for children may also be very different from that of adult leaders, owing largely to the age of group members. Each task, intervention, and skill must be adjusted to the age of the children in the group, as well as to the type of group. I now examine each of these leader components separately, using my clinical experience and research investigations.

COUNSELOR PERSONALITY

In my clinical work with children, I have noticed several personality traits that are critical for a leader's success. I highlight three of these because of their meaningfulness to groups with children: presence, self-confidence, and creativity.

Presence is reflected in enthusiasm about the group and, particularly, the children themselves. More than adults, children need to hear direct expressions of genuine love. They often do not distinguish well between anger, rejection, and lack of love, and they often interpret criticism and punishment as rejection. Many of the children participating in group counseling carry negative experiences from home, have issues with trust, and lack self-confidence. These children particularly appreciate a warm welcome and an openly expressed message of liking and loving. Moreover, children often perceive the group counselor as a parental figure whose love and feedback they highly appreciate. I have seen them fighting over the seat next to the counselor and expressing love to him or her in verbal and physical behavior. I suspect that the client—therapist alliance has a much stronger impact on children than on adults in groups, although this has not yet been investigated. One of the best counselors at my facility says "I love you" constantly to the children; her group members come to believe that they are loved and are highly attracted to the group. In her groups, there are no dropouts and the level of self-disclosure is very high. Moreover, her behavior sets a model for the overt expression of mutual liking among group members.

Another important counselor characteristic is self-confidence. In groups with adults, this is mainly reflected in risk-taking behavior (e.g., confrontation). In contrast, children challenge group counselors in many ways, as I show in my discussion of the resistance stage. There are also many discipline problems in the groups, particularly at the initial stage. Counselors who demonstrate the ability to face such threats to their confidence enhance the children's trust, both in the counselor and in the group. Children like to test the limits of adults; they know they can rely on a therapist who remains calm yet assertive, that he or she will control the group situation, and that they can be safe in the group under all circumstances. Self-confidence also helps the counselor to be open-minded and honest and to take risks, all of which are particularly important behaviors in adolescent groups (MacLennan & Dies, 1992).

In one of the groups at the center where I work, the children challenged the group counselor at the first session with the question, "Why us?" This is a common issue in children's groups, as they are not clients who selected therapy; rather, they are children referred to counseling because of social, emotional, or behavioral problems. For them, a group may carry a negative label or a stigma. Many novice counselors are afraid of this question, and exhibit insecurity at this point. Here is an example of a leader's sensitive and positive response to this question, posed by an elementary-school group: "I gave it serious thought. I wanted group members who can benefit from the group and also help each other. I consulted with each of you [at the intake interview] and got the impression that this will be a successful group." The encouraging message this counselor gave to her group was that they were each chosen for their capacity to be constructive in the group. She sounded positive, hopeful, and self-confident, and the children's reaction was: "Can't you see she wanted us?" This was, indeed, a good start for a group.

In a group of adolescent girls, Judy, the counselor, was challenged by Billy, a dominating group member who tried to take over. Billy started a game of Telephone, ignoring her leader. Judy hesitated for a moment, then invited Billy to express her feelings openly. Eventually, Billy expressed her disappointment in the activities Judy had introduced. Judy encouraged her to suggest an alternate activity, which turned out to be highly successful. Through this activity, the group progressed to a higher level of self-disclosure, and the leader avoided a power struggle without losing her status in the group.

Finally, a counselor who works with children must be creative and innovative in many ways. Children's group counselors need to prepare sessions that are fun and run smoothly; they need to guide the sessions in a flexible and creative way; and they need to offer a wide range of activities and methods to help children express themselves. Children are not necessarily in the mood to work, unexpected issues often crop up, and always, even in unstructured groups, creative methods must be used to help children express themselves. It is sometimes difficult to proceed with the group process through direct questions, particularly with younger children. The ability to apply creative methods that encourage group members to share their experiences is of utmost importance, because it reduces tension, embarrassment, and anxiety, and it increases playfulness.

COUNSELOR INTERVENTIONS

In respect to interventions in children's groups, Thompson and Rudolph (2000) mentioned similar tasks to those attributed to leaders of adult groups: directing communication traffic, facilitating the group process, blocking harmful behavior, protecting group members, supporting, linking, moderating discussions, summarizing, and giving feedback. R. R. Greenberg (2003) mentioned additional leadership tasks that are unique to children: maintaining discipline, keeping the group on task, establishing and enforcing group rules, encouraging full group participation, and moving the group in the direction of its objectives. Obviously, some of these tasks are more relevant at the initial stage of the group, whereas others are more relevant at the working stage or at termination.

The Initial Stage

In the initial stage, the counselor is particularly active in structuring the group process. This includes the task of creating a therapeutic group climate—that is, establishing group norms of emotional expressiveness and constructive interpersonal interactions that allow such expressiveness with minimal harm. As explained in Chapter 3, the most significant therapeutic factor for children is group climate and cohesiveness. It is hard to imagine children who would be willing to talk about personal matters and disclose emotions unless they felt the group is a safe place.

How does a group counselor achieve a positive working climate? One way is to demonstrate the facilitative skills of emphatic understanding, genuineness, and respect for group members. Counselors must show that they are caring by being nonjudgmental and accepting, and by providing encouragement, support, and guidance. Children learn quite well from modeling, particularly from a respectful authority figure. For example, a counselor may say to a silent group member something like:

> I know how embarrassing it may be to share private information in front of a group of strangers. I was not very brave either when I was your age. But you are an important group member, and I see you listening carefully to others. We will all be happy to get to know you a bit more.

As the counselor models facilitative behavior, group members begin to participate in the helping process and become more active helpers for one another (Thompson & Rudolph, 2000).

Another way to establish group norms of acceptance and support is through guidance and skills training. In group work with children, it is extremely important to attend to the development of norms and to reinforce expected behavior, especially during the first few sessions. For example, in response to a child who was playing with her cell phone, the counselor gently said, "You remember that we have an obligation to listen to each other. Careful attention and listening helps the speaker and helps us to better understand him." This became a group norm, and when such inappropriate behavior was repeated in the group, another member mentioned the rule instead of the counselor.

Unless children are prepared for group counseling experiences, they simply don't know how to behave in a group setting—how to relate to each other, ask questions, comfort and support, convey empathy, or provide feedback. This is not the typical language that children and adolescents use in communicating with each other, as observed in a study on interpretives in groups with children (Shechtman & Yanuv, 2001). The study showed that children challenge and provide feedback to other group members, but often in a nonconstructive way. They tend to criticize, offend, and blame rather than accept and support. These behaviors evoke nonproductive responses from group members. The study highlights the problematic interaction of young children in groups and calls for leaders to train group members in communication skills at the onset of therapy. In our interventions, my colleagues and I train children to talk directly to each other, to make eye contact, and to use a repertoire of emotions so that empathy can be conveyed clearly. We also teach children to refrain from premature guidance and advice, and to ask open questions and give constructive feedback.

Modeling and training are not always sufficient to achieve the goal of establishing a constructive climate. In some situations, the counselor must directly block a negative interaction and protect a vulnerable group member. One common difficult situation is when members try to force group norms, such as when they try to break another's silence. Once members start disclosing, they are eager to get others to do the same because they unconsciously believe that this will enhance confidentiality (if everyone tells a secret, then it becomes too risky to disclose secrets). Moreover, fairness plays a major role in children's, and particularly adolescents', lives; it is only fair to share the responsibility for the group's progress, they believe. Thus, at a certain point they become pushy. When pressure stems from such a rationale, it is usually expressed in a demanding and intolerant manner, which may be quite a threatening experience for some group members. Although sharing emotions and experiences is extremely important in counseling and psychotherapy groups, it is equally important that the group accepts a norm allowing members to move at their own pace (Smead, 1995). The leader must be very skillful in both encouraging all group members to share and protecting anxious group members from being attacked.

For example, in one group session the children were using picture cards to identify some of their issues. Two girls selected cards and disclosed meaningful information about themselves. Janet chose a picture of a forest to represent her complicated life; Marie selected a picture of two people holding hands to express her need for human contact. Toni, the next girl, hesitated for a moment, and Janet and Marie pressed her to go on. The counselor's intervention was, "We should give her the time she needs to make a decision. It may be quite stressful to make a decision under pressure. Remember, one of our rules was to respect individual needs." She protected a group member by blocking negative behavior and establishing group norms.

Very often, a therapist working with children needs to deal with discipline problems, which are more frequent in children's groups than in adult groups. Counselors usually prefer a nonauthoritarian style of leadership, and indeed, the climate that best fits the group atmosphere is democratic. Nonetheless, at times the therapist must be firm, as well as fair and friendly. To maintain discipline, a counselor may refer to the group rules, or she can use "I messages," thereby also demonstrating this very important means of communication. For example, one therapist said to a fourth-grade group, "Right now I feel that you are ignoring me." Because the relationship with her was warm and intimate, the group responded positively to the message and stopped the noise.

In short, structure is needed to maintain discipline, to develop group norms, to establish trust, and to reduce anxiety, all typical issues of the initial stage. But, at the same time, structure should not foster dependency or block spontaneous reactions. Group members need to be encouraged to speak when they feel a need (not only when they are invited to talk) and to become involved in the group process by taking over some of the leader's responsibility (Berg et al., 1998).

The Working Stage

In the working stage, group counselors are responsible for helping clients identify and define their problems and the related feelings and thoughts. They also assist clients with the exploration process, intensify identification processes and mutual sharing, help increase awareness and insight, offer alternative ways to behave, and encourage all group members to take part in this process. In groups with adults, it is easier to achieve these goals through a direct approach, such as asking a question about goals and difficulties. However, children need structured activities even in the working stage, and the younger they are, the more structure they need at this stage (M. S. Corey & Corey, 2006).

In our groups, my coworkers and I use structured activities mostly to stimulate self-disclosure and sharing; the rest of the time is spent processing personal and group issues. But although they function only as stimuli, these structured activities make a huge difference. Using an activity to generate discussion does not contradict the goals of developing awareness or increasing expression and exploration of feelings. On the contrary, it often facilitates the processing of meaningful personal issues, which would not come up following a direct question. Methods and techniques are explored in depth in Chapter 5; here I offer a few examples to illustrate the effectiveness of using structured activities at the working stage.

I have learned from experience that it is easier for children to select a card that reflects their problem than to respond to a direct cognitive question, such as "What is your problem?" In the picture card game mentioned earlier, Janet, in selecting the picture of a forest to represent her complicated life, responded on an affective level, which was then further explored. And Marie used the handholding figure to express her deep loneliness. Would they have been able to articulate their problems without this activity?

A group counselor who worked with children of divorced parents used photos from their family album as the stimuli to present their problems. Each child responded to a major difficulty in dealing with the divorce through that photograph. For example, Denise, who had presented her father as aggressive and threatening, brought a picture of him in a good mood, playing with her in the park, stating: "You see, he can be very different, warm and fun." This led to an exploration of her complex relationship with him, leading to a more balanced perception of him and reduced anxiety.

Another group leader used bibliotherapy (*The Soul Bird*; Snunit, 1999) to explore some of the children's secrets. In this story, the soul bird has many drawers in which personal secrets are hidden, and only the individual can open the drawer he or she wishes. Rather than inviting the children directly to share a personal issue, the counselor asked the girls to open one of their drawers. It was much easier to respond to this technique than to address a direct question about life difficulties. When Louise opened the drawer of anger at her father, who had abandoned her when she was a baby, she underwent a cathartic experience, followed by a sense of relief. I doubt that such experiencing could have taken place except though such a playful and indirect form of interaction.

This is not to suggest that sessions in the working stage always begin with a structured activity; in fact, many do not. By this time in the group process, most of the children feel free to take advantage of the group. The counselor must be flexible enough to let such processes occur, and be able to help clients work on their problems. In one session of a group of younger children, Eileen asked for help with a dispute she was having with her parents over visiting her grandmother's grave. The topic of death, which had already been briefly raised by Ken (whose dog had died), became the topic of discussion for the next few sessions. The counselor was surprised by Eileen's initiated self-disclosure, as well as by her interest in discussing an issue that is not commonly considered at this young age. She had to change her plan for that session, as well as for the next few sessions, and use a variety of helping skills to help Eileen explore the conflict, reduce her fear of death, and help other group members deal with this difficult issue.

At this stage of the group process, it is important to keep the group on task. The short-term task is to cover what has been planned for each week; the long-term task is to move the group in the direction of the agreed upon goal. Obviously, leaders of structured groups focus more on short-term goals, whereas those of nonstructured groups focus more on long-term ones. In groups my colleagues and I run, the exchange of self-disclosure, feedback, and support promotes such long-term goals as enhancing the children's abilities to express their concerns, difficulties, and problems; helping them understand these issues; and teaching them to help each other meet these goals. Thus, the focus is on both the individual's problem and the group process.

A crucial counselor task at this stage is to encourage full group participation, where members interact with others and are willing to share their feelings and experiences. Eliciting self-expressiveness in groups with children is easier than facilitating constructive interaction. As already mentioned, most children like to talk about themselves and release some of their emotional burdens. They seem to do so in quite a natural way, with little reservation (see Leichtentritt & Shechtman, 1998), unless their sense of trust was badly damaged. However, guiding children to respond to others with respect, empathy, and genuine interest is more difficult. This is a whole new language for most children, who need to be taught to use it. This is particularly true of children with an avoidant attachment style (see Shechtman & Dvir, 2006). Not only do such children disclose very little during the group process, they also react negatively to others' self-disclosure. Such interactions, if frequent, may impede group progress. When these issues come up, it is highly important to deal with them openly, to focus on the emotions involved using more advanced probing skills, to develop insight, and to translate that insight into action (M. S. Corey & Corey, 2006; Yalom & Leszcz, 2005).

For example, a group of children of divorce was stuck in a long silence following several very constructive sessions. Susie, the counselor, acknowledged the silence and asked members to think about reasons for it. Some complained that they had already shared and blamed the silent group members for being stuck. Susie led the group to explore their feelings. "What does it feel like to be stuck?" she asked. Some group members who had already shared said that they felt betrayed and regretted having shared; others said that they did not mind and felt good because they had gained so much; and still others expressed genuine interest in the stories of those who had not yet spoken and invited them to share.

Sandy eventually responded to such an invitation, sharing her difficulties in talking in a group. It often turns out that the silent group members are those with the most serious problems, making them reluctant to self-disclose in the group. The children in this group promised to be careful listeners, reassuring Sandy that they would keep her secret, and encouraging her to trust them. This enabled Sandy to talk about her mother's depression. As Sandy seemed uncomfortable, Susie asked the group for their reactions. Linda shared about her own mother's depression in a most natural manner, explaining that it is an illness and there is medicine for it. This seemed to "normalize" the issue and to make Sandy feel better. The group was very supportive; they reinforced her courage in sharing her secret with the group and offered their positive perspective of the situation: "You are lucky that both parents love you, want you, and fight for you." Sandy was happy she could open up in the group and felt empowered with a new perspective on her situation. Susie, for her part, was very careful to maintain a balance between pressure and invitation, and she had directed part of the discussion to sharing among the rest of the group, to prevent Sandy from feeling like the sole "actor on the stage," which she might have later regretted.

In sum, these examples demonstrate essential therapeutic factors in the group—catharsis and group cohesion—which the therapist must make every effort to enhance. In conflict situations, it is particularly important to remain hopeful and positive, as well as to convey the success of the group, the universality of problems, and the importance of catharsis and interpersonal learning. Most important, the counselor must model honesty and openness and the skills of listening and self-disclosure.

Termination

In the termination stage, counselors must prepare the group for separation, summarize gains of the group experience, and look at ways to transfer what they have learned to situations outside the group. There may be some anxiety and reluctance to terminate, and this may be reflected in regression in the level of participation through expression of strong emotions, such as sadness, mourning, or even aggression. The counselor must deal with these feelings with warmth and courage and without defensiveness. The leader's interventions are directed at helping clients go through separation, deal with unfinished business, evaluate their achievements following group experience, and say goodbye to each other. At this stage, the therapist will be using particularly active helping skills, such as information provision and guidance. More than in earlier stages, structure is required to complete these tasks. Therefore, the therapist continues to use a variety of methods, strategies, and therapeutic activities to achieve the tasks for the ending stage of group.

PROCEDURES FOR OPENING AND CLOSING GROUP SESSIONS

As it is of utmost importance to monitor children's feelings, the groups facilitated by my colleagues and I use a routine procedure for opening and closing a session, to focus on recent events. Every session starts with a brief exploration of expectations—and particularly feelings—as a result of the previous session. This is important to avoid impasses due to hidden issues.

For example, one group counselor opened a session by turning to a child who had disclosed in the previous session: "You left very excited last meeting. Can you share with us your feelings following this experience?" At another session, a counselor was concerned about absenteeism. She opened the session by saying: "Some people were absent last time. We all missed you. Can we share with them some of the main issues that we discussed?" To the members who had been absent, she asked: "How do you feel about having missed that session?" Yet another counselor referred to a difficult session in the previous week: "It was quite stormy here last time. How do you feel right now?"

These group sessions also end with evaluation of feelings or progress. It is extremely important to monitor children's feelings to make sure that no one was hurt and that there is no unfinished business. Sometimes a child may need an individual follow-up session, as suggested by M. S. Corey and Corey (2006).

This evaluation can be achieved in a number of ways. The counselor can use direct questions such as, "How do you feel right now?" or "What have you learned today about yourself?" Another possibility is to use feeling cards or feeling games. Yet another option is to administer a short questionnaire evaluating the session or inquire into each child's critical incident ("What was the most important thing that happened to you in the group?"). In addition, the children often receive an assignment for the following week, such as to practice some of the skills they have learned, to carry out a plan they decided upon, or to write a diary to express some of the feelings and experiences that they have during the week.

THE COUNSELOR'S HELPING SKILLS

Processing is a therapeutic endeavor in groups, just as it is in individual therapy. Therefore, in addition to leader tasks that are unique to the group process, the counselor must be trained in using effective helping skills. This is particularly true of those who conduct nonstructured groups. In structured groups, which are most often used with children (K. R. Greenberg, 2003; Riva & Haub, 2004; Smead, 1995), topics, activities, and materials are all prepared in advance, and the process is led mostly on a cognitive level. This provides confidence to the group counselor and increases his or her sense of self-efficacy. In contrast, in groups that are less structured, the process is less predictable, and the level of processing is highly emotional; therefore, the counselor's effective use of helping skills is particularly important.

Hill (2005) suggested a list of helping skills, including approval and reassurance, questions, restatement, reflection of feelings, challenge, interpretation, self-disclosure, information provision, and direct guidance. Although this list was compiled for individual counseling and psychotherapy, it is applicable to any therapy process. Based on comprehensive research, Hill (2005) suggested that certain skills are more appropriate for one stage of the therapy process and others are more in place at other stages. For example, at the exploration stage, the therapist is expected to use mostly encouragement and open questions to facilitate self-expressiveness and the sharing of past and present experiences. The employment of such skills helps both the counselor and the client get a better grasp of the latter's problem. As reflection of feelings facilitates affective exploration and cathartic experiences, this, too, is a needed skill in the exploration stage. At the insight stage, the counselor is expected to rely more on interpretive skills and self-disclosure. Interpretations, challenges, and feedback expand consciousness of self and help clients understand their difficulties, as well as the causes of their emotions, thoughts, and behavior. The counselor's self-disclosure helps clients develop insight. Finally, at the action stage, guidance and information skills are often used to help clients in instrumental ways to achieve therapeutic change.

It is interestingly that the same skills are used to address group issues, although they may be applied somewhat differently. For instance, they are conducive to using the here-and-now (Yalom & Leszcz, 2005) as a source for learning and emotional growth, a task that is unique to group counseling. As in groups with adults, therapists in children's groups tend to use helping skills more actively at the beginning stage of counseling, and then gradually reduce direct involvement and let group members take on some of the facilitation tasks (R. R. Dies, 1994; Yalom & Leszcz, 2005). Here are a few examples of how the counselor's helping skills can be used to address both a personal problem and a group problem.

One group was in its seventh session and, following some intense self-disclosures, the group put extreme pressure on the silent group members to talk. Annette said she found it difficult to share private information at that time. Her counselor could have approached this on a personal level and tried to explore those difficulties. She could have asked an open question: "Can you talk to us more about these difficulties?" She could have paraphrased: "You say it is difficult for you to share something personal right now." She could have reflected feelings: "You are a bit embarrassed at having to share." She could have self-disclosed: "I sometimes also feel uncomfortable about being intimate in a group of strangers." Or she could have related to the group, to the here-and-now interaction, using similar skills: "How do you feel about the group pressure to talk?" (question); "Does the group pressure embarrass you?" (question); "Does this silence right now suggest that some of you feel uncomfortable?" (reflection of feelings); "Can the group help somehow?" (guidance).

In a similar situation, Cynthia said she found it hard to self-disclose because she could only talk with people she was close to. The counselor responded with an interpretation: "So you expect the group to express positive feelings to you, so you can trust them more and then perhaps disclose." Cynthia's response ("Exactly") pointed to the accuracy of that interpretation.

In one group, when silence was somewhat prolonged, Sarah, who often tended to take the role of savior in the group, started talking. The counselor used an interpretation: "I can see silence bothers you. You seem to take responsibility for saving the group. Is this something that is familiar to you from other places?" This lead Sarah to explore her behavior outside of the group, where she felt considerable pressure to do things she really did not like to do.

Finally, in another group, Doreen, a teenage girl, said she was going to run away from home. The counselor helped her explore her difficulties at home, then used the following self-disclosure: "When I was in a similar situation, I went to talk with my parents." When Doreen replied she did not know how to approach her parents, the counselor introduced role playing to train her in the required skills. At the next session the following week, Doreen reported talking to her parents.

Group counselors often employ immediacy, i.e., disclosure of their techniques or tactics. On a personal level, a helper is often moved by a personal story and reacts emotionally: "I feel so sad listening to your story" or "I feel angry for the way you've been treated." On a group level, immediacy is used to share the counselor's intentions with the group. For example, after most group members have spoken, the counselor can allow for some silence, explaining: "I do not mean to pressure anyone to talk, but as some people need more time, I will wait for another couple of minutes," or "This time I will go around the circle, so everyone has a chance to say something." The use of immediacy not only conveys caring and empathy, but also models the use of emotions and empathy for group members.

Information and guidance are skills that are particularly important during the action stage. For instance, when exploration of Eileen's aforementioned conflict with her parents over visiting her grandmother's grave revealed that the real issue was her fear of death, the counselor used guided visualization to help her "leave the sack of stones someplace on the way." She also encouraged the group to share their advice of how to deal with the fear of death. When Doreen did not know how to approach her parents, role-playing was used to prepare her for a constructive conversation.

RESEARCH ON COUNSELOR HELPING SKILLS
IN GROUPS OF CHILDREN

Leichtentritt and Shechtman (1998) used Hill's (1986) Therapist Verbal Response Modes System to examine the verbal responses of a single therapist in 10 groups of elementary-school children. Six types of responses were investigated: encourages, directives, questions, paraphrases, feedback, and self-disclosure. Questions were found to be the most frequent counselor response; the counselor asked at least one question in 90% of the sessions. She used self-disclosure, feedback, and encouragement at least once in about 80% of the sessions, and she used directives and paraphrases in over 60% of the sessions. Overall, it appears that the counselor assumed an active role in the group process, using a wide variety of therapeutic responses.

The frequency of the counselor's responses was also investigated at three points of the group process: initial stage, working stage, and termination. On the average, there were about five questions per session, and about three self-disclosures and instances of feedback, throughout the process (paraphrases, encourages, and directives were less frequent). Moreover, all these responses were more frequent at the initial stage of the group and decreased with time. For example, the counselor began with about seven questions per session, reducing them to five in the working and termination stages. Similarly, although there were initially about 5 instances of self-disclosure per session, this dropped to 3.5 in the working stage, and to less than 3 at termination. The counselor's active involvement seems to be particularly necessary at the initial stage; with time, however, she can turn over some of the leadership to group members.

Finally, when the influence of the counselor's behavior on children's self-disclosure was investigated, it appeared that structured activities and questions were most effective: both produced about 90% of children's self-disclosure. This suggests the importance of structured activities in group counseling with children.

Two later expanded studies investigated these same therapist responses (Shechtman, 2004b; Shechtman & Ben-David, 1999) with several counselors. Results of both studies indicated the importance of questions (about 70%) followed by paraphrases; the remaining response types were infrequent. Self-disclosure was much less frequent in these studies than the first one (Leichtentritt & Shectman, 1998). This discrepancy in results may reflect individual differences between counselors; the first study was based on a single skilled and experienced counselor, whereas the later studies involved novice counselors. The child population was also different. The first study was of children with various emotional difficulties; the later studies included only highly aggressive children. Clearly, however, counselor self-disclosure (in addition to questions) is a valuable behavior that needs more attention, as it produced a high rate of children's self-disclosure. Although these therapist behaviors were not related to reduced aggression among the children, some were related to the children's behavior as measured on the Client Behavior Scale. For instance, encourages and challenges had some positive impact on effective participant behavior, whereas guidance had a negative effect (Shechtman, 2004a).

The Shectman and Ben-David study (1999) and the Shectman (2004a) study both compared therapist behavior in individual and group treatments. The findings suggested that the skills applied by counselors in groups are almost identical to those used in individual treatment. Indeed, the most widely used textbooks on groups provide lists of helping skills that are identical to those suggested by Hill (Hill & O'Brien, 1999; i.e., M. S. Corey & Corey, 2006; Gladding, 2003; Ivey & Ivey, 1999), although they also include some interventions that are unique to group processes (such as connecting and blocking). Perhaps these unique interventions deserve more attention in future research on groups.

Finally, a comparison between counseling groups and education groups (Shechtman & Pastor, 2005) indicated use of different skills to achieve goals. Therapists of the counseling groups used more encouragement, reflection of feelings, and interpretation. However, leaders of the educational groups used more guidance and information provision. This suggests that counselors use helping skills according to their theoretical orientation. As they work within an expressive–supportive modality applying an integrative theory, it makes sense that the therapists in the counseling groups used mostly encouragement, reflection of feelings, and interpretation. These are the skills that are more difficult to develop, requiring more intensive training.

SUMMARY

These clinical observations and illustrations clearly indicate that counselors of groups of children and adolescents must be warm people who can openly express and convey their love and caring for children. This is particularly true of the type of counseling and psychotherapy groups described here, where the therapy population is a vulnerable one. It is also clear that counselors need to be skilled in conducting the various stages of the group process and in helping the individual client go through the growth and change process. Although the helping skills used by the group counselor are similar to those used in individual counseling, the group counselor's role is extended beyond helping the individual person in the group. It is the group leader's role to guide the group process toward a climate of trust, positive interpersonal interaction, and mutual support. It is also important to be able to stop destructive behavior and protect the victims in the group. Finally, it is clear that adherence to the theoretical orientation offered here requires the counselor to use appropriate skills, such as encouragement, reflection of feelings, and challenges, more frequently than guidance and information provision. In short, the counselor's role in children's groups is much more active than that of the leader of adult groups.

Moreover, because of the clients' lack of maturity and history of difficult behavior, these processes may not be easy, requiring the counselor's understanding of child development and the acquisition of methods and techniques suitable to each child's age and needs. In contrast to leaders of adult groups, counselors for groups of children and adolescents must also possess a large variety of creative methods and techniques that can be adjusted to children's developmental stages. This unique component of the counselor's roles in children's groups will be discussed in the next chapter.

5 Activities in the Group: Methods and Techniques

Structured group activities are distinguished from leadership skills, functions, and roles, as they are entities unto themselves, with specific traits that define their nature. They are part of the leader's tool chest, aimed at promoting individual growth and the group process. They can be intrapersonal or interpersonal, verbal or nonverbal, depending on the persons who make up the group, the process that evolves, and the purpose for which the group is convened (Trotzer, 2004). The most frequent use of activities is in structured educational groups, although they are applied in all types of groups, particularly during the initial and termination stages. In group counseling and psychotherapy for adults, activities are needed less once the group reaches the working stage, when clients are usually ready to take an active part in the process and to spontaneously interact.

This is not the case when working with children and adolescents, who are not the usual clients in counseling and psychotherapy. Children typically do not choose to be in treatment, do not fully understand the therapeutic process, and do not possess the interpersonal skills needed to help themselves or someone else. Their attention span is limited, and their verbalization skills, particularly their ability to express emotions, are still under development. In counseling and therapy groups that focus on self-expressiveness, such as those in my practice, it is, in fact, the counselor's role to help young clients express feelings and experience catharsis, to enhance self-awareness and empathy, and to guide them in taking risks directed at behavioral change. This requires a creative leader whose tool chest is particularly rich in activities, and who is capable of employing methods and techniques skillfully and processing them effectively. Activities, methods, and techniques are only devices used to help stimulate and promote the therapeutic process (DeLucia-Waack, 1997). They should be applied only when necessary to further group processes.

Throughout this book, I demonstrate a variety of activities; however, some of them rest on a unique theory based on a specific body of knowledge and promote specific methods of treatment. This chapter thus refers to methods rather than activities, and focuses on three that have proven extremely helpful in group work with children and adolescents. All represent some form of the creative arts, which are highly advocated as an adjunct to counseling and psychotherapy. Gladding (2005), a leading proponent of creative arts in groups, suggested that the arts provide a channel for expression that weaves greater variety into the fabric of the group milieu. The positive energy of creativity, the multiple levels of communication, its playfulness, and its multicultural nature (Gladding, 2000) all make this an excellent method for treatment of children and adolescents. Specifically, I discuss the theoretical foundation and clinical applications for bibliotherapy, PhotoTherapy, and therapeutic cards, which my colleagues and I feel have proven to be extremely effective in our work with children and adolescent groups.

BIBLIOTHERAPY

Bibliotherapy refers to the use of literature in the service of therapy and is one method of the creative or expressive arts, along with music, drama, dance, and painting. All of these forms are helpful in counseling and psychotherapy with children and are often used in conjunction. As they encourage self-expressiveness, such methods are particularly suitable for use in expressive–supportive groups.

Beyond the creativity it generates, bibliotherapy has additional unique qualities. There is a great amount of psychological wisdom incorporated in books. Yalom (1998) argued that psychology started long before the advent of scientific methods, with novelists such as Tolstoy. As Kottler (1986) stated, "Without Shakespeare's plays, Dostoyevesky's novels, or James's short stories, our knowledge of anguish and conflict would be hollow, our self-revelation would be one-dimensional" (p. 35). Quality literature presents a wide range of human thoughts and emotions that readers can identify with, learn from, and apply to their own lives. A great deal of poetry, for example, expresses subtle and overt psychological insights about life situations that clients may come to personalize into their own lives. True self-knowledge and a greater understanding of the world then emerge. Clients realize that their problems are universal, as well as unique. They learn that they share a connectedness with many other people and cultures, which provides comfort and legitimizes their feelings and thoughts (Gladding, 2005).

When people read or listen to a story or poem or watch a movie in which human beings display their vulnerability, weaknesses, and strengths, they tend to identify with the characters' experiences, suffering, and pain, as well as their happiness. Through this identification process, the person experiences catharsis, sharing feelings and conflicts with the characters. These stories enhance understanding of the human situation and increase empathy for the suffering of others, which eventually may help individuals to understand themselves better. Although these processes occur in everyday experience without therapy, they can be used intentionally in counseling and psychotherapy as a means of focusing on a particular issue or conflict that is related to the clients involved.

Studies of bibliotherapy as a self-help therapy (also referred to as cognitive bibliotherapy) are relatively new. This type of bibliotherapy provides an opportunity for clients to generate alternative thoughts, feelings, and actions; to learn new skills; and to practice new behaviors (Jackson, 2001). Research findings on cognitive bibliotherapy are encouraging, pointing to a positive effect on various types of behavior problems. For instance, Ackerson, Scogin, McKendree-Smith, and Lyman (1998) found cognitive bibliotherapy to be effective in reducing depression among adolescents. Following a meta-analysis, Apodaca and Miller (2003) concluded that bibliotherapy is an efficacious method for helping clients with drinking problems. Indeed, a recent review of literature (McKendree-Smith, Floyd, & Scogin, 2003) concluded that cognitive bibliotherapy is an effective method for a variety of problems.

Cognitive bibliotherapy involves little or no intervention of a therapist, under the assumption that a direct dialogue between the person and the literature has a positive impact. The use of bibliography by my colleagues and I, which can be termed affective bibliotherapy, is quite different: we apply it as an adjunct to the therapy process. That is, counselors at my center use it as a tool to enhance experiencing constructively.

Affective bibliotherapy relies on psychodynamic principles. The basic assumption is that people use defense mechanisms, such as repression, to protect themselves from pain. When such defenses are activated often, individuals become disconnected from their emotions, unaware of their true feelings, and therefore unable to resolve their problems constructively. Both the literature and the therapist can help clients to reconnect to their inner selves. Through identification with literary characters, the individual is exposed to a wide range of emotions, of which he or she can recognize something in himself or herself. The therapist's role is to encourage such identification and to help the client discuss and understand these emotions in a nonjudgmental way. An accepting attitude towards the literary figure conveys an important message—namely, that emotions are accepted and understood. This in itself is therapeutic, as it legitimizes the client's feelings. When the discussion becomes more personal, the therapist also sends a direct message of acceptance to the client. These processes lead to a corrective interpersonal experience that allows for cathartic experiencing and reflection on these experiences. As in any effective therapy process, it is the client–therapist alliance that makes such an emotional process possible. In groups, it is the connectedness of the individual to the group, the group climate, and group cohesiveness that encourage such emotional experiences to occur.

I believe that therapist intervention in the interaction between participant and literature is particularly important when working with children. The infinite richness and complexity of the story may be overwhelming, threatening, and anxiety provoking to youngsters. The information conveyed to the reader may be misunderstood, misinterpreted, and even distorted, colored by the reader's private experiences. Therefore, my colleagues and I use books as an indirect means to offer therapy to our young patients. In such a bibliotherapy process, a triadic connection is fostered between the literature, participants, and counselor. The book creates distance between the client and his or her problem, thus permitting the therapist to guide the child to deal with troubling issues with more safety and less defensiveness and resistance.

Although long practiced in counseling, there is little research on affective bibliotherapy. My studies of aggressive children have demonstrated that this is an effective method to reduce aggression (for example, Shechtman, 2003) and to increase empathy (Shechtman & Birani-Nasaraladin, in press; for more on our research of aggressive children, see Chapter 14 in this book). A recent study compared expressive–supportive child psychotherapy with and without the use of bibliotherapy (Shechtman, in press). Bibliotherapy was found to be more effective in increasing empathy, and children worked more constructively in the therapy process; that is, they showed lower rates of resistance and higher rates of insight and therapeutic change. Although my empirical research on bibliotherapy is limited to aggressive children, my clinical experience is not. My colleagues and I use bibliotherapy for a variety of problems and at different stages of the group process, as illustrated throughout this book.

PRACTICING AFFECTIVE BIBLIOTHERAPY

There are numerous ways to use bibliotherapy when working with children. They can read stories and poems and then discuss them; they can listen to literature read to them; they can compose their own stories, tell their narratives, or write journals.

Selection of the literature is an important part of the therapy process and should be geared to the type of problem, the age of the child, and the purpose of the therapy. Some literary works are effective in eliciting the expression of emotions, and others are particularly helpful in generating alternative thoughts and behaviors. When these choices are made, it is important to consider the developmental stage of the group, the unique needs of participants, and the group goal (Trotzer, 2004).

Counseling and psychotherapy groups are a perfect setting for the use of bibliotherapy. In the initial stage of the group, the literature helps group members connect to each other, develop empathy, and enhance the language of feelings. Although with adults the method is used mainly at the beginning of the group, with children and adolescents it continues to be a useful device throughout the group process. For instance, in the initial stage the counselor may read a story or poem that deals with emotions to enhance expression of feelings. Toward termination, the counselor may use a story that deals with problem solving. In the working stage, the counselor may want to adjust the literature to a certain topic of discussion or to a particular focus of the group.

The following exemplifies the use of a book that I mention in several chapters: *The Soul Bird* (Snunit, 1999). This short piece describes the human soul as a vulnerable entity that sometimes hurts and is in pain and sometimes is happy and proud. It is made of lots of drawers that contain various feelings, and ends with the recommendation to listen to one's soul bird. This tale can be used on a group level to elicit feelings of the here-and-now towards the group, or on an individual level to deal with personal emotions. It can be read as one piece or used interactively. It may focus on various feelings, depending on the children's needs.

In one group of 11-year-old girls, Margie, the counselor, read the following paragraph:

Do you want to know what the soul bird is made of?
Well, it's really quite simple:

It's made of drawers.
These drawers can't be opened just like that—
Because each is locked with its own special key!
Only the soul bird can open its drawers. (Snunit, 1999)

Before Margie could pose a question, Gail said, "My biggest drawer is the one with secrets. There are simple secrets and dark secrets that belong to my family. This drawer should never be opened because then I will be very sad." To this, Ella responded, "I really get what you are saying. My biggest drawer is anger and sadness, but some of it has been released here in the group, much thanks to you, Gail. When you talked about your father, I felt like I wasn't the only one who felt this way." Margie then read the next paragraph:

When someone hugs us, the soul bird, deep inside, grows and grows
Until it almost fills up
That's how good it feels when someone hugs us. (Snunit, 1999)

And Gail responded, "My bird is very sad, sometimes very lonely. It wishes that someone would hug it, but that someone is never around." This triggers a cathartic experience for Gail, who continued, "You see, I said I would never open this drawer, but I just did." She assured the group that she had no regrets for revealing herself, and in the next session, she reported that she had spoken to her dad and confronted him about not attending her birthday party. She said she felt much better after this talk with him.

In the same group, at a later stage of the process, Margie used parts of the book to evaluate the progress each girl had made in the group. She went back to the drawers of the bird's soul, asking which ones the girls had opened, to what extent, and how they felt about it. She found that the girls had opened quite a few drawers, felt less tense, and were more capable of coping with life's frustrations. It seems that it was easier for them to respond to the idea of opening drawers than to a direct request to disclose secrets. The use of a metaphor made it less threatening and more playful.

When the counselor aims to identify goals for working in the group, it is possible to use a book such as *Like Fish in Water* (Lazarowitz, 1991). This book describes all sorts of fish—some live alone and others live in a group; some are big, some are small, and many are medium-sized. There are fish that follow the group and others that lead, and so on. Children can easily identify with one of the types of fish and thereby develop awareness of some of their weaknesses or difficulties.

In a group of six 16-year-old girls, Miriam selected the lonely fish because she felt rejected by classmates; Sheila chose a goldfish because she felt over protected; and Terry selected the swordfish because she cut off relationships too abruptly. This activity was used in the second session to help the girls identify an issue to work on. In the following sessions, each of these issues was processed, including thoughts, feelings, and plans for action. There was also an extensive exchange of feedback and provision of support, following self-exposure. All this had been triggered by an activity based on bibliotherapy at the initial stage of the group.

Toward the end of group sessions, when the emphasis is on problem-solving skills, my colleagues and I use the book *A Fence, a Sheep and a Man with a Problem* (Biran, 1999). In this book, a man who cannot fall asleep observes numerous sheep and how they cross a fence. One sheep jumps over the fence; another does not even notice there is a fence; two help each other; another pushes against the fence; and so on. Group members select the type of their coping strategy and discuss ways to change, if needed. In the same group of 16-year-old girls, but at a later stage, Miriam (who chose the lonely fish) identified with the sheep that avoids the fence. She grasped that by being so frightened, helpless, and passive in her response, she only encourages children's bullying. Following a cathartic experience and armed with support from the group, she chose the little sheep that cooperated with another to cross over the fence to represent what she wished to be her future behavior. In this way, she learned to ask for help and protection, which in itself was helpful for her. Sheila (who selected the goldfish) chose the sheep for which the fence lowers itself. She learned that her parents' protective behavior only weakened her, and that she had confront them about this. Finally, Terry (who took the swordfish) chose the sheep that runs head on into the fence. She realized that she got into many interpersonal conflicts and ruined relationships even with close friends. A very impulsive girl, she decided that she wanted to be like the rational sheep that figures out how it can get over the fence. Like the other books described, this one uses a metaphor to help the children to identify, verbalize and articulate their problems and to envision ways to cope with them.

In applying bibliotherapy in our groups, my colleagues and I usually use short stories, poems, or films that focus on a particular theme and apply a semistructured format to guide us in the process. First, we read the story or poem or show the movie. Next, we elicit as many emotions as possible related to the characters. This serves as a vehicle to enhance the language of emotions and understanding of them. Then we focus on understanding the dynamics of the situation or the behavior presented in the literature piece. We call this a mini-psychology lesson, in which we help children comprehend why such behavior occurs and what the consequences are. We also discuss possible alternative ways to achieve the character's goals. Finally, we apply the feelings and the new understanding to the children's own lives. The content of the book is selected according to children's problems or the goals of a particular session. Following is an illustration of such a process with young children.

The counselor read the poem "The Bad Guy" to a group of third and fourth graders, including Don, a boy with discipline problems who has been rejected by his classmates, and four other children with friendship issues. The poem describes a young child whose "bad guy sometimes enters him," causing him to behave destructively. When this happens, he loses control over himself; he screams, yells, and insults others, making everyone around him very angry.

The first step in the process is to identify feelings of both the child in the poem and the people that interact with him. Alice, who came from a warm family, felt that the child is anxious because people are too demanding. She felt that after an outburst, he would calm down, and there would be no need to be so harsh with him. In contrast, Don, the problem boy in the group, shouted out, "Can't you see?! He is stressed out because he can't get rid of the bad guy!" Each of these two children projected their feelings onto the literary figure, yet it is important for Don to hear Alice. The group further elicited feelings; fear, sadness, loneliness and anger were attributed to the boy, and anger, disappointment, and rejection were attributed to the persons surrounding him.

In the next phase, the group discussed the dynamics that led to the boy's behavior. Issues of lack of self-control and the consequences of such behavior were discussed. Alice believed that the boy in the poem was basically a good boy and that people needed to be more tolerant of children's mistakes. Don felt sorry for the boy because, although the boy wants to be good, he cannot control himself. Don worried that the boy would have no friends (projection again). Brenda, who was often a victim of Don's behavior, argued that lack of control was no excuse, and that she would also react with anger to such behavior just to protect herself. Tommy thought that the child should try harder. Overall, the group talked about misbehavior, what reactions it elicits, how to increase self-control, and how to fix a situation that went wrong, all this in an indirect way.

In the final stage of the session, the children moved to a direct process of sharing their experiences. Many related incidents in which the "bad guy" controlled their behavior. They explained how they strove to get rid of the bad guy, and discussed what could be done to correct a situation that goes wrong. For Don, this was an important lesson. He was exposed to various attitudes, some supportive, others demanding, as well as to ways to enhance self-control. It is hard to imagine such a lesson without the mediation of the literature.

PHOTOTHERAPY

"Photographs are footprints to our mind, mirrors of our lives, reflections from our hearts, frozen memories we can hold in silent stillness in our hands—forever, if we wish" (Weiser, 1993, p. 1). PhotoTherapy is defined as an interactive system of therapy techniques that makes use of client's interactions with ordinary photographs, such as their own personal snapshots and family albums, as well as photos taken by others. Its purpose is to help clients connect with feelings and memories too deep or complex to be fully reached or encompassed through words alone. Sight-based information is crucial to people's understanding of what individuals experience, and photos can make visible the ongoing stories of people's lives. Therapeutically, it is not only what is shown on the surface of a photo that is meaningful, but also what these visual comments mean, the stories they tell and the related feelings they evoke. In permanently recording each selected "frozen slice of time," along with the embedded stories captured within that unique moment, personal photos can serve as bridges for finding, exploring, and communicating about feelings and memories, current needs, and future aspirations. Photographs are emotionally charged, and one can never view personal photos dispassionately. Their significance resonates to and from people, over the past and into the future. Moreover, they provide information not only about the individual, but also about his or her social and family context, which is important information to understand a person's problems (Berman, 1993; Weiser, 1993).

PhotoTherapy is an adjunct to the therapy process aimed at invoking emotional experiencing and cognitive reflection. Photos are used as a nonverbal device to reach deeper meaning in the therapy process and to overcome cognitive barriers, such as denial and rationalization. As such, the technique is particularly suitable for clients who experience difficulties in self-expressiveness due to internal inhibitions or to communication difficulties. Children are therefore excellent candidates for its usage.

Practice of PhotoTherapy is more common than research on it. Norris-Shortle, Parks, Walden, and Hayman-Hamilton (1999) found that photos helped therapists establish rapport with withdrawn clients, learn about clients' problems, and increase interaction with them. In our own study of Ethiopian new immigrants (who both have language difficulties and come from a culture that does not encourage openness of feelings), my colleagues and I found that, during two sessions of intake interviews, individuals who were engaged with photos self-disclosed almost twice as much on a simple level and five times more on the intimate level (Shechtman & Zaghon, 2004). Although the study did not present results of psychotherapy, the findings are nevertheless meaningful, because in the initial stage of therapy it is the most difficult to elicit self-disclosure. Photos appeared to ease self-expressiveness in all areas studied: family, work and study, friends, and feelings. One young man brought a picture of his mom, who had stayed behind in Ethiopia. He said, "Every time I look at her picture, I feel so sad, so lonely. I cannot grasp the fact that she is not with me." This is a powerful expression of feelings that could not be expected in an initial interview with an extremely withdrawn population.

THE PRACTICE OF PHOTOTHERAPY

The basic technique of PhotoTherapy is to elicit photos of the client, photos taken by the client, self-portraits, and biographical snapshots, often of groups of friends or family. The first and last techniques are most often used with children and adolescents. When working with photos of oneself that have been taken by other people, the therapeutic work may focus on relationships with those people, or how they view the client. With family albums, the therapist can track life events of the clients, and help to understand family relationships and the individual client within this broader context. When working with photos, therapists commonly apply the technique of questioning: asking who is in the photo, requesting the client to relate the story behind the picture, inquiring into relationships between family members and the client, asking who is missing from the picture, and where the client would like to be situated in it. For example, as a result of asking who is missing from their picture, one of the Ethiopian girls discloses strong emotions and decides to get a picture of her father "before I forget what he looks like".

In the group process, the timing of PhotoTherapy is extremely important. When participants are asked to bring in photos at the initial group phase, they usually bring those that are less emotionally charged. If a child brings in a picture that is extremely meaningful, but the group is not ready to process it, it should be used again at a later stage of the process. Moreover, it should be acknowledged that the child has brought in useful information and made an initial commitment to work on his or her problem. When photos are used at the working stage, the selection of photos reflects how trusting and engaged group members are, and the material is processed on a deeper level.

In a group of adolescent girls whose parents were divorced, the PhotoTherapy activity was conducted deep in the working stage. As all group members wanted to share their photos, the counselor turned the pictures over and chose each one randomly. Gail had brought a photograph of herself at age 6 sitting on her father's lap, and she talked about her special relationship with him until he died. This is the first time she did not joke about her father's relationship with a young woman. She admitted that she missed him a lot and that she kepts his picture under her pillow.

Sandy had brought a picture of her mom's newborn baby. This was her way of sharing with the group that she did not live with her mother, because her mom became depressed after the birth; since then her father had had custody of her. For Sandy, this was a highly meaningful session; not only was this the first time that she spoke of her mom's illness, but Linda shared a similar story about her own mother, which put Sandy's situation into perspective.

Laura had brought a picture of herself at age 3 with both parents. She had trouble accepting the divorce and had continuously expressed a strong need to bring her parents back together, even though her father had just remarried and her mother accepted this marriage with no reservations. The girls helped Laura look at the situation in a different way; she saw that both parents were happier and that both offered her a home. This message seemed to have a positive impact, as she decided to accept her father's invitation for dinner.

PhotoTherapy in this group was obviously a powerful trigger that helped the girls share their most disturbing and intimate feelings and thoughts. Following the presentation of each picture, the photos were further processed. The girls were encouraged to express feelings and thoughts, to develop insight into the cause of their disturbing thoughts, and, when needed, to take action to improve the situation. The group members had an important part in each girl's growth, by sharing similar experiences and by providing feedback and suggestions.

THERAPEUTIC CARDS

Therapeutic cards are a special genre of games based on association and communication, also known as associative cards (Kirschke, 1998). "They serve as a springboard into imagination and creativity, a tool for learning and a catalyst with potential for directing its players into intense communication about themselves" (p. 11). This is an interactive game between the player and his or her cards, in which the individual associates with or projects onto the cards. These cards do not have an objective meaning; whatever each player sees in them is valid and should not be reinterpreted by other players.

The first of this genre of games was OH (2005), created by Canadian professor Ely Raman and his wife, Joan Lawrence. OH consists of two decks of cards: one with poker-card sized watercolor pictures depicting a diversity of everyday situations and objects; the other comprised of slightly larger frame cards, each with a specific word written 4 times along its outer edges. Cards from the first deck fit into the frame of cards from the second deck to form a set—an image surrounded by a word. When one set is not enough to help a client express his or her feelings or to understand a situation, the individual should be encouraged to take a few sets.

In one group of 13-year-old girls, Rhonda's abandonment issues with her mother emerged in the card game. She first picked a picture of a mother holding a baby with the word *Mother* surrounding it. She said that when she was young, perhaps her mother loved her. Karen, the counselor, encouraged her to pick another set of cards to express how she felt in her current relationship with her mother. Rhonda picked a picture of a group of people talking to each other, with one person standing apart, and framed it with a card that said *Strangers*, explaining, "My mom is now interested only in strangers. I do not fit into her life anymore." Karen then encouraged her to pick a third set that described how she would like things to be. Rhonda selected card of two women sitting close to each other framed by the word *Sharing*, and said, "I would like to share with her things that happen to me, but she is never around."

Rhonda's work was very powerful and inspired others to share family issues through the cards. The general group discussion focused on how to communicate feelings to one's parents. In the next session, Rhonda reported that she talked to her mother, who accepted her feelings and promised to change the situation. Other girls also used an open communication strategy with their parents.

It seems that the cards were a powerful trigger to express emotions, to articulate the problem, and to find an alternative coping mechanism. Pictures directly address intuition and emotions, often bypassing rational understanding. "It is this very quality of images that enables them to trigger reactions within us that cannot easily be expressed in words—and makes them so fascinating" (Kirschke, 1998).

The next set of cards (pictures only, without an accompanying word) is called SAGA. The themes are elements from fairy tales and myths well known around the world. "Fairy tales express in images something beyond isolated personal histories; namely, a collective stream of experiences which transcends the experience of any one person" (Kirschke, 1998, p. 44). They include the four elements (earth, water, fire, and air), animals, motifs of life and death, and archetypal persons (e.g., wise man, wise woman, queen, king). Each player randomly draws a card in turn, expressing the first association that comes to mind. In a group situation, the cards can then be used to compose a group story. This helps connect members and increase group solidarity. It can also provide feedback to individuals as to how they have contributed to the group story, the degree to which they have collaborated with others, what it was like to give up part of one's story, and the like. Following is an illustration of a group process initiated by SAGA cards.

The group was comprised of eight 13-year-old girls from a minority culture (Arabs in Israel) in which disclosure of private information and family secrets to a stranger is highly inhibited. The counselor began the second session with the SAGA cards, aimed at enhancing acquaintance between group members. She asked each girl to introduce herself using the cards. Saya chose one with a picture of a boat on a stormy sea, saying, "I am the boat. I am struggling with events in my life just like this boat." Leila challenged her about when she expected to reach the shore, to which she responded, "I will probably strive all my life and I'm OK with that because I do not drown." Rima selected a picture of a black and white puzzle to represent her positive and negative traits, both of which she accepted. When challenged about whether she tried to work on the negative aspects of herself, she responded, "To those who treat me nicely, I respond with kindness, but to those who don't treat me well, I can be very mean. Sometimes I feel I am too tough and I try to change, but I don't always succeed." Walla chose a card displaying a closed door because "my father locks me up every day at 5." Nassi selected a white egg "because my father locks me up all day and night." This was a powerful exchange of self-disclosure, unexpected at the second session and of this particular population. It is hard to imagine the girls sharing such intimate feelings without the cards. There was also identification among group members, and quite a few challenges. In other words, the cards helped the girls establish effective group norms and move to the working stage with little reservations.

A third type of therapeutic cards, Coping Cards, was created by Dr. Ofra Ayalon, an Israeli expert on trauma. This is basically a set of pictures presenting various traumatic situations: natural disasters, wars, interpersonal conflicts, and loneliness. The unique contribution of this set, beyond the focus on trauma and stress, is the additional focus on coping mechanisms. The set includes five cards that represent sources of coping: body, rationale, attitudes and beliefs, social connections, and imagination. As with the previously mentioned sets of cards, there is more than one way to play the game. Children can be asked to select a card that they wish to talk about, then choose one or more of the coping cards that help them. They can be asked to select a coping strategy that they would like to enhance. Or they can be asked to select several cards and look at the pattern of their coping style. Another way to play the game is to build a process of problem solving, ignoring the five coping mechanism cards. Children are asked to select six cards: one to introduce the stressful event, a second to represent the obstacle to solving the problem, a third card to show what helped the child find a solution, a fourth one to indicate who interfered, a fifth card to show who helped, and a sixth to indicate the solution itself. The child can then summarize the whole story and state goals for making a change. The fascination factor is that the whole scenario is outlined through pictures. This is a powerful technique for children and adolescents who find it difficult to verbalize their feelings.

Consider the next illustration of a group of girls who were victims of a terrorist attack on their bus on the way to school. The group intervention was held a year after the incident. Cindy, who was badly wounded and lost her best friend who was sitting next to her, had a particularly difficult time in the group. She refused to talk about feelings, saying that people must be strong and that this is God's will. But when she played with the cards, she selected images depicting fire, a group of threatening people, a man screaming, and a rope. The first three cards helped Cindy talk about the event itself and go through cathartic experiencing. The rope represented the restrictions that her family put on her against expressing weakness and anger. Coming from a religious family, she was expected to accept whatever occurred in her life, when actually she was very angry with the God who allowed this to happen. Only following this experience with the cards was Cindy able to admit to her anxieties, and realize how demanding it is to have to pretend to be strong.

SUMMARY

The three methods presented here—bibliotherapy, PhotoTherapy, and therapeutic cards— rely on psychodynamic principles, particularly processes of projection. Such processes help elicit conscious and unconscious thoughts and feelings, which may be difficult to reach otherwise. All this is achieved in a playful and nonthreatening climate. These methods are part of the tool chest that counselors of groups of children and adolescents use to help them navigate the group process. In one of our first studies, a colleague and I found that the leader's activities were the trigger that elicited most of the children's self-disclosure (Leichtentritt & Shechtman, 1998). A more recent study comparing therapy with and without bibliotherapy (Shechtman, 2006) indicated that counselors who employed this technique were more satisfied than those who did not, as it helped them to keep in focus and lead the therapy process. However, it is important to remember that structured activities are merely tools. "Losing sight of that fact will endanger the integrity of both the group process and the activity itself," concluded Trotzer (2004, p. 87). Activities and methods such as those described in this chapter should be used as adjunct to the therapy process, to stimulate participants to relate their stories to the group. Then the material that is brought up by these activities should be skillfully processed according to the three-stage model: exploration, insight, and action. Although this tool chest may be a nice addition to adult groups, it is a must in groups with children and adolescents, as children find it difficult to express themselves without games and activities, and because children learn much better through play (Cramer-Azima, 2002). Activities and games are part of the group leader's skills that are key to effective outcomes with children.

These methods play a particularly important role in the expressive–supportive form of therapy, because they are so helpful in encouraging emotional experiencing. Although the expression of feelings and catharsis is not the ultimate aim in groups with children, it is an important goal in itself, as it helps to reduce stress and achieve emotional relief, one of the main purposes of working with children and adolescents in groups (Dagly et al., 1994). The following chapters present the use of these methods in each of stage of group development.

6 Pregroup Planning and Forming a Group

Gladding (2003) attributed a number of advantages to counseling groups. Group members come to realize that they are not alone, unique, or abnormal in their problems and concerns. Through their interaction with one another, they learn more about themselves in social interactions. They can try out new behaviors and ways of interacting, because the group atmosphere provides a safe environment in which to experiment with change and receive feedback. Group members also observe how others attack and resolve problems, thereby picking up skills vicariously. Finally, the group may serve as a catalyst to help people realize a want or need for individual counseling or the accomplishment of a personal goal.

Based on my experience with the type of group advocated in this book, the most important advantage of groups seems to be the emotional and social support that participants gain. In these group experiences, children and adolescents feel accepted, cared for, loved, and valued. These are necessary conditions for personal growth and change (Rogers, 1980).

Yet, groups also have limitations and disadvantages, and they certainly are not suitable for all people and all problems. For example, many members' concerns and personalities are not well suited for groups. The problems of individuals may not be dealt with in enough depth in groups. Group pressure may force a member to take action, such as self-disclosure, before that member is ready. Groups may not succeed in developing the right climate for personal growth (Gladding, 2003).

Much of the success or failure in a group depends on the work done in the preplanning and forming stages. According to the American School Counseling Association (ACA) Code of Ethics (1998), the leader's tasks at this stage include member selection, group composition, and a detailed plan for starting the group.

MEMBER SELECTION

Some individuals who wish to be members of groups are not appropriate candidates. If such persons are allowed to join, they may become difficult members and cause the group leader considerable trouble (Kottler, 1994). Or they may join with others who are at an equally low level of functioning and contribute to regression of the group. When this happens, members become psychologically damaged, and the group is unable to accomplish its goals. The ACA Code of Ethics (1998) recommended that counselors screen prospective group members and work toward selecting those whose goals and needs are compatible with group goals. It is also considered important to include those who will not obstruct the group process and whose psychological well being will not be jeopardized by the group experience.

Little is known, however, about methods of screening that prove successful. Ritchie and Huss (2000) have suggested using individual interviews, group interviews, or questionnaire completion to screen children, but the extent to which these methods are effective is unclear. In a review of the literature on group selection, Yalom and Leszcz (2005) argued that neither individual interviews nor paper-and-pencil personality tests seem to be strong predictors. In contrast, observation of behavior in pretreatment sessions had some predictive value. They attributed this to the assumption that future behavior can best be predicted from observation of present behavior in similar situations, and cited group evaluation techniques, such as group assessment for predicting teacher success (Shechtman, 1992), as a possibility of screening candidates for group counseling. Another method that he cited as promising was the PM test developed by Piper and colleagues (2002) to screen candidates for outpatient and inpatient psychotherapy facilities. Piper et al. showed that the test was predictive of success in therapy, and offered two different therapy formats depending on the level of psychological mindedness: expressive therapy for clients with high psychological mindedness, and supportive therapy for clients low in psychological mindedness.

A recent study (Shechtman & Ribko, 2004) of over 400 university students in the field of mental health, divided into 27 groups, tested the prediction of client behavior in group counseling via two methods: (a) attachment style—including secure, anxious, and avoidant attachment styles (a self-report measure); and (b) assessment of initial self-disclosure in the first group session (an observational measure). Participant behavior in the group process included self- and counselor reports of self-disclosure, intimacy with group members, empathy towards group members, and productivity in the therapy process. Results indicated that attachment style predicted all variables reflecting participants' behavior in the group, and initial self-disclosure predicted most of them. Secure participants were more constructive group members than the other participants, and they disclosed more intimate information at the first session and along the group process, but there were only a few differences between anxious and avoidant participants. The conclusion of this study was that individual differences related to attachment may be a promising screening device, as is observation of behavior in the initial stage of the group.

The extent to which such knowledge can be applied to group counseling and psychotherapy with children and adolescents was tested in a recent study (Shechtman & Dvir, 2006). Seventy-seven middle-school children were assessed on attachment style and behavior in the therapy process based on session transcripts. Results indicated that attachment style did explain adolescent behavior in group counseling. Secure children showed higher scores on self-disclosure, and were more productive in their therapeutic work, less resistant, and more positively responsive to others' self-disclosure, compared to both anxious and avoidant adolescents. Moreover, avoidant adolescents had very low scores on self-disclosure, were highly resistant, did little therapeutic work, and had extremely negative responses to others' self-disclosure. Considerable differences were found between secure and avoidant group members: secure participants self-disclosed almost 10 times more often than avoidant adolescents; resistance rates were 15 times higher among avoidant participants; and negative responses to others' self-disclosure was 10 times higher for avoidant group members than secure members. Adolescents who fell in the avoidant category accounted for 22% of the sample and seemed to be the candidates most at risk for group work. In this study, as opposed to the earlier one, (Shechtman & Ribko, 2004) clear differences between anxious and avoidant participants were also found.

Differences between the two studies' results can be related to developmental issues. Children and adolescents are still in a process of psychological growth; indeed, my own clinical experience has shown that some children progress really late in the group process. Consider, for example, Maggie, a third-grade girl who was so withdrawn at the beginning of treatment that she would physically hide whenever emotions were brought up. At the end of her second year of treatment, she had the highest score on self-disclosure of the entire group (Shechtman, Vurembrand, & Malajek, 1993). Therefore, caution should be taken in applying knowledge about adults to decision making in practice with children.

The ACA Code of Ethics (1998), for example, focused on client rights and the necessity to provide information that enable potential group members to make an informed choice as to their participation in the counseling process, including information about leader's qualifications, purpose and goal of the group, expectations of group members, and confidentiality. Similarly, G. Corey (1995) suggested a list of 12 issues that participants should clarify before they enroll in a group, including a statement about the education and training of the group leader and disclosure about the risks involved in being in a group. These practices, although important, can be inappropriate for children and young adolescents.

Children and adolescents are unique participants, different than adults in group psychotherapy, particularly those children with severe problems. Imagine a group of angry and aggressive children or adolescents. Would it be wise to share with them the credentials of the counselor? How would one articulate the group goals? Would it be wise to state that the group aims at reducing the level of their aggression? Should one share with them the expectation to self-disclose and indicate the risks involved before the group even begins? Or consider a group for children whose parents have divorced. Do you want to tell them at that early stage that they will be expected to share private information and inform them of the risks involved? These are serious considerations for many other groups as well, particularly those involving young clients. Nonetheless, therapist need to screen children and adolescents referred by school personnel for counseling, mainly for placement considerations, assessment of their level of motivation to be engaged in a group, and assessment of their level of self-control.

Most children and adolescents are referred to counseling services following a professional staff meeting in which information is provided by teachers and other school personnel; this is usually followed by an interview of the child. Although the declared aim of the individual interview is to assess the child's motivation and ability to work in a group, and to explain expectations of the child in the group process (K. R. Greenberg, 2003; Smead, 1995), in my judgment, the main goal of the interview is to establish the necessary initial child–therapist bonding. Bonding is the most essential component in any psychotherapy process, particularly at the initial stage (Bachelor & Horvath, 1999), and it is crucial for children and adolescents, who are highly anxious when they begin working in a group. Moreover, most children who are referred to counseling exhibit problems related to trust, making it essential for them to begin bonding with the therapist before they have to deal with bonding with other group members.

The other merits of the individual interview with children are quite limited, and actually do not add enough information about the child to justify a decision to exclude him or her from group counseling or psychotherapy. Children who are not familiar with group processes often find it difficult to envision the process and their prospective behavior. They may be unrealistic about their expectations and those of the leader and interviewer. They may think it is easy to self-disclose, but once in the group, they may be intimidated by their peers. Conversely, they may think disclosure is an impossible task, yet find that the group interaction facilitates such behavior. And how can one judge what is too much or too little self-disclosure for a fifth-grade boy or girl who has never experienced a therapy group?

The entire debate about effective screening may be less relevant to children and adolescents, as the real issue is how to give a chance to all children who need counseling and psychotherapy. Unfortunately, it is precisely those children and adolescents who do not qualify to be participants in a group that seem to need the group the most. At the same time, it is the counselor's duty to secure the group process for all group members. To resolve this dilemma, my colleagues and I use the following yardstick: Unless children display exceptionally severe behavior, they should be given a chance. All children who wish to join a group should be permitted to experience it for three sessions. Sometimes, we even convince children who are reluctant to join a group to try it out, under the assumption that experiencing the group process helps both parties to make an intelligent decision. Only in extreme cases do we exclude a child from a group, prior to trying it out, as it is important to secure the safety of deviant children, as well as to promote the well-being of the other participants (ACA, 1998).

Thus, the forming stage (the first three sessions) becomes a trial experience for some children. Only rarely do children drop out at this stage. More often, nonfunctioning group members want to stay despite their difficulties. In such cases, I recommend first trying an individual conversation with the child, or use the assistance of a coleader to give the child special attention. If no educational methods work, and there is no choice but to exclude the child, this always involves an individual session in which all efforts are taken to limit the child's sense of failure and alternative treatment is offered.

These cautious practices of screening candidates to group counseling and psychotherapy are applicable mostly to younger children. The recruitment of adolescents involves greater freedom of choice. For them, groups are often advertised in the classroom, on the school notice board, or through flyers. This is an opportunity for adolescents, with whom teacher's have less intensive contact, to seek help. With such clients, it is easier to practice the ACA Code of Ethics (1998). They are mature enough to be informed of the goals of the group and to explore expectations of necessary behavior in the group process.

In short, because the focus of this book is on counseling and psychotherapy groups aimed at children who often demonstrate exceptional needs, it is strongly recommended that all these children be given the chance to participate in a group, in an effort to help them overcome their difficulties. However, to secure the group process, it must be properly designed and the leader must be properly trained. Group composition is one of the major considerations in the attempt to overcome the challenges in working with difficult children.

GROUP COMPOSITION

How does a group leader know how to assign participants to groups? The question that comes to mind is whether groups should be homogeneous or heterogeneous in respect to the type of problem, the level of difficulty, gender, and age of participants.

Homogeneous or Heterogeneous Problem

The professional literature on group therapy with children tends to favor focal groups—that is, homogeneity of problem (K. R. Greenberg, 2003; Rose, 1998; Schaffer, 1999; Smead, 1995). Because the cognitive–behavioral theoretical orientation is leading in treatment of children, the tendency is to form groups based on children's specific problems. Such interventions are structured, aimed at enhancing particular skills required for the particular problem. Participants have similar difficulties, which may ease self-disclosure, contribute to the understanding of the problem, and improve action to change behavior. Group climate and cohesion, universality, and altruism are all therapeutic factors that may be enhanced in a focal group. In short-term group therapy, where it is difficult to build such therapeutic factors, the universality of the problems accelerates their development.

I agree that a group has to have a common focus; therefore, the groups that are described in this book are composed around a major difficulty: aggression, withdrawal, learning disabilities, children of divorce, as suggested in the literature (Schaffer, 1999). However, the advantages of having a homogeneous group in terms of the type of difficulty can easily turn into disadvantages. A group has to be attractive, provide the necessary conditions for personal growth, and offer positive modeling. If it carries a negative label, and group members negatively affect each other, the result can be destructive.

For some of these groups, focusing on a homogeneous population seems to be justified. For example, it may be easier for children of divorce to be part of a group whose members experience similar difficulties, as they often feel alone with their problems. Their chances of gaining support and understanding from peers is much higher in such homogeneous groups. Moreover, these children may find it difficult to share their concerns with children from intact families. Thus, for children of divorce, a homogeneous group may be quite constructive, as the processes focus on issues relevant to all children. But even in this case, my concern is that children in the group will be labeled as problematic because their parents are divorced. This is particularly true of adolescents, who find it so important to be part of the mainstream.

To overcome this problem, children of divorce are placed in the same group as children who have experienced loss in the family. In this way, the focus is on the emotions related to loss, without stigmatizing children of divorce. The following documents an exchange between two group members: Jerry, whose parents were recently divorced and Martin, whose father has died.

Jerry: I hate my father, he never comes to see me even when he promises.

Martin: But, at least, you have something to hope for; things may change for you, whereas I know I will never see my father again.

Although each child has to deal with different emotions, they help each other. Jerry, who initiated this conversation, helps Martin to express his great sense of loss, and Martin puts Jerry's problem in perspective, providing hope for the future. Moreover, Martin may have identified with Jerry's anger, although he did not explicitly mention it, thus broadening the spectrum of emotions he could recognize in himself and legitimize.

A homogeneous population is particularly inadvisable for groups aimed at dealing with anger and aggression. Reporting on a summer camp composed solely of aggressive and violent youth, Dishion, McCord, and Poulin (1999) found not only that the intervention did not improve their behavior, but actually enhanced it. Common sense would advise that such a group composition would be a disaster. Highly aggressive and violent youths brought together for a short-term intervention in camp conditions are likely to develop antisocial norms, reinforce each other's aggression, and even learn new violent methods and techniques.

This is not to suggest that aggressive children and adolescents cannot be treated in group settings. Indeed, my colleagues and I do work with aggressive children and youth in groups, which have been found to be as effective in reducing aggression as individual treatment (e.g., Shechtman, 2003). Several factors probably play a role in this success, but the relevant one for this discussion is group composition.

Homogeneity of Level of Difficulty

The groups for aggressive children and adolescents that my coworkers and I conduct are comprised of children of different levels of aggression, including nonaggressive participants. The group is not labeled as treating aggression; rather, children are asked to join a group aiming "to deal with friendship issues." Although the aggressive participants are identified prior to group establishment, other peers from the same class or age level are invited as well. Although the aggressive children soon realize that the focus of the group is on aggression, the group is not labeled as such and members are not all aggressive, which helps mask the purpose of the group.

The interaction between the two types of participants is also very meaningful, as the aggressive children learn different perceptions of a social situation and alternative responses to it. Consider the following interaction, in which the group was talking about a conflict with a teacher. Stuart, a nonaggressive adolescent, suggested that he would talk to his father about it, to which Bobby, an aggressive child, responded, "I would never have thought of involving my father, or any other grownup." This led to a discussion of the need to allow others to help, even if some control must be sacrificed, and of how to identify supportive people in one's environment and solicit their assistance. Bobby identified his gym teacher as a supportive person and agreed to talk to him.

The proportion of aggressive to nonaggressive participants is about 70% to 30%, respectively. The latter are usually prosocial, sensitive group members whose modeling is essential. Moreover, the positive interaction between the two types of children usually carries over to the classroom, enhancing the aggressor's social status at school.

Homogeneous Versus Heterogeneous Gender Groups

Boys and girls seem to exhibit different needs and interactions in the group. In fact, they may display two different social cultures. In friendship relationships, girls tend to be more intimate, to disclose emotions and experiences more freely, and to be more empathic in reaction to other group members; boys like to be tough, instrumental, and active. Clearly, it would be easier to lead an all-girls expressive–supportive group, as the behavior required in such groups is more natural to girls.

Empirical studies point to gender differences in the impact of group therapy. First, research on groups of friendship enhancement in which many of the children are withdrawn, indicated that girls are more intimate than boys. Moreover, girls grow in intimacy with time, whether treated or not, yet only boys who receive treatment become more intimate (Shechtman, 1994). Second, a study on self-disclosure (Leichtentritt & Shechtman, 1998) found the girls' frequency to be initially higher than that of the boys, but in later stages of the group process, the girls reduced their level of disclosure to adjust it to the boys' level. However, in another study in which participants were asked to choose which therapeutic factors in the group experience were most important to them (Shechtman & Gluk, 2005), girls in mixed-gender groups selected the category of Awareness and Self-disclosure more often than boys (24% and 10%, respectively) and as often as girls in homogeneous groups (also 24%). That is, girls seem to value awareness and self-disclosure more than boys, regardless of group composition. Third, in a recent study on attachment and client behavior in counseling groups (Shechtman & Dvir, 2005), girls showed higher rates of intimate self-disclosure, were less resistant, and expressed less negative responses to others' self-disclosure.

Two divergent conclusions can be reached from the aforementioned studies. One is that an group comprised of all girls may be more suitable in counseling and psychotherapy for girls. The other is that boys are likely to benefit from the presence of girls in their group. However, considering that the effect of group therapy does not seem to be lost when girls are included in mixed groups, I recommend working with gender heterogeneous groups in counseling and psychotherapy with children and adolescents.

Age Homogeneity

Whereas heterogeneity is recommended in terms of problems and their severity, as well as in terms of gender, homogeneity is advised when it comes to age. For children, developmental needs and tasks are unique to different age groups. In addition, there is the issue of social status that is highly related to age. Sixth graders would consider it an insult to be with younger children, and may end up bossing them around. More important, there is also a practical consideration for grouping children by age or grade level; it is easier to take children from the same class and to conduct the group during regular school hours.

GROUP DURATION, FORMAT, AND SIZE

Counseling and psychotherapy groups in the school usually last about 8 months, comprising 15 sessions on average, although some are shorter. It is rare that children have the opportunity to be in a group more than 1 year; yet, on the occasions in which this does happen, these children become models for the newcomers, which is very helpful to the group process. It is obvious that summer vacation is an arbitrary cut-off point and that many children may need longer periods of treatment. The best way to solve this is through individual termination, but this practice is not conducive to the school setting.

Because most groups are short-term and the model used is expressive–supportive, close-ended groups are necessary to allow the necessary level of trust to develop in the group. Close-ended groups tend to promote more cohesiveness among group members and may be very productive in helping members achieve stated goals (Gladding, 2003). Yet, they may also be difficult for the children at time of termination, because the sense of loss is much greater. A time limit is established before treatment begins, of which children must be aware, and they are frequently reminded about the time limit and the date of termination (Schaefer, 1999).

Group size is another consideration related to children's functioning in the group. A very large group may be intimidating, may not allow trust to develop in a short time, and may prevent the counselor from monitoring all problem behaviors in the group. A generally agreed-upon number is 6–8 group members (G. Corey, 1995; Gladding, 2003), or even fewer (4–5) in the case of young children (K. R. Greenberg, 2003), but the right size varies by the type of problem the population suffers from, the length of treatment, and the age of the children. The group should have enough members to afford ample interaction and yet be small enough to give everyone a chance to participate frequently (G. Corey, 1995). When working with aggressive children and adolescents or those suffering form LD, it is recommended to use very small groups (4–6 members) to prevent behavioral problems that might impede the group process.

In a study on attachment and group functioning (Shechtman & Dvir, 2006), group size (which varied from 4 to 10 participants, with a mean of 7) was found to be related only to one variable: simple self-disclosure (e.g., disclosure of basic information about oneself) was more frequent in the larger groups. No difference related to group size was found in terms of intimate self-disclosure or the reaction to other's self-disclosure. Of course, a conclusion regarding the effect of group size on participants' behavior is premature, based on one study, and a range of group sizes that is normal for working with this age level.

PHYSICAL STRUCTURE

The physical space in which group counseling is conducted in the school is an important factor in creating an atmosphere of trust and cohesiveness. The physical structure should ensure the safety and growth of group members. It should also be attractive to promote attractiveness to the group (Gladding, 2003). In the school setting, the space and its furnishings reflect the value that the school attributes to such activity. When groups are conducted in a counseling center, with attractive furniture and decorations, the sense will be that this place is safe, rarely interrupted by outsiders, and that it is important to the school. In contrast, groups that meet in a different room or at a different time every session find it difficult to maintain attendance.

How children feel about the group experience is related to how the school administration perceives the intervention. If the administration finds such activity valuable, children will feel so, too. Therefore, before establishing the group, support of all people involved—the principal, teachers, and parents—must be ensured (K. R. Greenberg, 2003; Smead, 1995).

SCHEDULING

The best experiences my colleagues and I have had have been with groups conducted during regular school hours as part of the class schedule. This prevents dropping out and minimizes attendance problems. In schools where groups are highly valued, they can also be run successfully before or after school.

The older the children in the groups, the more they and their parents are concerned with them missing classes. Therefore, careful attention must be given to the scheduling of the group, so that participants do not miss much academic material or classes that they like (e.g., gym). When possible, my colleagues and I schedule the sessions before or after school to avoid conflicts of interest. In one of our groups for children of divorce, called the Breakfast Club, a light breakfast is served. Another adolescent group, The Restaurant, is scheduled after school, and the children take turns bringing in bread and cheese and making their own sandwiches.

Smart scheduling is easiest when children are drawn from the same class or at least the same age cohort. Being of the same age is also important for developmental considerations. As my colleagues and I are interested in homogeneous groups in terms of gender, and the groups are small (between 6–8 members), it is easiest to compose a group from one or two parallel classes.

Most of our groups run during 1 school year. They start a couple of months after school starts and continue until the end of the year. Considering holidays and field trips, the length of the group is about 15 sessions. Therefore, the most effective way is to schedule the group right at the beginning of the year, so it becomes an integral part of the school program. This provides continuity to the group work. Because they are close groups, they become an important source of children's support throughout the year.

BEYOND THE CHILDREN

The interesting and sometimes challenging issue my colleagues and I face in working with children and adolescents is that they are not our sole clients. Working with youngsters requires cooperation from important people in their lives—parents, teachers, and the school principal.

Most important is getting parents' agreement, if only because they have to sign the form of consent. K. R. Greenberg (2003) provided useful information regarding consent forms to be completed prior to the beginning of a group in the school setting. But even more important is the parents' attitude to the group experience. Parents can encourage a child to persist in a group or discourage a child from attending. Much depends on the child's problem, the parents' beliefs regarding therapy, and their general value system. One mother insisted that her daughter drop out of the group because "only disturbed children need a group." One of the parents' greatest concerns is the fear that family secrets will be exposed. This fear is present in many groups for children of divorced families. Another problem is their competition with the counselor over their child's trust. "How come my child is willing to trust a stranger rather his own mom?" they ask. Therefore, parents must be well informed about the group's goals and expectations. They must also understand the issue of confidentiality to avoid future conflicts. The best way to obtain parental agreement is to have an experiential orientation session with them, in which they are not only told about group goals and expectations, but can also experience an activity or two. Once they realize that the climate is safe and warm, they may more easily agree to have their child join. Some parents need more frequent contact with the counselor; this should be allowed without, of course, breaking the rule of confidentiality.

Teachers are also an important part of the group success. Those who believe in the child, the therapy, and the counselor cooperate more willingly. They make sure that the child arrives on time to the group, that assistance with academic tasks is provided when needed, and that the child's efforts to make progress are acknowledged and encouraged. My coworkers and I had an extremely aggressive child in one of our groups, who showed real progress in changing his behavior. One day on a field trip, someone pushed him towards the teacher. Her response was, "What a waste of time to put you into treatment. You will never change." Needless to say, this was so discouraging for him that he never wanted to go back to therapy. Teachers, too, must be convinced that groups are effective, and that they have a part in this success. Orientation sessions, or an ongoing successful group experience for the teachers, may convince them that the effort is worthy.

The school principal is usually the one to make the decision in favor of or against group counseling in the school. He or she may be afraid to take on an additional responsibility. One way to convince administrators is by presenting the accountability of such groups. Many of our experiences with administrative resistance to groups were associated with students with LD, as it seems illogical to take children who are academically behind out of class to send them to a group that does not deal specifically with scholastic learning. However, when outcomes of our research were presented to the school administrators and the rationale of our group work was explained, most often they accepted the idea and became actively engaged in the groups' success. School principals also need the agreement of their superintendent. All this must be taken care of before beginning the initial stage of the group.

SUMMARY

Preplanning is an extremely important stage for the group counselor working with children and adolescents, mostly because the counselor deals not only with the children, but also with significant people in their lives, and is limited by the setting involved. The group leader often works with referred clients, sometimes with little control over selection and composition processes. Group size and process duration also depend largely on the setting. In most cases the setting does not permit long-term groups, even though termination is often premature for some children. Thus, most of the groups my colleagues and I work with are short-term (about 15 sessions) and end with the school calendar. We compensate for the short duration by applying a policy of closed-ended groups rather than open-ended ones, as the former usually establish more intensive group cohesiveness, a central feature of the expressive–supportive model. The next chapter expands on how to achieve our goals in the initial stage of the group.

7

The Initial Stage

The first stage of the group process is called *forming*. A group of children who get together does not necessarily create positive relationships. If the children come from the same or parallel classrooms (as is common to groups in schools), past history and relationships, labels, and predispositions all play a role in threatening group cohesion. Such children generally have major difficulties with trust; indeed, a recent study (Shechtman & Dvir, 2006) found that 40% of the adolescents in 11 groups were insecure. The issue of trust is particularly problematic for many children at the forming stage, which largely resembles the strange situation (Ainsworth, Blehar, Waters, & Wall, 1978). At this stage, the group leader must actively provide structure to the group sessions, with the aim of achieving the goals of forming relationships, developing a language of feelings, establishing constructive group norms, and providing a sense of security.

FORMING RELATIONSHIPS

It is recommended to start with ice breakers to increase a sense of familiarity. I recommend activities involving pairs or threesomes instead of the whole group in order to gradually make participants comfortable in this unfamiliar situation. When children meet other group members in a face-to-face, intimate exchange of information, they already feel that they are in a familiar place. To increase the impact of such activity, it is recommended to exchange pairs several times, so that at the end of the session, each child has had an opportunity to meet all other children in person. The exchange of pairs can be navigated through music, which enhances the sense of playfulness. To make the conversation intimate, an intimate topic must be selected. The conversation will develop very differently if children are asked to just say something about themselves, than if they are asked to tell each other about a person or situation that made them feel angry or bad, an important event in their life, or a wish that they would like to come true. At the end of the session, my fellow therapists and I suggest a topic that raises positive feelings, such as a positive event in their life or a good memory, to let the children leave in a positive mood. Common feedback from such activity is: "We've known each other for years, but I didn't know that…". An emotional topic also sets the tone for emotions to be expressed and shared later on.

Familiarity with each other's names is an important start of a group. Learning the names can be achieved through therapeutic games. The Legacy of My Name is a game in which children are asked to tell how they got their name, what it means, how they feel about it, and so on. One child told the group that he was named after his uncle, who had died heroically in battle, and that he himself lived constantly with the fear that he was going to face the same fate. Another girl, whose name meant *beauty*, said she felt that she did not live up to the expectations of her name. It makes it easier to remember a name that is embedded in a story. This is also a game rich in information about the child's attitude toward himself or herself.

Another strategy my colleagues and I use to assist children in introducing themselves to a new group is through sharing a meaningful object. The children are asked to show or name such an object in their possession. This provides structure and permits self-introduction in a somewhat indirect way, making it easier on the child to share personal information. For instance, Ruth chose a piece of jewelry that she got from her father, who no longer lived with her. "This reminds me of him and also gives me a sense of being protected; that's why I never take it off," she said. This was an intimate self-disclosure that would not be easy to share without an object.

A variation of this game is to bring in a variety of objects, display them in front of the children, and ask them to introduce themselves through a selected object. Sam, an aggressive boy, selected a stone, "because I always want to be ready to repel an unexpected attack." Paul selected a book, because he likes it when his father reads to him. In this case, the children's presentation of self also served diagnostic purposes.

The use of therapeutic cards is another technique to introduce oneself. A variety of cards are displayed to the children (see Chapter 5), who are asked to select one that is meaningful to them. Linda selected a card of a queen, stating that she would like to be a queen sometimes and get more attention from people around her. Marsha selected the same queen, explaining that she is bossy sometimes and she would like to allow more space to others. Thus, the same card may have a different meaning to each individual. Introducing oneself through a card conveys personal meaning that helps group members get closer to each other.

DEVELOPING A LANGUAGE OF FEELINGS

As self-expressiveness is a central goal in our groups, the expression of feelings is constantly sought. However, a major problem in working with children is their limited vocabulary in the realm of emotions. A language of emotions needs to be directly developed in the group. Therapeutic games, cards, bibliotherapy, and photos are excellent methods to increase the language of emotions. Even a simple game like playing catch can invoke emotions if the child receiving the ball has to mention a feeling and expand on how he or she feels about this emotion. This is a good way to promote the norm that emotions are welcome and to experience the expression of emotions in a playful way. Using Feeling Cards is another way to increase the language of emotions. Cards with text or pictures representing various emotions are displayed on the floor, and the children are invited to select one that represents either here-and-now feelings or an out-of-group emotion, and to discuss them with the group. The cards may take different forms or be incorporated in a game. For example, the feelings can be written on little fish and the child is the fisherman.

A similar and highly popular game in our groups is "The Feeling Clock." The clock has emotions in place of numbers, and the hand indicates which feeling should be discussed. The game can be played so that the hand stops incidentally, and those who can connect to the indicated emotion share their feelings or experiences. Or a particular child can choose where to stop the hand and express his or her feelings accordingly. The leader can also take an active part in placing the hand on a particular feeling and navigate the discussion on either a personal or group level. The feelings can be changed periodically and so serve as a device to increase the vocabulary of emotions.

ESTABLISHING CONSTRUCTIVE GROUP NORMS

For a group to be constructive, appropriate norms of behavior beyond self-disclosure must be established. A culture of a therapeutic climate, which most children and adolescents are not familiar with, must be developed. To permit individual group members to work on their personal issues, group members need to learn to comply with the group rules, respond in a constructive way, and maintain confidentiality.

In groups with children and adolescents, rules and regulations are important issues, without which chaos will characterize the group. Yet, it is not easy to instill such rules because the group climate in counseling and psychotherapy groups is expected to be free and democratic. The usual recommendation is to include a discussion of the group rules at the first session (K. R. Greenberg, 2003; Ritchie & Huss, 2000). I feel, however, that premature discussion of rules has an adverse effect on group climate and is too similar to the classroom situation. Rules are better accepted when they are timed at the appearance of a problem, when children understand that the rules are created and maintained in response to their own needs.

Thus, when a problem arises, my coworkers and I play the Rule Game. Each child receives a blue scrap of paper on which he or she writes down one or more behaviors that would make him or her feel bad if they happened in the group. On another piece of paper in a different color, they write one or more behaviors in the group that would make them happy. These notes are completed anonymously. After all have been collected, they are read out and summarized into a few major rules. Each rule is discussed so that the children understand why it might be disturbing to a group member. Then the children discuss ways in which they can help the person that voiced the need. These rules are kept in a central place throughout the group sessions. When one is broken, the leader and group members have a reference to go back to and remind each other of the individual and group needs that have to be met in a successful group.

Another helpful activity is Fantasy Land. The children are asked to close their eyes and think about their group in terms of their fantasy land. They are directed to consider how it sounds, smells, looks, and especially feels. What relationships and what kind of behavior do they expect and desire in the group? With younger children, their fantasies can be first expressed through drawings, then shared with the group; the drawing helps them both express themselves and focus on the ensuing discussion. With older participants, drawing may not be necessary, and they can move directly to sharing their fantasies. Children and adolescents alike usually want a quiet room with no fighting or disturbances, one that feels calm and tension-free, and in which group members listen respectfully to each other. During the activity, the group also discusses its commitment to the needs that have been expressed.

CONSTRUCTIVE RESPONSE

The major difference between individual and group counseling is the interpersonal interaction among members that takes place only in the group context. Group members are expected to listen empathetically, respond through sharing and feedback, and encourage each other. These are behaviors that children and adolescents do not naturally possess, as observed in the Shechtman and Yanuv (2001) study. This study showed that the children used many unconstructive challenges and even the feedback they provided was often destructive. At this initial stage, therefore, my colleagues and I want to instill norms of interpersonal interaction that are responsible, positive, and empowering. Eye contact and direct communication are constantly promoted, and reactions to each other are shaped and improved to permit a constructive exchange of feedback. The following are a few activities to promote such interpersonal exchange.

Ball games are a simple and good way to increase interpersonal interaction, in general, and positive interaction norms, in particular, when designed to do so. For instance, the ball can be thrown to each group member, followed by a question of personal interest ("I am interested in hearing more about your responsibilities at home"). Another possibility is for group members to throw the ball to each other accompanied by a feedback response ("I threw the ball to Eva because I liked the way she shared her worries with me"). In this way, children become more involved in the exchange of interactions and take responsibility for the group process. They learn to show interest in other group members, to draw out silent group members, and to empower each other. The following three activities illustrate the empowerment process.

In the Personal Awards activity, awards are given out by group members to each other either for here-and-now interactions or for general achievements. Examples for here-and-now interactions are: "I give the award to Jan for introducing humor into the group;" "I give the award to Gail for sharing her secret;" "I give the award to Dina for being courageous." Examples for general achievements are: "I give you an award for improving your behavior;" "I give you an award for being a good friend;" "I give you an award for your achievements in sports." With younger children, we use a concrete award, which they hand to each other. With older children, we can use an abstract award. A variation of this activity is to focus on one child, to which the entire group gives (oral or written) awards. My coworkers and I often apply this technique at birthday parties, when we focus on the birthday child.

A similar empowering activity designed for older adolescents is My Tree, in which each group member first identifies his or her own strengths, then is empowered for them by other members. The first step is to draw a tree in which the roots represent abilities and the branches represent achievements. The second step involves identifying one's abilities and achievements. This in itself usually leaves participants empowered, as people tend to concentrate more on their weaknesses and deficits than their strengths. The third step focuses on expansion of both abilities and achievements through positive feedback from other group members. This can take place in pairs, followed by positive impressions of the partner shared in the group, or it can be done with the whole group from the start. This is a great activity to increase self-esteem, to encourage positive feedback, and to enhance a positive group climate.

Finally, another activity to promote positive interactions among group members is the Compliment Game, in which the children make positive statements to one another. This game can be played in various ways. One possibility is to have group members walk freely around the room with paper taped to their back, on which the others write compliments anonymously (or not). An alternative method is to write each child's name at the top of a piece of paper and pass that paper around. Each group members folds the paper after writing his or her compliment, so that it eventually looks like an accordion. In this variation of the game, everyone's compliments are hidden from each other.

SENSE OF SECURITY

Once group members start sharing personal information, the issue of confidentiality comes up. Groups function best when members feel that what has been said within the group setting will not be revealed outside it. To promote a sense of confidentiality and trust, the group leader needs to state this as early as the screening interview, repeat it during the first session, and reinforce it on a regular basis thereafter (Gazda, 1989). In the groups described in this book, the children not only talk about the importance of confidentiality, but also participate in a small ceremony to stress its importance. The entire group holds hands and promises to keep our secrets inside the group.

When there is a question about the betrayal of confidentiality within the group, it should be dealt with immediately. It is not easy to secure confidentiality in groups of children, as they do not always understand the devastating impact that revelation has on the group. Time needs to be taken to deal with this. Usually, the issue is brought up through a story in which a child was betrayed by his best friend. Feelings of the betrayed person are identified and the motives of the betrayer are discussed. The children then understand the difficulties involved in confidentiality and the devastating consequences of betraying that trust. Memories of betrayal are then shared and ways to avoid such pitfalls are discussed. The discussion closes with the ceremony of confidentiality mentioned earlier.

My fellow group leaders and I all know that confidentiality cannot be guaranteed, so we also talk about the possibility that a secret may sometimes leak out, as suggested in the ACA Code of Ethics (1998). But we also discuss the price people pay for holding back information, emotions, and experiences, leading to the understanding that solving a problem may be worthwhile even when a secret is uncovered.

SUMMARY

The initial stage is extremely important in groups of children and adolescents, perhaps more so than for adults, for several reasons. First, children and adolescents are not regular clients because they did not choose to be in therapy, but rather have been referred to it. As such, they may be less motivated to undergo a therapeutic process. Second, they are not familiar with the expectations of clients in therapy in general, and in group psychotherapy in particular, which makes it difficult for them to function constructively. Third, children and adolescents come from a unique culture in which positive interpersonal interactions are not within their normal group norms or skills. They need to be guided and assisted in developing and using interactions that are compliant with group counseling and psychotherapy.

Consequently, the group counselor must actively provide structure to the sessions at this stage, with the aim of forming relationships, developing a language of feelings, establishing constructive group norms, and providing a sense of security. Use of structured activities and therapeutic games is an excellent way to promote group norms, a positive and safe group climate, and a sense of personal empowerment. These lay the foundations for constructive later stages.

However, even though this preparation stage may be positive, it does not guarantee a smooth transition to the working stage. The working stage requires a deeper level of self-awareness and self-disclosure, which again raises the level of anxiety. Thus, a transition stage usually emerges, in which conflicts among group members are worked out, freeing the way to the working stage.

8

The Transition Stage

Successful completion of the initial stage of forming the group is likely to reduce some of the resistance of members, but not remove it entirely. A transition stage is inevitable, even necessary, in the life of a group. The expression of conflict and its resolution is key to the group's development. Yalom (1985) maintained that, unless conflict exceeds the tolerance of group members, it is a healthy process that brings "drama, excitement, change and development to human life and societies" (p. 352). In groups that last 10–15 sessions, the transition stage tends to begin in the second or third session and usually extends for one to three meetings (Gladding, 2003).

It is important to note that resistance continues after the transition stage, although it is evoked by different causes and manifested in somewhat different behaviors. In her work with adolescent groups, Hurley (1984) identified three forms of resistance typical of various stages in the development of the group. *Resistance in the service of defining group structure* is typical of the transition stage. It is aimed at testing limits, provoking the leader and defining issues of trust, safety and control. Resistant behavior at this stage takes the form of avoidance, laughing/giggling, distracting, and threatening. In contrast, *resistance employed to regulate group tension* is typical of the working stage of the group and is provoked by high self-disclosure of a group member. If such self-disclosure exceeds the optimal level of the group members' sense of security, counteracting forces are activated to ease tension, manifested by disruptive or distracting behavior. Finally, *resistance to deal with separation and termination*, typical of the termination stage, is manifested in high acting out behavior. This chapter focuses on resistance in the transition stage.

The transition stage begins with a stormy period, mostly because group members become anxious. As in any type of therapy, participants in group therapy deal with emotions, past and present experiences, and unresolved issues that are unpleasant, painful, and often threatening. Anxiety relates to the fear of exposing one's pain, of not sounding intelligent, of being overcome by intense emotions, of being misunderstood, of being rejected, and of not knowing what to expect (M. S. Corey & Corey, 2006). These emotions cause group members to resist the therapy process, just like clients in individual therapy (Hill, 2005). In an attempt to explain resistance in individual therapy, Mahalik (1994) suggested five dimensions: opposing expression of painful affect, opposing recollection of materials, opposing change, and opposing insight—all internal sources of resistance related to anxiety—as well as opposing the therapist.

In group therapy, the anxiety of members may be even higher than in individual therapy. In addition to intrinsically provoked anxiety, participants have to find their place in the group, find the direction of the group, and see if it fits their needs and expectations. This involves power struggles over issues related to the structure and the direction of the group, its goals, and members' expected behavior (M. S. Corey & Corey, 2006; Gladding, 2003). As group and individual goals begin to form, the issue of trust emerges. Members question the ability of the group to be of help, suspect the ability of other participants to keep secrets, and are reluctant to self-disclose.

Relationships among group members are also of concern. Group members question whether they will be liked and appreciated or judged and rejected. They are concerned about other members' reactions to disclosure of their dirty secrets; would they be considered abnormal or deviant? And sometimes they do not like the people in the group, the group is not attractive to them, and they hesitate to identify with it.

The counselor also enters into the equation. He or she not only evokes fears and transferences, but also needs to be shared by group members. Participants may question the ability of the therapist to like all of them, and to give the needed attention to each of them.

Resistance in adult groups is manifested in various ways, including silence, monopolizing, storytelling, intellectualizing, advice giving, and even hostility (M. S. Corey & Corey, 2006). Although some of these behaviors are found in individual therapy as well, the variety of forms of resistance seems to be larger in groups, particularly in groups of children and adolescents.

RESISTANCE IN CHILDREN'S GROUPS

A transition stage is mentioned in most of the reviews of child and adolescent group psychotherapy (Berkovitz, 1989; K. G. Dies, 2000; Smead, 1995). However, due to developmental differences, children go through the transition stage in somewhat different patterns than adults. Smead (1995) suggested that, unless children have an extreme lack of trust as a result of early traumatic life experiences, they tend to move more quickly toward the working stage than adults do. They seem to have less inhibition about self-disclosing, to be more spontaneous in their behavior in general, and to be less aware of the risks in facing negative experiences and feelings. In other words, the intrinsic motives of fears and anxiety are lessened in children's groups. This trend has been supported in a study (Leichtentritt & Shechtman, 1998) that showed that the initial level of self-disclosure in children's groups was high already in the first session (about 10 self-disclosures per session), and remained at about the same level throughout the intervention. Even with adolescents, early self-disclosure is quite common, as illustrated in the following scenario.

In the first session of a group of adolescent girls, the group was getting acquainted through a game. The girls threw a ball to each other and ask a personal question (e.g., "someone you like;" "a dream that you remember"). One question was "something you do not like about yourself." Although I would consider this too harsh a topic for a first session, the girls accepted it as a natural question, as can be seen in the following example:

Beth:	I'm too direct, sometimes it hurts others.
Karen:	Me too. And I'm stubborn—even when I know I'm wrong, I just go on fighting, just to win.
Helen:	I'm with you. I have a big mouth and I would like to change that.
Paula:	I am too weak and tend to be too submissive, which causes me all sorts of trouble.

This dialogue is more typical of the working stage, but it actually took place at the very first session.

Another example comes from a group of 9-year-old boys and girls, in their second session. They started this session with an activity focusing on here-and-now feelings. Most of the children expressed positive feelings (e.g., "we are like family;" "we are friends"), including David who, in addition, whispered, "I also wanted to say that I am extremely afraid of my father." This instance of self-disclosure was unexpected at this point of the group process and obviously emerged spontaneously from the child's need to express his pain. Jenny supported David by adding that she was also afraid of her father; the leader and other group members encouraged him to continue; and he went on to tell the group that his father often gets very angry and becomes extremely abusive: "He hits me with a big belt and it hurts." To this disclosure, Marty responded sarcastically ("Really?"), following which David refused to continue.

This is an unfortunate incident in the life of a group, yet a frequent one in a group of children. Apparently, David did not consider the risk he was taking, because he lacked the ego strength to inhibit himself. He must have had a great need to get the burden of his secret off his chest, and probably needed the support of his peers. However, this intimate self-disclosure received an inappropriate response because of several possible reasons: Marty might have been threatened by this particular disclosure; he might have felt less safe in the group; or he might have lacked the necessary skills to respond empathetically to the pain of another group member. His inappropriate response stopped David's exploration of his problem at that point.

This incident presents several characteristics of resistance in children's groups at the transition stage. Both children demonstrated limited inhibitions: David, in sharing his secret this early in the life of the group, and Marty in responding inappropriately. Neither behavior is frequent in adult groups. Hence, self-disclosure might be less inhibited in children's groups, but on the other hand, there is the danger of other forms of resistance, such as externalizing behavior—unrestricted verbal and nonverbal behavior—that intimidates other children and is difficult to handle in a therapeutic climate. Children do not communicate in the way familiar to most adults. They can be blatantly disruptive and often fail to follow common rules of courtesy in groups (Berg, Landreth, & Fall, 1998). In contrast to adult groups, children's verbal resistance is also spontaneous and unrestricted; they shout and scream, use abusive language, and reject group members openly. Nonverbal forms of resistance include playing with objects unrelated to the process (e.g., cell phones), moving around in the room, rocking in their chair, and pushing or hitting another group member (McClure, Miller, & Russo, 1992). These behaviors may be attributed to the children's lack of social skills necessary to negotiate conflicts (Arrington, 1987). Ghirardelli (2001) further suggested that personal objects brought to the group serve not only as symbols of resistance to the leader, but also as devices enabling participants to connect to their world of peers without having to resort to verbal communication.

Resistance may be directed at the group leader or the activity he or she introduces, but mostly it is directed at other group members. Because children's groups are generally conducted in the school, and group members are often drawn from the same class, they may know each other from previous interactions. In other words, they have a mutual history that sometimes impedes the group climate. Moreover, in contrast to adults who choose to seek help, most children are referred to group counseling, and they are often placed in groups that carry some degree of labeling; this probably makes the group less attractive to members. After all, who wants to be associated with a group of aggressive children, a group of children of divorce, or a group of underachievers? Thus, although many steps are taken to limit the issue of labeling (see Chapter 6), it still remains a factor that increases resistance in the initial stages. Here are a few examples of forms of resistance in groups of children.

RESISTANCE TO AN ACTIVITY

With children, and even with adolescents, structuring the sessions, particularly at the initial stages of the group, is an important strategy (Berg et al., 1998; MacLennan & Dies, 1992; Smead, 1995). In one adolescent group, the members were involved in the Personal Tree activity, in which each child is asked to draw a tree and name their strengths (as roots) and achievements (as branches). Marsha refused to draw a tree; she mades two attempts then destroyed her drawing. All efforts to support and reinforce her were rejected. She expressed dissatisfaction with her drawing and refused to participate. Although Marsha's resistance to the activity might reflect frustration with her drawing abilities, it could also be indicative of high expectations, fear of failure, and even anxiety related to poor self-image. This was certainly not the right stage to get into processing the real issue; at this point, the leader had to accept the child's resistance as targeted at the activity and offer an alternate activity that would allow her to proceed with the group process.

In another group of younger children (9 year olds), Dennis refused to draw the tree, but stated openly that he could not think of any strengths or achievements. The leader suggested that the group help him find his strengths. Dennis agreed to accept this modification of the activity, which gave him a strong sense of social support.

In the same group, following a discussion on empathy, the children were asked to write a letter to a child that was hurt. Anna, an immigrant to the country, refused to write a letter. She may have been concerned about language inadequacies and feared being criticized. To avoid power struggles or increased defensiveness of group members, children must be offered alternate ways to express themselves, so that they can continue with the group process.

RESISTANCE TO THE COUNSELOR

Resistance to the counselor is more common among adolescents than younger children. For adolescents, it is part of their oppositional behavior to authority figures. Elementary-school children usually become easily attracted to the therapist and seek her attention. Nonetheless, some children do not deal well with the competition over the counselor's attention and protect themselves from disappointment by resisting the therapist. Such may be the case in the next illustration.

Nine-year-old Myra was referred to counseling because of frequent disruptive relationships with her teachers. She was an adopted single child, and displayed high levels of distrust. As expected, she was presenting similar problems in the group; she interrupted the session by making noise and moving around restlessly. To the counselor's request to join the group, she responded, "I'll do what I want." It is not easy to maintain discipline in a democratic and therapeutic climate, and particularly difficult to face such direct provocations. Berg and colleagues (1998) stipulated that, in working with children, it is not easy to refrain from assuming a parental or teacher role. However, this counselor avoided an almost inevitable power struggle, and turns the situation into a learning experience.

First, Debra, the counselor, reminded Myra of the group rules that they themselves had drawn up and of the contract she had signed. Second, she invited Myra to explore her anger:

Debra:	You may want to tell me something I cannot understand. Are you dissatisfied with or disappointed in something I said or did? Please tell us what it is, so we can respond properly.
Myra:	Am I going to be punished here, too? Will you write a letter to my mom?

Debra reassured Myra that she would try to solve all problems in the group with the help of all members. This was a positive re-experience of human interactions for Myra, and she joined the group process.

Another example of resistance to the group counselor is drawn from a group of adolescents. Adolescents not only oppose authority, they also compete over the distribution of power and leadership, as is clear from the following scenario with Billy.

Billy was very active in the second session, in which she disclosed a private emotional experience with the group. But she started the next session by acting out and expressing resistance to Judy, the leader. She began by starting a game of Telephone in the group, ignoring Judy's presence. Judy felt excluded and rather intimidated.

However, identifying Billy's act as resistance, she tried to encourage her to talk about her resentment openly. It took a while, with much help from Judy, for Billy to express the following direct message: "Your activities annoy me." Judy encouraged Billy to express her feelings, tried to understand what was bothering her, and even accepted one of the activities Billy initiated. This is a positive re-experience of interpersonal relations, helping an extremely resistant group member gain confidence in herself, the group, and the authority figure. It turned out to be an excellent activity that accelerated the group process, because the girls were courageous, evoking high levels of self-disclosure.

Judy's reaction to this incident is interesting:

> When Billy started the game I knew it was about me, and that it was not positive. Knowing how vulnerable I usually am in such situations, and being hurt, at first I wanted to stop the game. But at the same time, I knew I needed to hear what they had to say. I am happy that my reason was stronger than my emotions, and I decided to open it up. From that point, I was not threatened anymore; I realized that it must be a normative part of the process. I left the session feeling stronger and realized that the interaction increased group cohesion.

This leader was a young counselor unskilled in running groups; in fact, this was her first one. But having the knowledge about group processes helped her cope with the situation. The literature suggests that the leader must balance support with confrontation, model appropriate behavior at times of conflict, and encourage self-expressiveness and risk taking. This is exactly what Judy did.

RESISTANCE TO A GROUP MEMBER

Resistance to a group member is a more delicate issue to handle than resistance to the therapist, because other children get hurt. Those who are used to being rejected or scapegoated are particularly vulnerable, and they are the ones who most often receive openly negative responses from the group. This is shown in the following group interaction.

In a particular session, the group was involved in identifying personal goals for working in the group. Nine-year-old Myra said, "My goal is to get rid of David. I don't want him here in the group." This was a difficult situation for Debra, the counselor, because she needed to protect all the group members by blocking negative interactions, and this was a nasty remark. Yet, at the same time, she did not want to cut off communication with the resistant child. Debra said,

> I assume that there is something that bothers you about David. Perhaps you can talk to him directly, and explain to him how his behavior affects you. Anyway, David is an important group member and he is staying with us.

Limits were set, the victim was protected, and the resistant group member was guided toward behavioral change.

RESISTANCE FOR INTERNAL REASONS

Resistance due to internal reasons is not easy to identify, because often these reasons are masked by more overt forms of resistance. Intrinsic resistance has to be handled with great caution because of the high level of anxiety involved. In fact, it should be dealt with at a later stage in the group, when both the individual and the group are more ready for therapeutic work. However, children sometimes talk openly about internal causes of resistance; in such cases, the fears and anxieties must be addressed (if not further explored) at this stage, as is illustrated in the following example.

Twelve-year-old Samantha shared with the group her sense of helplessness, "When I fail, I stop trying." But any attempt to hear more about her feelings or to get an example resulted in a long silence. Samantha might have been anxious about what she had already said, or she may have been afraid to deal with her issues more in depth. Whether her resistance was blocking expression of painful affect, recollection of past experiences, insight, or change, she was entitled to her privacy, certainly at this initial stage. She should have been acknowledged for her sharing and self-understanding and invited to continue whenever she chose to do so. It is extremely important to permit the client to set her own boundaries, to respect them, and to encourage the group to do so as well.

SUMMARY OF RESEARCH

In an attempt to investigate the type of resistance in children's and adolescent's groups, my colleagues and I conducted a preliminary study of 10 groups randomly selected from a pool of projects (five groups at each age level). Analyses were based on three (out of 15) audiotaped and transcribed sessions: second, seventh, and tenth sessions, representing the transition, working, and termination stages of group development, respectively. As this information has not been published yet, the descriptive data are presented in greater detail.

First, we looked at nonverbal resistance, which we broke down into two categories: (a) physical aggression, and (b) moving around and playing with objects unrelated to the session. These behaviors occurred only 12 times throughout the group process in both children and adolescent groups. Of these behaviors, 25% (three incidents) were expressed in acts of physical aggression, all of which occurred in the transition stage. Most of the moving around and playing with objects (about 60%) occurred in that stage as well. Overall, nonverbal resistance accounted for 7.4% and 4.0% (for children and adolescents, respectively) of their total resisting behaviors (n = 162 and 301, respectively).

Next, we analyzed verbal resistance. This accounted for 12% of the total speech of children and adolescents. Although the number of verbal resisting behaviors was much higher in the adolescent groups, when analyzed as a percentage of total speech (1246 and 2637), the resistance rate was similar (8.0% and 8.7%, respectively). These results are consistent with earlier studies (e.g., Shechtman, 2004a).

EXPLANATION OF THE DATA: SOURCES OF RESISTANCE

Breaking down the source of resistance into four categories—intrinsic (fear to recall, to express, to change; Mahalik, 1994), therapist, activity, and group (including members)—my colleagues and I found intrinsic factors to be the source of most of the resistance in both age groups (61% and 74% for children and adolescents, respectively; see Figures 1 & 2). The next most frequent category was resistance to the group (about 25% at both age levels). Resistance to a particular activity was about 11% in the elementary-school groups and less than 1% in the adolescent groups. Finally, resistance to the therapist was quite rare (about 2% in the younger groups and 1.4% in the older ones).

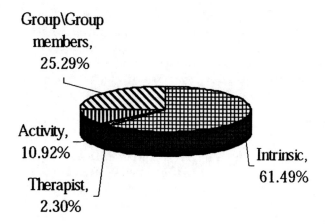

Figure 8.1. Sources of resistance: Children.

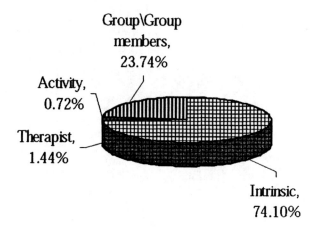

Figure 8.2. Sources of resistance: Adolescents.

These results suggest that children and adolescents do have intrinsic reservations about self-disclosure and so experience resistance to the group and its members, just like adults. What appears different from adult groups are the low rates of resistance to the counselor. Even the adolescents, who were expected to resist the counselor as a representative of authority figures, rarely did so. Between the two age levels, it is interesting to note the higher rate of resistance to activities among the younger children, probably because more activities are used for this age group. Moreover, adolescents seem to be more reserved; perhaps they are more conscious of the risks involved in self-disclosure.

EXPLANATION OF THE DATA: TYPES OF RESISTANCE

Along with my coworkers, I also investigated the type of behaviors in which resistance was manifested, based on four categories: verbal aggression (e.g., cursing, insulting), outburst of anger (screaming, shouting), distracting behavior (laughter, giggling, talking), and refusal to respond or act. In both age groups, the majority of responses fell into the refusal category (about 70% for both). The other three behaviors accounted for about 10% each in both age levels (see Figures 3 & 4).

EXPLANATION OF THE DATA: RESISTANCE OVER TIME

As we were interested in the transition stage in particular, my fellow therapists and I looked at the types of resistance at three points of time. As can be seen in Figures 5 and 6, refusal to respond was quite consistent over time in both age groups. Outbursts of anger and distracting behavior were high in the transition stage, but were sharply reduced with time.

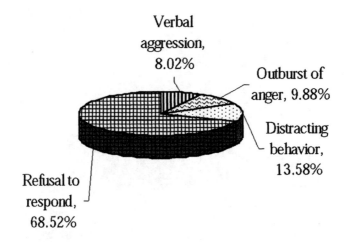

Figure 8.3.   Types of resistance: Children.

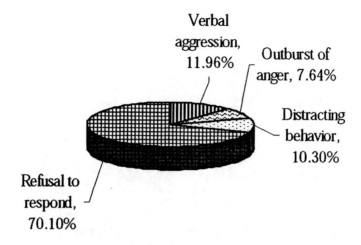

Figure 8.4. Types of resistance: Adolescents.

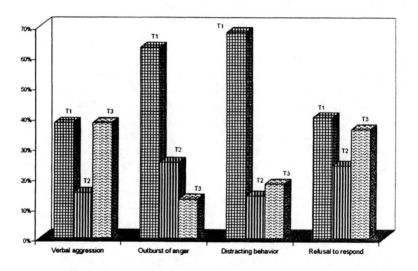

Figure 8.5. Types of resistance over time: Children.

Based on both measures—source of resistance and type of resisting behavior—it seems that both younger children and adolescents are worried more about dealing with personal issues and self-disclosure than with issues of power and structure, even at the transition stage. These results suggest that children and adolescents have similar reservations about dealing with intrinsic issues, just as adults have in therapy. Yet, at the transition stage, about one-third of their behavior is bluntly unpleasant, even aggressive, in respect to activities and the group or group members. Although this

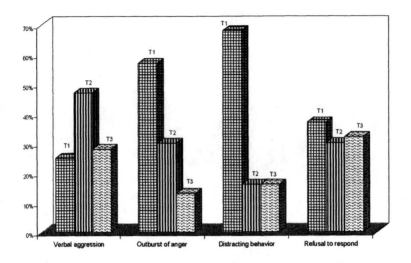

Figure 8.6. Types of resistance over time: Adolescents.

study is only a preliminary description of resistance in groups, the clinical implications are worth discussing.

There seems to be a transition stage in children and adolescent groups in which physical aggression, moving around, outbursts of anger and distracting behavior are present. Although these behaviors decrease with time, they must be dealt with skillfully at the transition stage. It is not clear from this data what the focus of resistance is; yet, it is clear that children and adolescents are occupied with fears and anxiety about self-disclosing that continue to pose a threat to them along the process. It is the counselor's role to reduce the level of anxiety at the initial stage of the group, to establish a climate of trust and secure confidentiality, to set norms for self-expressiveness, and to enhance group support.

SUMMARY

As with adults, resistance among children and adolescents must be dealt with openly and directly, but with warmth and empathy. Supportive confrontation (Cramer-Azima, 1989) is always the rule, including at this initial stage. Hostile behavior must be halted, and physical or psychological harm to others must be stopped firmly and quickly. This may be particularly applicable to groups of younger children, whose emotional stability may be precarious and who may act impulsively (MacLennan & Dies, 1992). Any attempt to deny, avoid, or try to repress such behaviors will cause them to emerge in later stages and interfere with the group process.

Myra is a typical example of a resistant young group member. Her resistance was manifested in almost every way: she was resistant to the counselor, to another group member, and to the activity. At first, Debra, the counselor, reminded her of the group rules, directed her towards direct communication, and suggested alternate activities, while providing warmth and concern. When Myra continued disrupting the group, Debra stated that she realized something was badly disturbing her, to a point where she was breaking the group rules, and invited her to share with the group her feelings of anger. When this did not help, Myra was offered individual counseling, but she chose to stick with the group and calmed down. In this case, the leader used confrontation combined with respect, support, and understanding. She set clear limits without getting into a power struggle. In her own behavior, she demonstrated desired group behavior and guided the child toward more constructive behavior.

These challenges at the early stage of the group are not easy to meet. They require appropriate personality traits, knowledge of how to intervene, and skills to conduct the interventions in an effective way. Facing such challenges may require greater group facilitation skills for working with children's groups "because they are developmentally more diverse and more likely to stimulate the subjective value of the facilitator" (Berg et al., 1981, p. 312).

The work done during the stormy transition stage is the foundation on which new norms of cohesiveness, belonging, collaboration, support, and self-disclosure are established. When relationships are based on intimacy and trust, group members are willing to take more risks and give more space to others (Gladding, 2003). This is the necessary climate to move to the next phase of counseling and psychotherapy, the working stage, which is discussed in the following chapter.

9
The Working Stage:
How to Enhance Emotional
Experiencing and Group Support

After resistance has diminished and trust in the group has increased, group members are usually ready for the working stage—the heart of any therapy. Resistance has not entirely vanished yet, and trust is not fully achieved, so both need to be further nurtured. However, some group members are ready to take a risk and share their difficulties or concerns with the group. Whether they have a need for relief or they want to help the group move forward (exhibiting altruistic behavior), they set the norms and models for other participants to follow. This stage may be an anxiety-provoking experience for some members, but the group and leader are expected to assist those members taking the risk by providing support, modeling self-disclosure, and instilling hope (Gladding, 2003).

When the working stage is reached, group members are focused on identifying their goals and concerns, and are willing to work both within and outside the group to address these concerns (Conyne, 1997; M. S. Corey & Corey, 2006). Therapeutic goals may be unique to the individual or common to all members, depending on whether the group is focal or not. In both types of groups, however, the focus of treatment is both intrapsychic and interpersonal (Yalom & Leszcz, 2005). That is, the interpersonal interaction among group members is used to enhance the release of emotions and to increase self-confidence, self-understanding, and behavior change (M. S. Corey & Corey, 2006; Yalom & Leszcz, 2005).

The interplay between individual and group goals is based on processes, unique to group formats (Fuhriman & Burlingame, 1990; Holmes & Kivlighan, 2000), referred to as *curative* or *therapeutic factors*. Yalom and Leszcz (2005) identified 11 therapeutic factors that are widely accepted, of which some (e.g., cohesion, interpersonal learning, catharsis) are universally valued as the most helpful across populations. In a recent investigation of which group processes are empirically supported, Burlingame, Fuhriman and Johnson (2004) found that interpersonal feedback and therapeutic alliance were the best predictors of client outcomes in therapy groups. In addition, group structure at the initial stage of the group, the leader's verbal style, and group climate were promising to good predictors. It seems that therapeutic relationships based on intimacy and trust enable and encourage individuals in a group to process issues of concern for them, and the feedback exchange helps them grow in self-understanding, gain insight, and make behavioral changes.

Although processing is the major mechanism in any therapy, in groups it has a dual focus: on the individual and the group. Processing in a group is defined as "an activity in which individuals and groups regularly examine and reflect upon their behavior in order to extract meaning, integrate the resulting knowledge and thereby improve functioning and outcomes" (Ward & Litchy, 2004, p. 104). It is the leader's major responsibility, at this stage of the group process, to help members recognize, examine, and understand their own behavior and that of others in the group, and to use group events and interactions to enhance personal growth (Gazda et al., 2001; Stockton, Morran, & Nitza, 2000; Yalom & Leszcz, 2005). How is this information applicable to group work with children?

THE WORKING STAGE IN GROUPS FOR YOUNG CHILDREN AND ADOLESCENTS

In the working stage, both young children and adolescents are usually able to share personal information, listen to one another, and be supportive of others' attempts to progress. They are able to express positive and negative feelings, to ask for help, and to help other participants process their issues by questioning, providing honest feedback, and contributing to their self-understanding and insight. They are also able to be more immediate and deal with the here-and-now context of things that happen in the group. They can better articulate their plans and goals for working in the group, and actually show some progress in behavior (Smead, 1995). Processing, according to Smead, is one of the most important aspects of the group, even though her groups have been structured and focused on specific topics. She emphasized the use of processing particularly at the end of each group session, during which members were helped to review various elements of the session, recognize what they learned, and identify ways in which they could use the learning outside the group.

O'Rourke and Worzbyt (1996) suggested support groups for children. They defined the goals of such groups as: "to help children explore their feelings, thoughts, and actions and to achieve new levels of understanding about their dilemmas, which will lead to more effective and responsible methods of self-management" (p. 4). They further stipulated that "the key to successful support groups is the bonding and emotional connectedness that takes place among children as they learn from each other and share positive and responsible ways to self-manage in the face of adversity" (p. 4). Thus, as in group counseling with adults, the working stage in children's groups, whether focal or not, uses processing on both the individual and the group level and in the interaction between the two.

In the children's groups facilitated by my colleagues and myself, in line with the three-stage model (Hill, 2005) and within the framework of the expressive–supportive modality, processing is based on the expectation that the children will identify problems of concern, be able to share some of them with the group, explore the issue, connect to the related feelings, develop insight, and when needed, make and activate a plan for change. As in individual therapy, this does not usually happen in one session, but this is the optimal cycle for a group member to complete. To facilitate such processes, the group has unique mechanisms, some of which are particularly meaningful in group counseling with children, owing to the unique developmental tasks and needs of group participants.

Cohesiveness—that sense of belonging and being accepted and supported—is most highly appreciated by children in groups (see Chapter 3). Young children and adolescents alike are particularly sensitive to issues of criticism and social rejection. As many of them come to the group following experiences of neglect and rejection, a positive social climate, together with accepting and supportive relationships, is the key to success. The group also encourages identification processes and the use of other group members as models. This is a particularly meaningful mechanism in groups of children, because children like to imitate and learn from their peers. The group also provides a sense of universality, which is important at this age because no child wants to be different or deviate. Finally, the group aims to provide honest and constructive feedback in a trusting climate that can greatly benefit individual members.

These group mechanisms help my fellow group leaders and I focus on emotional experiencing in a supportive climate, enhancing self-disclosure and cathartic experiences. That is, we lead the children to connect with and express their real emotions, because we believe that where it hurts is the root of the difficulty and the key to change. Furthermore, we help the children explore the meaning of their unique experiences, recognize the way these experiences affect their lives, and discuss ways to improve their lives. Often, the here-and-now experiences in the group are used to enhance understanding of the individual's needs and behavior.

VARIOUS FORMATS TO START THE GROUP PROCESS

There is more than one way to start the working stage and move it forward. One common way is through direct methods, often used with adult groups. That is, group members are asked to identify their goals for therapy through a direct question, such as:

> Here you are in a group of people who are willing to help each other with the difficulties in their lives. What would be a concern or difficulty you would like to bring to this place and take advantage of this wonderful group of people who are dedicated to helping each other?

Group members are asked to concentrate for a few moments with their eyes shut, and think about a goal to work on; they can write down their goal or draw it in symbols, then share it with the group when they are ready. The group members need to be assured that they can always change the goal if other things come up. This procedure serves to clarify goals for therapy, as well as to agree upon goals, procedures that are recommended by practitioners and professional organizations (Association of Specialists in Group Work, 1998). Moreover, sharing private information at this initial point of the working stage helps group members make a commitment to work in the group.

Such direct methods require cognitive and affective qualities that many adolescents, and certainly younger children, do not possess. As they are quite demanding and anxiety provoking; the literature has suggested using indirect and creative methods in working with younger clients (Berg et al., 1998; Gladding, 2005; Thompson & Rudolph, 2000). These techniques have already been discussed in depth (see Chater 5); here, they are related in the context of demonstrating the working stage with adolescents and younger children.

PROCESSES IN ADOLESCENT GROUPS

Goal Identification Through a Structured Activity

In a preadolescent group (seventh grade) comprised of eight children (two boys and six girls), the counselor started the working stage with an indirect activity to help participants identify goals for the group work. She read the book *Like Fish in Water* (Lazarowitz, 1991), which describes many sorts of fish: fish that live alone and fish that live in a group, small fish and big ones, and many middle-sized fish. The counselor had made all these types of fish out of cardboard and attached a magnet to each one, so that every child could "fish" his or her problem.

Miriam, an Ethiopian girl, hooked the lonely fish, admitting that she wants to be a fish that swims with the group.

Miriam:	They hate me in class, push and hit, call me names [Negro], and make fun of my disabled parents.
Terry:	It's because you let them do it. You are too submissive.
Miriam:	Yes, I am. I'm the weakest in class. I cannot fight back; I do not like fighting. I am afraid of them.
Jeanne: (to Terry)	It is easy for you to talk about submissiveness, because no one dares bother you.

Terry proudly agreed, stating that in the past she was the victim, but she would never go back to that place. Tom offered support, sharing his personal experience, "They do it to me, too. They kind of take pity on me because my father is sick. You shouldn't pay much attention to them."

This activity brought out one of Miriam's major current problems. I suspect that she would not have been able to articulate her problem without the game, because she is an extremely shy girl from a culture that restricts self-expressiveness, and also because she has some language difficulties. Once she expressed her problem, she received both feedback and support. Although not all feedback reactions were positive, she seemed to be able to handle this, probably because they were balanced with supportive responses. Moreover, her self-disclosure led to someone else's disclosure through the process of identification. Miriam could increase her sense of self-worth by assisting another group member.

Kelly selected a fish that was swimming in the middle of the lake. "I like to be in the center of events. I like to swim fast because I am competitive," she disclosed. Referring to an incident during recess, Terry suggested that Kelly should be the swordfish, because she hurt others. Kelly admitted that she could be very possessive and jealous about friends, because she was an only child and never learned to share things.

Again, I suspect it would have been difficult to articulate such a problem without the fishing activity. Moreover, Kelly explored her relationships with friends, a central task at this age, on both a cognitive and affective level, and even gained some insight.

Terry, who had picked on Kelly, joined in and shared that she is jealous, too, of her mother's attention. Miriam shared that she felt that her mom liked her brother more, "She does not kiss me the way she kisses my brother." Terry, who initially offered Kelly the swordfish, ended up taking it herself, because she was always on her guard and therefore was sometimes aggressive.

This group interaction started with a game intended to help members identify a problem worth working on in the group. However, it also provided an opportunity to release tension, express feelings, and give and receive interpersonal support and feedback. Emotional support was provided through identification and sharing similar experiences; instrumental support was provided in—and out—of the group, as reported by Miriam the next meeting. In response to the routine question of how the group feels following the last session, she said, "I felt better already. Even though I was picked on, I felt stronger, and the group members have been really helpful, protecting me on several occasions."

In sum, fishing the problem rather than verbally articulating it gave a more casual flavor to the task of identifying a problem for group work. It served as a stimulus for self-disclosure and release of tension. Following this, processing took place on both individual and group levels. Some adolescents reflected on their unique difficulties and enhanced self-understanding based on an honest exchange of feedback. Others received instrumental assistance with actual difficulties. The idea was for processing to involve as many group members as possible, but not to delve deeper into exploration, because this was only the third group session and just the beginning of the working stage. My suggestion is that exploration processes should be gradually introduced, for two main reasons: to keep anxiety low and to allow as many members as possible to participate in the group process from the start.

Goal Identification Through a Question About Emotions

The working stage does not necessarily have to start with explicit goal identification. As the goal of the expressive–supportive modality is to encourage children to deal with their emotions, other techniques that lead to self-expressiveness are useful as well. The following is an example of a group of Arab teenage girls in which the counselor opened the session by asking the girls to share one positive and one negative experience.

Leila told of an accident that she was involved in a few years earlier. She talked for a while about her experience in the hospital and the physical consequences of the incident, but eventually said, "The real problem was that I lost all my friends, and I really felt very lonely." This was the starting point for Leila to process her problems.

With tears in her eyes, she spoke about loneliness, sadness, and a sense of betrayal, even though it had been years since the accident happened. It was obvious that she was still hurting emotionally.

This was a cathartic experience for Leila. However, emotional experiencing is more than the expression of emotions, according to Greenberg (2002); there must be an additional component of cognitive reflection on the experience, so that understanding can be enhanced. Hill (2005) referred to cognitive and affective exploration, which eventually can lead to insight and finally to action, when needed. As is typical for this stage, the group went on questioning Leila about why she felt so lonely. First, she expressed mostly anger at her friends and disappointment for neglecting her in those difficult times. But as she continued exploring her feelings, it became clear that Leila isolated herself from her friends, as she wished to hide her limp from them. In fact, she had even changed schools. She said, "I was very popular in my old school and I just could not go back there limping." This was a new insight for her, which lead her to conclude, "I shouldn't really be mad, because I brought this on myself."

The group members provided feedback about how her behavior fooled them and highlight the fact that she was not disliked or rejected, but rather it was her choice at the time. They also asked about her sources of support, and when she told them that she is strong and optimistic, they praised her for it. For Leila, the experience was valuable; she had undergone catharsis and gained insight. At the same time, she received support from her friends, who reassured her that people did not reject her; they only misunderstand her. She was valued for her strength and optimism.

In this same session, Saya shared her own hospital experience. This identification process happens often in the group, but even though the frame of the story is similar, the experience may be very different. Saya focused on her fears, "I thought they were going to kill me," and shared how she hated and avoided hospitals. The lesson she learned from her experience is that life is precious, and therefore she has become extremely health conscious.

Walla reacted to the question of negative experiences by sharing her terrifying experience of her father's suicide. She started by saying that she had never talked about it with anyone, and began to cry. The group responded first with deep silence, but then encouraged her to go on, expressing their genuine interest in her. She told the group that her father suffered from substance abuse, felt very bad about himself, and eventually hanged himself. She was the one to find him and to cut the rope. Walla went into detail, crying the whole time. She clearly went through a cathartic experience. The girls cried with her and comforted her; they expressed their admiration for her ability to act cool (call the police for help) and be so strong. "I did not know you well, but I always felt that there is something impressive about your personality," Rima said. The girls inquired about the sources of her strength, and Walla mentioned the community, her mom, her religion, and a best friend. She felt much stronger following the cathartic experience. Relieved of this traumatic experience, empowered by her peers' reactions, and hopeful after realizing the sources of support available for her, she announced that she was determined to pursue higher education and become a psychologist, because her father would have valued that very much.

Saya also shared her experience with her father's death. She did not go into detail, but mentioned that she felt better now that the issue had been brought up. "It's good you can listen to others. This in itself is helpful," she said. Finally, Rima talked about self-image. "I don't like myself," she said. "My worst experience was being born." Rima was mainly concerned about her physical appearance. She felt that her brothers picked on her because she looked different from them. The group provided a lot of support, highlighting her positive character. She eventually admitted that she was more successful than her brothers in many areas. The group also suggested open communication with her brothers and parents, and they role played the scenario to increase her assertiveness skills.

Several points are worth highlighting in this group process. The group was nonfocal, composed of girls whom teachers considered to have some unique emotional needs. Overall, they were described as moody, sad, and quiet underachievers. The process described shows that each group member referred to a unique problem. Although processes of identification took place, and some girls followed the theme that was brought up by another group member, the issues still remained unique for each individual. Most of the sharing behaviors were limited in scope and mainly served purposes of mutual support. The process in this group clearly shows how intimacy encourages self-expressiveness, and that supportive interpersonal interactions empower group members and enhance self-understanding. Individual gains seem to evolve from both the cathartic experiencing and the emotional support.

At the session just described, experiencing and support were highly emphasized; these are typical processes in expressive–supportive groups. However, with the last speaker, the group also took on an instrumental task, trying to help Rima move toward the action stage and make some changes in her communication patterns with family members. This shows that, even in a nonfocal group, members find commonalities among themselves and mutual sharing takes place, but not at the expense of addressing unique problems. The group adjusts the working process to the specific needs of group members. Some only need encouragement to talk, others need help in developing awareness, and still others need assistance in changing their behavior.

SPONTANEOUS PROCESSES

Sometimes, no activity is needed to start the process, as the children bring in events from outside the group or even from within the group. Crisis situations happen to them all the time, and the group is a good place to bring them up, spontaneously, as evidenced in the following group process.

In a group of adolescent girls, Susan stormed into the session and complains about being picked on by her teachers. When she asked "Why me?" the teacher's answer was a sarcastic, "You are dazzling." "What does she mean by 'dazzling'?" Susan asked the group. She received the following feedback:

- "Because you are beautiful and have a strong presence."
- "Because you are provocative."
- "Because you dress provocatively."
- "Because you are always where there is trouble."

They even used examples from the group process to demonstrate the impact she has on people. They mentioned her domineering behavior in group, and how they were sometimes intimidated by her presence, which made them remain silent. But they also mentioned the importance of her responses to group members and how smart she was. The balance of positive and negative feedback seemed to be effective, because Susan summarized this interaction by thanking the group for being honest with her. "Now I know what I need to change so that people do not pick on me," she concluded.

For Susan, the group assumed at this particular session a crisis-focused intervention, in which an immediate problem of great concern to her was discussed. However, at the same time, the process of feedback was broadly geared to enhance her self-understanding and develop insight. The action stage was less present in the interaction, because Susan herself came up with the conclusion that she needed to make a change in her behavior. As suggested by Prochaska (1999), clients are at different stages on the change process, and therapy must consider these stages. In this case, Susan needed to enhance her understanding of self and she was at the preparation stage, ready to make a change. Perhaps at a later session, she might have needed more help with the action and maintenance stages.

At another session, in the same group, Ellen shared a dream she had:

> I get up in the middle of the night and call for my mom. As she does not respond, I go to look for her, but I can't find her. Only when I come back do I see her with her boyfriend. She points at me, laughing, and does not respond to my crying. She does not pay attention to me even when I go back into the house. She completely ignores me.

Several girls questioned Ellen about her feelings of abandonment in reality, to which she responded in tears, "I am always alone. She works late, then goes out. I really interfere with her life. Without me, she would probably be married by now." When someone asked if she has ever talked about this with her mother, Ellen responded, "I've tried, but it didn't work." After exploring her feelings further and having other group members share their feelings of loneliness, the leader invited Ellen to do some role playing. When she role played talking to her mother about feeling abandoned and lonely, Ellen got very angry. On an interesting note, someone mentioned that she has acted angrily in the group, too.

Bringing this issue to the here-and-now is a powerful technique to learn about interpersonal relationships (Yalom & Leszcz, 2005). Ellen understood and accepted the criticism, explaining, "It is not you that I am angry at, but rather my mother. I must talk to her because I ruin many relationships because I am so angry. I feel I can do it now." She felt relieved following this session and was thankful to the group. Armed with the support she received from them, she felt capable of confronting her mother.

Rose, a very quiet girl, continued this discussion, disclosing that she, too, felt very lonely, but could never talk about it before:

> You helped me tell my story, and I must say it helps me feel better, that there are other girls with similar problems. I was really afraid to talk in the group, but now that I have, I feel less frightened, and maybe I will be able to use this ability with other people in my life.

In the described session, there was catharsis, identification, universality, insight, altruism, interpersonal learning, and hope. The girls felt good about receiving help and about being able to give it to others. They also gained insight and practiced skills to resolve the problem, and it helped, as evidenced at the next session. Ellen reported having a very constructive conversation with her mother, and she felt that their relationship had improved. She was very relaxed and less angry. Rose shared her hope that things would improve for her soon. She also talked with her mother and was waiting to see the results. She was less optimistic, saying, "I know she will try, but she must work to support us, so I don't know how much she can change." This acceptance of existential factors was also important for Rose's progress.

Some participants in some situations have the ability to bring in material spontaneously and put it to work for the group. If the group is going through a healthy working stage, more of these experiences tend to emerge. Yet, for some individuals, even in a good working group, such spontaneity may be impossible.

Consider the following situation, which took place in the previously mentioned group. Elizabeth was a resistant and sarcastic participant. Deep in the working stage, following a lot of self-disclosure, it became clear that she wanted to share something with the group, but could not. For a few sessions she started to say something and soon stopped. Finally, in one session, she said, "I want to tell you something but I can't, I will start crying. Please ask me questions." Following several questions, she got to the issue of breaking up with her boyfriend. She told the story but could not express her feelings. She sounded confused and frustrated, and so was the group. She did some cognitive exploration and understood that she was in a risky relationship with an older guy, but could not talk about how she felt.

The counselor used the Echo Game, in which other group members stand behind the client and express for her feelings that she herself cannot verbalize. They expressed anger, disappointment, fear, confusion, and the like. Elizabeth picked those emotions that best represented her and expressed them, following which she understood that her boyfriend was pressing her to do things that were not appropriate for her age, and that he was threatening her and taking advantage of her. The group members also gave their opinions about the relationship.

This is an example of skill training achieved through emotional experiencing. Elizabeth eventually felt that she should end the dangerous relationship, because it would ruin her life.

PROCESSES IN CHILDREN'S GROUPS

It is well documented in the literature that younger children need more structure in the group process, including games and activities (Berg et al., 1998; Smead, 1995; Thompson & Rudolph, 2000). Although games and activities are helpful, they are not always necessary at the working stage, even with younger kids. Young children, too, can sometimes handle an open, nonstructured process with great effectiveness.

Goal Identification Through A Common Topic

The following demonstrates how the working stage of one group of 8 fourth graders (9–10 years old) evolved out of a spontaneously raised topic. The 4 boys and 4 girls in question were referred to the counseling center for a variety of difficulties. One had a severe learning disability; another was rejected by classmates; a third was a gifted child bullied by his classmates. In addition, there were two new immigrants, an angry girl, a withdrawn girl, and a child with no problem—a leader in his class (my coworkers and I often include normative children in our groups to help with the group process). This was a nonfocal group, with each child having his or her unique difficulty, yet they all had in common problems related to friendship.

Shortly after the working stage began, Ken brought up the topic of death, which lasted for the next six sessions (most of the working stage). He talked about his dog that had just died, and, as a result, the group began relating many more personal experiences with death.

Lois shared the story of her oldest brother, who was killed in an accident, and related how her parents refuse to talk about it. She felt that it was a secret that she needed to uncover, because it often distracted her. The group dealt with this serious issue through empathic listening; they shared experiences involving death and provided help. They suggested that she talk to her parents, discussing the issues openly, and that she try to put her fears into perspective.

Eileen talked about her grandmother's recent death. She told of a dispute with her parents about visiting the gravesite, but as the process of exploration evolves, it became evident that the issue was much deeper. Eileen's anger at her parents was masking fears that other significant people in her life could die, too. She was horrified by such thoughts and had nightmares. Aware that Eileen seemed to be in a crisis situation, the counselor ran a psychodrama activity, in which she told Eileen to imagine that she was walking with a sack full of stones; and, at a certain point, when it got too heavy, advised her to leave it someplace.

The therapeutic work with Eileen took several sessions. First, she shared her recent experience and expressed strong emotions. Following a cognitive and affective exploration process, she understood that the issue was not a conflict with her parents, but rather anxiety following the great loss of her beloved grandmother. This was when she went through a cathartic experience. The group members shared their concerns for their loved ones, and she no longer felt like a deviant. The group also offered many thoughts to cancel out her negative thoughts, and when this was not sufficient, the counselor used the guided visualization technique previously described. At the end of this process, Eileen felt much more relaxed.

This process was no different from that in an adult group. Whether Eileen would have independently selected this topic as her goal for therapy or whether she was reacting to someone else's initiative is beside the point. Regardless, it was a most meaningful issue for her and for the other group members. Eileen decided not to visit her grandmother's grave, in keeping with her parents' advice, because she did not feel ready. Lois talked to her parents and, for the first time, managed to open up the secret of her brother's death with some success. Ken, who had initiated the issue of death, talked to his parents about his feelings and received a new dog, and the group shared his happiness.

In children's groups, topics are often raised by one child and then continued by others. Most often, this is effective, but when the counselor realizes that the discussion remains on a superficial level, he or she can introduce an activity to change the topic. In the aforementioned group, it is quite possible that the group process would have evolved in a different direction if Ken had not brought up his dog's death. But this really does not matter in the type of group discussed here. Some children used the group to address a current issue, and others identified with this existential issue of death. They also had an opportunity to listen, develop empathy, and help others to feel better.

Goal Identification Through A Structured Activity

In another group comprised of girls from divorced families, the counselor started the working stage with an ancient legend in which many layers of hearts exist, and the most hidden one holds excitement. The counselor posed a question regarding a time when the girls had touched this hidden heart. "I was excited when my mom told me who my father was," said 11-year-old Dana.

This opening of the session was not different from asking about a major goal, yet it may have been influenced by the story. Dana went through a cognitive and affective exploration stage, with the group asking her many questions. She was able to refuse to answer questions that were intrusive (such as "What's his name?") and to focus on her feelings.

Dana explained that her mom decided to give birth to her even though her father disappeared, because she wanted Dana for herself. This impressed the group a lot; they emphasized the love her mother must have had for her, which made Dana feel proud and stronger. She later talked about her feelings towards the man she had known many years without knowing he was her father. She talked about missing having a father and then expressed a sense of being cheated, "Everyone knew, but nobody told me." When Jack hesitated to ask a question for a while, saying, "It may be too personal," Dana answered, "If I choose not to respond, I won't." Jack asked Dana what her expectations of this man were, and Dana hesitated in responding. When the silence was prolonged, the counselor shared her own experience as a child, when her father was away for five years during the war. She related how she had an image of a strong and capable man, but when he came back he was just a regular person and she felt disappointed. This self-disclosure on the part of the counselor, particularly the disclosure of her feelings, helped Dana to articulate her response. "I imagined him as a monster for a long time, because he abandoned me and my mom. And here I discover that he is a regular man, who can be kind and fun." For Dana, this was a constructive experience, which comforted and empowered her.

Other children shared similar experiences. Mary told of her anger at her father, who had abandoned her; she was full of hate and refused to forgive him. Melissa stated that it was not only fathers who are bad; in her case, it was her mother. Thus, there was a lot of sharing, each child from her own experiences and emotions. The activity used at the beginning of the session was a stimulus in place of an opening question; the rest involved processing feelings, experiencing, and reflecting on those experiences.

The illustrations and discussion of the group processes in children and adolescent groups that are presented here are based on clinical experience. Next, I present research of these group experiences conducted by my colleagues and I in children's groups that embrace the expressive–supportive modality. This adds a more scientific flavor to our cumulative knowledge on groups with children and adolescents.

RESEARCH ON GROUP PROCESSES WITH CHILDREN

Children as Helpers

Much of our research focused on client behavior in therapy. These studies addressed several questions, including: How effectively do children and adolescents work in group counseling and psychotherapy? What are the unique client responses in these groups? What is the change process in the children's responses over time? What is the relation between children's behavior in therapy and their outcomes? And how do these behaviors in the group in question compare to interventions in a different orientation? In all these studies my fellow researchers and I used several versions of Hill and O'Brien's (1999) measures of client behavior and therapist helping skills. We applied the helping skills to group members due to the dual role they play in the group, serving as both clients and helpers. As we use her integrative model of intervention, it seemed appropriate to use her scales to address those questions. The investigation of the process was based on transcribed sessions of many groups, and analyzed according to the guidelines suggested by Hill.

The first two studies used variables drawn from the Helping Skills scale (Hill & O'Brien, 1999). The first study, of elementary-school children (Leichtentritt & Shechtman, 1998) indicated that self-disclosure was the most frequent behavior among the children (occurring at least once in 90% of the sessions), followed by feedback (50%) and questions posed to other group members (30%). These results support clinical observations of the groups run by my coworkers and I: Children are engaged mostly in self-disclosure and cathartic experiences and learn through interpersonal interaction and feedback. As interpersonal interaction is such a fundamental mechanism in group, and our clinical observations pointed to many unproductive interactions, another study (Shechtman & Yanuv, 2001) focused on the quality of these interactions.

The Shechtman and Yanuv (2001) study looked at the three types of interpretives (interpretation, challenges, and feedback), because they bear potentially high risks to relationships. This study found challenges to be the most frequent response, followed closely by feedback; interpretation was rare. The nonfrequent response of interpretation was expected, considering the children's age and their limited psychological knowledge. This is more of a therapist's than a client's behavior, particularly at this young age. The frequency of challenges is disturbing, because children may perceive them as a personal attack and find it difficult to protect themselves. For this reason, the study investigated further the extent to which these behaviors were used in a constructive or unconstructive way, and the impact each had on children's responses: productive versus nonproductive. Generally speaking, a behavior was considered constructive when it was presented with care, acceptance, and empathy; and a behavior was considered nonconstructive when it was presented with criticism, a personal attack, or rejection. A productive response was reflected in a client's further exploration, insight, or action; a nonproductive response was reflected in silence, defensiveness, and anger. Results of the analyses indicated that challenges (constructive or not) mostly led to nonproductive responses, whereas feedback tended to generate productive responses, particularly when it was presented in a constructive way. Moreover, the participants' behavior became more constructive with time. Indeed, the statistical analysis showed that only feedback, constructiveness of the behavior, and time could predict a productive response.

This is an important study in terms of its clinical implications. The findings suggest that counselors should help children provide feedback rather than offer challenges, and that they should train children to use feedback in a constructive manner. Moreover, as time is a significant factor in producing constructive behavior, perhaps children must be guided to use feedback in later stages when they are more skilled in applying it and when group members are more ready to accept it.

Children as Clients

Several studies (Sason & Razin, 2003; Shechtman, 2004b; Shechtman & Ben-David, 1999) examined children's behavior using the Client Behavior System. Results indicated that most of the children's responses were simple response and cognitive and affective exploration (experiencing), followed by insight; the rest of the behaviors were infrequent. This suggests that children were mostly engaged in self-expressiveness, often on an emotional level, and that some also experienced insight. Moreover, resistance and simple response decreased with time, whereas insight and therapeutic change, although rare, grew significantly along the group process. No change was found in cognitive and affective exploration. A comparison of this type of intervention with cognitive–behavioral group psychotherapy (Shechtman & Pastor, 2005) indicated differences between the two types of groups. Whereas there was less resistance and more affective exploration and insight in counseling groups, there was more cognitive exploration in the educational groups. These differences were expected, owing to the different theoretical principles guiding the two types of treatments: In the counseling groups the process focuses on emotions and is geared toward the development of insight, whereas in the educational groups the focus is on learning and the development of problem-solving skills.

Several lessons can be drawn from these studies. First, it appears that the interventions used by my coworkers and I are in adherence with our theoretical principles. The studies support our observations and case illustrations showing that children are engaged mostly in talking about themselves, exploring thoughts and feelings. Second, these studies indicate that children and adolescents can and do work effectively in the group process. They use the time effectively, mostly focusing on affective exploration, but also gaining insight and undergoing some change. These patterns of behavior are similar to those of adult clients, who also engage more in self-exploration, with insight and therapeutic change being reported much less frequently.

Finally, as these behaviors are not related to outcomes (Shechtman 2004a), the question of what variables in the process do contribute to a child's progress remains open and requires further investigation.

SUMMARY

Both the clinical illustrations and the research highlight the processes in the working stage of counseling groups for children and adolescents. A great deal of self-disclosure, cathartic experiences, and cognitive/affective exploration takes place at this stage. Insight evolves over time, following self-exploration and sharing. There is also quite a lot of interpersonal exchange of feedback and challenges among group participants, even young elementary-school children. However, this exchange is not always constructive, leading sometimes to nonproductive responses. Leaders must train and encourage children to be constructive helpers.

It is clear that leaders take an extremely active role in the working stage, helping children not only to identify their goals, but also to explore their issues on a cognitive and emotional level, to develop insight into their behavior, and to make changes when necessary. Although children often express their concerns spontaneously, they usually need assistance to risk self-disclosure, articulate their problems verbally, and respond to others. Methods that enhance self-expressiveness (e.g., bibliotherapy), structured activities, and therapeutic games are all important mechanisms for achieving goals at the working stage.

Ironically, the more successful a group is in the working stage, the more difficult it is to end the intervention. As I show in the next chapter, it is the counselor's role to provide a constructive termination to the group.

10 Termination

Termination is more than the end of therapy; it is an integral part of the process of therapy and an important force in the process of change (Yalom & Leszcz, 2005). A successful ending of a group will have a strong impact on group members' self-esteem, sense of accomplishment, and self-confidence. It may also have a long-term impact on a person's future interpersonal relationships, on attitudes toward groups and therapy, and on a person's behavior. As every ending is also a new beginning, the successful end of the group may be the force for continuing personal growth in real life.

Accomplishing a successful termination process requires several sessions, as it involves a number of tasks: dealing with feelings of loss and separation; evaluating one's growth inside and outside the group, identifying areas in need of continued work, and developing plans and directions for continuing without the group (Berg et al., 1998; M. S. Corey & Corey, 2006). Each of these tasks requires appropriate leader characteristics, effective methods and techniques of intervention, and the effective use of helping skills, all of which are illustrated in the following.

DEALING WITH LOSS AND SEPARATION

Ending a successful group experience may be difficult for both the counselor and group members. Feelings of sadness and anger are common and need to be dealt with before the group ends. The more cohesive and intimate the group has become, the more difficult it is to say goodbye to each other and to the group leader (Bernard & MacKenzie, 1994). Following her group experience with children, M.S. Corey wrote, "It was as difficult for me to leave them as it was for them to see me leave, and we shared this sadness openly" (M. S. Corey & Corey, 1992, p. 289).

Due to the strong focus on emotional expressiveness, children in our groups develop high levels of cohesiveness and intimacy. They often feel that the group has become like a family to them; sometimes it is even a corrective experience of family relationships. For these children, saying goodbye to the counselor and to each other means letting go of significant relationships that they may not find elsewhere. Children in groups for divorce and grief, for example, may re-experience a sense of loss. Children who have relational difficulties with friends and peers, and have suffered rejection and loneliness, may find it particularly difficult to let go of a positive interpersonal experience. Therefore, processing feelings of separation in general, and separation from the group in particular, is crucial.

As with other issues discussed in earlier stages, dealing with separation can follow a direct question about separation experiences, or result from a structured activity. Although adolescents and even elementary-school children respond well to a direct question, structured activities usually elicit more affective reactions, and in some groups they are a must. For example, the counselor of a group of aggressive fourth-grade boys felt that a direct question was less appropriate, as the children were not highly verbal. Therefore, she used an art project to symbolize their perception of separation from the group. Paul created a cage, explaining that his heart is trapped in the group like an animal in a cage. George constructed a nest, explaining that he feels he is flying away from a protective nest. By using symbols, both children expressed their sense of attachment to the group in more depth than they would probably have done in response to a direct question.

Termination, according to Yalom and Leszcz (2005), involves three parties—the individual, the group, and the therapist—and for each it may be appropriate at a different time. Termination is an individual process, and each child may need to end treatment at a different time. Yet for groups, particularly those conducted in schools, external circumstances—such as the end of the academic year or the counselor's move to another place—dictate the date of separation. Thus, for some children, termination may be inappropriate; for others, it may even be harmful. The counselor's responsibility does not end with termination of the group; he or she must evaluate the progress of each child and each child's mental state at termination, and if needed, refer the child to another group or type of therapy.

PARTING THROUGH POSITIVE FEEDBACK

Part of separation is saying goodbye to each group member. In groups run by my coworkers and myself, this takes the form of giving and receiving feedback, which, according to M. S. Corey and Corey (2006), suggests how group members are perceived by each other and refers to incomplete goals and things that still need to be accomplished. These authors caution against being too positive, because it may send an inaccurate or even distorted message to the receiver.

In highly intimate groups, such as those of my colleagues and myself, feedback is mostly positive. Although this feedback may not be very accurate, I believe it is extremely important when working with children, as it sends them off to the outside world with more trust in themselves and others. It is a memory to be recalled at future difficult times, a source of encouragement and support. At this point, support is more important for these children than constructive feedback. Moreover, I do not trust all children to offer accurate feedback constructively; in a final session, when there is no time to process the communication, negative feedback can be harmful and have long-term negative effects. Therefore, in working with children and adolescents, my strong recommendation is to focus on a positive exchange of feedback and a highly warm ending of the group experience. The incomplete issues will have to wait for another opportunity.

As a way to say goodbye in the groups my coworkers and I run, we often have group members play the Post Office game, in which children send telegrams to one another, stating something positive. Or we have the children all walk around the room, writing positive feedback on a sheet of paper taped to each child's back. This feedback ranges from "You are a good friend" to more sophisticated feedback, such as "You are warm, understanding and courageous." These games create a boost of positive feelings about oneself, and offer something concrete that each child takes away.

The reactions of some teenage girls to the "telegrams" they received during the game of Post Office reflect the effect that such positive feedback has:

Andrea:	I didn't know I was so important to other group members. Thanks.
Joyce: [in tears]	This is the first time that I really felt a sense of belonging, that I am loved here. This was the best thing in school; I will keep it for my whole life.

This demonstrates the impact of positive interactions in the group that may bear long-term effects on group members.

To balance the highly positive feedback with some honest responses, my colleagues and I sometimes have group members play The Imaginary Present game, in which they give "presents" to each other, something that may be of help to a group member. For example, someone gave movie tickets to one group member who was overwhelmed with household chores; another gave a pair of scissors to help a group member sever her relationship with her abusive boyfriend. Although such messages may indicate some need of change, they are still handled in an extremely caring and supportive manner.

In most of the groups my coworkers and I run, the termination stage is even more structured, playful, and dramatic than these examples. Consider, for example, the following activity used in a fourth-grade group. The counselor brought in a long ball of yarn. Holding one end, she passed the rest to one of the children, saying something good about him. That child continued to hold the yarn and did the same with the next group member, until all the children in the group had received positive feedback and were holding the yarn. In this way, they created a "group rug," illustrating the importance of each member in the group, "Because if even one person loses his grip of the rug, it will fall apart," the leader said. This is an important farewell activity with an extremely positive tone, incorporating positive feedback exchanges between individuals and reinforcing the power of group intimacy.

EVALUATING GROWTH IN AND OUT OF THE GROUP

As the small group is a microcosm of the large world, the individual's normative behavior can be expected to be present in the group, particularly at its beginnings. It is important to acknowledge and reinforce any progress in behavior made in the group, as such change can impact relationships outside the group.

Leaders can use a direct question to spur evaluations of individual growth in the group, such as, "Can you think of ways you have changed your thoughts and feelings about the group and yourself?" But more precise and in-depth evaluations usually result from creative indirect methods, as can be seen in the next illustration.

The group was comprised of six teenagers (age 16), four girls and two boys, and they were in their final session. The counselor was using The Traffic Signs game to evaluate progress. She had arranged a cardboard road to represent the journey of the group, as well as various traffic signs. Each group member was asked to select two signs—one to represent thoughts and feelings at the initial stage of the group and the other to represents them at termination—and to explain their choices. Marge selected the Caution sign to represent her anxiety in the group and in life at the beginning of the intervention, as well as the Yellow Light to express her sense of hopefulness and her feeling that she was back on the road. Tammy, a dominant and bossy group member, chose the No Entry sign to represent her distance from the group at the initial stage. She said, "I did not trust anyone here, but now that I am convinced secrets did not spill out, I take the Yield sign, because I can show my vulnerability and give away some of my power". Steve took the same Yield sign to say that he had learned that he needed to get to know people before passing judgment about them, as in the case of his father's girlfriend: "I hate her only because she is Russian." He further explained that he had come to realize his intolerance in the group experience, when he judged Tammy for being bossy without actually seeing her vulnerability. This was stated to show his growth in tolerance, but it was also an apologetic message to Tammy and a nice way to finish open business in the group. Madelaine selected the Stop sign to present her assertiveness; "I now try to stop people from hurting me," she explained. Sharon took the same Stop sign, but for a very different reason: to stop time so that the group did not end. She also chose the Yield sign to present her progress in listening to others. Finally, Jan took the Curved Road sign to represent his family difficulties, and the Dead End sign because he was not sure where to turn. "I need some guidance," he said.

Very often, termination is not the right time for all group members, as in the case of Jan. Although the last session is not a good time to continue the counseling process, providing instrumental assistance at this opportunity is important. In this case, a short clarifying process helped Jan to decide that he should focus on achieving his personal goals (he was involved in music) rather than his parents' issues. For the moment, at least, he seemed to know which road to take.

In this particular activity, the focus was on here-and-now relationships and the progress made in the group, but the personal progress that each participant made in his or her life outside of the group was also discernible. Someone who develops trust in fellow group members may transfer this sense of trust to other relationships.

Steve's new awareness, gained in the group, about his tendency to judge people prematurely, had already been carried over to a real-life situation. Finally, Madelaine, who used to be victimized by peers, learned in the group to express her needs and had also acquired some skills of setting boundaries to other people's demands on her in real life.

EVALUATING THE GROUP EXPERIENCE

Feedback of how members feel about the group and leader provides information about the group's functioning, tells therapists what was good about the group, and reveals turning points in the group process. This information can be gathered through open-ended statements, as suggested by Berg and colleagues (1998): "this group…," "I like most…", "I feel…" or through open questions, as suggested by M. S. Corey and Corey (2006): "What changes have you made?" "How did the group help these changes to come about?" My colleagues and I also ask children to write about their critical incident in the group ("What was the most important thing that happened to you in the group?"), which is a more open question that brings out negative experiences as well. Direct questions to solicit a response to negative experiences can also be asked, such as, "In what way do you wish the group would be different?" or "Was the group experience hurtful in some way?"

In a group of adolescent girls, the counselor asked several direct questions that elicited some profound replies. In response to the question "What was the group for you?" the girls shared the following:

- A place to open up and share things [e.g., substance abuse] that we couldn't share with anyone else.
- A place to discuss issues that bother us in life [referring to family abuse].
- A place to learn about ourselves.
- A place to make close and intimate contact with people.

Following the leader's request to state "Something that you have learned about yourself that can help you in your life," Susan, the most domineering girl in the group, said, "I improved in my behavior a lot, and I get into less trouble in school. I am now more aware of my behavior and try to be less 'dazzling' and provocative. I've even changed the way I dress.". She was happy with the change in her behavior. At this point, the counselor asked the other girls to provide feedback to Susan. Their responses are quite positive:

- You seem to be more relaxed and quiet.
- At the beginning everyone was intimidated by you, but the things you said were very important to me.
- I also learned a lot from you, so I accepted your behavior.

Obviously, some very good things happened in this group. It became an intimate place where private matters could be shared. It was also a place where honest feedback was exchanged, which helped group members grow and make important changes in their behavior, both inside and outside the group.

Among younger children, structured activities and games are more appropriate for eliciting evaluation of the group process (as in other stages). Take the case of a small group of fourth-grade boys, including two ADHD children, in which activities and games were used throughout the group process, as well as at termination. In this group, the leader taped questions about the group process around the room. Under each question a continuum was drawn on the floor, from 1 to 10, and the children were asked to place themselves physically along each continuum. This group particularly liked and appreciates the physical action.

Most of these children placed themselves low on "My feelings toward the group at the beginning" and high on "My feelings toward the group today." Their explanations for their placement are interesting: "I didn't know what would happen here and kids were kind of interrupting" (response to the first question); "This was a place we could talk about personal stuff" (response to the second question). The children's evaluation of their own "Participation in the group" varied. Brad, the most difficult child in the group, placed himself on number 4, explaining, "I sometimes shared, sometimes listened, and sometimes interrupted." Brad's self-evaluation is important, as it reflects self-awareness that may eventually lead to insight and change.

The last question, "To what extent did things go wrong in the group?", was meant to address unfinished business in the group. Mark placed himself low on this question, mentioning an incident in which Greg made fun of him during a particular activity. This became a good opportunity to discuss the issue again and, as a result, Greg apologized. It was also an important lesson for Mark, a particularly sensitive child, to speak up when someone hurts him.

In another group of young children, the counselor gave each child two cards; she asked them to use one card to write something positive from the group that they would like to take with them, and the other to write something negative that they would like to leave behind. The children mentioned such positive experiences as "We learned to help each other;" "We replaced anger with direct communication;" "We learned to listen to each other;" "We said good things about each other;" and "We learned to solve problems." Ken, for example, shared that, following a group discussion, he talked to his parents about his sadness following his dog's death and asked for a new puppy. The group was happy to hear that his parents, in fact, got him a new dog. The things the children say they want to leave behind are fears, pain, fighting, and the like. The idea of leaving bad feelings behind is interesting and suitable for younger children. It conveys the message that the end of the group may also be the end of negative emotions.

Finally, in a group of teenage girls, the leader turned the last session into a mystic event by using candles to say goodbye. The room was dark and the girls sat around the candles. Each girl lit a candle for herself and summarized her gains in the group. She then presented it to another group member or the leader. Wendy, for example, mentioned her academic gains and her improved relationships with teachers. She said she was more relaxed and optimistic about life (in the group, she talked about the loss of her mother). Then she presented her candle to Nancy (who had a disabled brother) and said,

From the beginning I knew that you had something painful to share, and that it was too difficult for you to express. It was very important for me to hear you, as I would not have been able to feel comfortable sharing if you didn't share, too. I think you are a very strong person and I admire you for the way you treat your brother.

This activity also gave the girls an opportunity to say goodbye to their group leader. Nancy thanked the counselor for protecting her from further abuse (the counselor heard about it in the group and referred the case to the authorities). Vivian gave her candle to the leader, thanking her for being accepting and nonjudgmental, unlike most people. Most of the girls in the group told the leader she was a role model that will remain with them in good times and bad.

In this process of summarizing the group experience, unfinished business between group members, with the leader, or with the group as a whole often comes up. It is important to resolve these issues as much as possible, as they not only damage the impact of the group experience, but also tend to be carried over to future groups and to life in general.

For example, a group of teenage girls were interacting in an extremely positive manner until Evelyn stopped the excitement, saying, "You're exaggerating!" The other girls were quite angry, but the counselor invited Evelyn to elaborate on her comment, saying "You must feel very different." After a brief silence, Evelyn admitted that the group experience had been OK for her, but not that great, because she had not shared her greatest secret, and now she regretted not having taken full advantage of the group. She seemed to be disappointed in herself, but put some of the blame on the leader for not helping her. The leader responded with empathy, "I am sorry you are a bit disappointed and that I was not careful enough to read your unspoken need. If it can help you, I can see you in private and try to help.".This was an important closure to Evelyn's feelings, and a gentle message to her that it was hard to guess her unspoken needs. Often, clients try to use the last moments in the therapy process, but it is too late. On this occasion it was, indeed, too late to take care of Evelyn's needs in the framework of the group, but at least she could express her true feelings. This in itself was a great accomplishment, and a more effective ending of her group experience.

In another group, a conflict between Gary and Johnny, two best friends, was affecting the group. The two boys were not talking to each other and for a long while both refused to discuss this in the group. But when termination started to take place, the other children felt that the conflict was threatening the unity of the group and pressed the two to resolve the issue before the group ended. Gary and Johnny eventually admitted that they could not even remember how it all started. They expressed positive feelings about each other and noted the difficulty in being the one to make the first move. In the final session, they shook hands and invited one another to come over during summer break. Not only was this an important lesson to all the children in dealing with forgiveness, but it also gave them great satisfaction to have helped resolve the conflict as a group, enhancing their sense of social self-efficacy.

MAKING PLANS FOR THE FUTURE

Retention of gains in therapy is one of the most difficult stages (Prochaska, 1999). For children to secure the gains they have achieved, they need to be able to make a connection between the group and real life, and to transfer the knowledge and skills that they acquired in the group to their life outside and to their future. Some plans and skills need to be polished before leaving; role playing and other techniques can help children apply the knowledge and skills to their lives (Berg et al., 1998). K. R. Greenberg (2003) suggested giving homework to children following group sessions. My colleagues and I do not assign homework routinely, but at termination some type of homework may help transfer the knowledge gained in the group to real life.

The next illustration is of a group of teenage girls in a special education setting. All came from dysfunctional families, were underachievers in school, and exhibited both externalizing and internalizing behavior. They needed a lot of help expressing their feelings and, even more so, needed instrumental assistance in behavior change. This focus on behavior change was also reflected at termination, in regard to applying the lessons learned from the group to their lives. At the session in question, the girls were dealing with critical incidents in the group and the lessons that could be learned from them and applied in real life.

At the beginning of the group process, Suzanne was extremely immature and withdrawn. At termination, she reflected on her critical incident, which occurred in a session in which she brought in a puppet but refused to show it to the group. The girls had been angry and abusive at first, but, with the counselor's intervention, they managed to communicate with her directly and explain what made them so mad. Following this constructive communication, Suzanne shared with the group an incident in which her mother physically abused her. It soon became clear that she communicated with her mother the way she did in the group, and she was able to reflect on how she angers her mom. From the group experience she took the newly developed skill of direct communication. In this final session, the counselor challenged her by having her role play her next confrontation with her mother. This was aimed at enhancing her ability to apply her acquired understanding and skills in real life.

Kathy tended to monopolize the group. She took the role of the counselor's helper, and often abused her power; at one point she turned the entire group against Sally. The critical incident Kathy mentioned was her fight with Sally. From this experience she grew to understand that, although her goal was to help others, she sometimes did not do it in the right way. She took from the group the skill of communicating verbally and directly, listening rather than moralizing. The counselor asked her to provide feedback to each group member using an "I message," as an exercise to strengthen her communication skills.

For each of the girls, the critical incident was taken a bit further, transferred to real life situations. The leader used this final session to refine some behaviors that needed polishing.

SEPARATION FROM THE LEADER

The leader's separation from the group and the group members is extremely meaningful. The counselor never becomes an equal participant in the group, certainly not in groups of children and adolescents. To perform all required tasks, the leader needs to be an authority of sorts for the participants, and, as a result, the content of his or her communication with the group and each individual in it has a particularly strong effect. At termination, the leader should encourage positive feelings toward the group and its individual members and convey hope for their future. The following is an example of a leader's goodbye statements, first to each individual, then to the group as a whole.

Laurie presented written feedback to each of her group members, along with a candle. Here are some examples:

> Dear Marissa, you are very special, strong, and assertive, which I value. In the group you were the "guardian angel." You helped people express themselves, you were a great listener, and always supportive. Good luck.

> Dear Tina, Each time you spoke I was impressed with your wisdom. You moved the group forward with each interaction, always in a gentle way. I appreciate your sharing with the group some of your difficulties, which actually point to your strong personality.

To the group Laurie said the following:

> We all knew that the time to end the group would come, and yet it still hurts. I can see how difficult it is for you to say goodbye, as it is for me, too. You were a wonderful group, each of you is so special, and each made a profound contribution to the success of this group. I thought about you from meeting to meeting, I came to respect you for your courage to deal with the difficulties in your life, and I appreciate your willingness to share your pain in the group. We went a long way together, with ups and downs, but we reached this successful ending. I wish you the best and send my love to each of you.

SUMMARY

The more successful a group is in the working stage, the more difficult it is to end the intervention. When working in highly cohesive close-ended groups, where many of the children are insecure in their attachment style or have a history of neglect and rejection, termination can be an extremely painful experience. It is, therefore, important to discuss loss and separation before the group ends.

This ending stage of the intervention also has a number of powerful positive aspects. One important aim of the group is to help the children grow psychologically through learning about others and self, and termination affords them an opportunity to evaluate the group experience and each member's personal growth in the group, enhancing their self-understanding. Helping children transfer what they have learned in the group to their lives outside the group is an additional necessary task to be completed at this stage. Finally, there is the goal to empower the group participants through positive feedback. Positive feedback provided by group members is an extremely intensive experience, not only because it is given by peers who are so important in children's lives, but also because it is provided by persons whom they have learned to trust and whose opinion they value. Armed with such positive feedback, children and adolescents can continue maintaining the gains they have achieved and take the steps necessary for further progress. The gains achieved in such group processes will be further discussed in Part III.

III Accountability and Processes With Various Groups

Introduction to Part III

Group counseling and psychotherapy have long been practiced with children and adolescents who present various difficulties. The most common issues such groups address are social interactions/skills, anger management and aggression, academic achievements, divorce, and bereavement (K. R. Greenberg, 2003; Holmes & Sprenkle, 1996; O'Rourke & Worzbyt, 1996; Schaeffer, 1999; Smead, 1995; Thompson & Rudolf, 2000). More recently, my fellow therapists and I evidence a broader scope of groups for children and adolescents, including cancer patients (Stamko & Taub, 2002), the sexually abused (Jones, 2002), and traumatized children (Aronson, 2005; Scheidlinger & Kahn, 2005; Webb, 2005). However, most of the literature is descriptive, and although the impression of clinicians is that these groups are effective, an evidence base is still largely missing. Moreover, little is known about processes in these groups.

Hoag and Burlingame made an interesting attempt to summarize the evidence for the effectiveness of group with children and adolescents. First, they offered a narrative review suggesting that, overall, group counseling and psychotherapy helps children cope with various difficulties and improves their adjustment behavior (Hoag & Burlingame, 1997a). However, several reservations regarding the methodological soundness of these studies were raised, as many were based on a single-group design, employed too small a population, had no control or comparison group, and lacked follow-up measurement (Dagley et al., 1994). Therefore, the conclusion regarding the effectiveness of these groups was only tentative. Following this attempt, Hoag and Burlingame performed a meta-analysis based on 56 outcome studies regarding children and adolescents, published between 1974 and 1997. Various types of groups were assessed, including prevention programs, counseling groups, and psychotherapy groups, most of which measured outcomes of adjustment, disruptive behavior, and self-esteem. Results indicated that group treatment was significantly more effective for children than wait-list and placebo control groups (effect size = .61). That is, they found that the average child or adolescent receiving group treatment is better off than 73% of those in control groups. These results were supported by previous meta-analytic studies performed on children's groups (e.g., Weisz, Weiss, Alicke, & Kloz, 1987) and they are similar to the effect size of adult groups (.54; Hoag & Burlingame, 1997b). Based on the meta-analysis, it was possible to confirm the efficacy of child group psychotherapy.

To demonstrate how expressive–supportive therapy works in groups with children and adolescents, Part III illustrates the processes in the groups that this book has focused on and provides research outcomes. It is also my goal to show the effectiveness of these groups, to provide an evidence base for this type of therapy. Attempts were made to establish rigorous methods of research, including both outcome and process measures, and to provide systematic results of an investigation of these groups. This systematic effort came at the expense of broadening the scope of problems investigated. More research is clearly needed to evaluate many more groups that involve children. Nevertheless, the findings of the studies discussed in this part of the book are important in that they support the model of expressive–supportive therapy for children and adolescents.

11

Group Counseling for Lonely Children and Adolescents

Creating and maintaining friendships is an essential developmental task during childhood and adolescence. Children who lack social skills and the ability to use them effectively often fail to develop mutually satisfying peer relationships and are neglected or rejected, whereas more socially competent children are generally happier, have a more positive outlook on life, do better academically, and have fewer emotional problems (Elliot & Gresham, 1987; Forman, 1993; O'Rourke & Worzbyt, 1996). Yet, development of social competence is largely neglected, argued Duck (1991):

> Despite the fact that friendship is one of the most important far-reaching and continuous lessons of children's lives, it is a lesson that we leave irresponsibly to chance alone. It is a lesson, therefore, in which accident and coincidence have a persistent, uncorrected influence and where they can turn and twist a personality for life. (pp. 134–135)

Duck called for intentional intervention in which children's friendship can be enhanced.

To achieve such a goal, one first needs to define friendship. It is clear that friendship is more than a social skill; it is recognized today as part of a comprehensive set of social competencies (Beelmann, Pfingsten, & Losel, 1994), although the content of this set varies somewhat among researchers. Based on extensive research, Buhrmester and Furman (1987) identified five competencies that children need to establish and maintain stable and healthy friendships: initiating social relationships (ability to call friends, make play dates, and the like); providing support (ability to be empathic to a friend and make him or her feel better when he or she is upset); assertiveness (ability to confront a friend in an attempt to stop nasty behav-

123

ior); self-disclosure (ability to share private information about the self); and conflict resolution (ability to disagree without having a fight, or to forgive a friend). Although some of these competencies (e.g., conflict resolution) are dependent on skills, and therefore are sensitive to training, most seem to be related to personality characteristics and cannot be easily learned. For instance, should self-disclosure be considered only a skill? Actually, it is a behavior that requires self-confidence, trust, and attachment security. Similarly, can empathy really be enhanced through training alone? The literature suggests that empathy is highly motivational (Hoffman, 1997); a person who has developed both the cognitive and affective ability to empathize may nevertheless choose not to. Even assertiveness skills, although commonly considered to be enhanced by training, require a basic level of self-confidence and self-esteem. In fact, even the ability to initiate a friendship requires some level of trust in self and others. These arguments raise serious questions about the methods by which children can be helped in improving friendship relationships.

A different typology of friendship skills has been suggested by Duck (1991), who delineated four types of skills children must acquire to achieve friendship: social skills (understanding the ecology of attraction); interpersonal competence (learning to handle other people within a disruptive conflict); communication competence (ability to communicate skillfully and persuasively); and relational competence (ability, especially within close relationships, to skillfully deal with intimacy, privacy, and trust). Although these categorizations overlap to a certain extent, relational competence is recognized as a unique skill distinguishable from other social competencies, and as the core of friendship. Cassidy (2001) argued that relational competence mainly involves attachment security and reflects four main abilities: to seek care, to give care, to be comfortable with self, and to negotiate. People with a secure attachment style demonstrate all these abilities more than anxious and avoidant people, he said. Moreover, he suggested that intimacy is also related to truth, as intimacy requires open communication and sharing one's deepest nature. Thus, a close friendship requires intimacy.

Berndt (2004), who investigated close friendships extensively, defined them as "a specific new type of interest in a particular member of the same-sex who becomes a chum or a close friend" (Sullivan, 1953, p. 245). Intimacy in friendship is about helping and sharing, support of self-worth and esteem, and mutually satisfying activities (Sharabany, 1994). Close friendships help children feel more important and more confident. Their friendships also enhance children's sense of reality, improve their relationships with other peers, and reduce the chance that they will be victimized by their classmates (Berndt, 2004). Not having any friends increases the child's tendency for anxiety, depression, and social withdrawal (Ladd & Troop-Gordon, 2003). In fact, having a close friend is the most important source of social support at this age, argued Reis and Shaver (1988).

These competencies cannot possibly be acquired through skill training and problem-solving techniques; it is the basic nature of a human being that must be transformed. This may happen in groups that value intimacy, where people can experience positive and supportive relationships.

SOCIAL COMPETENCE TRAINING

Social competence training is most often conducted in a group format (see review in Riva & Haub, 2004). A meta-analysis of social competence training programs (Schneider, 1992) indicated that most studies employed a small group format. Another meta-analysis concluded that these programs used a variety of techniques that address behavior, affect, cognition, and interpersonal relationships (Beelman et al., 1994).

When the most common group programs are inspected, however, they seem to be high in cognitive social skill training. For example, the I Can Problem Solve program (ICPS; Shure, 1992), which has been extensively investigated, shows positive outcomes. The ICPS employs social skill training and a problem-solving approach, and has been found to reduce impulsiveness, increase participation, and improve problem-solving skills. Another frequently mentioned program is the Skill Streaming Curriculum developed by Goldstein and McGimis (1997). This, too, focuses on problem-solving skills, using such techniques as modeling, role-playing, performance feedback, and generalization—all cognitive–behavioral skills. Although conducted in a group setting, these programs actually focus more on content than on the group process. Basically, learning is achieved by training individuals within a group format.

Some counseling groups aimed to develop friendship are also presented in the literature; these are mostly short-term, focused educational groups. Although these programs use a group process orientation, they are highly structured, focused on particular content to be learned, and are based to various degrees on cognitive–behavioral techniques, such a modeling, positive reinforcement, coaching, practice, and problem solving. Minilectures, imitation, discussion, problem solving, and homework, serve as major formats of intervention. The following reviews two of these programs more closely to highlight the differences between them and the counseling groups promoted in this book.

O'Rourke and Worzbyt (1996) presented an eight-session group intervention in which children got an opportunity to develop such social skills as sharing, giving compliments, providing feedback, empathizing, asking for assistance, and asserting themselves. This highly structured program is designed to develop awareness of social difficulties, recognize responses that are helpful and unhelpful in friendship, recognize the 3 R's (right, reality, and responsibility), find ways in which to connect with others, state personal goals for improving friendships, deal with peer pressure, and develop assertiveness. The program is tailored to the needs of children with social deficits, and is based on learning processes, coaching, and training.

Of similar orientation is the counseling program suggested by Smead-Morganett (1994) to enhance friendship relationships. Her goals were to help children clarify the concept of friendship and loneliness, increase awareness to what kind of behaviors are damaging to friendships, enhance the ability to give and receive help, encourage apologizing behavior, help children enhance cooperation on tasks, and increase the skills of ending friendship. These goals are achieved through structured sessions, using a variety of materials, such as books, paintings and charts. For instance, Session 4 ("getting and giving help") aims at enhancing awareness of the need to give and receive help, as well as helping children ask for help and practice this skill. The session begins with a discussion that focuses on the things that children need help with. The skill is then practiced in the group, by having children consider the things they can do to help other people, as well as draw a chart of good things they did during the week. The children then discuss what they learned, state what it feels like to ask someone for help or be asked for help, and indicate what they think they will get out of helping others and what others will think of their helpfulness. It is clear that, although feelings are invited, they are not the focus. Cognition gets the most attention, as this is a learning process, and discussion remains mainly on the conscious level.

These two programs are effective short-term school interventions and are accountable in several areas of social competences, but their effectiveness in enhancing relational competence and close friendships is questionable. This chapter shows how the counseling groups run by my colleagues and I, grounded in expressive–supportive theory and applied methods designed to fit the age groups in question, focus on intimacy in friendship, and lead to positive outcomes that transform the children's ability to maintain close relationships.

THE DEVELOPMENT OF SOCIAL COMPETENCE IN INTIMATE GROUPS

Although the groups my colleagues and I facilitate are considered short-term (an average of 15 sessions), they focus on the group process rather than on skill training. Group processes are driven by mechanisms that generate change in group counseling and psychotherapy—also known as therapeutic factors (Yalom & Leszcz, 2005). The uniqueness of these mechanisms is that they are based on interpersonal interactions. Group cohesion, for instance, cannot develop unless group members interact with each other, share personal experiences and feelings, and provide assistance and support. Interpersonal learning cannot take place without observing other's behavior and learning from others. Mutual feedback exchange helps group members learn from each other. Although, in principle, catharsis can be achieved without interaction, it is much more common in a group setting where people connect with each other, identify with each other, and even imitate each other's behavior. Cathartic experiences involve high levels of self-disclosure, which in turn evoke altruistic self-disclosure of other group members. The universality of experiences helps group members express and release emotions, as well as understand themselves better. The social support provided in the group and the progress made by others instill hope among participants. Peers and the therapist sometimes provide useful information. In such interactions, socializing techniques are developed in a natural process. Moreover, the central ingredients of close friendships—sharing one's true self, providing support and encouragement, being considerate and empathic—are the very ones that characterize the process in our groups.

Thus, rather than teaching children and adolescents about friendship, my fellow therapists and I encourage them to experience close relationships. In other words, learning occurs, but not through coaching, training, or rehearsals, but rather by experiencing corrective interpersonal relationships. Although self-disclosure may occur following modeling, it is more likely to be evoked by the expressed pain and sorrow of another group member. In the latter case, it becomes an act of altruistic or reciprocal behavior, intended to help someone in need (Derlega, Wilson, & Margulis, 1993). Empathy, too, is more likely to be enhanced by someone's expression of pain than as the result of structured guidance to be empathic.

This is not to suggest that my coworkers and I do not employ structured activities in our children's groups, as is recommended (Thompson & Rudolph, 2000). In fact, structured activities were found to be the most frequent stimulus for self-disclosure in our study (Leichtentritt & Shechtman, 1998). For instance, at the initial stage, we use ice-breakers to make children feel more comfortable in this strange situation and to establish rules that maintain order, including the issue of confidentiality (K. R. Greenberg, 2003; Smead-Morganett, 1994). However, in our groups, these activities have an additional purpose: to focus on emotions, enhancing the language of feelings and establishing norms of emotional expressiveness, self-disclosure, mutual nurturing, and support. Group interaction is the key to success, and promoting it becomes the leader's central task at this stage. Activities are designed not to elicit a particular content-based reaction, but rather to encourage self-exploration and enhance cathartic experiences. Working within a comprehensive three-stage model, we help children in the group explore their particular difficulties in friendship relations, help them develop insight into the causes of their difficulties and, finally, in the action stage, help them make some necessary behavioral changes. Thus, we, too, use cognitive–behavioral principles, but only in the last stage of the therapy process, as suggested by the integrative models of change (Hill, 2005; Prochaska, 1999). Even though the activities we apply may look similar to those used in other groups, the process is different, as the following cases illustrate.

THE DEVELOPMENT OF SOCIAL COMPETENCE
IN AN ELEMENTARY-SCHOOL GROUP

A group of 10- and 11-year-old girls was meeting for the first time. First sessions are always aimed at getting acquainted, creating a positive climate of trust, and establishing group norms. This group was focusing on self-introduction, in which each member tells the legacy of her name. Janice asked to skip her turn. This should, of course, be allowed because my colleagues and I value the private boundaries of members; it is most important to protect them from group pressure or misuse of power. But, on the other hand, we also suggest that relating to what others say is important, so the child knows he or she was heard and does not feel neglected. In this scenario, Rita said to Janice, "I just wanted to tell you that you have a pretty name, that you are a very nice girl and that I am very glad you are in my group." Although Janice remained silent, it was clear from her body language that she felt more comfortable and relaxed. The fact that she was not ignored was important to her, as she was so often ignored in social situations. This interaction also served as a building block for self-esteem. Moreover, from the perspective of Rita, who provided the feedback, it was an empathic response, an effort to initiate a relationship and to provide support—all social competences required in a friendship relationship.

This activity (The Legacy of My Name) and another icebreaker my colleagues and I often use (Sharing a Meaningful Object) are aimed at producing emotions. For instance, during the latter activity, Doris shared the earrings she got from her grandmother who had recently passed away. Doris was extremely emotional talking about her feelings of longing for her grandmother. This served as an opportunity to exercise self-disclosure skills. Sandra, a highly withdrawn, quiet and rejected girl, joined her on the topic of death, sharing that her mother passed away en route to Israel. The rest of the group was quite shocked, but they reacted with interest and empathy.

This was the first time that Sandra experienced close relationships with peers. What made her disclose her greatest secret? I suggest that it was not the activity itself, but rather her identification with Doris' expressed pain. This was an opportunity for a highly reserved person to practice self-disclosure in a most natural way. Sandra later shared with the group the internal struggle that she was going through; she told them that she never talked about her mother with other people, even her father, so it was buried deep inside herself. Being a rejected child, she did not trust anyone enough to share such a secret. She was surprised that it came out, as if she completely lost self-control. Ultimately, she was proud of taking the risk. She reported feeling more relaxed, closer to group members and, most importantly, she also shared her secret with her close friend and thus strengthened that friendship, so that she did not feel as lonely anymore.

In a later session, Lois thanked Sandra for sharing her story, as it helped her to open up in the group. Patti said to her, "When you cried, I felt very sad." This was an expression of empathy without teaching or training. It evolved in a natural manner following emotional interactions and the intimacy shared in the group. Such supportive responses are building blocks for the development of self-confidence and trust in self and others.

At another session, Karen entered the group session in a stormy mood. She was furious because someone in class insulted her parents. She responded by fighting back and was punished by the teacher. She was so emotionally aroused that she could hardly speak. The girls insisted that they wanted to help her. They were silent for quite a while, refusing to move to another subject. Margaret said that it was impossible to leave Karen in this emotional state. The girls encouraged her to speak up, and Cindy hugged her. Karen eventually calmed down and shared the incident and her feelings of being hurt. The reactions were empathic; several girls stated that they would also be hurt.

Karen, an aggressive and rather rejected girl, suddenly experienced a different type of interpersonal interaction with peers. She was accepted, understood, and cared for; and, as a result, she was able to express herself verbally. She talked about her emotional arousal and lack of self-control. Armed with social support, she was able to think of alternative ways to resolve a conflict. Conflict resolution skills, which are important for successful maintenance of a friendship, require supportive interactions before insight can be developed and behavior can begin to change. And for the other group members, this was an opportunity to practice the provision of support.

Deep in the working stage, Natalie and Kathy were still silent. Naturally, the group members who already shared were trying to pressure them to talk. The resulting tension led the counselor to remind the group that forcing someone to talk is not an acceptable group norm. "There must be other ways," she said. Nancy took the lead, inviting Kathy to talk in a very pleasant way, "I am curious about you and would like to get to know you better, but I kind of hesitate to approach you because you are so reserved." This invitation was accepted, and Kathy, a lonely, sad, withdrawn child, shared with the group the tragic death of her father and her mother's subsequent depression. Up until that point, no one knew of her life experiences. The release of her secret was a highly cathartic self-disclosure, which opened the way for trust building. The girls responded with great empathy. Cindy hugged Kathy, saying it was painful to listen to her story. Patti shared her feelings of longing for her father, and Marissa invited her to come over to her house. In this exchange, the group members expressed emotions, experienced empathy, and initiated a new friendship.

At termination, the friendships established in the group were obvious. When they played the Post Office game, they sent warm telegrams to each other. "You are my friend and I love you, but sometimes, only sometimes, you insult me and I do not feel good," said Kathy, the silent withdrawn girl, who was now able to express both love and vulnerability in a close relationship that started in this group. Karen wrote to Kathy, "It really helped me when you talked about your dad. I learned about my relationship with my dad. I wish we could go on sharing some things between us." Finally, Sandra, who shared her secret about her mother's death and was encouraged to celebrate her birthday despite this, said that she would like to continue her relationships with each of the girls and celebrate her birthday with all of them the next year.

In this group, most of the therapeutic factors were present:

- Thank you for telling your story, it helped me, as now I don't feel so shameful about my family. (universality)
- I never saw my mom, I don't even have pictures, because in Ethiopia there were no photos. I really miss her and talk to her at nights, crying. (catharsis)
- Whenever you feel you miss your mom, please share it with us; we would like to help. (cohesiveness)
- My greatest secret is my anger, but much of it I released here in the group, thanks to you, Kathy. When you talked about your dad, I realized that we are in a similar situation and I really liked your response. (interpersonal learning)
- I went home and called my dad. He seemed to be happy I called, and I was proud of being able to do it. (recapitulation of a family experience)
- I don't think my father will change much, but at least I can accept him as he is and let go of some of the anger. (existential factors)

It is these therapeutic factors that increased the girls' abilities to make friends and that addressed the main components of social competence, particularly those related to relational competence and to friendship.

THE DEVELOPMENT OF SOCIAL COMPETENCE
IN AN ADOLESCENT GROUP

A group of 10th-grade boys and girls with friendship difficulties was comprised of four shy and submissive adolescents and two quite externalized girls. In the second session, following a story that the leader read to them, they were asked to select a type of fish that best represented them. Miriam, an Ethiopian girl, selected the lonely fish and talked about her sense of rejection. She said, "They hate me, they hate to see me, they hit and push me, pull my hair and call me names only because I am dark-skinned."

Terry suggested that Miriam was bullied because she was too submissive. Miriam agreed, explaining that she felt weak and was quite frightened. She continued exploring her feelings until she realized that it was her peers' disrespect that makes her feel so hurt. The reaction of group members varied. Some expressed similar feelings and experiences of victimization; others pointed out that her submissive behavior must be changed. "You have to protect yourself; ask for help," Jeanne said. Many agreed with this line of thought and suggested sources of help.

Thus, Miriam went through a cathartic experience with support from her fellow group members. Her self-disclosure was initiated by the metaphor used in the story (structured activity), which generated an emotional experience in an extremely withdrawn girl. She also elicited the disclosure of similar feelings by others, which reflected their empathic reaction in an altruistic attempt to support her. Finally, she received feedback from her peers about her submissive behavior, and was even guided to use a different approach. Armed with the social support provided in the group, and released of suppressive emotions, she could start looking at her difficulties with more hope. She realized that she is not the only one who is bullied. Such a sense of universality is another way of perceiving support.

In the next session, Miriam reported that things had changed for her. First, she realized that no one had disclosed her secret, which increased her trust in the group. Being so mistrustful of her peers, she expected the whole school to know her secret, but this did not happen. Second, she felt closer to the people in the group, so she spent time with them during breaks, and on several occasions they protected her from classroom bullies.

At termination, Miriam said that she felt stronger about setting her boundaries. In a game in which traffic signs are used to show progress made in the group, she selected the Caution sign to express her progress in assertiveness, "Now they have to be more cautious before they bother me." She seemed to feel empowered by the group process. This newfound assertiveness can be ascribed to the interpersonal interactions she experienced, rather than to coaching in assertiveness skills.

In the next session, still using the same book and the fish metaphors, Kelly picked the fish that swam in the middle of the lake, expressing her need to be at the center of things, surrounded by people who love her. She characterized herself as competitive and influential. Terry seemed to disagree, saying, "You are more of a swordfish because you sometimes hurt others." Understanding that this remark was made following a fight she had earlier that day over a boyfriend, Kelly shared the incident with the group and admitted that she was rather possessive about friends. She realized that, being an only child, she had never learned to share. At this point, the counselor opened the discussion to involve more children. Many expressed their difficulty in sharing love (of parents, best friends, etc.). At the end of the session, Kelly admitted that she always knew that her behavior was wrong and that her mom always insisted that she must change, but she did not really want to. But in this group she felt comfortable enough to discuss it and was surprised to find that others seemed to feel the same way. She did not feel different anymore and could deal with a commitment to change. At termination, she took a Stop sign, explaining, "I have learned to slow down, not to require all the attention for myself. I try to let other people talk without being critical. I've learned to let others 'swim in the middle of the lake,' too.

In this scenario, like the one described earlier, self-disclosure was initiated by a structured activity (story), but the rest of the learning occurred through interpersonal interactions, particularly the here-and-now exchange between two group members. In both cases, the adolescents involved gained assertiveness and empathy.

Perhaps the best way to learn about the increase of relational competence in a group is through feedback at termination. Steve, a rather silent group member, used the Yield sign to express his growth in tolerance, claiming, "I tend to judge people by first impressions; that's what I did here too. I learned that people are different and that I need to take the time to learn more about them." In other words, initially he was highly protective and defensive; and these newly acquired skills should help him initiate and maintain friendships more easily. Tammy selected the Stop sign to express her lack of trust at the group's beginning and the Yield sign to express her progress in divulging her vulnerability. She was a highly aggressive girl at first. It was clear that she too was self-defensive, but in time gained trust in others. Trust appears a general outcome across groups and children, and as the literature suggests, trust is the heart of successful close friendships.

SOCIAL COMPETENCE AS MANIFESTED
IN CHILDREN'S FEEDBACK

My fellow groups leaders and I gather feedback about the group process in two central ways. We routinely ask children about their learning experiences in the group at the end of each session, as well as in a more formal and structured manner at termination. We also accumulate data on the therapeutic factors that help children grow. These two sources contain valuable information about the enhancement of social competence, as defined in the literature, in counseling and psychotherapy groups for children.

Critical Incidents

A study of critical incidents in children's groups (Shechtman & Gluk, 2005) accumulated many clues indicating how friendship competence grows in group counseling based on responses about the most significant factor the children had experienced in the group:

Larry:	The most important thing was that I told a secret in the group and they [the counselor and children] helped me … and now I am friendly with all of them.
Bob:	The most important thing was that I was helped in the group. … When I had a problem we discussed it and everyone tried to help … and I also helped others.
Counselor:	How?
Bob:	By joining in and sharing my experience. I learned to behave … to listen … to be a good friend.
Counselor:	What helped you to be a good friend?
Bob:	I learned to be helped and to help others.
Tommy:	It felt good to help someone with a problem … I could give him advice and it was helpful.
Terry: (a very difficult child)	They helped me when I had a problem … I understand other children more and now I have more friends that I can play with.
Shelley:	I was once shy and I am not anymore.
Ruth:	I used to think I was ugly and that people do not like me. But in the group, people said I am pretty, a good friend, sensitive, and understanding, and I believe them, because in the group we only say the truth. So now when I look in the mirror I do not see the ugly me that I used to see before.

This is only a sample of what children have said following group treatment. It is clear that they grew in trust of self and others and became more truthful. The support that others provided and their own ability to support others permitted such growth of trust. It is obvious that they acquired the friendship competencies needed in a close relationship and felt more at ease in intimate friendships.

Feedback at Termination: Elementary-School Children.

A group of 10 year olds was playing with feedback cards and wrote the following:

- We learned to listen to each other.
- We learned that it is easier to ask for help than to be angry.
- We learned to help each other.
- We learned to comfort children when they were sad.
- I learned from what children said about me.

The group then continued with a more open discussion, in which numerous gains were expressed. Ken said that he learned to be assertive; he talked to his father about his feelings following the death of his beloved dog and was able to ask for another dog. Lois recalled how she shared a family secret about her brother's death, and, as a result of group support, she became assertive enough to bring the topic up with her parents and make them open up the secret. Gary told of how he resolved a long-standing conflict with Johnny, another group member who used to be his best friend. He concluded that forgiveness is much easier than he had thought, and he hoped to use it in other relationships. Finally, Mandy, a very shy girl, admitted that she eagerly awaited every group session because she could talk about her private issues. In sum, virtually all social competencies needed in a friendship relationship were present in this group: assertiveness, self-disclosure, provision of support, and conflict resolution.

Feedback at termination: Adolescent groups.

A group of adolescent girls was playing with picture cards. Each participant was asked to select a card that represented the progress she had made in the group. Carrie selected a card with a clown on it, explaining, "I let myself be me in the group. I gave up my mask that I use outside the group, but even there I do not use it so often anymore." Tina chooses a card with two bows tied together. She said,

> I feel connected to this group, and to each of the members. I disclosed here things that I don't mention even to my family, and so did others. It was so intimate here ... I learned to listen and I know I was understood. ... This experience will help me in the future with friends, with resolving conflicts, particularly with fights that I used to have so frequently.

Mary talked about the quality of the people in the group, "I have learned that, if you listen carefully, you get to really know others more and learn to appreciate them." Sarah related her own difficulties, "I could not always share private things, but it was so important for me to listen to other people. I have learned so much from each of you." Sharon selected a picture of a house, saying, "I felt here like family, more than family. At first I was worried that people would give away our secrets, but everyone shared and secrets did not leak out. I learned to trust the girls in the group." Cathy said she gained mostly from listening to others' resolutions, "I got ideas that I would never have thought of on my own." The girls then moved on to reflect upon the role each of them took in the group. They mentioned mostly self-disclosure and supportive behavior. For instance, one girl said, "I talked about my family, and my boyfriend, really serious and intimate issues. I also listened carefully, and when I had something similar, I shared with the group. I thought it would help the person if I shared with her how I dealt with it."

These older girls expressed friendship gains in a more sophisticated way than the younger children previously described. Overall, the general theme was of acquiring trust and being able to share intimate information with each other. The girls appreciated both their risk taking in disclosing themselves and the trust that other group members developed toward them.

THE EVOLUTION OF SELF-DISCLOSURE

The last statement quoted in the previous section explains how the process of self-disclosure evolves in such a natural way in groups. Early in the group's life, catharsis experienced by altruistic or highly disclosive members evokes a need in members to respond emotionally, either by joining in and sharing personal matters, or by responding with affection and warmth. Self-disclosure is a reciprocal process (Derlega et al., 1993), and with time even very withdrawn or shy people feel the need to participate in such interactions. Hidden or overt group pressure, or even group norms, make participants feel obliged to disclose their own feelings as part of the deal of being a group member. But most of all, it is the altruistic need to help another person, or an empathic response to suffering so openly expressed, that evokes such behavior.

Even an extremely withdrawn person may eventually progress in self-disclosure skills in an intimate group, as Maggie's case shows. Maggie was anxious and depressed when she first joined a group of third graders selected for the criterion of friendship difficulties. The group included both shy, internalized members and aggressive, externalized ones. In the process, my fellow therapists and I unexpectedly discovered that eight of the nine children suffered physical abuse in their families. Maggie was the most withdrawn of the lot. She refused to join the circle or touch another child in a group game, and she did not communicate verbally with anyone. But she wanted to be in the group and usually sat in a corner, listening from a distance. Eventually, she moved to sit in the circle, but still hardly participated in group discussions. We followed this group in a two-year study.

At the end of the first year, Maggie had accumulated 12 statements of disclosure, but mostly on a simple informative level. The rest of the group was far ahead of her, talking about very intimate issues, like family relationships, parental neglect, and abuse. The counselor actually considered removing her from the group at the end of the first year, but because my colleagues and I felt that she might take this as an insult, and because she did not interfere with the group process, we let her stay. In the middle of the second year, Maggie finally started participating. She disclosed her abusive background and released strong emotions of anger and pain. Our research findings indicate that, in the second year, she not only gained the most in self-disclosure at an intimate level, but also showed the highest level of disclosure of all the girls. How did this happen?

Maggie opened up only after she gained trust in the group. Considering her abusive background, it is clear that she needed time to build some trust again. The fact that the group accepted her as she was, despite her deviant behavior, and did not pressure her, was extremely helpful. It is hard to believe that modeling or training would have helped her overcome her traumatic experiences. She needed to gain trust, and the warmth and intimacy developed in this group provided her with the ingredients needed for trust to grow. The feedback she received from one group member was particularly on the mark: "You made the most impressive gains in this group. Do you remember how you were first hiding under the table? And now you became a leader in this group. I like you and want to continue being your friend." This is the type of experience needed to gain in relational competence and in friendship abilities.

The feedback that my coworkers and I gathered, both from critical incidents and at termination, not only shows that children grow in social competence, but also provides clues as to how this happens. It is clear that the group interaction and the presence of therapeutic factors are key. This is very different from the processes in educational groups or even counseling groups that focus on teaching. These latter groups cannot possibly develop this type of intimacy, which children cherish so much.

RESEARCH OUTCOMES

So far, I have related clinical experiences to indicate growth in relational competence in our counseling groups. What remains is to prove that the method is effective. The following descriptions of research findings provide empirical evidence for the efficacy of such groups in increasing close friendships.

Self-Disclosure

Using a single case study design and in-depth analysis, Shechtman, Vurembrand, and Malajek (1993) investigated the evolution of self-disclosure in a group of eight third-grade girls along two years of treatment. Certain activities initiated by the counselor were found to produce unique types of self-disclosure. For instance, the Feeling Wheel, which elicits personal feelings in the here-and-now or the there-and-then, was used deep in the working stage; it produced 17 emotionally disclosive responses in one session. Similarly, the Personal Mask activity (which deals with self issues) elicited 14 responses in the area of self-exploration and 13 expressions of feelings. Birthday celebrations produced frequent emotional responses or raised many friendship or self issues, depending on each girl's unique difficulties.

The expression of feelings was the dominant behavior in both years of the treatment (39% and 42% of responses, respectively). Friendship was a stable subject along both years, and self issues became frequent only toward the end of the second year. Most of the disclosure was of an intimate nature (compared to simple self-disclosure), which can only be a result of the therapeutic mechanisms of catharsis, interpersonal learning, a strong sense of belonging, and altruistic behavior (M. S. Corey & Corey, 2006; Yalom & Leszcz, 2005). The fact that feelings and the self were two dominant topics suggests that catharsis and interpersonal learning were the two most frequent therapeutic factors (Yalom & Leszcz, 2005). It is the length of treatment that allowed self to emerge, which is the goal of treatment, because change may occur essentially through the self.

Friendship Intimacy

Intimacy in friendships was a construct that my colleagues and I measured quite extensively. It was clear that children develop close, intimate relationships in our small groups, because such relationships form the basis of our group processes. It was not obvious, however, that relational competence could grow during the group process or be transferred to friendship relationships outside the group. The rationale for our expectation of such a transfer was that processes in counseling and psychotherapy groups of the type we employ are similar to processes in dyadic friendships. Both involve the expression of feelings, satisfying social needs, reducing social fears, talking and learning about the self, and becoming close (Reis & Shaver, 1988).

Self-disclosure is the fundamental behavior, key features of which involve expressing emotions, sharing private experiences, and disclosing personal secrets. In turn, such disclosure fosters liking, caring, understanding, and support, both in dyadic friendships (Reis & Shaver, 1988) and in groups (Yalom & Leszcz, 2005). Thus, the same capacities are at the root of friendship and of therapy processes.

Intimacy as an outcome variable was measured in three successive studies (Shechtman, 1991, 1993; Shechtman, Vurembrand, & Hertz-Lazarowitz, 1994) involving over 300 children who were referred to counseling groups for various social difficulties. Results indicated that children receiving treatment increased in intimacy with their best friend significantly more than children that were used as a control. Significant gains were also found for self-esteem (Shechtman, 1993). This significant positive correlation between gains in intimacy and self-esteem supports the assumption that intimacy and trust are just two sides of the same coin (Grunebaum & Solomon, 1987). In the third study of the series (Shechtman et al., 1994), growth in friendship intimacy was confirmed by the friend's perception of that relationship. This correspondence between self-perceptions and another's perceptions indicates that children receiving treatment were realistic about their friendship relationships, supporting Yalom and Leszcz's (2005) finding that group treatment leads to growth in reality testing. This last study also differentiated between friends inside and outside of the group. Results were significant for the best friend outside the group, but that relationship was deeper when the best friend remained the same over the course of the school year. This is not surprising, considering that the development of true closeness takes time. Only after the friendship is well established is it possible to apply the skills of self-disclosure, empathy, and feedback acquired in group therapy. Thus, taken as a whole, these three studies of preadolescents consistently point to the positive impact of counseling and psychotherapy groups on the ability of children to transfer their new-found capacity to foster intimate friendships to larger social settings.

Social lives of boys and girls appear to be quite separate, and each gender seems to have different characteristics. Boys are aggressive, competitive, and brave. They value physical toughness and interact in groups. In contrast, girls live in a more private world that promotes psychological closeness mostly in dyadic or small groups. They play in cooperation rather than in competition and are higher in friendship intimacy (Zabatany, McDougall, & Hymel, 2000). My coworkers and I therefore tested whether the impact of group counseling and psychotherapy on intimacy in friendship differed between boys and girls. Thus, the whole set of data (over 300 children) was analyzed for possible gender differences in growth in intimacy (Shechtman, 1994). Results indicated that girls grew in their sense of intimacy in a same-sex friendship, although more in treatment groups than in control groups. In contrast, only treated boys demonstrated growth. It appears that girls grow in intimacy in a somewhat naturalistic developmental process. In contrast, only boys receiving treatment significantly grow in this domain.

Why do boys change despite their unique cultural codes? My cofacilitators and I tend to attribute this to the group codes and norms in our groups, which challenge their boys' culture. Support for this line of thought was provided by Zabatany and colleagues (2000), who showed that socializing activities increased boys' intimacy and sports activities suppressed it. Group counseling provides opportunities for socializing activities and explicit norms of supportive interpersonal interactions. This is reflected in boys' behavior both in and out of the group. Our observation of group sessions revealed that boys at this age self-disclose as much as girls do, almost from the start of therapy (Leichtentritt & Shechtman, 1998).

A more recent study (Shechtman, Friedman, Kashti, & Sharabany, 2002) investigated growth in friendship intimacy among 174 adolescents. Results indicated that adolescents in treatment grew in intimacy with their best friend more than adolescents in the control group, and that the bulk of this growth occurred after treatment was over (measured at follow up). Gender had no impact on how the intervention affected adolescents who received treatment. However, in contrast to studies on preadolescence, the adolescent girls had higher intimacy scores than the adolescent boys. It seems that the two gender cultures become more separate at this age.

SUMMARY

This chapter focused on friendship relationships, an ability that relates to one of the most important developmental tasks for children at preadolescence and adolescence. However, although many clinicians and researchers refer to social competence as a multivariable, my colleagues and I focused on a unique construct of social competence named intimate friendship. This social ability was expected to be successfully developed in groups due to the similarity of behaviors manifested in close friendships and such groups. Moreover, intimacy in friendship is particularly difficult to alter, because it involves more than skills. Intimacy requires trust in self and others, qualities that can be transformed by re-experiencing positive relationships.

Overall, these intensive studies consistently show the accountability of the counseling groups that my colleagues and I facilitate in enhancing relational competence and close friendship. They strongly support our clinical experiences in these groups, and suggest that more efforts should be taken to employ such friendship groups in preadolescence and in adolescence. This is important not only to help young people to accomplish their major developmental task of intimacy, but also to establish fundamental competence for future intimate relationships.

12 Group Counseling for Students With LD

Today I can tell you that I am a student with learning disabilities of every possible sort. I graduated from elementary school knowing that I am a problem child and that learning is not for me and will never be. I know that everyone thought I was just lazy; no one thought that it is simply difficult for me. The letters jump in front of my eyes and I can hardly combine them into a word and I don't understand what I read. With time, learning became more complicated and I just did not manage. I was ashamed. What could I say? That I cannot read and write? When I manage to write I cannot read my own handwriting. Once in class, the teacher came over, looked at it, and said, "What a scribble!" Then I understood very quickly that it is better to be considered lazy and even arrogant than stupid.

These are the words of Dan, spoken in one of the sessions of a group of seventh graders designed for students with LD. His monologue has many of the elements characterizing students with LD: the learning difficulties and the fear of admitting them, the shame and embarrassment, the threat to his self-image, and the disappointment of self and others. Like many students with LD, Dan used misbehavior to mask his disabilities, because the most devastating feeling is to feel stupid. And no one really expected him to change—until that moment. In a group of children with similar difficulties, who talked openly about their difficulties and expressed similar feelings of frustration and embarrassment, Dan was able to admit for the first time that he had LD, and to understand the ways he compensated for his lack of success in academic achievement.

Following identification and expression of his emotions, Dan was also able to state goals for possible change. Yet, the issue he brought up was not his academic performance, but rather his problems with friendship. Because he was not well accepted by his classmates and felt quite lonely and rejected, he had joined a group of youngsters on the verge of breaking the law. He did not like what they did, but nevertheless went along with them. He asked the members of his counseling group to help him in his efforts to resist these youngsters. The group appeared to provide him with a new sense of belonging and support that he needed to be able to disengage from his so-called friends. Armed with social support, he made the decision to give up his mask and deal with his issues in an open and direct way. He indeed became the best learner in the group, demonstrating progress in behavior as well as in scholastic achievements. In classes where he had a supportive teacher, Dan did extremely well.

Although Dan could gain a sense of universality in another type of group as well, it was the unstructured form of treatment focused on emotions, rather than pre-planned content, that broadened for him the scope of issues to deal with. He could select the issues that were unique to his life, which helped him reduce the emotional burden and free his energies to cope with his difficulties.

George, another highly intelligent boy in the same group, was not so lucky. He repressed his difficulties and presented instead a clear lack of interest in learning. He blamed most of his teachers for being boring, and unfortunately convinced his parents that school was not worth attending. George missed school a lot, which gave him an excuse to fail, as he could not make up the material. Any reason was more acceptable than admitting that he had LD. Even the universality in the counseling group did not help, and in the third session he left the room. A week later he came to see the counselor, complaining that he could not feel his legs. He was extremely frightened but hesitated to call his mother. Eventually his mother came and, under pressure, admitted to giving him a drug without consulting a doctor, because she did not want anyone to know that her son was "crazy." She took George home and he never came back to this school. His hyperactivity and LD remained a family secret; so threatening was the issue for him and his parents that they almost damaged his health.

Finally, Sandy, a teenager in another group, shared his experience of being interviewed in the process of admission to a new school. He badly wanted to be accepted to this vocational school, where he had a better chance of succeeding; in fact, it was his only chance of receiving a high school diploma. Upon arrival at the school, he found out that there were several tests to take and an interview with the school principal, which scared him. In the counseling group, he reported that he skipped some of the tests because "they did not seem relevant" and he did not cooperate in the interview because "the principal was mean." Like many other children with LD, Sandy had developed a sense of helplessness, and gave up his chances for admission even before trying. He played it cool and disguised his fears as lack of interest, when actually he wanted very much to be admitted. Why? Because it was easier to reject than be rejected. It felt better to say "I am not interested" than "I cannot make it." The group worked very hard to help him explore his real emotions and admit that it was actually very important for him to be accepted there. They also helped him develop some insight into his distorted behavior. Finally, they encouraged him to take a second chance and ask for another interview with the school principal. In a role-play, he practiced the skills of a constructive and open interviewee and was encouraged to emphasize his real desire to be admitted. In the end, Sandy was successful and was accepted into the new school.

LITERATURE REVIEW

There is considerable empirical evidence that children with LD differ from normally achieving children in terms of behavior and personality variables. Due to difficulties in academic achievements and lack of appropriate social skills, they experience more negative affect, which in turn impairs their academic and social performance (Yasutake & Bryan, 1995). They often demonstrate high rates of anger, anxiety, and depression (Fisher, Allen, & Kose, 1996), low self-efficacy (Zimmerman, 1995), low self-esteem (Elbaum & Vaughn, 2001), high rates of loneliness and rejection (Margalit & Efrati, 1996), and low self-control (Bender & Wall, 1994). These are affective processes that have negative impact on school performance (Grolnik & Ryan, 1990). Indeed, research has widely documented the relation between cognitive and affective variables in learning and points particularly to the aforementioned variables (Dohrn & Bryan, 1994). Often, therefore, researchers have concluded their studies with the recommendation to treat students with LD in small groups.

Many schools, however, do not assume the role of mental health support and focus instead on excellence in education. These schools normally treat children with academic dysfunctions by offering increased teaching assistance and support, failing to recognize that the learning process contains both a cognitive and an affective component (Epstein, 1994). In view of the multiplicity of difficulties that children with LD face, as well as the salience of the affective component, it is clear that these components also need to be treated.

When schools do assume the role of helping these children with their affective difficulties, it is usually provided within a cognitive–behavioral orientation with a strong focus on learning and social skills (Kazdin & Weisz, 2003). Cognitive-behavioral treatment (CBT) group is defined as therapy that uses the dynamics of the group format, in addition to common cognitive–behavioral techniques—such as challenging thoughts, setting goals, problem solving, and risk assessment (White, 2000)—to change distorted, maladaptive, and dysfunctional beliefs, attitudes, and behavior (Van Dam-Bagger & Kraaimaat, 2000). Even though practiced in groups, it is a task-oriented model, content focused, and largely structured, designed to seek problem resolution for the individual; the group provides validation (Petrocelli, 2002). The model places an emphasis on the learning process, skill rehearsal, modeling, self-talk, and relaxation techniques (Kendall, Aschenbrand, & Hudson, 2003).

EDUCATIONAL/PROBLEM-SOLVING GROUPS

One such educational program was developed in Israel (Alyagon & Bracha, 1996). The program is aimed at developing coping skills with academic tasks and social adjustment. Based on the problem-solving model (Kazdin, 2003), the intervention includes three major topics: strength building (sessions 1–3); examination of coping patterns at times of difficulty, frustration, and failure (sessions 4–6); and practicing with the problem-solving model (sessions 7–15). For example, in the initial stage children draw their own portraits, note some of their strengths in each part of their body (e.g., "I am a strong runner"), and then share a few of the strengths with the group. An example of an activity in the middle stage is having the children engage in the Facing a Difficulty activity. Cards with sentences describing a difficulty in school are presented ("I did not understand my homework;" "I failed the math test), and each child is asked to select one and share with the group his or her way of coping. The group then discusses similarities and differences in coping strategies. Finally, in the third stage of the group, the children practice the problem-solving model. For example, they are presented with a picture of a boy facing a wall, and are then asked to identify the problem, to find alternatives for coping, to evaluate the pros and cons for each option, and to select the best solution. Finally, they are asked to apply the problem-solving process to one of their own social or learning problems. Such programs are effective and help children with LD cope better. However, in this book I offer counseling groups, which operate in a different way.

COUNSELING GROUPS

In congruence with the expressive–supportive model, the groups my colleagues and I facilitate are aimed at releasing negative emotions, sharing disturbing experiences, and exploring personal difficulties not necessarily related to learning or social difficulties. Cathartic experiences are encouraged and used in the process of affective exploration. Insight is intensified by sharing the personal experiences of other group members and the leader, as well as through the exchange of constructive feedback. Action is intensified by exploring one's own coping strategies and by considering alternative strategies offered by others.

Although the process is largely unstructured, activities are offered for each session. The initial stage (sessions 1–6) is aimed at building self-esteem, similar to the educational groups, but it also contains activities designed to build relationships and group cohesion, to develop a language of feelings and self-expressiveness, and to develop norms of interpersonal interaction, the exchange of feedback, and support. At the working stage (sessions 7–13), children share personal experiences of their choice, not limited to learning problems. One child might select test anxiety as an issue to explore, another might consult the group on a social difficulty, and yet another may choose to talk about his relationship with his father. That is, each child raises his or her unique concern or problem. Finally (sessions 14–15), children summarize gains in the group, declare goals for future improvement, and say goodbye to each other.

This counseling form of group intervention differs from educational groups in several major respects. First, the intervention does not focus on LD, and is not structured around specific issues of LD. The assumption is that students with LD are, first and foremost, children who may have various developmental or situational difficulties, including LD. Second, the focus is on emotions, because my coworkers and I believe that the roots of the difficulty and the key to change lie within the affective domain of human functioning. Finally, therapeutic interaction among group members and positive interpersonal support is strongly encouraged, as we believe that change in the individual is more a function of the group interaction than of learning specific skills.

ILLUSTRATION OF THE PROCESS

One counseling group consisted of seven eighth graders: five boys and two girls. Five participants had been diagnosed as learning disabled with emotional difficulties. Three of these were also diagnosed with ADHD and medication has been recommended for them. One boy and one girl did not have learning disabilities, but had been evaluated as troubled children. The group met for 15 one-hr sessions after school in the counseling room.

The group, labeled "Children Help Children," was introduced as an opportunity to talk about thoughts, feelings, and difficulties in children's lives. Participants were told that they had been selected owing to their ability to help themselves and others. Such a positive presentation of the group encourages members at the onset of therapy and instills a sense of hope. It conveys a message that no one is going to teach them something that will make them fail yet again. For children with a history of failure and getting into trouble, such a positive welcome is extremely important.

The activities at the initial stage aimed at developing the language of feelings, building trust, and developing group norms. The children played the Circle of Emotions game, in which a circle is divided into four parts. As they stood in each part, they stated a feeling they had in the here-and-now about the group. Both anxiety and excitement were expressed. The children were a bit anxious about the unknown, but were also happy to be selected, and they were looking forward to the activities and games promised. They then played the My Ideal Group game to establish norms of constructive work. They mentioned issues such as arriving on time, not leaving the session, expressing honest feelings, and treating everyone with respect. Shari, the counselor, added the issue of confidentiality, and they closee the session with the We Promise activity, in which they all promise to keep secrets in the group.

In the next sessions, the children continued developing a climate of trust. They played the Legacy of My Name, which made them feel more intimate with each other, and they interviewed each other in pairs to promote self-disclosure. Processing of the difficulties in this activity revealed interesting self-learning. Kathy admitted, "I am afraid to be the first to disclose." Timmy said, "I was afraid that no one will invite me." And Jordan stated, "I was afraid I would be rejected and so I preferred to wait to be invited." These reactions are typical of children with LD, reflecting their deep sense of social rejection, low trust of self and others, and low self-esteem.

The next session focused on identifying emotions. Many children in general, and children with LD in particular, lack a language of emotions. This limits their ability to express emotions and to understand them. The children played with picture cards and with a Bingo of Emotions to enhance their vocabulary and their identification of feelings. Susan said, "I am frustrated and feel hopeless because I fail the science exams." Johnny said, "I feel lonely and I don't feel good about it (but now I don't feel that lonely)." The group seemed to already take a place in his life and ease his sense of loneliness. Larry expressed his pride for being able to perform on stage, singing and dancing, and the group members responded with encouragement and reinforcement, reflecting the beginnings of spontaneous feedback exchange. Shari, the counselor, felts that they could now move to the working stage and deal with some of the major issues they had presented—namely, loneliness, a sense of failure, and low self-esteem.

The next session, therefore, centered on self-esteem. The counselor asked the children to give themselves awards for things that they appreciated in themselves, and she encouraged group members to enhance their sense of worth by expanding upon the given award. Here are some of the reactions following the activity:

- "I feel good because, although I do good things, I never expressed them in front of others."
- "I found that I had the patience to listen to others and was interested in what they said."
- "I usually talk only with my mother about personal issues, because I trust no one; here I had an opportunity to share with other people and it felt good."

Then Susan said, "I know that people always see the dark side of me, they hear my screaming and talking back. Now I shared for the first time something good about myself." This lead to several spontaneous reactions among group members. "I am in your class. I can help you when people say something negative about you," Kathy said. "You are kind of a leader and a very important group member," added Larry. Timmy stated, "I did not know you are so vulnerable. On the surface you seem so cool. I like you more this way." "I am sensitive, too. I feel much like you," said Marc. This had been an extremely meaningful session for Susan. Supported with social acceptance, her self-esteem was enhanced and she became less restless in the group.

One of the next sessions took place in the music room. Following a session that seemed too superficial to her, Shari was looking for a way to make this one more creative. The children were at first confused in the large room and looked to her for guidance. Children with LD easily get distracted and need clear limits, but Shari decided to let them figure out the rules. After a few minutes in which they inspected the drums, each picked one up and started playing, trying to connect with the other group members. Timmy suggested that they play a feeling game, in which they should take turns using the drum to express their feelings, and the others will have to guess what the feeling is. The group gladly accepted the idea. Jordan began by banging extremely hard on the drum. The group identified anger, and he said, "Too often people do not listen to what I say, so I like to get on people's nerves." In response, Larry also beat on his drum with much anger, saying, "I'm with you. We are not treated fairly. The teachers don't like us." Others soon joined and created a quite angry communication. This was followed by an open discussion of their difficulties with schooling and with authority figures in the school.

Shari felts that this was a turning point in the group process. Group cohesion was enhanced, and the children actually took over leadership of the group in a very constructive way. They were able to follow the rules of a constructive group with minimal intervention of the leader, which is not very typical of children with LD and particularly those with ADHD. Indeed, when, in the next session, a new girl asked to join the group, they refused. Susan explained, "I know she may feel bad, but we need to be honest in this group, and honestly, I would not feel comfortable with a new group member." Marc, an extremely withdrawn boy, added, "At this point, I can talk about everything in the group. I feel connected, and I've gained a new friend. I don't want to change it." Johnny confirmed this, "I've been with him for years, but only here in the group, when he talked about his feelings, did I discover what a good person he is. We are very close friends now."

At termination, Shari asked the children about critical incidents in the group. The drum session was mentioned as one that helped them to connect. "Since then I feel close to the people in the group, and when I have a bad day, I turn to them," said Larry. Other children mentioned interpersonal learning, group cohesiveness, acceptance and support, and catharsis.

All of these children had behavior problems. Teachers described them as having severe attention and discipline problems, a high level of arousal and aggression, low self-esteem, extreme withdrawal, high anxiety, and loneliness. These issues came up in the process, but the attention deficits and discipline problems were hardly there. Rather, their interactions were typical of a regular group with social and emotional difficulties. These gains may be attributed to the counselor, who was sensitive, supportive and creative, as well as to the group, which created cohesiveness and norms of support.

A second illustration involves a group of seven 16-year-old girls, all diagnosed with LD, who dropped out of middle school and were in a special vocational program. All had a long history of failure in school. Nonetheless, the dominant issues that come up during the therapy process were relationships with parents and peers, and only towards the end of the intervention did the issue of LD emerge. The girls in this group spoke of parent–daughter relations characterized by lack of communication, harsh discipline, mistrust, and even violence. They related how they had reacted by lying, drinking alcohol, taking drugs, driving without a license, and running away.

The initial sessions of this group were dominated by anger directed at their parents; few feelings were expressed on a deeper level, and there was little evidence of insight. This low level of communication changed in the fourth session, when they worked with the book *The Soul Bird* (Snunit, 1999; see Chapter 5 for details). Martha shared her basic strategy of constant lying to her parents and expressed feelings of sadness and fear for not being able to be honest with them. Other group members presented a variety of coping strategies, mostly negative. Only after Mindy, the counselor, insisted that the group was not really listening to Martha's feelings and not hearing her sadness and pain did they start listening and sharing similar feelings. After several role-plays, it became clear that the girls had replaced their hostile reactions to their parents with a more open communication pattern.

At another session, Judy, the most silent group member, shared her experience of extortion:

> I am very lonely most of the time; I do not have friends, and when these two guys asked me for my money, I gave it to them, even though it left me hungry all day and I had to walk home [it took an hour]. The next day they asked for more money, which I did not have. They said they will come back tomorrow. They were nice and friendly, and I wanted to give them the money, but since I did not have it, I did not come to school for several days. Eventually, I consulted with the school counselor and I did not see them anymore.

Judy's motivation to give away her money was typical of children with LD, because of their sense of loneliness. She misjudged the situation, perhaps because of her low self-esteem or even her cognitive difficulties. The group offered powerful support for her courage to speak with the counselor and for being who she is:

- "This is the first time I hear you. You are so delicate. I liked listening to you."
- "I would also be afraid to report them and I admire your courage."
- "I was very moved when you talked and liked the way you expressed yourself. You were interesting."

Such feedback is meaningful beyond the reported incident. Judy felt valued and liked, and considering her sense of loneliness and history of withdrawal, this was an important group event for her.

At another session, the girls were playing with SAGA cards (for details, see Chapter 5). Karen selected a card of a clown and one of a prison. She said she felt happy when she got away from her troubles and came to the group. But she was sad because she felt rejected by classmates ("not here" she added); she felt used by other girls who took from her but never gave back or invited her over: "I am slow in learning and have no confidence to respond even when I know the answer. This has been going on since third grade. It makes me feel frustrated, even violent sometimes." This self-disclosure lead to a wide sense of identification and other girls expressed similar feelings. Donna shared her sense of incompetence, even stupidity, and Gail told of her poor self-image and low expectations for the future. There were also supportive, warm, and caring reactions. Donna acknowledged Karen's honest self-disclosure and expressed appreciation of Karen's great ability to articulate her feelings. Carla empathized with her regarding her low sense of self-efficacy, but urged her to continue striving for academic achievement, because it would make a better life for her.

In the next session, Carla raised the topic of academic success, but Mindy, the counselor, noticed that Carla was also expressing much anger. When she reflected on those feelings, Carla began to cry. After a long silence, she shared with the group a recent incident in which her mother was violent, and told them that she had left home and refused to go back. The most disturbing message she had received from her mother was that she was disappointed in her and had lost all hope for her future. Carla felt that her mother's attitude had a devastating impact on her motivation to make an effort. To deal with the situation constructively, Mindy used a book that offered various coping patterns. Carla selected the strategy of avoiding the problem rather than dealing with it. The group provided her with immediate feedback, pointing out that she was choosing to run away. She understood the feedback and agreed to involve the school authorities and confront her mother. Eight days later, following her mother's visit to school and constructive confrontation with her, Carla returned home.

In sum, children with LD have common problems including academic difficulties, social isolation, and low self-esteem. Yet, they also have unique difficulties, some of which are more disturbing to them than academic achievements. There are developmental and situational problems that seriously hinder their performance in school. It is true that, through progress in schooling, some of these problems may diminish, but how does one keep students on task when they feel so vulnerable, so helpless, and so hopeless? When asked at termination what they take from the group, LD children mention friendship, connectedness, warmth, and support. This is not to suggest that they do not need to develop more effective coping and problem-solving skills. Such skills are indeed a part of the group process, but what appears more effective is the exchange of empathy, the provision of social and emotional support, and the enhancement of self-esteem. These interpersonal processes are highly related to academic achievement, as the clinical experience and research show (see the following).

THE UNIQUE CHARACTERISTICS OF GROUPS WITH STUDENTS DEALING WITH LD

Most children with LD have difficulty functioning in a group, as in life. Following continuous experiences of academic failure and stormy relationships with authority figures in the school and at home, they find it hard to trust the counselor. They are frustrated and angry and have little hope that things can change for them. With peers, too, they often have a history of failure, so it is not easy to trust other kids. Those children who also have an attention disorder and hyperactivity find it even more frustrating, because they are unable to control themselves, even when they want to behave well.

An example is the case of Sam, who had ADHD. He insisted on attending the group, but found it difficult to calm down. He walked around the room restlessly, interrupting the discussion. At a certain point, Jodie, the counselor, suggested that he leave for a few moments to calm down, but he refused and continued wandering around the room. At the end of the session, when Jodie gave out imaginary awards, she rewarded Sam for his persistent participation in the group, despite his difficulties. In return, he gave her an award "for being accepting and so different from other teachers." I know that many psychologists would consider this to be reinforcement of negative behavior, but this counselor chose to focus on the bright side, on the positive intentions of the child, and rightly so. I fully agree with Malekoff (2004) that working on the strengths of the child rather than the deficits is much more effective in producing change in a child or adolescent's behavior. Indeed, this was a turning point in Sam's behavior in the group. He was encouraged by Jodie's positive attitude and made great efforts to control himself.

Support and acceptance are not always sufficient, however. For example, in another group in which three of the six boys were diagnosed with ADHD, it was more difficult to progress with the group process, because several children had similar difficulties controlling themselves. Ed wanted very much to be in the group. Being a very intelligent boy, he understood the group rules, but found it difficult to control himself. His attitude to his peers was critical and rude; he insulted the other group members with abusive language and he bullied some of them. At one point, he disclosed a secret but immediately regretted this, and did not show up the next time. When he was convinced that the secret had not leaked out, he came back, destroying the delicate discipline that had since been established in the group with much effort.

Margo, the counselor, felt that he was a threat to the group process and asked him to leave. In a later private conversation, Ed convinced her to give him another chance. But the next time, Ed recognized that he could not control himself, and he left the group for good. Whether it was the difficult group composition (50% ADHD boys) or Ed's particularly difficult disabilities that created the problem, it was impossible to keep this boy in the group despite the very sensitive therapeutic approach.

In general, it is more difficult to conduct counseling and psychotherapy groups for children with LD because of problems of attendance, discipline, and attention. Therefore, the groups should be kept small, and much attention should be given to group composition. Pregroup screening and individual interviews may help eliminate prospective members who would not benefit from the group. If possible, coleading can be very helpful, so that one leader can provide individual attention to the very needy group members. Just sitting down next to a highly aroused or restless child can help. Despite these difficulties, groups for LD children are successful. My colleagues and I know this from children's feedback and our research outcomes.

CHILDREN'S FEEDBACK

Attending a faculty meeting a year after her group terminated, a counselor noted that all the children from her group were doing extremely well in school. Excited about this positive feedback, she decided to investigate how they were actually helped in the group. She contacted them and interviewed each. Here are some of their responses:

Wendy: Following each session I felt more confident, less anxious on tests. I am also more open with my friends, and get to establish closer and deeper relationships with them.

Ruth: The meetings helped me change socially and in school. I am happier, less stressful during exams and I have more friends. My improvement in school also improved my relationships with teachers. I liked the group because it enabled me to express my feelings. I learned a lot about myself, and I realized that other people also have similar problems.

Delia: They asked me what this group is, and I really didn't know how to define it. We simply talked and we helped each other a lot. I used to be very moody; today I am different. I talk more freely with girls and I've improved in academic achievement. Now that I've overcome both social and academic difficulties, I know I can overcome any difficulty. I kind of trust myself more, and when needed, I know where to turn for help. I learned to admit to my difficulties and, when needed, to make a change. I also learned to think before I act, and this is the most important thing I learned in the group.

This feedback incorporates all the goals that my colleagues and I have for such groups. The children resolved social issues, increased academic achievements, enhanced trust in themselves and others, increased self-confidence and self-efficacy, and gained self-control. In some respects, such gains have unique meaning for children with LD, but in many other respects they reflect developmental issues of any children their age.

In a group of younger children, feedback was obtained through a game. The counselor displayed various objects and asked the children to select the one that best described what the group had been for them. Gary selected a box of chocolate, because it was such a sweet experience. Cindy chose a package of rice to express the connection between group members. Corey selected a seesaw, expressing the ups and downs in the group, and indicating that they ended at on top.

This is only a sample of feedback provided by children to show the efficacy of such groups. More can be learn from our intensive research on groups of children with LD.

RESEARCH OUTCOMES

The first study (Shechtman, Gilat, Fos, & Flasher, 1996) on children with LD was aimed to measure self-esteem, social status, and self-control of 142 low-achieving children of whom two-thirds were diagnosed as learning disabled. Academic achievements were measured only as a by-product, because of the well-known association between academic achievement and social and emotional variables. The sample population of 142 children was randomly divided into experimental and control groups. Although both groups received 4–6 weekly hr of academic assistance by expert teachers, only the 73 children in the experimental group also participated in group counseling of an expressive–supportive nature. They were grouped by age level, creating 11 mixed-gender groups. Results indicated an overall significant difference between the experimental (counseling) and control groups, with higher gains for the former on all measures: scores in language and math, self-concept, locus of control, and social acceptance, and these gains were sustained at follow-up.

Although gains on socioemotional measures were expected in such groups, academic achievements were beyond our expectations. The average grades of the experimental group moved from failing to almost average (math: from 50 to 63 at termination and to 65 at follow-up, 6–9 months later; language: from 58 to 68 to 69, respectively). There was no change in the control group. These gains were confirmed in national tests, which are usually perceived as more objective measures than teachers' grades. In addition, my colleagues and I compared the percentages of experimental and control failing pupils who received passing marks (60 and above) at the end of the intervention and at follow-up. Results indicated that about 70% of the pupils in the experimental group who initially failed received a passing math grade at termination, and this percentage remained constant at follow-up. Parallel percentages for the control group were 15% and 12%, respectively. The improvement was equally clear for language; the proportions of pupils in the experimental group whose grades improved from failing to passing was about 80% and 60%, in comparison to 13% and 10% in the control group.

The results of this study clearly indicate the contribution of group counseling of an expressive–supportive nature to children's progress in academic achievement, as well as on social and emotional variables. Gains in academic performance after treatment of affective variables, without specific focus on academic issues, make the results particularly interesting. Althoug 4–6 weekly extra-help sessions focusing on scholastic performance did not significantly improve grades or test scores, the addition of the weekly group session did. Because there were no initial differences between the experimental and control groups, and because the only obvious difference between them was the group treatment, it is reasonable to attribute the outcomes to the intervention. The progress made on the affective and social variables, although not directly linked to the outcomes on academic achievements, may provide some explanation for these outcomes. The children involved in the study displayed affective difficulties along with LD. Improved self-esteem, self-control, and particularly social status can positively affect children's academic achievements. Indeed, children's feedback on the group experience clearly supports this assumption.

These results bear a significant message for educators who normally address learning dysfunctions with increased teaching assistance. It seems that these children's social and emotional needs must also be addressed. Another important message is that counseling groups of an affective focus are effective. This is important to state in light of the prevailing modes of cognitive–behavioral treatments.

Another study (Shechtman & Pastor, 2005) expanded on the previous research by comparing counseling treatment of LD children to cognitive–behavioral group therapy. The study comprised 200 children from second to sixth grade. All were diagnosed with LD and were receiving treatment in a learning center. Some received 1-hr assistance with academic achievements twice a week; others received academic assistance along with CBT group treatment or affective group counseling; and the rest were on a waiting list for academic assistance and, meanwhile, received one of the two group treatments. Thus, the 200 children were randomly assigned to five comparison conditions: academic assistance only; academic assistance + group treatment (both types); and treatment of both types without academic assistance. Two more comparisons were made between all children who received CBT and all children who received affective group counseling. The last two comparison groups entailed a reclassification of the second and third groups, to allow the comparison between treatments.

In this study, too, my fellow therapists and I measured academic progress, this time with the expectation that affective groups would have a positive effect on achievements, but questioning whether it is the particular type of intervention offered that makes a difference. Overall, all children moved from a failing (around 40) to a passing (around 60) grade in reading, following all types of treatments. However, progress was significantly different for the comparison groups. The group that received only group treatment gained more than the group that received only academic assistance, and of the two types, affective therapy was more effective than CBT group treatment. A similar result was obtained for progress in math. The most striking result was that academic assistance was least effective in generating gains on scholastic achievement; affective therapy, which does not focus on learning, achieved the highest gains.

Results on affective measures were along the same lines, which, of course, could be expected. One would not expect progress in adjustment behavior, self-efficacy, or social status following academic assistance only. Indeed, all group treatments were more effective than no group treatment, but on most of these measures, too, affective group counseling was more effective than CBT groups.

In this same study, my colleagues and I also analyzed the process of client and therapist functioning, to help us understand results. We found less client resistance and more affective exploration and insight in the affective therapy groups, and more cognitive exploration in the CBT groups. These results provide evidence that the two types of treatment indeed do what they aim to do. Affective group therapy is meant to focus on affect and to achieve some insight; and the climate of sharing and trust usually reduces resistance. Conversely, cognitive therapies focus on cognition, thoughts, and perceptions. Moreover, as affective exploration and insight are considered more constructive behaviors (Hill & O'Brien, 1999), they may also explain some of the advantages seen in the outcomes for the affective therapy groups.

As expected, therapists used different skills in the two types of treatment. There was more encouragement, reflection of feelings, and interpretations in the affective therapy groups and more information and guidance in the CBT groups. Leaders operated within their theoretical orientations and used their helping skills with particular aims. Because reflection of feelings, encouragement, and interpretation are also more appreciated by clients (Hill & O'Brien, 1999), this result, too, may explain the effectiveness of affective group therapy.

These results are congruent with the feedback we received from the LD children. They seem to tire of being reminded of their academic failure. The affective and social issues seem to be of more concern to them than their academic performance. Perhaps it is time to address the real issues of this population.

Support for the importance of the affective processes in the group experience was found in a recent study (Shechtman & Sender, 2006) involving a large number of students with LD. Results indicated gains on social competence following group treatment compared to a wait-list group. More important, however, was the finding that these gains were associated with children's bonding with other group members (although not with the counselor). This result adds strength to the importance of relationships in the group, as reflected so clearly in children's feedback.

It is interesting to note that it was not only with children that we obtained these results. A study conducted on mothers of children with LD (Shechtman & Gilat, 2005) compared educational groups based on information provision to counseling groups of an affective focus. On all measures of parental stress, mothers in the counseling group gained more than mothers in the other group. They reduced their level of stress, gained control of the child's behavior, and perceived them as less problematic than the other mothers. Moreover, children's feedback confirmed the progress made in mother–child relationships. Another interesting outcome was the progress made by fathers on all these dimensions, although they themselves did not take part in the intervention. It seems that the influence of the group on mothers had a broad effect, including the father and the child. The process measures in this study indicated that catharsis and interpersonal learning were the therapeutic factors most valued by the mothers, supporting the type of intervention provided to them (Gilat, 2004).

SUMMARY

This chapter described counseling groups for children with LD that focused on their social and emotional concerns rather than their academic difficulties. The clinical illustrations point to the importance of processes that are free of preplanned content and based on self-expressiveness and intensive interpersonal interaction and support.

The results of research conducted by my colleagues and myself clearly support affective group counseling for children with LD and for their parents. Such groups appear to be more effective than training groups, which are more commonly used. The implications of these results are both theoretical and practical. Theoretically, it seems logical to conclude that students with LD are, first of all, children or adolescents; they also have LD. Thus, they display a wide range of emotional and social needs, along with the disability. Addressing these needs seems to be more effective than providing academic assistance. Practically, it appears that such groups can be conducted in a school setting. They are not much longer than educational groups, and trained counselors can lead them effectively. They should also be recommended on the grounds of cost effectiveness; both types of groups, conducted by a total of eight counselors, were more effective than individual assistance given by 60 special education teachers.

More research with this unique population is important. It is interesting to compare groups for children with LD to groups for children without LD, in respect to both outcomes and processes. It is particularly interesting to compare client behavior, content of problems, therapist interventions, and therapeutic factors. Such information would help counselors work more effectively with this population.

13 Group Counseling for Children of Divorce

INTRODUCTION OF THE PROBLEM

Perhaps the two most difficult experiences young children confront are the loss of a parent through death and the divorce of parents (Guldner, 1999). The U.S Bureau of the Census (1999) reported that, each year in the 1990s, over one million children experienced the divorce of their parents. Although not all children are harmed by their parents' divorce, most of them need emotional or instrumental assistance at some point in their lives.

Research on children of divorce has suggested that these boys and girls are at risk for one or more of the following: aggression, anxiety, anger, sadness, guilt feelings, depression, insecurity, loss of self-confidence, loss of self identity, and lower academic achievements (Amato, 2001; Kelly & Emery, 2003; Oppawsky, 2000; Riva & Haub, 2004). Longitudinal studies have indicated that a child may still be disturbed by the parents' divorce many years after the event (Wallerstein & Blakeslee, 1989; Wallerstein & Lewis, 2004).

Wallerstein (1983) identified six tasks that children must negotiate in dealing with the divorce of parents: acknowledging the reality of the marital rupture; disengaging from parental conflict and distress and resuming customary pursuits; resolving the loss; resolving anger and self-blame; accepting the permanence of divorce; and achieving realistic hope regarding the relationship. Addressing these variables may facilitate the child's coping and adjustment.

Children of divorce often have no one with whom to share their concerns, fears, and loneliness. Small groups are an excellent resource for addressing such problems; they are often the single most important factor in the child's ability to cope with divorce trauma (Hage & Nosanow, 2000; Smead-Morganett, 1994). Indeed, a literature review by Dagley and colleagues (1994) found that group intervention programs designed for children and adolescents of divorced families have become quite common. Riva and Haub (2004) reviewed some of the more popular programs: the Children of Divorce Intervention Program (COPIP) (Pedro-Caroll & Cowen, 1985), Rainbow for Children (Skitka & Frazier, 1995), and Spectrum (Skitka & Frazier, 1995), among others. The results of research that evaluated these programs were positive: treatment children reduced depression and anxiety, improved beliefs about parental divorce, increased scholastic competence, and increased general adjustment.

Most of the researched intervention programs are short-term psycho-educational groups, highly structured and focused on issues relevant to the problems typically faced by children of divorce. They are content based, focus on learning the problems that children face, and provide training in skills necessary for coping with those problems. As they are short and structured, they are easy to practice in the schools and therefore are favored by school counselors and parents.

EXAMPLES OF PSYCHO-EDUCATIONAL GROUPS

The following description of two psycho-educational programs for children of divorce aims at highlighting the differences between such groups and the counseling groups suggested here. As psycho-educational groups, they are excellent examples of how to help children of divorce avoid more serious problems by imparting information to increase understanding of divorce-related issues and by guiding and training the children in life skills needed to cope with the stress of parental divorce.

The CHANGE club was developed by Guldner (1999). CHANGE stands for the basic tasks that children of divorce need to accomplish: Communication, Healthy self, Adjusted relationships, Needs, Guidance, and Emotions. This structured eight-session program uses therapeutic games and activities to help children grow in these six domains, with each session focusing on one of the domains. The second session, for instance, centers on communication: "The goal is to foster communication. This session focuses on how children are communicated with about the separation/divorce, and how children can acquire the information they need to help them cope with this crisis in their life" (Guldner, 1999, p. 35). To achieve this goal, children examine their own reactions to separation; play the game Gossip Rumor to demonstrate broken communication; role-play communication with parents on difficult issues; play the Sculpture game, in which they physically position themselves in relation to family members (played by peers in the group) to express the level of intimacy with each; and close with punch and cookies, review what has been learned, and pick the topic for next session.

As emotions are the focus of the counseling groups suggested in this book, I also review the seventh session, dealing with emotions: "The goals of this session are to identify emotional feelings and to find beneficial ways of managing these feelings" (Guldner, 1999, p. 47). First, the leader presents five cards to the children, each bearing a word representing one of five feelings: fear, anger, sadness, joy, and love. The task is first to understand the feelings, then to select the one that they have experienced most since their parents' separation. The children then discuss how they and others in their lives express these feelings, how it feels, and what the consequences are. Next to focus on sadness and fear, each child uses a drawing of a crying child and writes his or her thoughts in a cartoon bubble above the child's head. They then use a story to discuss shame and guilt, and close the session in the routine way with cookies and punch. The program is informative, facilitative, and creative; it builds on the common ground of children of divorce, helping them to adjust to their difficult situation.

A similar popular program, Skills for Living, has been offered by Smead-Morganett (1994), who has delineated eight goals for intervention:

- provide a safe, secure, and reinforcing environment where children can learn new skills to help them cope with the divorce;
- teach some factual information about divorce that will help children deal with their emotional issues more effectively;
- give children the opportunity to express their negative feelings about the divorce and what is happening to and around them;
- encourage children to share their thoughts and feelings with other children who have experienced similar thoughts and feelings;
- teach the skills of assertively expressing feelings and needs to family members;
- teach children effective ways of managing their stress;
- reinforce social support systems that may have been lost due to the divorce;
- teach children to identify behaviors and situations that enhance ineffective emotional and behavioral responses. (p. 83)

To achieve these goals, Smead-Morganett (1994) has structured each meeting, including goals for the session, materials, activities, and process questions. For example, the goals for the first session are adjusted to the beginning stage of a group; they include: creating a climate of trust; establishing rules and the group contract; enhancing positive feelings about the self; and highlighting the universality of the problem. Ice breakers are used to establish a positive group climate, and confidentiality is required of all participants. To enhance positive self-feelings, each child is asked to draw a self-portrait, tape the picture on the wall and state positive things about himself or herself, sort of a "show and tell about me." Finally, the process is based on such questions as, "What did you learn about yourself?" "What do you like or don't like about yourself?" "What did you learn about other people and about families going through divorce?" In the next sessions, participants learn about family change, why people divorce, feelings about divorce, assertiveness, issues of stepparents, dealing with stress, and saying goodbye.

Again, as feelings are the focus of counseling groups run by my colleagues and myself, it is useful to also review the session that emphasizes emotions. According to the *Skills for Living* (Smead-Morganett, 1994) book, the objectives of this particular session are to help children identify feelings, express them, and accept them. To achieve these objectives, Smead-Morganett has suggested using a Feeling Face Chart that displays pictures and words of varied intensities, with the aim of enhancing the children's understanding of feelings in general and their own in particular.

She also has offered pictures representing family situations that allow the children to talk about how people feel. Processing focuses on what they have learned about feelings in general, their own feelings, and feelings of other group members.

These psycho-educational group programs are highly structured, have a predetermined goal and plan, and focus on the central issues of families of divorce. The group is used as a context for individual learning and highlighting the universality of the situation. In what way, than, are the counseling groups of my coworkers and I different?

COUNSELING GROUPS FOR CHILDREN OF DIVORCE

In keeping with the theory of group counseling presented in this book, the groups for children of divorce that my cofacilitators and I operate are of an expressive–supportive nature. They are minimally structured to permit each individual to bring up the main issues of concern for him or her. In other words, the process is client-centered rather than content-centered. Moreover, these groups directly promote the expression of emotions. As anxiety, loneliness, and depression are the main feelings typical of these children, we believe that these emotions must be expressed and tension must be released before further learning can occur. In accordance with the three-stage model (Hill, 2005), only after emotional experiencing is made possible do we apply processes in which insight is enhanced for those children who are capable of developing insight into their thoughts, feelings, and behavior. It is not until nearly the end of the therapeutic process that children are encouraged to take action and make changes in their behavior that could help them cope better.

Interaction between group members is another major component of counseling interventions by my colleagues and I. Group members are encouraged to share emotions and personal experiences through altruistic behavior and to provide emotional and social support. Altruistic and courageous self-disclosure creates intimacy among group members and enhances identification and modeling processes. We believe that children's progress depends on an intimate group climate, on reexperiencing positive peer relationships, and on emotional and cathartic experiencing, more than on learning processes or the provision of information and guidance. Indeed, studies conducted by my coworkers and I on therapeutic factors in children's and adolescents' groups have indicated that these were the mechanisms of change in our groups rather than problem identification and change (Shechtman, 2003; Shechtman, Bar-El, & Hadar, 1997; Shechtman & Gluk, 2005; see also in this book).

Following are illustrations of processes in counseling groups with children of divorce. As the example selected from *Skills for Living* (Smead-Morganett, 1994) referred to elementary-school children, my first illustration refers to this same age group.

AN ELEMENTARY-SCHOOL GROUP

The group was comprised of six 11-year-old children, one boy and five girls. As in any group, the beginning stage was geared to the development of a climate of trust and the establishment of group norms: confidentiality, self-disclosure, and interpersonal support. In this group, members took turns bringing in pieces of literature for the start of each session. As bibliotherapy is a projective technique, my colleagues and I assume that each child would select something meaningful to his or her life; this would also serve as a strategy to increase children's involvement and responsibility in the group.

In the third session, Gail brought in a story about loneliness, explaining that she often felt like the girl in the story. She first talked about her relationships with her classmates. Jack, who was in her class, responded with his own self-disclosure: "It is not easy for me to say this ... but I used to reject kids and give them a hard time. I don't know why." Gail insisted that he still did and that it made her feel bad. This was the beginning of self-exploration and open communication between two group members.

In an attempt to broaden the scope of the discussion to family relationships, the counselor asked the children to think of similar feelings they might experience in other places. Gail, who lived with her grandparents, said she often felt like this at home, particularly since her grandfather passed away. Although she spent a lot of time with her grandmother, with her grandfather gone, she felt her father's absence even more. To this, Jack responded, "I wish I had a grandma to be next to when I wake up; I get up lonely every morning." A connection had been made here between two rival group members through the expression of a mutual sense of loneliness. There was expression of strong feelings, made possible by Gail's courageous self-disclosure. Jack's response was quite unexpected, as he was known to be highly withdrawn and somewhat harsh.

The next session started with a game called We Follow The Steps Of.... The purpose of the activity was to encourage and empower group members following experiences they had in the group. In this case, the counselor wanted to reward the two courageous group members previously mentioned, as well as to reinforce the norm of group participation. Dana chose to "follow Gail's steps" of openness "for opening her heart to us;" Ruth chose to follow her friendly behavior; and Jack chose to follow her improvement in behavior. Gail appreciated Jack's acceptance of her criticism and his kind response this time. The counselor expressed her respect for Jack's expression of feelings.

Following this opening activity, the children played a therapeutic card game called SAGA (see Chapter 5). The counselor asked them to pick a card that was meaningful to them and to share that meaning or the associations that emerge with the group. Gail selected a card with a picture of an old wise man, and continued talking about her grandpa, whom she missed so much. Dana took a card of a person looking across the street at a house, which made her think of her father, who was disconnected from her life. Madelaine chose a lonely wolf standing on the edge of a mountain, but refused to explain why. As the other children were not ready to share their cards, the counselor stepped in and shares her own card, of a lonely elderly woman. She told the children that, as she got older, she felt how much she missed her son, who lived abroad. She expressed sadness and longing for him. Jack was the first to respond to her self-disclosure. "Can I ask you something personal?" he asked. "Do you think maybe your son doesn't love you?" She responded with a yes, continuing, "It feels sometimes like he does not love me." The children tried to comfort her, but she stopped them, explaining that she should not take the time of the group for her own sake. She then turned to Jack, asking, "Is this something you feel about your mother?". He responded, "Yes, she could fight for me, like my father did. But she did not even try. She just told my father he can have me." The counselor told Jack that when his mother met with her, she expressed her love and longing for him. But he is not convinced at all, saying, "Then why doesn't she ever write that she loves me or says she's sorry?" It was obvious that Jack was experiencing a crisis that needed further attention, but time was up. Nonetheless, the counselor served as a model for self-disclosure, which permitted Jack to express his pain.

At a later session, Dana, who had grown up with her mother in a single-parent household, disclosed her discovery of who her father was and explored her relationship with him. She was very puzzled; although she was curious to know who her father was, now that she had discovered his identity, she was not sure that she wanted him to be her father. She went through a cathartic experience as she explained her mixed feelings, "He left my mom when she gave birth to me; he did not support her when she needed help; and he did not even try to get to know me all these years." For years she had hated him for abandoning her, and now she suddenly discovers that he has been around all this time and had another family in the same neighborhood. Jack asked what she expected of him, but she did not know how to respond. The counselor then disclosed another of her past experiences: When she was a child, she was separated from her father for five years. She imagined him all this time as tall and strong, and when he came back from the war an ordinary man, she was very disappointed. This disclosure gave Dana the leeway to talk about her own expectations. She said she expected a monster, but discovered an ordinary man "sometimes even fun to be with." At the end of this session, Dana felt clearer about her expectations and relationship with him. But she now felt very angry that her whole family knew who her father was, but never told her. She felt betrayed by everyone she was close to. The group members played an important role in assuring her that this conspiracy was meant to protect, rather than hurt, her. Several group members shared similar responses from their parents, who had promised to give them additional information when they grow up. This sense of universality was helpful to Dana in resolving some of her unfinished business with her family.

The next few sessions focused on difficult relationships with an abandoning father. Gail, Madelaine, and Francine all shared their anger and need to punish such a man and take revenge. Ruth, on the other hand, said that she maintained a relationship with both parents because the issue was between her mother and father and should not involve her. She accepted their divorce and tried to take advantage of both homes. This mature reaction helped to develop a new avenue of discussion, in which the children tried to detach themselves from the parental conflict. Some of the anger had decreased when Jack suddenly stated angrily, "You always talk about fathers as the bad guys, but what about mothers? They can be very mean, like on my birthday." It was clear that the next session should focus on him.

The counselor brought it up, apologizing that they could not attend to Jack's comment the week before because they had ran out of time. She assured him that she had thought about him ever since. She directly asked about the birthday incident. Jack said,: "She did not even call, and I'm glad. I did not feel bad at all." From his responses to several questions, it became clear that she had called a month earlier to ask him what present he wanted, but he refused her offer. The group responded wiith great empathy: "What nerve she has;" "You don't ask about the present you want;" "Children may feel uncomfortable about responding to such a question." As Jack had been denying his true feelings, the counselor decided to role-play the conversation between him and his mother. Like in a psychodrama, they set the stage for the role-play, and Jack provided the two actors with information: his mother had to act emotional and the boy must feel insulted. Following the short role play, the girl who played his mother reveals, "It was painful to be rejected by your own son." The girl who played the son felt sad and abandoned, commenting "Why did she forget him for so long?" Jack could identify with her expressed feelings, saying, "Yes, even if I rejected her, she should continue calling me." He accepted the counselor's interpretation that he needed to test her love because he was so unsure about it.

The counselor now moved to the action stage, asking the group members how they could help Jack change his feelings in this situation. Some suggested talking to his mom directly, others suggested writing her a letter, which Jack preferred. So they wrote a group letter, with each child adding a sentence:

Hi Mom.

I want to talk to you.

Today I felt that I have the courage to do so.

I feel that I am anxious about our relationship, because you don't show that you care about me.

I expect you to call more often even if I do not respond, to show that you really love me.

I am very sad even though I don't always show it, because I do want a relationship with you and I need your help.

I don't want to mislead you; I still want to stay with dad, but I also want to know I have a mom.

I am also sad that my sister did not call. You could at least encourage her to call me.

I don't think that I want a relationship based on presents. I cannot trust you.

Love, Jack.

Jack summarized the experience as follows: "I agree with what you all said, but, although I accepted the idea of a letter, I don't feel I can send it. I felt I could trust the group, I know they will not disclose my secret." The counselor reassured him that he did not have to send the letter, and that the group just wanted to express their understanding of his situation. Indeed, the group helped Jack to stop denying and to connect to his real feelings, which were anger, frustration, disappointment, and anxiety. When Francine corrected him, saying: "You don't hate your mom, you miss her," he started crying. This was an extremely accurate interpretation that helped him identify his real emotions. The sharing of mutual feelings and the empathic reactions of group members had provided him with a sense of power. Mobilizing the expression of emotion is a crucial part of the counselor's role. In this case, the counselor was able to involve all group members in exploring feelings and helping each other with their personal issues, including the use of her own disclosures to help along the group progress.

Many of the goals declared in the structured psycho-educational programs were achieved in this process. The children dealt with the reality of marital rupture trying to accept the permanence of divorce; they expressed anger and resolved the loss; and they achieved realistic expectations (Wallerstein & Blakeslee, 1989). They did all this in a safe supportive environment, shared thoughts and feelings, and enhanced the ability to manage stress (Smead-Morganett, 1994). Yet the process was different in several ways. First, the focus was on experiencing. Each child experienced his or her own narrative, which was different and unique, despite the similarity of background. Experiencing led to an improved understanding of the given situations. Sometimes actions were taken with or without the encouragement of the group. Second, the group was highly interactive, including the counselor. The children and their counselor helped each other through altruistic self-disclosure, universality, modeling, and interpersonal learning (Yalom & Leszcz, 2005). Finally, the process was unstructured, but the leader used activities to enhance the therapeutic factors.

AN ADOLESCENT GROUP

The second example is that of an adolescent group comprised of seven girls, aged 12–13. Most of the parents had been divorced for many years; only in one case was this a newly divorced family.

Gail's parents had been divorced for 6 years, following an ugly separation. She did not get along with her mother, with whom she lived, and liked her father very much but had trouble communicating with him "because his girlfriend is always around." In the first session, she described an ideal relationship with her father; she was the only one in her family who accepted his relationship with a young woman who could be his own daughter. The only problem was that he was never available; there were so many things that she wanted to say to him, and she needed to find an opportunity. But, unfortunately, the next day he died of a heart attack. Gail missed a session, but arrived at the next one all smiles, as if nothing had happened. She played the role of a clown, denying her emotions. Yet, outside the group, teachers and children complained about her unpleasant, even aggressive behavior. It was clear that she needed to connect with her true feelings, but it seemed too painful. For a while, the counselor let her get away with this, but at the working stage, she decided to challenge Gail about her behavior. The group was playing with a set of therapeutic cards (OH), and Gail selected one depicting a man lying on a hospital bed. She talked about her father's death and her own role in the hospital in an informative, emotionally detached manner. At a certain point, in an attempt to capture her feelings, the counselor asked Gail to imagine standing there next to her father, talking to him. This lead to a cathartic experience. She cried heavily, leaning on the group leader as another girl hugged her, but did not speak at all. The group was deeply silent, attuned to Gail's experiencing. At the end of the session, she felt relieved, "as if I exploded." In the next session, she reported that she felt rather relaxed throughout the week and had no outburst of any sort. A classmate confirmed this report. Gail still occasionally played the role of clown, but in her reactions to other people she was warm and honest.

The next time Gail experienced catharsis was in a session with PhotoTherapy. She brought in a picture of her father holding her in his arms when she was 3 years old. She again cried heavily, but this time was able to use a vocabulary of feelings. She expressed her sadness and pain, shared how much she missed him, and disclosed that she slept with his picture. The other girls in the group supported her for being able to connect to her real feelings and for putting the clown away. They told her that she was a better friend now, more attentive and sensitive to their needs. She admitted that she had changed; she was less provocative and aggressive.

Denise's parents had been divorced only 2 years, and the family was still threatened by her father. She was basically afraid of him and tried to avoid him. The first time she referred to her father's aggression, she spoke in an informative and accepting tone. "Growing up in an abusive home himself, he could not be any different," she stated to justify his behavior. As Denise herself was a violent girl with little control over her own behavior, she was suspected of identifying with him. In the next session, a group member who had missed the previous one asked for an update and Denise immediately offered to tell her story again. However, this time she did not provide the basic outline, but rather told the real story. She shared with the group an incident in which her father tried to choke her on one of her visits to him. Since then, she had avoided him when he came for visits. In tears, she shared how terrified she was of his anger. In the therapeutic card game, she selected a card on which a girl sat in a corner protecting her head. However, in PhotoTherapy she brought in a picture of her father that was very different from what she had described earlier: he was in a park, in a good mood. "You see, he can be very different, warm and fun," she added. The girls reinforced her for her mature way of seeing him, looking at both the dark and the bright sides. She felt less fearful and less sad. She talked about her own progress in controlling her behavior, her plans to improve her schoolwork, and her belief that she would be a good mother to her own kids.

Linda's parents had divorced 6 years previously. Linda remembered a lot of fights between them, so she preferred it this way. She saw her father regularly and functioned well in school. In the group, it became clear that she was, indeed, well adjusted. The picture she selected from her family album was of her class, with her in the center, really popular. In the group, she was an excellent participant. She took little time for herself but was helpful to others. She was good at articulating questions to other group members, and, indeed, received feedback from the group about being a central figure, despite her shyness.

Nora's parents divorced when she was very young and both were remarried. She was not allowed to see her father due to court restrictions. In the fourth session, she insisted on sharing her story. She told of a memory of her father and grandmother coming to see her in school; as they were not allowed in, they threw the gift over the fence. Nora was in real pain as she told this story. She also expressed disappointment in her stepfather, "He does not love me." All this time she was in tears. The group was very supportive, but they also tried to understand why her rather was forbidden to see her. They suspected abuse, but she insisted that her mother felt that he was irresponsible and so she tried to protect her. The therapeutic card she selected had two clasped hands; this represented her mother's hand keeping her away from her father. But when Denise talked abut her abusive father, it reminded Nora of rumors she had heard about her father; she also remembered her mother's promise to tell her a secret when she is 18. It seemed that Nora was struggling between repressed memories and her wish to see her father. The group was not the right place to open up this issue; however school personnel confirmed there was sexual abuse in her case.

Jane had been raised by her mother in a single-parent household and did not know who her father was. She was quite lonely and was anxious to get into this group. She seemed shy and withdrawn. At the beginning of the group she was quite invisible. From the start she tried to talk, but each time someone else took a turn and she submitted and kept silent. Finally, the counselor made time for her. Jane told the group that she did not know her father and that her mother responded angrily whenever she brought the issue up. She shared a vague memory of playing with a toy a man had given her when she was five. She envisioned him sitting on the sofa and was obsessed with attempts to remember his face because she thought it was her father. She was angry at her mother for not cooperating, and at her father for abandoning her. She was very sad and emotionally aroused as she spoke, not like her usual communication style. The other girls were attentive and supportive, and Jane became the center of the group for a while. The girls asked questions, showed empathy, and encouraged her to be more assertive with her mother. She was very thankful to the group and reported feeling relieved. The next time Jane spoke, it was through the therapeutic cards. She selected a card of three judges sitting at a table, explaining that her mother constantly criticized her and had extremely high expectations of her. The group encouraged her to talk to her mother and explain how she felt, and they role-played the conversation.

In another session, Jane communicated by showing a picture from her album in which she was riding a horse. She explained that she loved animals and that they substituted for friends. During this process, the group provided feedback about her behavior with friends; they told her that she was always submissive, avoidant, and therefore lonely. They also offered her friendship, encouraged her to initiate relationships, provided positive feedback, and pointed to her behavior in the group (here-and-now). She accepted this feedback by suggesting that she might try riding horses in a group, rather than by herself. In the last group session, she was the one to bring in a cake. She had become more assertive, and when someone asked for the puppet she was holding (which someone brought to the last session), she assertively refused. Most importantly, she reported insisting that her mother reveal to her who her father was, and she did.

Sandy was a baby when her parents divorced, but she lived with her father. She saw her mother on a regular basis and had a good relationship with her. As it was unusual for the father to receive custody, the group was occupied with the question of why she did not live with her mother. For a long while, Sandy insisted that she did not know, then Laura asked, "How come your mom doesn't fight for you?" It was then that Sandy told the group that her mother had been fighting for 6 years, but her father managed to prove each time that she was unstable. For the first time in her life, Sandy disclosed the secret that her mother was depressed following her birth. She was extremely ashamed about this. But when Linda responded by saying that her mother was depressed too, this normalized the situation. The group pointed out to Sandy that she was lucky because both of her parents wanted her. This seemed to change her perception of her situation, because she reported having good conversations with both parents that week. She talked with her mother about her childhood and they laughed a lot. Her major accomplishment in the group was that she came to realize that both parents really love her.

Laura was six when her parents divorced, and both had new relationships, but she felt bad about both. She presented psychosomatic symptoms and fainted quite often for no physical reason. She was still coping with anger at her father, and was preoccupied with his upcoming wedding. She fainted just before the wedding and refused to attend it. The picture from her family album showed the whole family with her held in her father's arms. She was still holding on to the fantasy of her parents reuniting. The group responded mostly to her anger. They showed her how much her father really wanted her to be at the wedding and to be part of his new life. They also dealt with her misperceptions regarding his stepdaughters. They challenged her about her avoidant behavior and encouraged her to be more friendly and cooperative. She finally agreed that she was fighting a hopeless battle. She realized that her parents would never live together again, and was ready now to accept this as fact.

In general, although all of the girls had enough time to adjust to the divorce, they were at different stages and faced unique issues, despite the common background. Gail struggled with unfinished business and Denise with anxiety due to her father's violence. Nora fought repressed memories and rumors of sexual abuse and Jane was confused about her faceless father. Sandy struggled with denial of a depressed mother, and Laura struggled with her father's upcoming wedding. In the open unstructured process, each group member could focus on her unique problem rather than sharing similarities. Because each girl concentrated on her own major difficulties, they were all able to undergo cathartic experiences and release some of their strongest negative feelings. Finally, they gained considerably from the interpersonal interactions. Linda, for example, was well adjusted to the situation of divorce, but being able to challenge and support other group members was to her great advantage, as well as to the group. She might have gotten very little in terms of learning about dealing with divorce, but she gained a great deal of self-confidence from her interaction with group members. All this was accomplished in a short-term group consisting of only 14 sessions, led by a novice school counselor. Thus, it is possible to conduct such groups within the school schedule and by school personnel, to the benefit of these children.

RESEARCH ON GROUPS OF CHILDREN OF DIVORCE

I now discuss two studies on groups for children of divorce, both of which were process research. As they have not been published, they are described in greater detail than previous studies cited so far.

One preliminary study of a single case (Sagi, 2000) compared an educational group and a counseling group. Both groups were comprised of five adolescents each, with mixed genders, and were led by the same school counselor, a novice in mental health. One group followed the educational program developed by Morganett (1990), and the other one was a counseling group of an expressive–supportive type, as described in this book. For the investigation, two scales were used, developed by Smead and Morganett: Dealing with a Divorce in the Family (Morganett, 1990) and Coping with Divorce (Smead, 1995). The first scale measured attitudes toward divorce—for example, "I think people who get married should never get divorced." The second scale measured coping skills—for example, "I think I can learn to cope with my problems." A comparison of scores at the beginning and end of the intervention revealed that the adolescents in the counseling groups gained significantly more on both the attitude scale ($M = 2.80$–3.05 and $M = 2.75$–3.24, for educational and counseling groups, respectively; $Z = 2.70$, $p <$ .01) and the coping scale ($M = 2.60$–3.05 and 2.75–3.24, for educational and counseling groups, respectively; $Z = 2.35$ $p < .05$). In addition, transcripts of the second, fifth, and seventh sessions were analyzed using two verbal behaviors of the Client Behavior System (Hill & O'Brien, 1999): Cognitive Exploration and Affective Exploration. In the educational group, cognitive exploration was more frequent (a total of 56 responses), compared to the counseling group (a total of 39 responses). In contrast, frequency of affective exploration was less frequent in the educational groups (12) than the counseling group (27).

This study had many limitations, including the single-case design, the small group size, and the unequal numbers of boys and girls in each group. However, the results suggest that counseling groups of a nonstructured type may be at least as effective as educational groups for children of divorce. Further investigation is definitely needed to arrive at a conclusion regarding the effectiveness of counseling groups. The process investigation was even more interesting, as it points to adherence of the intervention to the theoretical orientation offered in this book. Results indeed indicate that psycho-educational groups are geared to learning, however counseling groups of an expressive–supportive modality are geared to experiencing. A replication of this study on a larger sample is needed to confirm the different processes in the two types of groups. Further research, which will connect such processes with outcomes, will permit a conclusion regarding the accountability of each type of group. Such research is largely missing in the professional literature.

A second study (Shechtman, Halevi, & Avraham, 2005) compared self-disclosure processes in counseling groups for children of divorce and for children of intact families. The assumption was that the self-disclosures made by children of divorce would focus more on their family and feelings than would self-disclosures made by children in the other groups. The study was comprised of 32 elementary-school children, 16 from divorced families and 16 from intact families. Children in each category were broken down into three small groups for the intervention. Self-disclosure was measured through the Self-Disclosure Preadolescence Scale developed by Vondracek and Vondracek (1971), based on transcripts of audio taped group sessions. The original scale included eight domains of self-disclosure, on two levels of intimacy (simple and intimate), of which this study used three domains: Family, Friends, and Self.

Results indicated that children of divorce discussed mostly family issues, particularly on the intimate level. In fact, intimate self-disclosure on family issues was about eight times more frequent in these groups than in the groups of children from intact families ($M = 3.19$ and $M = 0.31$ for the divorce children and the other children, respectively; $\chi^2(1) = 19.13, p < .001$). Thus, when children of divorce are free to select a topic of concern, they choose mainly family issues, even though the intervention is not specifically structured around such content. One could speculate that the counselor directs the conversation according to the type of children in the group. However, the transcripts showed that the counselors in both groups used the same techniques—cards, pictures from the family album, and bibliotherapy—yet the conversation developed in different directions.

The advantages of unstructured interventions is that children are not limited to a previously selected topic and are free to bring up their major concerns in the here-and-now, as illustrated in the aforementioned cases. As they get to pick the issue of their greatest concern, there is a greater chance that they will undergo cathartic experiences, considered the key to emotional healing (K. R. Greenberg, 2002; Hill, 2005; Spiegel & Claussen, 2000), focus on their main problems, and try to understand and resolve their unique issues. It is important to reiterate that these two studies refer to processes only. More research is needed in regard to outcomes of such groups for children of divorce.

SUMMARY

Groups for children of divorce are quite common in the school setting, as it is clear to educators that these children are coping with a great deal stress, for which they need support. However, most of the group interventions offered to these children are psycho-educational and focus on specific content drawn from knowledge of the difficulties they go through. As with other issues, in this case, too, my colleagues and I offer children of divorce unstructured counseling groups in which each child can deal with his or her unique difficulties. We have found that, despite the uniqueness of the problem for each participant, there is a lot of commonality; children help each other by sharing feelings, experiences, attitudes, and ways of coping.

Research in this area is very limited, which does not permit a conclusion regarding the efficacy of these groups for children of divorce. Nonetheless, the two process studies and the clinical illustrations indicate that the type of group my colleagues and I offer is well suited to children of divorce.

14 Group Counseling for Aggressive Children and Adolescents

Joe was a member of a group for aggressive children. He was angry, considered the most aggressive child in his class. His parents were divorced and there was a history of parental abuse. At the very first session, during the getting acquainted activity, he expressed his great need to protect himself. When the children were asked to select one of the objects displayed in the room that was meaningful to them, he picked a rock, explaining, "I need to be ready for any event." In a later session, following the reading of *The Soul Bird*, he chose to open the drawer of anger, explaining, "When someone bugs me or is angry with me, the drawer of anger immediately opens up, and I have no control over it." Joe felt he was a victim of his parents' relationship, which made him extremely angry. At a later session, he stated, "I wanted to hit them back, but I couldn't, so I hit someone else; it helps me get rid of the anger. ... It is so natural for me to hit, almost an automatic reaction."

These are a few statements that Joe made during the group process, which help one understand the profile of an angry and aggressive 10-year-old boy. Aggression was modeled to him at home; he was a victim of physical abuse and always on the defensive. Being strong and a threat to others was a safer position than being victimized, so he hung on to his aggression; these were secondary rewards that were hard to give up. Moreover, it was a pattern of behavior well established and difficult to change. It was not easy to challenge this boy's perception of life and feelings of frustration and anger, and it was difficult to make him stop his aggressive behavior.

But Joe did change. Teacher evaluations indicated a dramatic reduction of aggression in his case. Analysis of session transcripts showed that the number of statements he made endorsing aggression dropped sharply over time, and were virtually absent in the last three sessions. Moreover, his responsiveness to others, statements of empathy, and insight increased with time. Joe provided an explanation for this change in the last session, when participants were asked to summarize the group experience:

166

"When I can talk about things that bother me and people listen to me, I am open to listen to others. When they yell, I yell back." In the group he demonstrated high levels of self-disclosure, and received highly empathic and supportive responses from peers and the group counselor. Under such conditions of acceptance and respect, he could see the risks of his behavior and make plans for change (for a full description of the group process and outcomes, see Shechtman, 1999).

Parental and family characteristics, particularly social interaction processes, are fundamentally related to antisocial and aggressive behavior (Dodge, 2002; Pettit, Laird, Dodge, Bates, & Criss, 2001). Harsh discipline and psychological control have been found to be highly related to aggressive behavior (Dishion & Patterson, 1997). Dodge (2002) provided an explanation of how parents influence their children's behavior. He suggested that socialization experiences are stored in memory as knowledge structures, which then serve as a proximal guide for the processing of social cues, which in turn results directly in social behavior. Other (e.g., Eisenberg, Fabes, & Murphy, 1996) studies on parental socialization techniques have shown that mothers who are punitive, nonattentive to needs, and devalue their children's difficulties raise angry and antisocial children, whereas mothers who are attentive, encourage the expression of emotions, and help their children solve their difficulties have children high in social competence and empathic behavior. A recent study (Birani-Nasaraladin, 2004) found that the degree to which a mother is stressed, punitive, and devalues her child's stress is positively related to the child's level of aggression; in contrast, encouragement and attendance to feelings are negatively related to children's aggression. Moreover, a change in maternal socialization responses was found to be directly related to the reduction of aggression on some of the measures (Shechtman & Birani-Nasaraladin, in press).

In short, parenting style that reflects warmth, high involvement with the child, and consistent discipline may prevent childhood aggression. However, it has been well established that, in addition to family factors, there is a wide range of additional variables, including biological, individual, peer, school and neighborhood, all affecting a child's level of aggression (Farrington, 1997). Unfortunately, therapists do not have control over many of these risk factors; they have only the child, and the question is how one can help aggressive children and adolescents in schools.

Most of the interventions offered are drawn from cognitive–behavioral theories. They suggest that cognitive processes intervene between risk factors and antisocial behavior (Dodge, 1991; Eron, 1997). Aggressive children seem to be different from other children, particularly in their social information processing, argued Dodge (1991). As a result, interventions focus on training children in cognitive problem solving skills. Although I agree that aggressive children are driven by faulty misperceptions and lack of problem solving skills, I believe that aggression is a complicated behavior resulting from multiple sources and therefore must be addressed by a multiorientation approach.

A COUNSELING INTERVENTION OF A COGNITIVE TYPE

Most of the cognitive-based interventions offered to children are labeled anger management, rather than aggression control. Fleckenstein and Horne (2004) suggested the following outline:

First, develop awareness to anger, evaluate the function of their anger and replace anger with more effective responses. Second, learn relaxation skills to self-calm and develop self-talk that will calm the proactive response. Third, learn problem solving skills. Finally, increase the effectiveness of communication skills. (p. 555)

The components of this intervention are drawn from cognitive orientations that currently prevail in most interventions with angry and aggressive individuals. However, to be effective, aggressive people need to be motivated to make a change. "Perhaps the best predictor of a positive outcome is the willingness of a client to honestly examine and admit the consequences of poor anger control," argued McKay (1992, p. 164). My colleagues and I have, indeed, identified motivation to be the key factor in the treatment of aggressive children, which led to the development of a unique group intervention with them.

INTERVENTION BY MY COLLEAGUES AND MYSELF

Dodge (1991) made an important distinction between proactive and reactive aggression. Proactive or instrumental aggression refers to intentional, deliberate, controlled, goal-oriented misuse of power to achieve an external goal. Reactive aggression refers to a less controlled outburst of anger that appears to be a defensive reaction to frustration or threat. A subcategory often seen in schools is bullying, which is a proactive type of aggression used mostly to gain social power, targeted repeatedly at a weak victim and performed in a group (Olweus, 2001). Sometimes it is difficult to distinguish the various types, because accumulative frustrations may become the basis for proactive aggression and for bullying. Broadly speaking, proactive aggressors are more frequently engaged in violent and delinquent behavior, and reactive aggressors are the common population in the school settings, with whom my colleagues and I most often work.

Due to established patterns of aggression, secondary gratification, lack of emotional empathy, and difficulties connecting with their own emotions, aggressive children do not find it easy to acquire newly learned skills. When my coworkers and I first meet our aggressive students, most are unaware of their negative behavior. In fact, they perceive themselves as victims who only react to the provocations of others to defend themselves. It is impossible to offer them a change process without going through a whole therapeutic cycle. That means first creating a strong client–therapist alliance; then exploring their emotions that lead to aggression, looking at the consequences of their behavior and enhancing insight into their motives and acts; and finally working on behavior change. Motivation is the key to success.

As explained in earlier chapters, my coworkers and I work within a theoretically integrative approach (Hill, 2005; Prochaska, 1999), with a strong focus on emotional expressiveness. As the program progresses and motivation is raised, we move to the cognitive theories, providing instrumental assistance to promote behavior change.

However, the intervention with aggressive children differs from most groups discussed earlier in the book. First, the program is more structured than the usual nonstructured groups my coworkers and I conduct. This is necessary in light of the unique focus of the group and the disciplinary problems that these participants present. We found that aggressive children demonstrate four central areas of deficits that must be addressed: they are unclear about how to handle anger, have issues revolving around power struggles, are unaware of the consequences of their actions, and do not know how to solve problems or control themselves. These four themes establish the content of our semistructured intervention for aggressive children.

Second, because of the high level of resistance to change, my colleagues and I believe that an indirect method of treatment is less threatening and more appealing to these children. Therefore, we use bibliotherapy as an adjunct to the therapy process. Through the process of identification with literary characters, children recognize familiar feelings, release disturbing emotions, and connect with their own feelings and behavior. The stories, poems, and films focus on the four themes just delineated. Several poems are used to discuss emotions that lead to aggression and its control. In one poem, a boy is angry because he is frustrated; in another, he is jealous. Each of these poems is a trigger to discuss reasons for anger and ways children react to it. Two pieces of literature deal with power issues: a story that relates to the need for social power and a poem that deals with the difficulty to forgive. A film and a story are used to demonstrate the long-term consequences of aggressive behavior. Finally, problems of self-control are discussed through two poems; in the first the monster of each child is explored, and in the second they become their own commanders (develop self-control).

The children like the program because they enjoy stories, poems, and films, perceiving them as playful rather than therapeutic. In his book, *The Wonder of Boys*, Guerian (1997) suggested that all children love stories, but aggressive boys actually need them to reconnect with their own emotions. Pollack (1998) argued that boys are incapable of expressing feelings or even connecting with them. Without attending to one's emotions, it is difficult to develop self-awareness, which is a first step to change. Moreover, it seems easier to develop empathy to literary figures than to real people. Even tough children who have great difficulty relating to another person's pain may soften up in response to the suffering of a literary character. Finally, the literature presents coping skills and alternative behavior to aggression that children may identify with and learn from. In sum, through the use of literature the children develop the ability to express their difficulties and emotions, enhance their ability to empathize with the suffering of others, and gain more control over their own behavior—all leading to reduced aggression.

In this 10-session program, stories are adjusted to the participants' age level, but the content and method of intervention is similar. The process is comprised of several phases. First, the leader reads the literary piece to the children. When this reading is clear and accurate, the children go through an identification process in which similar feelings are aroused. Next, feelings of the literary character are identified. A lot of the feelings that come up are projections made by the children; however, more feelings are gathered to increase the repertoire of emotions. This also enhances empathy and perspective-taking skills. Then, a discussion of the dynamics underlying the characters' behavior is held. This is an opportunity to enhance children's understanding of social situations and problem-solving patterns without much threat. Finally, children are invited to share similar emotions or experiences. This is when the direct therapeutic process begins. The children are encouraged to express themselves, explore their feelings, and look at reasons for their behavior. When they admit that they have a problem, clarifying processes are used to help them examine pros and cons of their behavior. At this point, they are attached to the counselor and the other group members, and are more capable of learning from the feedback of others. The turning point comes when they realize the price they pay for their aggression; it is then that they are ready to make a change, to discuss alternative behaviors to aggression, and to commit themselves to make an effort to give up their aggression.

In addition to the use of bibliotherapy, these groups operate within an integrative orientation, and include the therapeutic factors necessary in a group, such as catharsis, interpersonal learning, and group cohesiveness. To promote interpersonal learning, the composition of a group is crucial. A group made entirely of aggressive boys may have a negative influence, as reported by Dishion and colleagues (1999). Therefore, my colleagues and I add nonaggressive children to the group and, when possible, put aggressors and their victims in the same group. The following illustrates the importance of a heterogeneous group composition.

The group was comprised of five 12-year-old children—three aggressive (2 boys and 1 girl) and 2 nonaggressive (a boy and a girl). They had just heard a poem about a group of older children who hit a younger child because he was cheating. The three aggressive children argued that the younger child must hit back; Mary stated that he must protect himself, and Roy and Tony agreed, explaining that if he doesn't, he will always remain a victim. In contrast, Susan and Randy, the two nonaggressive children, said that the problem could be resolved without a fight, for instance, by repeating the rules of the game to the younger child or just giving in. "Sometimes it is smart just to forget about it," Randy said. When they later discussed their own experiences, Roy said, "Now I think that if I just gave in to the little boy when he cheated me at the card game, I would not have gotten into trouble." Tony responded; "I always get punished by my father because of my cousin. Maybe it's not worth it." Mary shared her pride in managing a dispute with her mom by giving in. The aggressive children, having had an opportunity to hear different perceptions from peers, and as a result of how the counselor led the session, were able to change some of their perceptions.

DESCRIPTION OF A GROUP PROCESS

The group was composed of four fourth-grade students: two aggressive boys, one victimized girl, and one girl without problem. Jimmy was the perpetrator and Alice was often his victim. For several sessions, Jimmy expressed his endorsement of aggression. He seemed to be proud of being strong and liked to present a threat to others. In the second session, the students discussed the poem "The Inner Anger," in which a boy finds it difficult to tolerate the anger growing inside him. Although the discussion still focused on the literary figure, Jimmy said, "I would break the TV.". Later, however, when they were asked to share related experiences, he could not think of any. This session highlighted the importance of using an indirect approach with aggressive children. Jimmy certainly identified with the boy in the poem and reacted spontaneously, but was still resistant and could not admit to his aggression at that early stage of the group.

In the next session, the group discussed another poem on anger. Jimmy seemed quite restless and was picking on Alice. She complained to the leader, who in turn encouraged her to talk directly to Jimmy. Alice told him that she was hurt, to which he responded, "Who cares?" The leader intervened, suggesting that Jimmy may have had an unfortunate slip of the tongue and forgotten the rule of "no insulting" in the group. By saying this, the leader continued to build an alliance with Jimmy while blocking his negative behavior. At this point, Jimmy was aware of his behavior but unwilling to make a change. Alice, on the other hand, found the courage to confront him.

The fourth session focuses on uncontrolled aggression through discussion of a monster that controls one's behavior. Jimmy thought the boy was using the monster as an excuse and that he could actually control it. Jacqui confronted him about his own lack of control, and, in contrast to earlier sessions, he was not resistant; later in the session, he even admitted that he sometimes lost control. When Alice talked about how she relaxed, Jimmy said, "I don't know how to relax." Jimmy was definitely progressing, but not yet willing to make a change.

The fifth session focused on forgiveness, starting with a poem. First, the group identified feelings of the literary figure (confusion, anger, fear of losing power). Then the children discussed the dynamics of forgiveness (the need to continue being angry, the need to be in power) and ways to deal with forgiveness (change perception, think empathically, share feelings). Finally, the leaders asked the children to relate to forgiveness by placing themselves on a continuum from 1 (*never forgive*) to 10 (*always forgive*). Jimmy gave himself a 5, admitting that he found it difficult to forgive. Alice gave herself a 10, crying as she explained, "I always give in. I forgive children even when they insult me." The leader comforted her and turned to the group for responses. Donna recognized Alice's pain, and Jimmy, who seemed quite moved by this scenario, said, "I think she is crying because of me, too. I pick on her and hurt her quite often, and she keeps on giving me things that I don't deserve." The counselor suggested that Jimmy talk directly to Alice, and he continued, "I can try to think before I hurt." Mark confessed that he, too, had similar experiences with Alice and asked for her forgiveness. This session was a turning point; Jimmy has progressed to a new stage of change following an exchange of honest and genuine interaction among group members. And Alice was encouraged by the boys' responses.

The last group session ends with the poem "My Own Commander," focusing on the topic of self-control. Following the discussion, Jimmy declared that he had made a decision to control himself, but honestly raised reservations about his abilities to do so. The leader turned to the group to generate their encouragement, and the other children provided support: "I think he can make it," "He can if he tries hard." Armed with the group's support and trust, Jimmy decided to give it a try and make an effort. The group discussed how self-control indicated power rather than weakness (cognitive restructuring), and offered ways to control anger and relax, such as sharing with a close person, writing about it, participating in sports, and watching TV (sublimation techniques). At termination Jimmy declared that he was progressing, "This week I wasn't angry even once. I did not lose my temper, which is good." "What is good?" asked the counselor. "That I am beating the anger; this feels good." Beating the uncontrolled anger had become a challenge to Jimmy, signifying progress to the stage of change.

Jimmy was a difficult case, and yet progress seemed to take place. It is hard to conclude from this scenario if Jimmy would indeed change his behavior, but the empirical evidence that complemented this study indicated progress on all dimensions measured: He increased dramatically in empathy and decreased the level of aggression by self- and teacher report (see Shechtman, 2001). That is, evidence for actual change in behavior is quite salient. Of course, it is difficult to generate a conclusion from a single case; more can be learned from intensive research on this program.

OUTCOME RESEARCH

My colleagues and I have done research that involves mostly boys, as they make up the majority of aggressors in the school. Several studies (Shechtman, 2000, 2003; Shechtman & Nachshol, 1996) involving hundreds of aggressive boys, from regular and special education settings, measured the change in level of aggression following treatment. These studies employed a quasi-experimental design, mostly using Achenbach's (1991a, 1991b) self- and teacher reports. Results indicated a significant difference between experimental and control groups following treatment, with a significant reduction of aggression in the former and an increase in the latter groups. Attitudes endorsing aggression did not decrease following treatment, but they increased in the control group, which led to a significant difference between the groups.

Two additional studies (Shechtman, 2003; Shechtman & Ben-David, 1999) were conducted with the aim of comparing outcomes for individual and group treatment using the described program. Results of both studies showed that children who received treatment had a reduced level of aggression compared to children in the control group on both measures, regardless of the format of treatment (individual or group). These findings suggest not only that the intervention is effective, but also that counseling groups are preferable to individual therapy, because they produce comparable results and are more cost effective.

The results of these studies are also important from a theoretical point of view. Although groups for angry and aggressive children are recommended in the literature (Alpert & Spillmann, 1997), reservations have also been raised regarding the negative influence that aggressive children may have on each other. In fact, Dishion and colleagues (1999) reported results of studies showing such negative effects. The finding that group counseling is as effective as individual treatment challenges those reservations. Overall, these studies have suggested that expressive–supportive therapy is effective with aggressive children and adolescents.

PROCESS RESEARCH

Change Process (Prochaska, 1999). As questionnaires are sometimes criticized for being subject to social desirability or the halo effect, particularly in the case of children and adolescents, my fellow researchers and I were interested in observational data as well. As we routinely transcribe the sessions of each group, we were able to look at the processes in them. We were particularly interested in the change process. Using Prochaska's (1999) theory of change, it was interesting to track change among our treatment children.

Two studies investigated the change process of aggressive boys, both indicating that as treatment progresses, children move to higher stages of change. The first study (Shechtman & Ben-David, 1999) showed that in the first four sessions, 20%–25% of the children were at the unawareness stage, and 20%–45% were at the stage of awareness with no intention to change. Motivation to change increased from 12% to 36% over these sessions, but there was almost no attempt to take action toward change. The fifth session seemed to have been a turning point. Unawareness decreased with time, until only 3% of the children remained at this stage in the last session, whereas 20% remained in the stage of awareness with no intention to change, 40% were at the preparation stage, showing some motivation to change, and 21% reported making efforts to restrict their aggression. Overall, almost 47% of the children reached the last stage at some point along the group process, and 83% expressed motivation to make a change. Undesirable statements (lack of awareness and no wish to change) decreased with time, whereas desirable statements (wish to change and attempts to modify behavior) increased during the process of treatment, as can be seen in Figure 7.

This pattern of change was also tested in a correlation analysis between session number and the percentage of statements at each stage of change. Results indicated a significant relationship between the expected process of change and the course of treatment, particularly for behavior in the first and last stages (lack of awareness and attempts to modify aggression, respectively).

The results of the second study (Shechtman, 2003) also indicated that at the onset of therapy, only a few children (about 10%) had reached the preparation or action

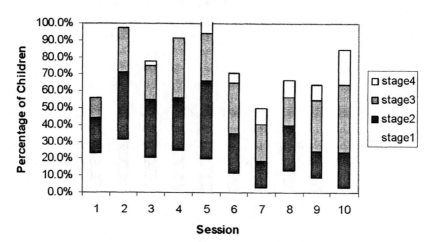

Figure 14.1. Percentage of children making at least one statement representing a stage of change, by group session (Shechtman & Ben-David, 1999).

stage. In contrast, at termination, most children had reached one of these two advanced stages (close to 80%). These results were similar for individual and group treatment (see Figure 8).

A regression analysis concluded that the probability of reaching a higher stage of change increases significantly as treatment progresses. This not only replicates earlier results, but also stresses the importance of the duration of treatment. More research with longer periods of time is required to see if longer periods of treatment would engage more children in the change process.

It is clear that most of the children were unaware of their problem behavior when my colleagues and I first met them. Any attempt to teach them skills at this stage was doomed to failure. Thus, a therapeutic process based on establishing a therapist–client alliance and group cohesiveness was needed before trying to modify behavior. These results also indicate that about half of the treatment children do not modify their behavior, and many are stuck in the preparation stage. Perhaps many need a longer process than 10 sessions.

Nevertheless, overall, the results of the change process support the outcomes seen from the questionnaires. Moreover, the similarity of processes in individual and group treatment explains the equal outcomes of treatment in these two formats.

Participant Feedback

When the boys treated for aggression were asked about the mechanisms that helped them make a change (Shechtman, 2000), most mentioned catharsis as their most meaningful experience (52%), interpersonal learning was next (38%), and socializa-

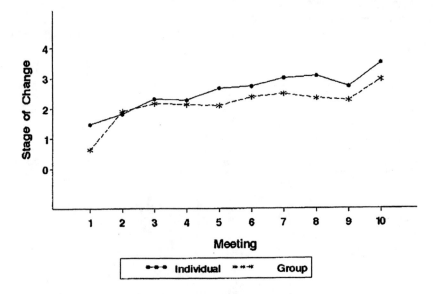

Figure 14.2. The change process as a function of treatment sessions in individual and group treatment (Shechtman, 2003).

tion techniques were third (26%). Interestingly, group cohesiveness was infrequently mentioned (12%) in this study, in contrast to studies on other groups (see Chapter 3), but this makes sense: These groups are relatively small and focus more on behavior change of the individual within the group, rather than on an interactional style (Yalom & Leszcz, 2005). Moreover, based on clinical experience, it becomes very clear that being able to expresses oneself in an accepting climate is the most important component of treatment (see the introductory illustration in this chapter). Because the focus is on aggressive behavior, there is obviously less group support. This may also explain the relative infrequency of group cohesion as a therapeutic factor, as cohesiveness in children's groups is primarily a function of supportive reactions (Shechtman & Gluk, 2005).

Treatment of Mothers of Aggressive Children

As parental characteristics, particularly social interaction processes, are related to children's aggression, an attempt was made to treat mothers of aggressive children as well. The study in question (Shechtman & Birani-Nasaraladin, in press) compared mother-and-child treatments with child treatment only and with a no-treatment control group (25 participants in each treatment condition). The intervention was based on the same program previously described, adjusted to participants' level (e.g., literature for mothers was different from that of the children). Results indicated that, compared to the control group, both treatment conditions were effective in reducing aggression, but the mother-and-child groups showed significantly higher gains on the self-report measure. Moreover, results of treatment measures after 3 months pointed to sustained progress. This is definitely not a long enough period to prove the long-term effectiveness of a program; nevertheless it is an important outcome, because it at least puts to rest the suspicion of a halo effect.

Mothers showed improved parenting responses following intervention, and their gains were correlated with the child's reduced aggression on some of the subscales. These results replicate and support earlier studies. They also show that mothers can be helped to change harsh disciplinary techniques. Finally, they indicate that change in maternal strategies may reduce aggressive behavior of children. The study highlighted the effectiveness of a broad-based treatment for mothers of aggressive children, a conclusion quite in opposition to common beliefs favoring cognitive–behavioral treatments.

The Unique Contribution of Bibliotherapy

Finally, as the treatment of aggression uses bibliotherapy as an adjunct to treatment, my colleagues and I were interested in the unique contribution of this method to treatment outcomes. Although the study (Shechtman, 2006) was based on individual treatment, its results are relevant. It included 48 aggressive clients with an age range of 12–16. These adolescents were randomly assigned to experimental (bibliotherapy + helping sessions) and control (helping sessions only) groups. Both operated with the same integrative theoretical orientation, the only difference being the addition of bibliotherapy. Results indicated that, in the experimental group, children exhibited greater empathy than their peers in the control group; counselors reported higher satisfaction; children reported therapeutic change at termination more frequently; and they had higher frequencies of insight and therapeutic change on the Hill and O'Brien (1999) measure. These results suggest that bibliotherapy may make a unique contribution to the treatment of aggression.

SUMMARY

Overall, all these studies consistently and widely support this type of group treatment for aggressive children. The outcomes indicate its effectiveness in reducing short-term aggression, although lasting effects need yet to be proved. The process research suggests that children are progressing throughout the course of group counseling and psychotherapy and are working effectively along the process. Working with parents seems to be an effective avenue that deserves further exploration. When children are asked for feedback on the intervention, they mention cathartic and emotional experiencing, learning from each other, and gains in socializing skills most frequently. Following is feedback by Leon, a 15-year-old highly aggressive boy:

> I feel much better now and much less stressed. It helped me that I could talk and explain myself; it is different from when I get punished or when they yell at me. ... I would recommend to other children who have problems to join such a group because it might help them just to talk about their difficulties; it will make it easier for them to handle their stress.

These outcome and process research results provide strong evidence for the effectiveness of an integrative theoretical model for the treatment of aggressive boys. The focus on affect is diametrically opposed to the cognitive–behavioral treatments currently prevailing in work with aggressive children. Yet, expressing strong emotions in an accepting climate, and reflecting on them, seems to be the path to raising motivation to change, which can then be followed by a cognitive discussion of ways to reduce aggression.

15 Group Counseling for Adolescents of a Different Culture: The Case of Arabs

Multiculturalism has become an important discipline and a primary source for explaining human development and functioning (Lee, 1997). Pederson (2000) predicted that multiculturalism will be the "fourth force" (p. 183) in counseling, following the psychoanalytic, humanistic, and cognitive–behavioral forces. Mental health professionals agree that awareness of cultural influences is essential for understanding clients, and they use common knowledge about each unique culture to predict their behavior. However, these predictions are rarely investigated scientifically.

In the context of group counseling and psychotherapy, cultural influences can clearly impact behavior and the group process. Self-disclosure is a fundamental behavior in groups, the force that underlies all therapeutic factors (Yalom & Leszcz, 2005), and is expected of all members. It is a sign of motivation to work on personal issues and trust in group members and the leader. Participants in group counseling are expected to undergo cathartic experiencing and altruistically share personal thoughts and feelings. Moreover, they are expected to provide honest and direct feedback to each other, challenge individuals in the group, and take risks. But all these are Western ideas about group processes that may not fit other cultures. The Asian culture, for example, values thoughts and doing more than feeling. The expression of feelings, therefore, is not appreciated, and direct verbal communication is not valued. Altruistic and spontaneous sharing of personal information or challenging individuals in the group may also be inhibited. And as the leader is perceived as an authoritative expert, group members may refrain from initiating a move or taking risks, assuming that it is the leader's role to conduct the group (see DeLucia-Waack & Donigian, 2004).

These different behaviors are driven by culture, defined as a set of concepts, values, beliefs, expectations, and norms that particularly affect interpersonal behavior (Hifstede, 1997). Culture is not only external but also within the person, limiting the individuals' behavior more than any demographic variable (Pederson, 2000). One's multicultural identities—the race, ethnicity, and groups one belongs to—deeply affect one's ways of thinking and behaving, even how one responds emotionally (Ivey, Pederson, & Ivey, 2001).

Non-Western groups have common cultural codes of behavior and restrictions that stem from the social structure of their families and communities. These are often collectivistic societies (as opposed to the individualistic Western society), in which the welfare of the collective is more important than that of the individual. Family structure is based on hierarchy, obligation, and duties, and independent behavior or expression of emotions that might disrupt family harmony is discouraged. The family is patriarchal; males—particularly the father and eldest son—have dominant roles. This is how the Asian culture is often described (Chi-Ying Chung, 2004; Sue & Sue, 2003). As a result of these different social structures and cultures, all major professional associations (American Psychological Association [APA], American Counseling Association [ACA], Association for Specialists in Group Work [ASGW]) expect group leaders to provide services that are culturally responsive. The implications include structuring the group and making it more didactic, assuming a more authoritative leadership position, and using appropriate interventions (Chi-Ying Chung, 2004; Rivera, Garrett, & Brown-Crutchfield, 2004).

The Arab culture, which is the focus of this chapter, perfectly fits the description of these non-Western cultures. On the whole, it is considered a collectivistic society in which the family, community, and religion are more important than the individual (Al-Kernawi, 1998; Barakat, 1993). Moreover, the family has a clear hierarchical structure, in which the father is the head of the pyramid and men are more important than women (Jackson, 1997). As family harmony must be maintained under all circumstances, mental health problems are usually unaccepted and kept a secret; they are perceived as a threat to the family's reputation and honor. For this reason, and because the family is the provider of all types of support, individuals with problems are expected to turn to the family for assistance rather than to professional help (Dwairy, 1998; Masalla, 1999; Savaya, 1998).

Owing to these cultural structures and norms, one might expect Arab children and adolescents to inhibit their behavior in groups and for this to be reflected in the content of their disclosures. However, both the research and the practice conducted by my colleagues and myself indicate that very little of these reservations hold true. It should be noted, though, that all our groups are homogeneous in respect to ethnicity and are led by Arab counselors. Homogeneity helps members with group cohesiveness (Yalom & Leszcz, 2005), which in turn encourages other necessary behaviors. Moreover, the counselor is familiar with the culture and aware of sensitive issues in the group process. These two factors are extremely important for the success of these groups.

RESEARCH ON GROUPS FOR ARAB CHILDREN AND ADOLESCENTS

First, my colleagues and I investigated the desire to participate in a counseling group and willingness to disclose personal information during the process (Shechtman, Haddad, & Nechas, 2000), comparing 50 Arab and 50 Jewish adolescents. The former group was comprised of two seventh-grade classes in one Arab school, and the latter was comprised of two seventh-grade classes in a Jewish school, each in a major Israeli city (one with a predominantly Arab population and the other Jewish). As the children were unfamiliar with the concept of groups and how they operate, a video was developed for this study. The video presented the fourth session in a counseling group, including scenarios of self-disclosure in three areas: self, family, and friends. Two versions were prepared (one in each language), and each videotaped group comprised (Arab or Jewish) university students who had been trained in the group process. The film lasted 45 min, following which viewers completed a 12-item questionnaire specifically developed for this study. The questionnaire examined intentions to join a group and disclose private information in the areas of self, family, and friends. For example, in the family scenario, Machmud disclosed a family secret. Respondents were then asked, "Do you respect Machmud's self-disclosure in the group?" and "Would you behave like Machmud if you were in the group?" Similar items referred to the other two areas of self-disclosure. In addition, there were items referring to general expected behavior in the group.

Results indicated differences between the ethnic groups only in two areas of disclosure: family and friends. In both areas, Arab adolescents were more reluctant to self-disclose, as expected. However, no differences were found on the other items. The Arab children were willing to attend a group and actively participate in it, just like their Jewish counterparts. The conclusion of this study was that psychodynamic groups can be safely offered to Arab adolescents, although caution must be taken when dealing with family and friendship issues. Leaders must be prepared to block any pressure on Arab participants to disclose in these two sensitive areas.

In contrast to this first study of intentions, a second study (Shechtman, Hiradin, & Zina, 2003) examined actual behavior in group counseling, investigating 106 ninth graders (54 Arabs and 52 Jews) who participated in 10 counseling groups. All the groups were led according to the psychodynamic orientation presented in this book, with a strong focus on emotional expressiveness. Sessions were recorded and transcribed, allowing measurement of the actual level of self-disclosure. This study used the same three areas of disclosure as in the first study, with the addition of feelings. (Feelings are distinguished from the area of self in that the latter refers to thoughts, expectations, ideas, character, and the like, whereas the former refers solely to the expression of emotions.) In contrast to expectations, it was the Arab group that showed the highest level of self-disclosure. Only on friendship were results equal to those of their Jewish counterparts. Self was the most frequently mentioned topic of disclosure and family was second.

How can this gap between intention to disclose and actual self-disclosure be interpreted? First, it is possible to attribute the results to developmental needs. Adolescents of both ethnic groups struggle with many issues for which the group is a viable place to provide support and guidance. Because they have less opportunities to express themselves honestly and openly, the counseling group might have offered a rare desired opportunity for these adolescents. Second, group processes may be stronger than cultural inhibitions. Once individuals belong to a group in which cohesiveness is developed and norms of self-disclosure are established, the small group becomes the reference group rather than the culture.

This study further analyzed participants' responses to other members' self-disclosure along two dimensions: positive affiliation and negative affiliation. Positive affiliation included responses of affirmation, understanding, loving, nurturing, and protecting; negative affiliation included ignoring, attacking, rejecting, belittling, and blaming. On both scales, the Arabs scored higher than the Jews, although in both groups positive affiliation was higher than negative affiliation (76% and 70% of responses were positive for Arabs and Jews, respectively). Thus, not only did the Arab adolescents self-disclose, they also responded more positively to other's self-disclosure; but at the same time, they also responded more negatively. Such behavior indicates an ability not only to disclose, but also to be engaged in a spontaneous exchange of feedback among group members—a necessary behavior in group counseling. Finally, no interethnic difference was found on any of the outcome scales (Adjustment). That is, counseling groups were equally effective for Arab adolescents as they were for Jews.

The implication of this study is that counseling groups of an expressive–supportive nature should be offered to Arab adolescents. Such groups are really needed and appear to be effective. Even though Arabs might initially express reservations, they seem to become engaged in the group process and gain from the experience. Because these adolescents are not expected to reach out for counseling, it should be offered to them. Nevertheless, there are certain practical aspects that must be taken into account. In groups that express reservations regarding self-disclosure, it is necessary to adjust leadership style, methods of intervention, and techniques. Leaders must also protect members who continue showing reservations, as it is not easy to give up cultural norms.

A third study (Shechtman & Halevi, 2006) investigated university students in a counseling program. There were three groups of Arab trainees ($n = 39$) and two of Jewish trainees ($n = 37$) of the same age, all led by the same experienced counselor. The study included outcome and process measures. Results showed that the Arab trainees reported greater intentions to disclose than their Jewish counterparts. Being in training, these participants were also asked whether their goals for the course were mainly educational (e.g., to learn about groups) or personal (to participate as a group member). Most of the students said they preferred personal goals, with no difference between ethnicities.

Based on transcribed sessions, my colleagues and I also compared the two ethnic groups in terms of the frequency and intimacy level of their self-disclosures in four areas: self, family, friends, and feelings. No difference was found on any of these measures, neither in frequency nor in the level of intimacy. That is, there was no difference between Arab and Jewish participants, not only in their intention to disclose or in their expectations for group counseling, but also in their actual self-disclosures during the group process.

Finally, an analysis of client behavior (Hill & O'Brien, 1999) was conducted, measuring resistance, simple response (collapsing Hill's, original categories of agreement, appropriate request and recounting), cognitive exploration, affective exploration, insight, and therapeutic change. Results indicated that simple response and cognitive exploration were more frequent in the Arab group; resistance, insight, and therapeutic change were less frequent there. The lower rates of resistance and the higher rates of simple response and cognitive exploration are in keeping with findings that Arab participants initially intended to disclose more in the group and focused on personal goals, just like their Jewish counterparts. Their lower rates of insight and therapeutic change raise a question regarding the type of therapy that is most appropriate for this population, as suggested in the literature (Dwairy, 1998). However, the difference between the two groups, although statistically significant, was quite small.

Overall, these three studies suggest minimal differences between the ethnic groups. Moreover, Arabs seem to be more willing to participate in a counseling group and to be capable of functioning effectively. The clinical experiences my colleagues and I have had support these research results.

CLINICAL DATA

First, I discuss a group, comprised of 13-year-old girls, that was conducted in a very conservative Arab village. It is the third session, and the group was celebrating Saya's birthday. These celebrations are common in groups my colleagues and I run (see Chapter 3); they are essentially an opportunity to empower the birthday child. The girls have brought symbolic little gifts but mostly are engaged in providing positive feedback:

- I love Saya and I brought you a nice stone, so that when you look at it, it will remind you of how much I love you.
- I gave you candy because you are sweet and you make others' lives sweeter with your empathic reactions.
- I wrote you a letter expressing my appreciation and love for you.

Saya's reaction was, "I am really excited. It was my happiest day. I did not know that so many girls love me." Feelings were clearly expressed openly and directly with much ease.

The culturally expected restrictions did not apply, perhaps because only positive feedback was expected, but the next activity revealed that the girls were actually capable of much more. They were asked to share a meaningful object that they had brought from home. One girl brought a watch that she had received from her father for her 10th birthday. "It is precious to me because I feel closer to him than to my mom; my mother is always stressed and does not listen." Several other girls joined in, sharing their relationships with their parents. Thus, although the family was expected to be quite taboo for group discussion, these girls raised the topic without any reservations, as early as the third session.

Rima had brought a doll she received from her uncle just before he died. She was anxious to share the story of his death with the group, crying all this time. It was obvious that Rima was going through cathartic experiencing. Following her, two other girls shared the loss of their fathers. They expressed feelings of sadness, longing, and jealousy. The counselor closed the session in a positive tone, asking about their sources of support. They all mentioned the extended family, a male figure from the family who took responsibility of the family, religion, and faith. "My mother always says that it is God's will and that this was his faith," said Rima. The girls appeared to be capable of sharing highly emotional issues and responding with spontaneous warmth and empathy. Also interesting were the coping mechanisms that they mentioned, which are unique to the Arab culture.

In the seventh session, the girls were asked about pleasant and unpleasant experiences, as an opening activity aimed at reexperiencing difficult situations. Two cathartic experiences were evident in this session. Leila talked about the bad accident she had a few years before, after which she had several operations and ended up with a limp. She mostly talked about being bullied because of that limp, and she expressed a great sense of rejection and loneliness. Following cognitive and affective exploration of the situation, and armed with much support from the group, she was able to develop insight:, "Perhaps I am responsible for this situation because I did not want to see anyone; I was scared and sad."

Following this self-disclosure, Walla shared her father's suicide. She had never talked about it outside her family, because committing suicide is forbidden in her culture. But she insisted that she wanted to share the incident with the group. She went into detail, describing how she found him hanging and cut the rope, "I keep going back to this scene, I find it hard to concentrate on my studies, and I have nightmares." The group reacted with much support and encouragement, admiring her cool response to the tragic scene. When asked about her sources of support, she, too, mentioned her family, religion, and faith.

In sum, this is a typical group of girls with few reservations about expressing themselves, sharing altruistically, or providing support. Moreover, the girls were even able to confront each other, a behavior that is not typical of people of this culture. They all talked about family issues, including some deep family secrets. Thus, the expected cultural inhibitions were not evident in this group, even in respect to the content of disclosure.

Another group was comprised of 15-year-old Arab girls. Here, too, there did not seem to be reservations about expressing feelings or sharing personal experiences, although some of the conflicts expressed revealed problems that were culturally related. The third session started with here-and-now feelings. The counselor presented a chart with facial expressions and asked the girls to select the one that best fit their feelings at that time. Nassi expressed sadness following a conflict she had with her older sister. She was crying, extremely upset by her sister's anger. The counselor reflected on her sense of helplessness for not being given a chance to explain herself. However, Iman, another group member, insisted that she should give in and apologize, "because she is older than you." The advice Nassi received from the group included sending her sister a letter and involving a third party. She chose the latter option.

It was only the third session and these girls are already talking about personal experiences related to family. They seemed to build group cohesiveness in a similar way to other groups. But the content of the problem revealed the issue of family hierarchy; older siblings have a unique status, and to some girls at adolescence this may seem really unfair. The resolution of the problem is also interesting, involving indirect action, often through a third person. This suggests that, although the girls seemed able to express their needs in the group, this becomes more difficult in real-life situations where the social structure is clear and norms are well established.

Later in this session, Nawal shared her sense of confusion. She felt that her peers were friendly with her only because of her father, who was highly respected in the village. "It bothers me that people are nice to me only because they want to get something," she said. The group members seemed to be disturbed by this comment, but did not respond. The counselor acknowledged Nawal's feelings, using an interpretation, "You want people to appreciate you for what you are." The response is, "Exactly. I think I have many qualities to make me a good friend." "It seems you are a bit lonely," the counselor continued reflecting her feelings. Nawal admitted that she often felt lonely because the girls misunderstood her quite often. She had spent a few years abroad and, since her return to the village, did not feel a sense of belonging. It was hard for her to give up the freedom she was used to and to accept all the cultural restrictions. She felt that she was different and that people rejected her because of that.

The leader now reflected on her anger; "You sound angry right now," she said. Nawal admitted that she was angry at her peers who criticized her and because of the gossip about her. She openly asked the group for help, "How can I be more easily acculturated in this community?" The group responded with silence, despite the counselor's attempt to elicit the girls' reactions. The counselor reinforced Nawal's courageous self-disclosure and asked the group to respond to her request for help. This was a perfect opportunity for interpersonal feedback, but the girls did not take it. They found it difficult to admit that they, indeed, refrained from getting closer to her, behavior that might have emerged in a group from another culture. They also found it hard to defend themselves against the accusations they just heard.

As the group did not take the role of feedback provision, the counselor tried an interpretation, "Is it possible that your disappointment makes you turn some of your anger against the girls?" After a relatively long silence, Nawal admitted that this might be an accurate interpretation:, "Maybe I make them feel uncomfortable because I don't accept their behavior." Following her expressed self-awareness, the girls were ready to respond, but no one confronted her or provided honest feedback. Maya gently asked her if she ever tried to invite a friend to her home; Nassi advised her to initiate a mutual activity with a friend. Nawal seemed to be open to and appreciative of these suggestions.

At a later session, Salwa shared with the group her grandmother's poor health and cries. Nassi offered her a tissue and patted her on the back. For a long while, Salwa described her pain watching her grandmother deteriorating so rapidly. The counselor challenged her about the anger she heard in Salwa's voice. Salwa admitted that she was angry at her family, particularly her mother, who was disappointing her by her lack of care for her aging mother: "I have learned in this group that we cannot always solve our problems, but we can at least provide support and care. But even this little bit my mother does not give her. I love my mom, but in this case she really disappointed me." The counselor acknowledged Salwa's strength but also her stress, and the group moved into the instrumental support phase, trying to help her find a way to share the responsibility and ease the stress. Interestingly, in this particular case, not only were family issues expressed, but someone even dared to criticize her mother! Other group members shared the death of family members, including the counselor. When Nassi asked her how she coped, she shared with the group her love of writing, and several of the girls identified with her.

Family criticism and family secrets became more frequent as the group progressed. In the 11th session, Iman talked about the restrictions in her home, mainly imposed by her oldest brother. He controlled every move she made, the way she dressed, and who her friends were, and he was violent with her. Her parents had no control over him. "Actually, my mom loves him much more ... she says I should obey him because he is my oldest brother." The counselor reflected on Iman's distress and helplessness, and engaged the group in advising her to find someone who might have some influence over her brother. Again, the indirect way of involving a third person emerged. Iman selected her grandfather, because he was old and respected.

Overall, the girls talked freely about themselves and expressed strong emotions of anger, disappointment, and loneliness. The only group behavior that seemed difficult for them was the provision of honest and constructive feedback. The group process evolved in a very natural way: a few brave or altruistic group members started self-disclosing, followed by group members who were more reluctant to talk at first. The content of self-disclosure was common to many of the girls in the group: typical issues of adolescence, but with their unique manifestation in the Arab culture. This universality probably encouraged mutual sharing. The leader played an important role in this group. She used many active helping skills, such as encouragement, open questions, and even challenges. She also demonstrated her own expression of feelings and self-disclosed some personal information. It seemed that these techniques helped the girls go through emotional experiencing. However, the leader, too, refrained from guiding the problem-solving processes toward assertiveness or more direct communication. Coming from the same cultural background, she herself might have been restricted in direct and assertive communication. It is even more likely that she was sensitive to the girls' difficulties and did not want to lead them toward a conflict with their cultural values and their everyday lives. After all, when they left the group, they went back to their families and communities. This was an important way to show culturally responsive and responsible group leading skills.

Another Arab group was self-referred and comprised of both genders. The inclusion of boys was unusual, as most of the groups that my colleagues and I run for Arab youths are composed solely of girls. Overall, girls are known to seek therapy more than boys, but the striking difference in numbers here suggests that this may be a cultural artifact as well. Perhaps in a hierarchical society, in which men must be strong and reliable, they perceive therapy and the expression of feelings as a mark of weakness. It was, therefore, quite unexpected to find Arab boys volunteering to join a group. But as the group progressed, it became clear that the boys, too, had many problems in their families and that power struggles and violence disturbed them a great deal.

The group was comprised of six boys and four girls, all from the same high-level class. Due to previous acquaintance with the counselor, 20 children volunteered to participate, but only 10 were admitted, following a short individual interview.

Although all the children attended the group of their own free will, and it was made clear to them in the interview that self-disclosure will be expected, resistance to self-disclosure is high, particularly among the boys. For example, in the Legacy of My Name activity, Sa'alem said, "I don't know much about my name; I never asked and it really doesn't interest me as long as I have a name." His sarcastic response suggested that he saw this activity as nonsense. Yusuf stated, "I like that I am ambiguous; people don't really know who I am, how I feel, or what I think." This was not an easy starting point for a group. The process was slow, and in the fifth session the counselor decided to draw out the resistance through an activity that encouraged group members to talk about their fears. Ahmad said that he is afraid to be disappointed, because someone might disclose his secret. Tariq and Soheib indicated that they will disclose difficult issues only to the counselor in private. Sa'alem said, "I generally don't trust people or get close to others easily. So I don't think I will disclose personal issues here." This processing of resistance is very helpful, permitting the group to move on to the working stage.

Soheib, who insisted that he would only talk about personal issues in the counseling room, started the sixth session by sharing his distress and lack of control, particularly in respect to relationships with family members. He described embarrassing situations in which he lost his temper, "I hit my younger sisters and immediately regret it; I don't even know why I do this. ...Yesterday, I yelled at my mom so loud that my uncle came in to see what was going on." Soheib explored the reasons and situations that aroused this reaction, and came to the conclusion that he was imitating other men in the village. Examining the pros and cons of his behavior, Soheib realized that he lost more than he gained, because he hated himself when he got out of control. He decided to make an effort to change his behavior. He admitted that it was not easy for him, because he was used to using anger to his own advantage, but he would continue trying. To the group he said that their mutual sharing has been important because "it made me feel like I am not crazy."

Soheib's disclosures opened the door for Tariq, who was the focus of the next session. Tariq, too, stated earlier that he would never talk about his issues except in private. But when Soheib told his story, Tariq shared anger at his father; so in this session, the counselor asked him if he would like to share more about it with the group. He rambled quite a bit, expressing fear, shame, and embarrassment. He was particularly concerned about involving other people. But after the group encouraged him, and following a long pause, he eventually described the horrible circumstances in which he lived, with an extremely abusive father who was violent toward him, his siblings, and his mother. "I hate him," he said, "and anyone in my position would hate him too." He described one incident in which his father tied him to a tree and beat him in front of others "just because I got an 85 on an exam.". He was bothered by the lack of sense in this act, and felt completely helpless. "He does not love me," and there was no one to help him because he was the oldest sibling in his family. "No one can tell him what to do." Tariq's disclosure obviously helped him undergo cathartic experiencing. He accepted the counselor's suggestion to appeal to professional services, but also added, "If you will give me time, I would like to talk more. There is so much that I still have not told you. This is the first time I have shared these experiences."

The need to share the secret and his emotions was very strong, and the process of being accepted and respected was extremely powerful.

In the eleventh session, it was Ahmad who wanted to share with the group, even though earlier in the process he was very concerned that his secret would leak out. He started by asking group members to listen to him, to try to understand and respect his feelings, and to keep his secret. He told of a love story, how his girlfriend left him for someone else but wanted to come back. He was still in love with her and was probably willing to take her back, but the other boys in the group were extremely resistant to his choice. They expressed "macho" values that he could not accept. Even the girls who took his side were not able to convince the other boys that a girl could change her mind and still love him, and that forgiveness was possible.

These descriptions are all of boys who shared personal issues with the group, went through cathartic experiences, and were able to provide honest feedback. It took them longer than the girls, but eventually they released extreme stress. It was a good and healthy process, despite initial cultural reservations. Once the process started working, there was no difference between this and any other group.

SUMMARY

Developmental issues came up in these Arab groups, just as in many other (Jewish) groups described in this book. Issues with parents, difficulties in school, friendship problems, and loneliness were all manifested in these groups. Situational difficulties were also present, but they were somewhat different in content from the issues that are revealed in Western adolescent groups. A high frequency of problems with family members was evidenced, including abusive relationships. Many family restrictions and psychological controls seem to bother these youngsters. Very few external sources of support were available to them. These adolescents not only worked well in counseling groups, they actually needed them even more than other adolescents.

For instance, Ahlam's mother asked her to drop out of the group because she was concerned about its stigma and fears that participation will damage the family honor. Ahlam was caught between her mother's pressure and her own desire to remain in the group. She shared her dilemma with the other girls, telling them how helpless she felt. After a lengthy exploration of the conflict, Ahlam said, "I need you. Without you I have no one to share with. Here I feel important." The group helped her deal with her mother's resistance, and she eventually convinced her mother to let her stay in the group.

Although Dwairy (1998), a clinical psychologist in Israel, argued that the Arab population preferred short-term cognitive behavioral therapy, if at all, the cases in this chapter show that it is not only safe to conduct affective groups with Arab adolescents, but it is imperative considering the magnitude of problems and the lack of external sources of support. To all the Arab participants, the counseling groups provided social and emotional support, enhanced well being, helped to released stress, provided a chance for corrective interpersonal relationships, increased self-esteem, and enhanced problem solving skills. These are the commonly accepted goals for child and adolescent group therapy (Weisz et al., 1987) and were all achieved in a non-Western culture. Perhaps these results may be attributed to the level of acculturation. Living alongside a Jewish population, some modification in Arab cultural values and norms might have taken place.

The really important finding here is that behavior in the group was not restricted. On the contrary, Arab children and adolescents disclosed really big secrets. The leaders worked with them within the same theoretical orientation as did all the other group leaders presented in this book, and used the same interventions and leadership style. Although they were sensitive to content that reflected cultural values and social structure, they did not turn the groups into educational groups. This does not imply in any way that cultural knowledge and sensitivity are not important. It does argue, however, that culturally expected restrictions need to be tested before modifications in group orientation and models are made. It may be that group processes are stronger than cultural restrictions, and in groups that develop constructive group norms, the group norms will become the reference culture for group members. More research is needed in the area of multiculturalism and group counseling.

IV Summary and Conclusion

Introduction to Part IV

Clinicians and researchers alike have claimed that group psychotherapy is not yet a mature profession (Hoag & Burlingame, 1997a; Yalom & Lesczc, 2005), particularly child group psychotherapy (Barlow et al., 2000). Counselors are often not sufficiently trained to work with children's groups and there is not enough research to support claims for the effectiveness of child group counseling and psychotherapy. Clinicians tend to be more reluctant to work with groups than to provide individual treatment, because of the anxiety inherent in the role of group leader. This is primarily due to the greater public exposure of self, less sense of control, and fear of being overwhelmed. Researchers are also reluctant to study groups, mainly because of the complexity of such research, but also because of the lack of professional prestige afforded to group counseling and psychotherapy owing to the weak scientific base of the profession (Yalom & Lesczc, 2005).

It is understandably more difficult to meet the high standards of current methodologies in group research. The need to gather large enough samples in which the group (rather than the individual) is the subject of analysis, to secure control groups that do not receive services, and to control individual differences within the group, as well as the limited instruments available to measure group processes, all interfere with the progress of the profession. The obstacles in child group counseling and psychotherapy are even greater, because children find it difficult to complete questionnaires, self-reported information is often unreliable, questionnaires developed particularly for children are scarce, and it is difficult to obtain permission from school authorities and parents to investigate children. It is, therefore, no wonder that research in child group counseling and psychotherapy lags behind adult groups (Barlow et al., 2000).

Yet, perhaps most important, the problem is a clear lack of proper training in the profession. Many teaching programs for mental health professionals do not offer group therapy training at all, or offer it as an elective. This not only provides inadequate training, but also causes professionals to devalue the group therapy enterprise (Yalom & Lesczc, 2005). An effective educational process for group counselors and psychotherapists requires close interweaving of clinical and research orientations. Trainees need to observe groups, to experience them, to be supervised in their group work, and to perform their own research on groups. This model, which has been applied in the training program developed by my colleagues and myself, serves as the basis for this book.

In the words of Yalom and Leszcz (2005), "The moment demands a whole new generation of well-trained gardeners, and it behooves us to pay careful attention to the education of beginning group therapists and to our own continuing professional development" (pp. 543–544). It has been my intention throughout this book to move in this recommended direction, and to raise a generation of child and adolescent group counselors and therapists who are enthusiastic about groups, understand the process, and lead the group skillfully. As this book demonstrates, it is possible to train counselors to conduct short-term nonstructured counseling and psychotherapy groups successfully in the school and elsewhere.

16

What Does the Data Tell Us About Group Counseling With Children? Future Directions

This chapter summarizes the accumulated knowledge on group counseling and psychotherapy with children and adolescents based on the clinical experience and research findings of my colleagues and myself. I agree with Yalom and Leszcz (2005) that, to specialize in a specific type of group, one needs to know first the basic group therapy principles. Accordingly, most of the chapters in this book start with the general principles of group counseling and psychotherapy. Only then does the discussion move to deal with the unique characteristics of group counseling and psychotherapy with children and adolescents.

According to Yalom (Yalom & Leszcz, 2005), once the basic group therapy principles are salient, they can be applied to any specific clinical situation by taking three steps: (a) assess the clinical situation, (b) formulate clinical goals, and (c) modify traditional techniques in response to the new clinical situation and the new set of clinical goals. These three steps serve as a framework to summarize the data my fellow researchers and I have accumulated on the population of children and adolescents participating in group counseling and psychotherapy.

ASSESSMENT OF THE SITUATION

When assessing the clinical situation, one needs to consider setting, group composition, age, specific problem, length of treatment, and group size. The most common setting for group work with children is the school. According to several reviews of literature, about 75% of such groups are conducted there (Hoag & Burlingame, 1997b; Kulic et al., 2001; Riva & Haub, 2004). There are several reasons for groups to become the treatment of choice in the school. In that setting, children are naturally organized in groups and perceive group interventions as part of their daily routine. Thus, clients are available, almost a captive audience, and their attendance can be relatively easily monitored. Indeed, most of the groups described in this book were conducted in the school. This reality affects group processes in several ways.

Atypical Clients

Children and adolescents in groups conducted in the school are not typical clients of therapy, because they are usually referred by school staff rather than seeking therapy themselves. This may affect their level of motivation and their expectations of the group. Being referred to counseling implies that "something is wrong with me," yet most times the child is unaware of his or her problems; resistance, therefore, is inevitable. Moreover, most children and adolescents have no experience in psychotherapy and do not know what is expected of them in the group. Very often, the counselor is also a teacher in the school or a member of the administrative team, which may be quite puzzling to a child in respect to expectations regarding behavior. It is, therefore, imperative that children and adolescents participating in groups in the school be well informed about the nature of the group and expected behavior. Dual relationships (i.e., the need to distinguish between the teacher–student relationship in the classroom and the counselor–client relationship in the group) must be clarified, and the group has to be appealing and attractive right from the start. A trained group counselor knows how to deal with these issues.

An ethical issue that must be discussed is respect of personal boundaries. As the children and adolescents who are referred to counseling services do not choose to be clients, caution is needed in regard to what is expected of them. Both the counselor and group members must be tolerant about each child's participation in the group, respecting individual boundaries of privacy and self-disclosure. More so than with self-selected clients, it is the counselor's responsibility to secure a climate of trust and to make sure that the group experience is a positive one for each child. In process-oriented groups, this is not an easy task at all. Although in psychoeducational groups the prepared structure helps monitor the boundaries, in process- oriented groups such limits do not exist. On the one hand, the counselor wants to encourage the children to express themselves, but on the other hand, he or she must take into consideration that these children were placed in therapy rather then selecting therapy, and therefore extensive pressure to participate actively in the group may be unfair. This is a fine line for the counselor to walk in navigating the group, requiring sensitivity and respect of the individual's boundaries.

Confidentiality

A related issue is confidentiality; in a setting where participants know each other and spend time with each other on a continuing basis, confidentiality is a major threat. Children, particularly the younger ones, may release all inhibitions in the group and then regret it. Consider, for example, a child who discloses about his abusive father. Such information may be used by peers and classmates inappropriately, sometimes with malevolent intentions. The counselor must monitor children after a high level of self-disclosure or cathartic experience, checking their feelings both immediately following the experience and at the beginning of the next session. In extreme cases, children may need immediate individual assistance. The counselor must also work very hard to secure confidentiality—establishing it as a major rule in the group, consistently referring to it, and dealing with it rigorously when it is breached. In one group, a young girl complained that someone had revealed the secret she had shared with the group. She threatened to leave because she could not trust the group members anymore. The therapist, an experienced counselor, was furious; after discussing the problem with the children, she expressed her strong feelings of betrayal and stopped the session, explaining that she must think about whether the group can continue at all. This was an unusually dramatic reaction of a calm and accepting counselor. She later explained that she wanted to send a very clear message to the children about the importance of confidentiality, and as these were very young children (fourth grade), she needed a powerful response. Indeed, the children were shocked, and at the next session they were determined to keep the rule of confidentiality. The leader went even further and discussed with the children ways to share an experience with someone without revealing the person involved, and this was further role-played. Thereafter, there were no breaches of confidentiality in this group.

Nonetheless, confidentiality can never be totally guaranteed. Therefore, the counselor must also make the children aware of the danger of information leaking and encourage them to take personal charge of what they disclose. My co-facilitators and I have dealt with confidentiality breaches often, but we have also learned that, at a certain point, the children don't care, as evidenced in the following response of Dana: "I don't care that other people know my parents are divorced. It should not be a secret anyway, and I am pleased with the group's help." In another case, Jeff said, "People now know that my father is abusive, but I don't care, as I stopped being a victim." Thus, the children learn that the advantages of the group may exceed the disadvantage of uncovering one's secret. This is an important lesson for group counselors and therapists who are anxious about the issue of confidentiality.

Mutual History

Another factor related to the school setting is the children's familiarity with each other before and during the group experience. A mutual history can be both good and bad. If friends join a group together, they may find it easier to adjust to the group and its demands. Friends help reduce the level of anxiety at the earlier group stages, provide constant emotional support, and sometimes protect a child from others' pressure, negative feedback in the group, or bullies outside of the group. For example, Jamie was a quiet and withdrawn child who was a victim of bullying by his classmates, because of his somewhat deviant physical appearance. He asked to bring along his best friend, Mark, who was also quite a withdrawn child. Mark was helpful in expressing many experiences that Jamie could not express himself. Mark's presence, alone, was a reassuring experience. And although he might not have been referred to the group, being a withdrawn child, he gained from the experience.

At the same time, pregroup familiarity has its disadvantages. It may lead to subgrouping, which usually impedes the group process. Moreover, if the children have a common negative history, many of their difficulties are carried over into the group. Recall Myra, for example, who was obsessed with her attempt to kick David out because of their negative relationships outside of the group. Another example is that of Gary and Johnny, who did not speak to each other because of a dispute outside the group. For a long time there was tension in the group, which caused unease among members. Eventually, they insisted that the two boys talk to each other and resolve the conflict, which they did to the great satisfaction of the group. There are also victims of bullies or scapegoated children in class who may continue being scapegoated in the group. This can be a devastating experience for children whose main need is to re-experience positive relationships. It is imperative for the counselor to know the dynamics of the group and to pay attention to interactions of members which may impede the growth of the group and the individual.

Stigma

Counselors are also concerned with the group stigma, part of which can be eliminated with proper consideration. Stigma is a problem for many reasons. First, attraction to the group is a major component of group climate, and it is hard to imagine that children would be attracted to a group with a negative connotation. After all, who wants to be identified as part of a group of aggressive children or students with learning disabilities? Second, children—particularly adolescents—are extremely anxious about their self-image and peer acceptance. Being part of a group with a stigma is likely to keep potential participants from joining or maintaining their membership, and may even increase their social rejection.

The best way to deal with stigma is to conduct many groups. The more groups that are held in a given school, the less this comes to be considered deviant. In one of the schools my colleagues and I work with, Adele, a highly experienced group counselor, is employed part time. In the 10 weekly hr of her employment contract, she conducts 10 groups, reaching out to about 100 children. Not only is this an efficient use of her time, but groups have become so popular in her school that there is a waiting list to join. No stigma of groups is evident in this school.

One way to neutralize the stigma of group therapy is to break a classroom into small groups, allowing children to select the one that best answers their needs or interests. If one perceives group processes as growth experiences, geared to enhance well being, it becomes clear that one does not need a special deficit or problem to benefit from a group. Under such arrangements, groups are the most natural setting in the school.

The leader can help reduce the stigma by carefully choosing a label for the group. My coworkers and I call many of our groups The Friendship Club, which actually refers to a wide range of difficulties (aggression, LD, lonely/shy), but under a friendly name. Group names may be neutral, such as The Breakfast Club, The Sisters, or The Brothers, and may be chosen by the leader or group members. In fact, choosing a name for the group can be an effective activity to enhance group cohesiveness. To a certain degree, the label of the group masks some serious deficits or problems, but soon the children realize that participants are problem children of some sort. One additional way to deal with the problem is to combine children with special needs with normative children.

Composition

Normative children in a group not only serve as a buffer; they also add quality feedback to the group process, and often have an impact on the classroom group dynamic, thus helping a needy child outside the group as well. How are these children reached? Sometimes my cofacilitators and I invite a child to join the group; at other times, a child asks to bring a friend along. These children benefit from the group experience in many ways: through the very fact that they were selected, through the help they offer to others, and through their usually high status within the group. But most of all, they, too, have an opportunity to deal with some of their own issues and experience psychological growth. Parental consent is sought for these children, as for all other group participants, and parents usually do not object, particularly if scheduling is seriously considered to avoid missing important school subjects.

Scheduling

The older the children in the groups, the more they and their parents are concerned with them missing classes. Therefore, careful attention must be given to the scheduling of the group, so that participants do not miss much academic material or classes that they like (e.g., gym). When possible, my colleagues and I schedule the sessions before or after school to avoid conflicts of interest. In one of our groups for children of divorce, called The Breakfast Club, a light breakfast is served. Another adolescent group, The Restaurant, is scheduled after school, and the children take turns bringing in bread and cheese and making their own sandwiches.

Smart scheduling is easiest when children are drawn from the same class or at least the same age cohort. Same age is also important for developmental considerations. As I recommend homogeneous groups in terms of gender, and the groups are small (between 6–8), it is easiest to compose a group from one or two parallel classes.

Most of the groups my colleagues and I facilitate run during one school year. They start a couple of months after school starts and continue until the end of the year. Considering holidays and field trips, the length of the group is about 15 sessions. Therefore, the most effective way is to schedule the group right at the beginning of the year, so it becomes an integral part of the school program. This provides continuity to the group work, and, being close groups, they become an important source of children's support throughout the year.

Beyond The Children

The interesting and sometimes challenging issue in working with children and adolescents is that they are not the sole clients. Working with youngsters requires cooperation from important people in their lives: parents, teachers, and the school principal.

Most important is getting parents' agreement, if only because they have to sign the form of consent. But even more important is their attitude to the group experience.

They can encourage a child to persist in a group or discourage a child from attending. Much depends on the child's problem, the parent's beliefs regarding therapy, and their general value system. One of the parents' greatest concerns is the fear that family secrets will be exposed. Another problem is their competition with the counselor over their child's trust. Therefore, parents must be well informed about group goals and expectations. The best way to obtain parental agreement is to have an experiential orientation session with them, in which they are not only told about group goals and expectations, but can also experience an activity or two. Some parents need more frequent contact with the counselor; this should be allowed without, of course, breaking the rule of confidentiality.

Teachers are also an important party in the group success. Those who believe in the child, the therapy, and the counselor cooperate more willingly. They make sure that the child arrives on time to the group, that assistance with academic tasks is provided when needed, and that the child's efforts to make progress are acknowledged and encouraged. Teachers, too, must be convinced that groups are effective, and that they have a part in this success. Orientation sessions, or an ongoing successful group experience for the teachers, may convince them that the effort is worthy.

Finally, the school principal is usually the one to make the decision in favor of or against group counseling in the school. Informing the principal about the goals of the group and the process is imperative for success in group work in the school setting. Providing evidence of success is a useful way to convince him or her, as I have learned from my experience with LD students.

FORMATION OF CLINICAL GOALS

After assessing the clinical situation, one needs to set applicable goals (Yalom & Leszcz, 2005). Group interventions comprise groups that vary widely in format and objectives, from psychoeducational prevention groups, to counseling growth-engendering groups, to psychotherapy aimed at character change (Gazda et al., 2001; Gladding, 2003). Each of these types of groups may have different objectives and necessarily apply different techniques. One study (Shechtman & Bar-El, 1994), which compared psychoeducational groups with counseling groups for ninth graders in one school, found that the goal of improving classroom behavior was more effectively achieved in psychoeducational groups conducted with the whole class, however, self-esteem was increased more in the small counseling groups. As the focus of this book is on counseling and psychotherapy groups, the question that arises is: What are the clinical goals of these groups?

The definition of group psychotherapy with children and adolescents may help answer this question. Like many other researchers in this domain (e.g., Hoag & Burlingame, 1997b), my colleagues and I accept the broad definition of group psychotherapy for children and adolescents suggested by Weisz and colleagues (1987): "Any intervention designed to alleviate psychological distress, reduce maladaptive behavior, or enhance adaptive behavior through counseling, structured or unstructured intervention, a training program, or a predetermined treatment plan" (p. 543). This definition does not refer to a specific deficit or problem behavior, but is rather concerned with the reduction of stress and pain and with the child's improved sense of well being. Throughout this book are many illustrations of reduced stress and improved sense of self achieved in our groups through cathartic experiences and emotional support. Our observations and the children's feedback point to these two components as the fundamental conditions for their change.

Thus, the major goals of groups run by my coworkers and I are to release stress and help the child feel better with his or her issues, whatever these might be. These goals are achieved through structured or unstructured activities that help group participants express emotions and disturbing personal experiences in an all-accepting, supportive environment. However, catharsis alone is insufficient in the therapy process in both individual (L. S. Greenberg, 2002) and group therapy (Yalom & Leszcz, 2005). Clients need to understand their experiences. Therefore, the second goal is to enhance understanding of the problem situation or behavior. Reflecting on the cathartic experiences through a process of cognitive and emotional explorations helps to develop awareness and insight. This stage of change is not always evident in adult therapy, as insight is relatively rare (Hill, 2005). It certainly does not always occur in children or adolescent groups. Much depends on the age of the group participants; the younger they are, the less frequently they are able to develop self-awareness. It also depends on the type of problem. For example, in the case of aggressive children and adolescents, it is not easy to develop insight because they are particularly defensive, often starting from a state of total lack of awareness. Research suggests that insight was quite rare in this population; in one study (Shechtman & Ben-David, 1999) it was present 12% of the time for each of the six variables measured. In a second study (Shechtman, 2004b), it was even lower (about 2% for eight variables), although a significant increase in insight was evidenced during the therapy process (Shechtman, 2004a). It appears that, at least with this type of population, therapists may need to complete treatment without insight. Perhaps a greater emphasis on action is needed with them. We suspect that with young children the situation would be similar, even with other issues, which implies that a more active action stage should occur in these groups. Indeed, even with adults, an action stage is needed to challenge long-standing patterns of behavior (Hill, 2005; Prochaska, 1999). Children and adolescents need instrumental assistance in transforming motivation to action and in maintaining the changes achieved.

Another reason for the low proportion of insight may be the counselor's lack of helping skills. Throughout our process research, my fellow researchers and I found that counselors used questions most frequently; other important helping skills, like encouragement, reflection of feelings, and challenging were quite rare. To develop insight in clients, it is these very skills that are required (Hill, 2005). A recent study (Shechtman & Gat, 2006) found that counselors used only 40% of those helping skills that can be classified as effective. Much of these results may be attributed to the inexperience of many of the novice group counselors involved in our studies. These results suggest that more rigorous training is required for leading a group successfully, a condition that rarely exists.

So far, the goals declared by my workers and I seem to be appropriate for individual therapy, and they are indeed drawn from the literature of individual therapy.

However, these goals in a group context are achieved through group processes rather than client-therapist interaction. Therefore, on the group level the goals are to establish a climate of warmth and support, close connectedness among group members and the counselor, mutual sharing of private information, and provision of honest and constructive feedback. These mechanisms are necessary to achieve individual goals in a group context (Yalom & Leszcz, 2005). In contrast to psychoeducational groups, which focus their intervention on particular content to address a unique predetermined need or problem, our groups focus on the issue the child brings up at a particular session. The group process strives to go through the whole cycle of change, but even if the group can only help the child to reduce stress and improve feelings about the self and others, this is construed as an accomplishment.

MODIFYING TECHNIQUES

Age plays an important role both in determining the goals and conducting the sessions. Developmental psychology has suggested that children develop in cognitive, social, and emotional stages (Piaget, 1986). They have specific needs at each stage, specific tasks to accomplish, and certain abilities suitable to their age. An understanding of normal child development is therefore essential for effective group treatment (Kymissis, 1996).

Preschool children have a short attention span, a low level of abstract thinking, difficulties in verbal expression, limited perspective-taking skills, and problems controlling their own behavior. For them, play would be the major instrument used in therapeutic groups. Slavson (1945/1986) was probably the first to develop groups for young children. This activity group therapy is based on psychoanalytic tenets, nondirective, and devoid of verbal interventions. Play therapy, puppets and dolls, storytelling, bibliotherapy, and picture drawing are techniques to permit reexperiencing of earlier conflicts in a safe environment (Huth-Blocks, Schettini, & Shebroe, 2001).

Elementary-school children (ages 7–11) are industrious, eager to learn, and demonstrate abstract thinking and competent verbal skills. They are capable of empathy and self-awareness. The peer group provides support in the initial emancipation from the family and serves as a prime source of self-esteem. Games, sports, crafts, and writing become the building blocks for a sense of self-confidence and can be implemented in the group therapy process, along with other techniques (e.g., creative drama, story-telling, therapeutic cards; Lomonaco, Seidlinger, & Aronson, 2000).

Adolescents (ages 12–18) struggle with separation from parents and the development of self-identity. Self-awareness and empathy are now developed, permitting close relationships and friendships. Peers become an extremely important source of support; therefore, groups become the treatment of choice (Cramer-Azima, 1989; Malekoff, 2004). Commonality of problems leads to a sense of universality and permits discussion and problem solving of many disturbing issues. Although adolescents appear to be best equipped for group work, they may also be the greatest challenge for group counselors. In their struggle for independence, they are often resistant to authority. Their struggle for a clear identity leads to inflexibility and intolerance. Although talk therapy is used at this stage, the counselor must structure at least part of the sessions to regulate the anxiety and allow freedom of expression (Kymissis, 1996; Nichols-Goldstein, 2001).

Modifying the techniques of treatment is critical to the success of the process. Unfortunately, leaders are usually untrained to use helping techniques that are specifically designed to fit the children's age level (Dagley et al., 1994; Pollack & Kymissis, 2001). The four techniques my colleagues and I use most frequently are bibliotherapy (sometimes combined with other forms of art, such as music or drawing), PhotoTherapy, therapeutic cards, and therapeutic games (on the first three, see Chapter 5). These techniques are helpful at all stages. In adult groups, a leader may use some of these techniques at an early stage of the group and at termination, but in the working stage clients are expected to initiate self-disclosure, spontaneously raise goals for improvement, and interact with each other. However, in children's groups, all these functions can be facilitated through the use of techniques also at the working stage. Using techniques does not replace the leader's function of processing. The games are used to facilitate group processes. Throughout this book I demonstrate many examples of techniques and activities that were adjusted to the children's age, the type of problem, and the stage of the group development.

In sum, my colleagues and I have assessed the clinical situation, formulated clinical goals and modified techniques accordingly, following Yalom's (Yalom & Leszcz, 2005) suggestions for adjusting the group core factors to the unique population of children and adolescents. However, proper adjustments, when made, do not guarantee the effectiveness of such groups. It is our responsibility to show that such groups are accountable and worth employing with children and adolescents. Outcome research becomes important in achieving this goal.

OUTCOMES

Overall, there are more clinical demonstrations than research studies pertaining to the effectiveness of groups with children and adolescents (Barlow et al., 2000). The few reviews of the outcome research indicate that such groups are effective (Hoag & Burlingame, 1997b; Holmes & Sprenkle, 1996; Prout & Prout, 1998; Whiston & Sexton, 1998). However, these reviews include all types of groups: psychoeducational, counseling, and psychotherapy, as well as various treatment orientations, with cognitive–behavioral treatments being the dominant ones. Although the groups my coworkers and I facilitate deal with similar issues to those reviewed in the literature, including friendship, aggression, learning difficulties, and divorce (Dagly et al., 1994; Holmes & Sprenkle, 1996; Schaeffer, 1999), we worked within a somewhat different model than most of them. Therefore, it is our obligation to demonstrate the effectiveness of these groups.

Outcome research indicates that group counseling of the type illustrated in this book yielded positive outcomes with respect to a large range of problems. The friendship groups produced more intimate relationships with friends, both among elementary-school children (Shechtman, 1991, 1993, 1994) and adolescents (Shechtman et al., 2002), and these gains were particularly impressive for boys

(Shechtman & Vurembrand, 1996). These results are based not only on self-reports, but also on a friend's response, which confirmed the growth in intimacy (Shechtman et al., 1994). Throughout the book, the reader has witnessed numerous cases of such processes of individual growth.

These are important outcomes, as intimacy is a unique construct in close relationships, distinguished from general interpersonal relationships. A child who does not have a close friend is missing a major source of social support and suffers loneliness. Intimacy is not just another ability or skill that can be taught; it is related to trust in self and others, and as such must be reexperienced in positive relationships with people the children can trust to carry over this sense of trust to a dyadic relationship outside the group. This need is effectively addressed in the groups my colleagues and I run, as they are characterized by intimacy and trust, the same ingredients that make up close friendships. The group process emphasizes a nurturing and supportive environment, close relationships, and self-disclosure. These components seem to establish the basis for trust, which is eventually transferred to close dyadic relationships outside the group. Along similar lines, our research also indicated progress in a construct closely related to intimate relationships—namely, self-esteem, which is just the other side of the same coin (self-trust). Our research has shown that self-esteem was enhanced in treatment children compared to wait-listed children (Shechtman, 1993; Shechtman & Bar-El, 1994).

Self-esteem and related variables (e.g., social acceptance), which are more commonly studied in the child group literature, were further explored in research my colleagues and I conducted on children with LD. This is another fascinating example of outcomes, because children with LD are usually assisted only with their academic difficulties. Although they are sometimes trained in social skills as well, rarely are their emotional difficulties addressed. Our groups proved to lead to improvement in several areas: self-esteem, social status, and adjustment behavior (Shechtman et al., 1996; Shechtman & Pastor, 2005). Most interesting, however, were the positive outcomes in academic achievements, even though this was not the focus of the therapy. Not only were the children who received treatment different from wait-listed children in the progress they made in math and language, but these gains continued growing after termination. Furthermore, most of the children studied (about 70%) received a passing grade in both of these subjects; only one-third of the children in the control group improved to this point, and most of them continued to fail. It seems that the nurturing and supportive climate in our groups enhanced personal growth; self-confidence and self-efficacy may explain the gains in academic achievement.

Studies of group treatment of aggressive children point to reduced aggression (Shechtman, 2000, 2003, 2006; Shechtman & Birani-Nasaraladin, in press; Shechtman & Nachshol, 1996) and increased empathy (Shechtman, 2006; Shechtman & Birani-Nasaraladin, in press). Moreover, research showed that such groups are equally effective as individual treatment (Shechtman, 2003; Shechtman & Ben-David, 1999). These results are important clinically and practically: they suggest that such groups are safe and effective, despite recent reservations regarding group work with aggressive children (Dishion et al., 1999), and that they are cost-effective. Considering the large number of aggressive children in the schools, this is an outcome that should not be underestimated.

Groups for children from a non-Western culture (Arabs) are also effective, despite the cautions raised in the literature against giving psychodynamic treatment to individuals from such a culture. Research by my colleagues and I found no difference in outcomes on an adjustment scale between Arab adolescents and adolescents of the Jewish majority group, which represents a Western culture. The process research of this study indicated that children from the Arab culture function well in the group process, presenting the necessary functions of self-disclosure and feedback provision (Shechtma et al., 2003).

Overall, the groups that my coworkers and I conduct, for a varying population of children and problems, appear to be effective in all our studies. All these studies employed relatively large samples, an experimental design, and sound multiple measures. We may conclude, therefore, that groups of the type presented in this book are safe and productive, and may be employed by counselors and psychologists in the school setting and elsewhere. In our most recent study (Shechtman & Pastor, 2005), we showed that these groups were not only effective compared to a control or wait-list group, but that in the case of LD children, they were more effective than CBT groups. Although this study needs further replications with various problem children, it certainly adds to the validity of our group intervention.

PROCESS RESEARCH

An even more interesting question is why these groups are effective. In other words, what processes in the group may explain the positive outcomes? Process research is hardly mentioned in the professional literature on groups with children and adolescents (Barlow et al., 2000). In a recent review of the adult literature, Burlingame, MacKenzie, et al. (2004) suggested a model for conceptualizing group treatment variables that affect outcomes (p. 648). I borrow this model for this discussion, applying it to groups with children and adolescents.

According to the model, outcomes are affected by several levels of variables. At the primary level are the variables of formal change theory and small group processes. The second level is the group leader, and the third level includes the patient and structural factors. All these variables are interrelated and believed to affect outcomes. As patient and structural factors were discussed earlier in this chapter (see the section on Clinical Assessments), I elaborate here on the first two levels of the model only.

Theory and Group Processes

The two variables on the primary level are the theoretical orientation used (e.g., cognitive–behavioral) and the therapeutic properties of the group. Both must be recognized as potential influences of group outcomes. Many groups mainly emphasize theory. Such emphasis is an extension of individual therapy, provided in a group format, but the group itself is not considered a source of influence. In contrast, an emphasis on group processes suggests that the group itself is the vehicle of change and that group interaction is a primary mechanism of change. In an attempt to identify those process variables that predict outcome, Burlingame, MacKenzie, et al. (2004)

found interpersonal feedback and alliance with the therapist and group members to be the best predictors in groups for adults. Early group structure, leader verbal style, and group climate were also good predictors of outcomes. How, then, are these fundamental sources of influence on outcomes (theory and group processes) manifested in groups with children?

In regard to theory, my colleagues and I use an integrative orientation (Hill, 2005; Prochaska, 1999) that includes psychodynamic, humanistic, and cognitive–behavioral principles adjusted to the stage of client change. Although borrowed from individual adult therapy, it is successfully applied to children and adolescents in groups. Our research (Shechtman, 2004a, 2004b; Shechtman & Ben-David, 1999) has indicated almost no differences between client and therapist behavior in individual and group therapy, and the frequency of each behavior is quite similar to that reported in the adult literature (Hill & O'Brien, 1999); only the insight stage is less represented in our groups. This is to be expected of children, particularly the younger ones. I believe that children can gain a lot from the group experience just by releasing stress and being empowered by positive interpersonal feedback and a positive climate. Thus, we use the expressive–supportive modality with them; we encourage them to express and explore feelings and events, and provide both emotional and instrumental support.

Group processes play a central role in groups such as those conducted by my colleagues and I. Although humanistic-oriented principles are strongly presented in our groups, they are not just an extension of humanistic therapy. Group cohesiveness appears to be the major mechanism, at least from the children's perspective. Broadly defined, group cohesiveness includes attraction to the group, a climate of support and nurturing, close relationships, and a good alliance with the counselor. These seem to be the ingredients that help children and adolescents grow. Indeed, they value them as the most important components of change (Shechtman, 2003; Shechtman & Gluk, 2005), and they were found to be related to outcomes (Shechtman & Sender, 2006). Although interpersonal feedback is the most important factor in adult groups, and is considered a path to change in adolescent groups (Cramer-Azima, 1989), our research shows that with younger children the process of interpersonal interaction process is not always constructive (Shechtman & Yanuv, 2001). This outcome has important clinical implications for the group counselor, whose role it is to help children develop the skills of constructive feedback. Group structure and the use of structured activities and techniques have also proven effective in this respect. In fact, structured activities triggered most of the children's (and the counselor's) self-disclosure (Leichtentritt & Shechtman, 1998). In numerous clinical examples, the reader could witness the helpfulness of structured activities, particularly at the early stages of the group.

The theoretical orientation and group processes that my coworkers and I use are two highly interrelated components, as self-disclosure increases a positive climate and a supportive climate increases self-expressiveness. A balance between theory and processes is necessary to consider work in a group as group work. The adherence of our groups to these two fundamental principles was tested in a recent study (Shechtman & Pastor, 2005), in which we compared processes of our groups with psychoeducational groups. Several differences were found between the two types of group treatments in regard to both the counselor's helping skills and clients' behavior. As expected, leaders in our groups used encouragement, reflection of feelings, and interpretations more frequently; leaders in the educational groups used more information and guidance. Participants in our groups presented behaviors of affective exploration and insight more often; participants in the educational groups presented cognitive exploration more frequently and were also more resistant. Moreover, the slope of change suggests that resistance decreased more sharply in our groups than in the comparison groups; however, insight increased more sharply.

Leader Behavior

The leader is the next component that influences outcomes in the model discussed, mediating between the two fundamental principles of theory and process, on the one hand, and patient and structural factors, on the other. The counselor is the pivotal force in determining the degree to which the theoretical components of the formal change theory are thoughtfully integrated with small group process principles. To connect between the two forces, the leader must preserve effective change processes, patient–therapist roles, and modify techniques (Burlingame, MacKenzie, et al., 2004). Although most leaders of adult groups have at least some training in conducting groups, the counselors for groups of children most often lack specific training. Most APA programs do not require group therapy as a mandatory course, let alone groups that specialize in children and adolescents. As a result, these counselors often apply their knowledge about adult groups to the work with children.

As this book shows, a therapist of child groups needs a unique personality, a clear understanding of developmental psychology, and a wide range of skills. The difficulties that children and adolescent pose, particularly at the early stages of the group, require the counselor to possess a rich tool chest to successfully conduct the group. In reality, however, counselors who work with children in groups do not have the proper training, and as a result, groups are often used as a setting for skills training. Familiarity with techniques and activities is insufficient; the counselor must also know how to utilize them to develop individual and group processes of growth. This is probably the most difficult part in training group counselors to work with this unique population, as it requires cognitive knowledge and understanding of psychology of children, group principles, and methods and techniques.

I believe that experiencing such a group from a client's perspective is needed to grasp the distinction between work in a group and group work. However, even this experience does not guarantee that counselors use the wide repertoire of helping skills necessary to be effective (Shechtman & Gat, 2006). Observing group work of skillful leaders, conducting a group under supervision, and pairing with an experienced coleader are additional steps toward becoming a successful group therapist (Yalom & Leszcz, 2005). In addition, my colleagues and I involve trainees in research on group psychotherapy; each trainee investigates both the outcomes and process of his or her own group. We have found this to be a useful way of increasing one's understanding of the unique features of group work with children and adolescents.

SUMMARY, CONCLUSION, AND FUTURE GOALS

I now summarize the implications of the model suggested by Burlingame, MacKenzie, et al. (2004) for children and adolescent groups. It is clear that to conceptualize a model that will explain outcomes of child and adolescent groups, a great deal of further work is needed. Researchers need more outcome studies and many more process studies to answer the question of what affects outcomes, and both types of studies need to be enhanced in scope and sophistication. I now discuss these needed studies within the model suggested by Burlingame.

To validate the integrative theory of change that my colleagues and I use, we need more comparisons of treatment orientations and their outcomes, as we did in our recent studies on children with LD (Shechtman & Pastor, 2005) and their parents (Shechtman & Gilat, 2005). Although we used relatively large sample scales and adequate research designs, comparisons were usually made between children who received treatment and those who received no treatment or were wait-listed. This design allowed us only to conclude that the groups we offer are effective and can be reliably used. However, a more sophisticated research should involve a comparison with another treatment orientation; this will add to the validity of the formal change theory.

More sophisticated research is also needed on the unique processes of groups with children and adolescents. My colleagues and I have observed in these groups similar therapeutic factors to those that appear in the literature, but the emphasis and interpretation of these factors is different. The emphasis that elementary school children gave to group cohesiveness was particularly strong and the interpretation of group cohesiveness was somewhat different, much more focused on encouragement and support. In adolescent groups we found that socializing techniques emerged as a frequent therapeutic factor, which we hardly find in adult groups. This is a reasonable finding for adolescents, who are seriously occupied with peer relationships. In short, our results suggest that different age groups may stress different therapeutic factors. As therapeutic factors are central to our understanding of outcomes, they should be further explored in each age group, preferably using a uniform definition and scale; right now, the definition of group cohesion is not clear, and the different scales may produce different results.

Other processes must also be investigated to understand how the group process affects outcomes. Several studies investigated client behaviors (Hill, 2005) borrowed from the individual therapy literature. Although this helped my colleagues and I understand the behavior of the children in our groups and helps us point to the adherence of our intervention to the theoretical orientation, we have thus far failed to find direct connections between these processes and outcomes (Shechtman, 2004b). We need to identify other process variables focused more on the group process than individual behavior (e.g., interpersonal variables), as they seem to be the best predictors of change (Burlingame, MacKenzie, et al., 2004). We found evidence in this direction in a recent study (Shechtman & Sender, 2006), which suggested that bonding with group members was related to gains in social competence.

Researchers also lack sufficient knowledge of how leader behavior affects outcomes. Using the Counselor Helping System (Hill, 2005), my colleagues and I have found that counselors in individual and group therapy use very similar skills (Shechtman, 2004a). The same study also indicated that questions are helpful to young clients, whereas challenges are disruptive. Despite the importance of this information, therapist behavior was not found to be directly related to children's outcome. It seems that additional variables must be identified and tested for a direct connection between process and outcomes.

The literature regarding patients lags far behind. In the adult group literature, for example, research has shown that patients with bulimia, social phobia, schizophrenia, and cancer have a *very good* to *excellent* prediction of success (Burlingame, MacKenzie, et al., 2004). Moreover, researchers know that patients with low PM gain more from instrumental group therapy, and patients high in PM do better in expressive groups (Piper et al., 2002). In contrast, knowledge about the prediction of outcomes of children in groups is quite limited. Research by my coworkers and I on attachment style as a predictor of an individual's functioning in a group showed that secure children function best in groups, however avoidant children function the worst. This, of course, does not say much about their outcomes. Thus, much more research is needed here.

In regard to structural factors, my colleagues and I have found that group size did not affect how participants work in the group process (Shechtman & Dvir, 2005), and that structured activities are essential to produce effective group functioning (Leichtentritt & Shechtman, 1998). This is, of course, not enough; there is much more to learn about structural issues in group counseling and psychotherapy with children.

Lastly, researchers need to expand upon the concept of outcomes itself. What is considered an outcome? Is behavior in a group an outcome? Is satisfaction and mood following participation an outcome? Is the acquisition of a particular skill or knowledge considered an outcome? I argue that rigorous research of outcomes should be perceived in a broad perspective. It is not the knowledge of a particular skill that needs to be measured, but rather its manifestation in actual behavior in real life. Not only should the client's report of progress be taken into consideration as an outcome, but reports of other related individuals must be sought. For example, in a study of parents of LD children, my colleagues and I investigated outcomes for mothers who participated in the groups, as well as fathers and children who were not involved in the group. As expected, mothers who participated reported lower stress and more control over both the child with LD and his or her non-LD sibling. However, the interesting finding in this study was that the father and child (who had not participated in the group) also showed gains. These results point to a broader impact of groups, thus adding power to the outcomes.

This is our modest contribution to the evidence-based psychotherapy (EBP) war (Norcross, Beutler, & Levant, 2006) that is being waged in the professional literature. It is a war because both researchers and practitioners disagree on the definition of EBP. As most of the literature that supports current EBP principles (60%–90%) is based on cognitive–behavioral theories (Norcross et al., 2006), it is not surprising that treatment manuals, controlled research, a focus on specific disorders, and specific validated treatment methods are required to consider a treatment EBP.

EBP efforts are worldwide because therapy cannot be a jungle for clients and therapists. My coworkers and I join these efforts by focusing on the research component of the EBP definition, and point to the efficacy and accountability of our integrative expressive–supportive group therapy. Although replications of studies are needed, more long-term follow-up measurement is required, and clinical progress (as opposed to statistical progress) is missing in several studies, taken overall, our research clearly supports group therapy without manuals and with no focus on specific symptoms. We embrace the humanistic goals of helping a person to grow, rather than helping him or her to resolve a specific problem, and show that this approach is accountable. This is our modest contribution to the EBP of a humanistic approach. It seems that we have just started traveling down a road hardly traveled. Much more sophisticated research is needed in the arena of child and adolescent group counseling and psychotherapy. It is our hope that more researchers will join us on this journey, and that more practitioners will be encouraged and become skillful in practicing such groups in the school and elsewhere.

Although I recognize the pressure on counselors within and outside the school to conduct short-term cognitive–behavioral groups, my impression is that the type of groups proposed in this book are not practiced widely enough, mainly because counselors and therapists are not trained to conduct them. It is not difficult to see the threat posed by groups that are nonstructured and process-oriented. This is one of the greatest obstacles to group therapists working with adult groups as well (Yalom & Leszcz, 2005). It is my hope that child and adolescent counselors and therapists will use this book as a training guide and find it an inspiration to take the risk and conduct such groups, as so many children in our society are awaiting an opportunity to be helped in their painful process of growth.

Appendices

Appendix I
Illustrations of Group Processes with Exceptional Populations

___

INTRODUCTION

This appendix describes group processes undertaken with several unique populations having exceptional goals. Owing to the nature of these populations, it was not clear how effective the expressive-supportive modality would be. Nevertheless, my colleagues and I decided to give it a try, and the results were often surprising. The following brief descriptions are followed by a more detailed discussion of each group.

The first group was comprised of physically and mentally challenged adolescent boys. It could not be taken for granted that a group process would evolve with this population. Limited mental ability can hinder self-exploration and the development of insight, and it can limit the understanding of other people's situations. In addition, these youngsters seriously lack social skills, not only because of their mental deficiencies, but mainly because they are highly isolated socially. Owing to their physical limitations, they have little chance to establish and maintain friendships after school. Moreover, they come to the special education setting from various geographic locations, which makes it even harder for them to get together after school. Even within the school, because of the large variability in their capabilities, they learn individually, with little interaction between themselves. Still, they are adolescents with severe identity problems, with major stressful life events, and with a natural need for human contact and intimacy. We therefore decided to accept the challenge and see if we could turn these individuals into a group.

I found the process in this particular group exciting and rewarding. These adolescents seemed to function well in the group; they released some of their emotional burden, gave and received support, and became more intimate with each other. Counseling these boys in a group demanded a great deal of love, patience, and creativity, but it was a growth experience for the counselor. Here is how she described her experience with this group:

> I learned what it means to get involved with them. I felt how meaningful they became in my life, how dear they are to me. But most important was that they taught me what authenticity means. I learned to feel comfortable, to be honest, and to express my feelings spontaneously without being afraid. I understood that my feelings had an important value in the group process. I became a better and richer person.

The second group was multicultural. It involved three Arab girls—refugees in Israel—and seven Jewish girls, all learning in the same class. The three minority girls were not accepted among their classmates simply because they were Arabs. The timing was also bad; it was during the Second Intifada, when any Arab was considered an enemy and a terrorist. The group was established with the aim of facilitating their acceptance in the classroom. A small group is a good place in which to establish a dialogue between two rival groups. The situation was too delicate to resolve in a large classroom. It was not an easy process, as the Arab girls were fearful and had ambivalent feelings as well. They had a serious problem with their own identity and with cultural restrictions that served only to increase their segregation. Yet, they, too, needed to belong, to be accepted and understood.

The group seemed to largely achieve its goals. Even if great friendships did not develop between the Arab and Jewish girls, the daily bullying stopped. The Arab girls received an open invitation to join their classmates during school activities. They came to understand why they were initially excluded, and the degree to which it resulted from their own behavior. They also realized that the Jewish girls had problems, too, although different ones. These new relationships were transferred to the classroom. Here is how the counselor summarized her experience with this group, "This was a new, challenging, and exciting experience. I realized the enormous power of the group and the great responsibility of the counselor in making the group a safe place and yet an effective means to peace."

The third group was comprised of very young children (age 8). Often I am asked if such young children can effectively take part in a nonstructured group that is not focused on specific content and is not meant to teach specific skills. This group indicated that 8-year-old children can, indeed, be effectively involved in an expressive–supportive group. They shared personal experiences, disclosed secrets, supported each other, and challenged one another. Most reported personal growth and change of behavior that was supported by the observations of the other children, the counselor, and the school staff. All this was achieved in just ten 45-min sessions. The counselor summarized her experiences with this group as follows:

> From my group experience I have learned the value of self-disclosure. Self-disclosure is made possible when group cohesion is established, and the existence of cohesion enhances self-disclosure. I was proud to see that I can enhance both.

GROUP COUNSELING WITH PHYSICALLY HANDICAPPED AND MENTALLY CHALLENGED ADOLESCENTS

Description of the Group Members

This unusual group was comprised of five adolescent boys, ages 16–17, all physically handicapped and mentally challenged:

- Gary had had head surgery, which damaged his motor and mental performance. He walked with crutches.
- Wayne was in a car accident in which he received head injuries and also lost his mother. His motor and mental functioning were limited. He walked with crutches and also had a severe speech impediment.
- Andy had muscular dystrophy. Although he could walk independently, he needed support.
- Jan, too, had muscular dystrophy. He was new to the school (after attending a regular school) as a result of recent rapid deterioration. He was confined to a wheelchair and was mentally challenged.
- Larry was born with cerebral palsy, and was also confined to a wheelchair. His mental performance was limited, but his verbal expressiveness was relatively good.

Their counselor was Wendy, a graduate student in a counseling program.

Goals and Expectations

The goals of the group were to create a safe place for these boys, where they could experience a sense of intimacy and belonging, express their concerns, share similar difficulties, and develop social skills. Considering their limited mental ability and lack of social skills, it was not clear whether such goals could be achieved. The following is a description of their group process.

Pregroup Planning

The group was held in a special education facility for physically handicapped children, and the five oldest boys were invited to join. Dubbed "The Social Club," the group met in the counseling room once a week, for a total of twelve 45-min sessions. Owing to the participants' limited mental ability, lack of social skills, and high level of anxiety, Wendy used one therapeutic game throughout the process to stimulate the discussion in each session. This was a board game on which players move based on the throw of a die. They could land on three possible spaces: (a) Select a card and answer the question on it (e.g., "What do you do when you are sad?"); (b). Share something about yourself; (c) Ask someone in the group a question. These three instructions are geared to enhance self-expressiveness and self-disclosure and to increase interpersonal interaction. Due to the boys' limited motor and mental abilities, Wendy had to help with the reading of the cards and movement around the board.

Description of the Sessions

The first session was introductory. It began by having the adolescents and counselor introduce themselves. Having provided some structure, Wendy then asked the boys about their expectations of the group. Andy talked about releasing stress, sharing what was in one's heart, and knowing that no one will disclose their secrets. Gary expected the group to be a place to share private information, "to raise issues that cannot be discussed in another place." Wayne had difficulty expressing himself verbally, and, following several attempts to understand him, Wendy suggested that he write down his thoughts. He wrote, "Group is good." Larry did not want to be in the group, and Jan could not come up with a goal. Wendy acknowledged the difficulty of being in a group, and moved on to the topic of sharing favorite foods. Larry continued to resist; he was unable to find any food that he liked.

Most of these boys seemed to look forward to the group and to have reasonable expectations, despite their limited mental performance. Larry, the resisting participant, came from a highly functioning family, and although he had the best verbal skills in the group, he did not feel connected to the other group members. Still, he did not drop out and, in fact, was the first to arrive at the next group session.

At this second session, after a brief outline of group rules, the boys started playing the board game. Wayne was first, and the die landed on the instruction to select a card. His card instructed him to discuss "what a good friend is." He looked embarrassed and pointed to Andy. Wendy asked him to verbalize what he meant and Wayne, despite his extreme speech difficulties, said, "He is a good friend." The counselor further challenged him to express what he meant by a good friend, and Wayne wrote down, "nice, good hearted, fun." Only one other group member was able to join the discussion, expressing his agreement to what was already said. Wendy expanded the discussion by adding that good friends give each other mutual support. Andy then acknowledged that he, indeed, wanted Wayne to feel good and to be happy.

Gary was next; he landed on the instruction to share a personal experience. He then told the group about a visit by his girlfriend. Nobody believed the story and they actually got quite angry at him, accusing him of lying to them. They felt betrayed and insisted that there was no room for lies in the group. Larry was particularly troubled and reacted aggressively. Wendy reflected on the situation, suggesting that Gary badly wanted to have a girlfriend and wanted the group to believe him, and that Larry could not tolerate the lie. The counselor, like the boys, knew that Gary was fantasizing about a girlfriend; she also understood how vulnerable the boys were about the subject, and decided to drop it at this point.

Larry seemed happy with the reflection of his feelings. He took the next turn, and, in contrast to his previous resisting behavior, cooperated. He received a card saying "What do I do when I feel sad?" First he talked about his sad moments, particularly his loneliness and boredom, and shared his coping mechanism: music. The type of music that helped him appears to be a common theme for the boys and generated a group conversation. Wendy emphasized this similarity to increase group cohesiveness.

In this session, important progress had been made in terms of Larry's cooperation with the group. He risked speaking up against Gary and his fantasy; he was willing to play the game; he shared his feelings; and he even offered the group a topic for mutual sharing. As Larry was more verbal than the others, he probably served as a model to the other boys and felt good about his altruistic help to the group.

The third session started with Jan, the new boy in school. He insisted on being the first player, but was unable to respond to the instructions. Wendy gave him time, and after a relatively long pause, he mentioned his previous school. The boys, most of whom had attended the current school since kindergarten, seemed to be very curious about his different background. They ask questions about that regular school and also about how he felt in the new school. He talked about the pressure of exams and failing grades in his previous school. The boys tried to support him by offering good reasons for being happier in the current school: "The teachers are nicer here;" "There are no tests," they say. Jan seemed to be embarrassed by so much attention, and Wendy reflected on his embarrassment. The boys were not familiar with the term, and, following Wendy's explanation, they all shared embarrassing experiences. Taking away the focus from Jan was helpful; he seemed relaxed. Wayne shared with the group that he, too, was once in a regular school. This information appeared to surprise the group, as they were not familiar with his past. He shared with the boys his accident, following which he transferred to the special education school. The group was attentive and curious. A sense of cohesion seemed to be building. Wendy praised them highly for their good listening skills.

In this third session, progress had taken place in the group process. Jan, the new boy in school, who had avoided participation in the group process until this point, shared his experience of transition to a new school, and Wayne joined him in sharing a similar experience. The transition to a special education setting is a difficult, sometimes traumatic one. Both moved to the special facility because of deterioration in their health, which was an additional devastating event. This was Jan's way of connecting with the group, and Wayne has responded with altruistic self-disclosure. The group responded with empathy to both stories. Group cohesiveness seemed to be growing.

The fourth session focused on wishes, as one boy was instructed by the game to talk about a wish. Most of the boys wanted concrete things, like a DVD or a television. Only Larry expressed a wish to be "like everyone else," "to be independent," "not to be dependent so much on my mom." After a relatively long silence, Larry continued to share the difficulties his mother faced now that he was growing. Wayne joined in, but was too excited to express this verbally. He wrote, "Dad all the time." He then further explored his difficulties, moving from one situation to another in his home for which he needed his father's assistance. He spoke very slowly, the words rambling, but the group was attentive and tolerant. Wayne seemed relieved following his self-disclosure, and proud of being able to express himself orally. The group seemed to connect well, even though not everyone was able to share feelings at this point.

The fifth session started with Gary, who had to ask someone else a question. He addressed the question "Do you sometimes feel lonely?" to Andy, then acknowledged his own sense of loneliness. Several group members identified with this feeling, but their ways of coping were different. They discussed various activities that they could do within their limitations. Larry expressed his acceptance of his physical handicap, "I know I will never be like other kids, so I try to enjoy whatever I can do." This statement seemed to represent an existential factor, which was important for the boys' healing. More than the coping mechanisms, it was important to be able to share one's sense of loneliness in a group in which such feelings are universal. It was also helpful to the group to hear Larry accepting his handicap, rather than fighting it. These two processes were therapeutic for all the boys.

The sixth session focused on character. One of the instructions of the game was to describe some of one's own traits. As the boys were not familiar with the term, Wendy offered an example of her own. She shared her lack of courage to take risks. Following this, Wayne disclosed his fear of falling out of bed at night. Apparently, this is a common fear of children with a physical handicap. Indeed, several of the boys shared similar fears and suggested ways to deal with them. It was obvious that the boys were generating alternative coping skills. Wayne, who initiated the topic, discovered a creative way of coping that was not offered in the group and seemed to be proud of himself.

The seventh session was noisy and ineffective. There were fights and disturbances until Wendy shared her feelings with the boys, using an "I message" in which she expressed her sense of being disregarded and disrespected. The boys calmed down and permitted a group member to talk, but it was quite late. Many factors can explain such a problematic session, such as the relatively high self-disclosure in the previous session; after all, it is not at all easy to talk about fears, especially in adolescence. There also might have been external factors in the school that could affect the boys' mood. Moreover, difficult situations can be expected of normal adolescents, let alone exceptional ones. One group member's bad mood can cast a shadow on the whole session. The counselor must not be discouraged by such an incident, and should continue with the process as planned.

In the next session, Wayne entered with a big mark on his face. He immediately tried to share the incident with the group, but found it difficult to express himself. He was so devastated that he refused to write down what he wanted to say and continued struggling with the words. He mentioned the words "father" and "it hurts." Eventually, the message got through; his father hit him because he tried to go down the stairs by himself, which he was not permitted to do for reasons of safety. The boys reacted with much anger at his father and cited the law that protects children from abuse. Wayne was able to accept reflection of feelings of hurt and insult, but rejected the reflection of being fearful of his father. In other words, he trusted his father, but hurt physically and emotionally. The group responded with much support. "I hope you feel better by tomorrow," Gary said. "Tell your father that he is not allowed to hit you," insisted Larry. Jan, who only rarely participated in the group, promised to keep Wayne's story a secret. They all agreed to keep it a secret.

Wendy described the session as exciting, first, because the group proved to be a natural setting for the relief of emotions. Wayne did not hesitate to tell the group what happened; in fact, he seemed anxious to share the incident, expressing trust in the group. Second, the group reacted with maturity. The boys were attentive; they communicated directly with Wayne, maintaining eye contact, and they provided support and advice. They all insisted that he tell his teacher and principal, so that they can discuss the incident with his father and prevent another one from happening. Wayne accepted their advice and told his homeroom teacher, and actions were taken with his father. All these things point to the cohesiveness of the group.

In the ninth session, Larry asked to start. He picks a card that instructed him to think of a character trait that he shared with a family member. He mentioned anger. "I easily get angry and explode, just like my mom," he said. To explain what he meant by this, he mentioned his broken wheelchair, which limited his movement and took a long time to fix. He mostly shared with the group his daily difficulties moving around. Then Gary shared a mutual trait with his father, "My Dad talks so much, he never listens to me, and I like to talk, too." He explained that it bothered him that he could never express himself. The group took this statement to the here-and-now, accusing Gary of not letting other people in the group talk. The focus was on feelings of disappointment and disrespect when people do not listen to each other. The message was clear; Gary's lack of listening skills, as reflected in the group, hurt group members just as he himself was hurt in his relationship with his father. The group members seemed to feel good about the chance to teach him a lesson, yet in a gentle way, following his own self-awareness.

The tenth session began with the tragic incident of a classmate with muscular dystrophy whose health has deteriorated so badly that he was taken from school in an ambulance. Andy and Jan, who both had this same disease, were extremely upset and repeatedly gave a detailed description of the event. Wendy reflected on their feelings of concern, fear, and uncertainty, but the boys were too anxious to respond to this reflection. Larry tried to help the group, suggesting that they begin the game, but actually he refused to pick a card and instead shared his continuing problems with his broken wheelchair. Without it, he could not be mobile, and this caused him to be stuck at home and bored. He was particularly concerned about the approaching summer vacation. Andy joined him and shared a recent incident that left him feeling lonely and bored, too. His twin brother, who apparently spent a lot of time with him, had company and they all went out to play, leaving him behind. Wendy offered an interpretation of his feelings of abandonment, connecting these to the incident of the sick student that they had discussed earlier. Andy's response was, "It is indeed frightening." This was the first time that Andy has expressed a feeling in such a spontaneous manner, and he received warm reinforcement from Wendy. She expressed her own excitement following his self-expressiveness, saying "I felt you deep in my heart." Andy seemed very pleased with this response.

Several interesting processes were evident in this group session. First, it showed how external factors affect adolescents' behavior in the group; in this case, it was the expression of fears. Whether it was these external factors or the group's progress in general that facilitated the overt expressiveness, it is clear that a turning point had been reached. The boys no longer needed the game, as they now take the initiative to share their experiences with the group. Moreover, when the group seemed to be stuck with the external incident, one boy took the initiative to move the group ahead. Finally, a free expression of feelings took place in the group.

Session 11 started routinely, with the board game. Jan picked a card with the question, "Who do you feel close to?" He immediately mentioned his mother. The boys joined in, each one sharing whom they felt close to in their family. Wayne landed on the instruction to share something personal. He told the group about the pains in his hand, which limited his mobility even more. Gary landed on the instruction to ask a question. He turned to Larry and asked him, "Why don't you want to be my friend?" Larry responded that "We're just not like each other" and explained that they have different natures. Gary then said, "But in the group we often see similarities between us." Larry did not respond. This was a brave yet risky exchange of communication. Gary asked a direct and honest question, and Larry, who usually got easily irritated by Gary, responded thoughtfully and respectfully.

In this session, one could witness the group's maturity. Group members easily connected to the question on Jan's card. Wayne shared his physical difficulties spontaneously, a topic that these boys did not like to share. The highlight of the session was, of course, the direct question posed to Larry and his respectful response. The improvement in social skills was evident for both parties.

The twelfth and final session focused on termination. First, Wendy asked the boys how they felt about the group ending. Wayne and Andy said they were sad; Gary asked if they could meet during the summer; and Jan felt sorry that the group was ending (Larry was absent). Next, Wendy invited them to imagine that they were playing the board game, and each of them picks a card with the question, "What did you get out of the group?" Wayne said strength; Andy said friendship; Gary said patience; Jan felt closer to his classmates. Next, they said goodbye to each other and exchanged wishes. Finally, Wendy expressed her love for and appreciation to the group. She told them that she had learned a lot from them, that she shared with them the excitement and the sorrow. She then gave each of them a decorated stone with a personal note and suggested that they can hold it whenever they felt that they missed the group. She shook hands with each boy as they left. On her way out, she met Larry, who came to school sick just to say goodbye. "It was most important for me to say a personal thank you," he said, and shook her hand.

The termination session was indicative of how the boys enjoyed the group, became closer, and grew in social skills. The group goals had been largely achieved, despite the unique and challenging participants. The greatest initial concern was that these boys would not be able to interact with each other, which might inhibit the establishment of a group. However, this did not prove to be the case. Like in many groups, in the initial stage, the boys hesitated to disclose, interacted through the counselor, and were intolerant, particularly to one group member. However, as of the third session, the increase in self-disclosure was palpable. The boys talked about meaningful issues in their lives. Many of the common therapeutic factors were evidenced in this group. The sense of loneliness, dependency on others, and feelings of helplessness were universal, and awareness of this universality motivated the boys to acknowledge their feelings and release their burden. The development of socializing skills was also observed. During the group process, the boys learned to show interest in and concern for others, initiated interpersonal communication, and strengthened friendship ties. For example, Wayne and Larry became closer friends following the group experience. Some of the boys also went through cathartic experiences—Larry, when he disclosed his dependency on his mother, and Wayne, when he revealed his father's abusive act. Self-understanding increased for Gary, who, following feedback from the group, came to understand how his talkative behavior irritated others, and for Larry, who grasped that he gets easily irritated and was able to control his behavior during the exchange with Gary. The boys also learned from each other and from the counselor; for example, Wayne's brave struggle to express himself encouraged Jan to speak up. They also provided information to each other, particularly in the session where coping with fears of falling was discussed.

Conclusion

Very little has been published in the literature on groups for children with physical and mental challenges. Learning in a special education facility, they are mostly accustomed to individual work. Moreover, their mental deficiencies and lack of skills limits their interaction with others. Therefore, the effectiveness of such groups could be questioned. On the other hand, these boys, like so-called "normal" adolescents, needed close friendships and a sense of belonging. The group addressed these needs, helped them release emotional stress, and increased their interaction skills. I believe it was a most meaningful experience for them, and would like to encourage such groups in other special education settings.

COUNSELING A MULTICULTURAL GROUP

Description of the Group Members

The group was comprised of ten 13-year-old girls from one eighth-grade class in a school in northern Israel. It was established with the aim of facilitating acceptance of three Arab girls from families of the South Lebanese army that had escaped to Israel after the Israeli army pulled out of Lebanon. Because the South Lebanese army cooperated with the Israeli army during the war, these families were in danger after the Israelis left, and thus they received political asylum. Their children found it difficult to adjust socially; they were often rejected by their Jewish classmates and under certain circumstances, like after a terrorist attack, they were bullied. In addition, being refugees, they had problems with their own identity.

The three Arab girls—Crystal, Angie, and Nelly—were invited to join the group, along with seven Jewish girls from the same class. Two of these girls, Yael and Lior, needed emotional assistance—Yael because of her mother's recent death and Lior owing to problems in her family. The other five girls (Anita, Mor, Chen, Karen, and Natalie) were normative classmates. The group was introduced to them all as a place in which to discuss issues of adolescence and to improve interpersonal relationships. All the girls had a short interview, during which they expressed interest in joining the group. Sessions ran once a week for 10 weeks, during the regular school day.

Goals and Expectations

The major goal of the group was to increase the inclusion of the three Arab girls in their class. Through the mechanism of social support provided in a small group, the Arab girls were expected to release some of their stress. We also believed that, by getting closer to each other in the small group, some of the attitudes of the Jewish girls would change. Finally, we assumed that the change in attitudes in the group would carry over to the classroom, so that the rejection and bullying would stop.

Description of the Sessions

The first session started with an activity of getting acquainted. The girls were asked to share the legacy of their given name. There was quite a lot of embarrassment, so they asked the counselor, Shelly, to begin, and only then did they follow her modeling. Natalie went first; she explained that she was born in France, and that she loved her name because it made her feel special.

Mor related that her name meant "myrrh," which is a sweet scent, and that it suited her, because she was good looking and liked being a girl. Lior said that she was born a healthy baby, so her parents gave her the name, which means "light." Mor, who was her friend, confirmed that she was, indeed, a beacon of light and wished her happiness. This was the beginning of a spontaneous exchange of mutual support. Shelly, the counselor, took this opportunity to reinforce the norm of interpersonal support and she reflected on Mor's empathic skills.

Crystal, one of the Arab girls, explained that she was named after her grandmother, and that, in their tradition, it was the father who selected the baby's name. Karen stated that this was not fair. A short discussion of cultural differences evolved, following which the girls agreed that cultures are different in their customs and that this should be accepted. The girls also added information, telling her that crystal is an expensive type of glass. Crystal smiled; she already seemed to feels better with this small gesture.

Nelly, another Arab girl, barely whispered her name. It was clear she did not feel comfortable speaking to the group. She only said that she had the name of a celebrity. The group seemed detached from her.

Angie, the third Arab girl, related that she was named after a famous singer with whom her father was in love in the past. She thought that she got special attention from him because of the name. Yael mentioned that this was the first time that she had heard Angie's voice.

Anita was next; but before she could begin, the group started to giggle, which seemed to embarrass her. It turned out that her name was the title of a popular television comedy show. Anita expressed her embarrassment and admitted that she did not like the connotation. The girls who giggled apologized and suggested a nickname for her.

Yael said that her mother gave her the name because she liked it, and tears welled up in her eyes. The girls and the counselor understood that she was crying because of the recent loss of her mother. Shelly promised that the group would be there for her whenever she needed them, and, to continue in a more positive tone, she mentioned that Yael in the bible was a smart, brave woman. The girls acknowledge that the Yael they knew was very brave. It helped her to hear this.

Chen was named after her grandmother, which made her father's favorite. Karen said she got her name simply because her mother liked it.

Overall, a positive climate seemed to have been established. The girls had been quite open about the legacy of their names, and they had also been supportive of one another. Shelly, the counselor, worked hard at modeling and encouraging the necessary language of acceptance and empathy.

The goal for the second session was to establish a group contract. This was achieved in two stages. First, the group was divided into pairs to discuss the pros and cons of self-disclosure, and the experiences that come up were further discussed in the group. There were both positive and negative experiences regarding self-disclosure, but the overall attitude was positive. Next, Shelly took a large sheet of paper and wrote down one behavior that each participant contributed. The three main themes that were suggested are confidentiality (keeping secrets), attentive listening, and respect. It was concluded that there would be no pressure on any group member to participate, but at the same time the girls were encouraged to contribute to the group process as much as they could. They came up with the central norms needed for an effective group process. Shelly added her expectation for them to avoid missing the group sessions and to come on time.

The aim of the third session wsa to increase group cohesiveness. The activity was for each girl to present herself through a drawing. First, each participant drew symbols that best represented herself; then, they shared this in pairs; and last, each girl presented her partner to the group.

Nelly, one of the Arab girls, did not initially participate in the drawing phase, but, after some encouragement from Shelly, she drew a computer and a bouquet of flowers. She was first to introduce her partner, Angie (also Arab). Nelly told the group that Angie liked TV and liked to dance. The other girls addressed many questions to Angie following this introduction. They did not know much about her and seemed very curious. Her most meaningful response was, "I like TV because this is the only place I have some control over my life". She went on to describe her father's overwhelming control. She was not independent; she could not dress the way she wanted or go to a sleepover party. The girls reacted with empathy. One said she found it difficult to see Angie suffering; another wanted to help but did not know how; a third is angry at Angie's father, and a fourth girl suggested that she should confront her father. Angie responded with great maturity. She was not angry at her father, because she knew he was only protecting her, and he did not understand the norms of Israeli culture. The girls insisted that she should talk more openly with her father. Karen asked Shelly, the counselor, to intervene on Angie's behalf. Feeling that Karen was trying to pull her into a power struggle, Shelly firmly concluded that she could see Karen's concern for Angie, but that Angie had to decide how she wanted to deal with this, and then Shelly would be happy to support her efforts, if she wished.

Next, Angie introduced Nelly. The group was impressed with her drawing and reinforced her for it. Someone responded to her interest in chat groups and invited her to join her list. She smiled but did not take her up on the offer. On the whole, both Arab girls received quite a lot of attention and support.

The next pair comprised two Jewish girls, Chen and Lior. Chen was challenged about her snobbish behavior. The girls felt that she was parading her academic success and this hurt other people's feelings. Chen listened carefully and concluded that she had learned something important about herself. She offered her help to anyone interested, and Yael accepted the offer. The group was pleased with the way the feedback was provided and they reinforced Chen for being able to accept their feedback so graciously.

Considering the short time left in this session, the other girls had to hurry. Yael's symbol was a bird, because in bad times she "flies away." Anita drew a big heart and some butter to represent her lack of assertiveness. Crystal drew a microphone and a baby, because she liked to sing, and because she wants to remain a baby protected by her parents. Mor drew the moon and stars to represent her relationships with her classmates; she felt that she was too dominant. Karen was occupied with her sexual identity. To help her with a somewhat embarrassing issue, and because she showed resistance to the counselor, Shelly disclosed that she, too, had similar issues; she was considered a muscular woman and often wondered about it. This self-disclosure reduced some of Karen's resistance. Finally, Natalie presented her piano, which served as a source of support at difficult moments, when she was stressed or angry.

Overall, it appeared that the goals of this session were met: the girls became closer, learned about each other, and made good use of interpersonal skills. The three target girls participated well in the process, got positive responses, and one even received an explicit invitation.

The fourth session addressed the issue of prejudice and stereotypes. It began with a 10-min film in which a mixed young couple tried to rent an apartment, but was rejected when the owner discovered that the man was Ethiopian. The girls immediately applied this theme to their situation involving the Arab girls. Mor mentioned that the Arab girls were not invited to their parties and said that she felt bad about this. She was not sure how the girls felt about it. Shelly suggested a direct dialogue. Crystal said that she did not care, as her father would not let her go anyway. In an attempt to elicit emotions, Shelly disclosed an incident in which she was not invited to a teacher's wedding and told of how she felt lonely and rejected, and lost faith in herself. After her modeling, the following exchange ensues:

Shelly: (to Crystal)	If Mor invited you, even though your father does not allow you to go, how would you feel?
Mor:	That she is my friend.
Shelly:	So, how do you feel when you are not invited? (Crystal does not respond.)
Karen:	See, she doesn't react. How can you be friends when the other person doesn't respond?
Shelly:	So what do you want to say to Crystal?
Mor:	I want her to answer if she wants us to be her friends.
Shelly:	Do you want to be her friend?
Karen:	Yes.

Mor:	Yes, me, too.
Natalie:	If I were them, I would hate the Jews.

Most of the responses were empathic, but Natalie added the implication that the Arab girls also played a role in their segregation. She complained that they withdrew from the group and did not make efforts to connect.

Natalie:	They do not like us.
Karen:	They feel stuck with us.
Anita:	That is not fair. We do not really invite them.
Shell: (to the Arab girls)	Did you know that this is how the girls feel about you?
Angie:	We never talked about it.
Shelly:	What do you think now?
Angie:	It's not easy. They are all together and we are alone.

Angie further explained that by belonging to a minority, it was hard for her to make the first move. Karen complained that the group was dealing with an issue that obviously made the three girls feel uncomfortable. Shelly insisted that open communication might help. Anita, following the lack of response from the Arab girls, felt that Karen may be right. But on the other hand, she said, "if we do not talk about it, we will never resolve the problem." Following her statement, most of the Jewish girls supported the Arab girls and expressed their wish to help. The latter were embarrassed but also empowered, and the following dialogue took place:

Angie:	We were always excluded. It is strange to hear those thoughts. I don't know what to say.
Crystal:	I feel really good. It was good to listen to Karen ... she seems a bit .....
Mor:	Against you?
Karen:	No, I am not against you. Your segregation sometimes bothers me, so I don't speak nicely.
Shelly:	Do you express anger because of the distance they keep?
Karen:	Not anger, but I feel I want to bug them.
Shell: (to the Arab girls)	Did you ever think that this might be her way of becoming closer?
Crystal:	No, I thought this is a sign of rejection.
Shelly:	And how do you feel now?
Crystal:	Perhaps she cares about us.
Angie:	I feel that there are nice girls here.
Nelly:	I am really OK.

The Jewish girls felt that the group had become more cohesive, that it was important to continue with the discussion, that it felt good to hear from the Arab girls. But Karen had mixed feelings: "I came out sounding like the bad guy, but I understand I am not perfect." Shelly reinforced this mature response and praised the girls for their courageous exchange. The group was clearly approaching the working stage.

This session led to the idea to schedule a class meeting with the parents of the three Arab girls, so they could explain to the Jewish children the supportive role that the South Lebanese army took. This was particularly important against the background of the Intifada, a time when every Arab was perceived as an enemy.

The sixth and seventh group sessions focused on coping patterns. The girls used the book *A Fence, a Sheep and a Man with a Problem* (by Y. Biran, 1999). They first listened to the story, then selected the sheep whose pattern of coping was similar to their own.

Anita picked the sheep that is strong and not afraid of difficulties. She supported her choice with examples from her life, such as working hard to improve her grades and ignoring remarks about her name, which eventually caused people to drop them.

Mor chose the spoiled sheep for which the fence gets smaller when it approaches. Yet, because she was sure that she often joined others in their efforts, she also selected another sheep that cooperates with the others. She cited the time when her parents refused to let her go on a school trip, and described how she gained the support of her teacher and principal and eventually was allowed to go.

Karen selected the sheep that rams straight into the fence, explaining that often she used force to achieve her goals, even though she knew this exacted a price. The group challenged her about this pattern of coping. She admitted that she was stubborn. The girls also recognized the pattern in the here-and-now, when they dealt with the Arab girls. They also mentioned her initial resistance to Shelly. Karen was left with the question of whether she wanted to continue with this pattern or make a change.

Natalie picked the intelligent sheep that deliberates between its choices. She said it took her forever to make a decision. The girls then tested her recent decisions and discovered that she was pleased with all of them. Her conclusion was that she was making good decisions and that she only needed to have more confidence in herself. The girls responded with surprise regarding her choice. They felt that she was a strong person and they often consulted with her. Natalie felt empowered by the feedback.

Yael selected the two small sheep that helped each other, because this was how she was coping with the loss of her mother. She relied on others and shared her feelings with them. The girls perceived her as strong and courageous, and actually more willing to help than be helped. Crystal, the Arab girl, shared with the group that she was absent the week before, and that it was Yael who took notes for her in the classes she missed. This was a beginning of a new friendship, probably following the exchange of communication at the last session. This was also the first time in the group that Crystal initiated communication.

Angie followed her modeling and shared with the group the sheep she picked. She chose the sheep that ignores the problem, feeling that this sometimes helps. In an attempt to make her aware that ignoring or repressing a problem is not always effective, Shelly asked her to choose a sheep that she would like to be. She picked the confident sheep.

Finally, Chen chose the sheep that jumped over the others. She admitted that she would do anything to succeed, because the world was extremely competitive. The group challenged her as to her limits. She assured the girls that she would never hurt a close friend.

The feedback in this session was very good. The girls clearly felt closer to each other, both in and out of the group. The counselor reinforced them for their honest interactions, particularly the ability to support and challenge at the same time.

The plan for the seventh session was to start without an activity, but the girls asked to revert to the pattern they already knew. So Shelly handed out two cards to each girl; she instructed them to write down on the first card something they liked to hear someone say to them, and on the other card, something that made them angry when they hear it.

The focus of this session was on Mor, whose mother was pushing her to be a model, whereas Mor was hesitant:

> I like it that I am good looking. It often helps me, but it seems like it is more important for my mom than it is for me. ... I don't agree with others that I am that good looking, I am too short to be a model. ... I am not sure this is what I want to do. ... It is as if the beauty takes over. ... I never heard my mom say something good about me except that I am pretty. ... It is the money involved that makes her feel that way.

Mor understood that the same statement made her both happy and sad. She liked to be good looking, but she wanted to be appreciated for her other qualities as well. She wanted attention from her mother as a person, not as an object, and she did not want to be pushed into making a decision. These were the insights that she gained in the session.

Mor then moved on to talk about her relationships with friends. In this arena, too, she was not sure whether girls wanted to be friends with her because she was popular or because they liked her for who she s. She responded positively to the challenge to receive feedback from her friends in the group.

Chen:	You are very pleasant. It is good to be with you. You are never pushy or aggressive.
Anita:	You are considerate and sensitive. You always sense when something is wrong, even before I say anything.
Lior:	You are well behaved. Even with the teachers you are polite.

Mor felt good with the feedback and laughingly suggested that they teach her mother how to see her. The group offered to take this a step further and confront her mother with a good and honest conversation. Mor said she would think about it.

At this point, Karen expressed her disappointment for focusing so much on Mor. The girls tried to dismiss her complaints, but it was the counselor who encouraged her to speak up and express herself. Karen explained that she was concerned about Crystal and Angie, the Arab girls, as they had no chance to speak. It was good to see her concern for the girls. Her resistance had been channeled in a positive direction, which was good for all—Karen, the counselor, and the group as a whole.

Most of the girls enjoyed the focus on one person. They felt that it moved the group towards greater intimacy:

Natalie:	I have learned many things today. I always envied Mor, but I don't feel that way now. I also learned more about her; she is much more modest than I thought. I feel closer to her now.
Crystal:	It was important for me to listen to Mor. I felt good.
Nelly:	The fact that I don't talk much does not mean I do not like the group. I feel good.
Shelly (to Nelly):	Can you hear the invitation to talk? You are invited.
Nelly:	OK.
Mor:	For me it was important that you all listened to me. I apologize to Karen if she is hurt.
Karen:	Although I disagree sometimes, I want you to know that I am happy with the group.

The group was progressing, so that they could give space to someone else. There was great concern for each other. The girls were considerate, supportive, and challenging.

The next session was based on bibliotherapy. The girls received little poems from a book on adolescence and were invited to choose one portion of a poem. The focus of the session was on Lior. She selected a piece that talked about the telephone and a personal diary as best friends. She disclosed that she was keeping a diary, as they did not talk about feelings in her family. "People in our family live apart with little interaction among them. ... They don't seem to be happy with each other," she added and tears welled up in her eyes. Angie (the Arab girl) hugged her. Armed with this support, Lior disclosed her big secret: her retarded brother, who was a great burden on her, who her family was ashamed of, and who was a target of constant concern. Nobody but him got attention from her parents, particularly her mother. She could not share her concerns or feelings because they were not accepted. Nothing could measure up against her brother's problems. Shelly acknowledged her feelings of loneliness, but also highlighted the impact that it had on her personality. In the group, Lior appeared empathic, concerned, and encouraging. The girls also contributed positive features, such as tolerance and reliance. Lior agreed that she was very mature. She felt relieved and thanked the group for listening and for their concern. Shelly added that Lior now had good friends besides the diary. The group was very pleased and seemed more cohesive than ever.

The ninth session was the beginning of termination. Each of the girls made a collage of herself, and then they added feedback to each other. The result was a group picture full of positive feedback. The next step was a summary of their experience in the group. They all felt that it had been effective, interesting, and helpful, but also too short. They felt that the group had much potential but they did not get to hear everyone.

The last session was a party which the girls organized themselves, with games and food.

SUMMARY AND CONCLUSION

The group was established to help integrate three Arab girls in the classroom. The selection of participants included two other girls who were expected to benefit from the group because of difficult life circumstances. The rest of the girls were normative and were invited to help with the integration goal.

The process revealed that two of the three Arab girls adjusted to the group norms. They gradually increased their participation in the group conversations and sometimes even initiated the contact. The important achievement for them was the open feedback that they received from the Jewish girls. They were wanted, they were welcome, but they also needed to show some interest in the relationships. Even if nothing changed in practice and the girls continued to be left out of sleepover parties, the sense of isolation and rejection had certainly decreased. Indeed, the homeroom teacher who had initially asked Shelly, the counselor, to help her out with the Arab girls' segregation, reported that there was more interaction between the Arab and Jewish girls both in class and during recess.

It was important for the Arab girls to hear that their Jewish peers also had difficulties, although of a different kind. There was one opportunity where one of these girls provided emotional support to a Jewish girl; this in itself was a healing process.

Of the two Jewish girls who were expected to benefit from the process, one underwent a cathartic experience and the other briefly touched upon her difficulties. Both, however, gained from the group support provided to them.

It is interesting that some of the normative girls, who were expected to help with the process, got a lot out of it. One talked about her relationship with her mother; another learned that her appearance intimidates others, and a third learned how her anger was misunderstood. They all grew in the process, without having recognized specific difficulties. It seems that one does not have to have a special situation to benefit from a counseling group, certainly not in adolescence.

The main therapeutic factors were evidenced in this group process; there was catharsis, interpersonal learning, self-understanding, altruistic behavior, hope, skill acquisition, advice, and guidance. Nonetheless, group cohesiveness seems to have been the basis for all these factors. Only when the group was close enough was it possible to go through cathartic experiences, and these experiences of self-disclosure further enhanced the cohesiveness in the group.

The advantage of a small group is clear. A dialogue with the three Arab girls would probably be impossible within a large classroom. We could see how intimidated the girls were even in a small group. Addressing the issue in a small, intimate group as a first step turned out to be effective, as these relationships carried over into the classroom and to life in school in general.

The counselor played an important part in the success of the group. She was an effective listener; she was not afraid of challenges, and, above all, she dealt with resistance with sensitivity and respect. She understood well the roles she assumed as a group leader. She gave first priority to establishing group cohesion, norms of mutual support, and interpersonal feedback. Behavior in the group was closely monitored to avoid discipline problems. She encouraged self-disclosure, self-exploration, and insight. She appreciated emotional experiencing and led the girls towards that end. The group gradually took over and she stepped back. She was good at monitoring the group process and the mood of participants. As a result, we evidenced an effective group process that needed more time to fully achieve its goals.

GROUP COUNSELING WITH YOUNG CHILDREN

Description of the Group Members

The group was comprised of six 8-year-olds (two boys and four girls) from one third-grade classroom in a school in an affluent neighborhood. All of these children were identified by the school staff as having social problems. One interesting note is that most of the children were able to identify their difficulties accurately, as evidenced in the way they stated personal goals for the group:

- Nelly, who was quite an angry girl, said she would like to learn to control her frequent outbursts of anger.
- Tom, who was frequently involved in fights and had discipline problems, wanted to reduce his aggression.
- Lily, a rather withdrawn girl, wanted to learn how to cope with criticism without hurting so much.
- Angelina, who had severe communication difficulties, said she wanted to be less critical of her friends.
- Sasha, a shy and withdrawn boy, wanted to have more friends.
- Ella, an extremely rejected girl in the class, was unable to come up with any personal goal.

Goals and Expectations

The goal for this group was to enhance the interpersonal skills of these young children. However, instead of using an educational skills training approach, my colleagues and I used the same expressive–supportive modality illustrated in this book. We believed that the children would be willing to share personal events and disclose feelings, and that a positive and supportive climate could be achieved. We also expected some of the issues to be brought to the here-and-now of the group. It was clear, though, that due to their young age, the counselor should be more active and use a great variety of therapeutic games.

Description of the Group Process

As in many other groups, the goals for the first stage were to create a climate of trust, to increase group cohesiveness, and to establish constructive norms to work in a group. These goals were initially achieved through icebreaker exercises and getting acquainted activities, and later through the establishment of group rules. For example, one activity was to get to know each other better through a mutual interview in pairs.

Mindy, the counselor, instructed the children to wander around the room, stop on her signal, and then pair up with the child standing next to them. Then the partners interviewed each other for about 5 min apiece. Finally, they introduced their partner to the group. This activity achieves several goals. Getting acquainted with at least one child in the group helps reduce anxiety, increases the sense of support, and enhances listening skills.

Ella was quite resistant in the first few sessions. She displayed disinterest in the group and made some nasty remarks. Yet, she chose to be first to introduce her partner, Nelly. The two had discovered that they shared a love for animals. Nelly then introduced Ella to the group, detailing the kinds of animals that Ella liked. But Ella was not satisfied, because Nelly had forgotten to mention one of the animals she liked. She got upset, complained, and became grouchy.

Ella:	I also said cats! She doesn't remember everything!
Nelly:	Sorry, she also likes cats.
Ella:	Now it's OK!
(in a bossy tone)	

It was obvious that Ella lacked several social skills. She had little empathy, had difficulties compromising, and was harsh in her responses.

The other two pairs did much better. They mentioned more personal issues (e.g.," I have a little brother who makes me mad;" "I like to have friends come over, but sometimes I get into fights with them.") and expressed more concern for each other (e.g., "Did I mention everything?"). Overall, the children were able to share personal information, to initiate questions, to listen carefully, and to present each other in a respectful way.

Group rules were established in two major ways. One was through an activity in which personal needs in the group were identified. Mindy instructed the children to mention one behavior that they would like to see in the group and one that they would not want to see. There was pretty much of a consensus regarding the focus on group cohesiveness; the children said they wanted to be able to share without being criticized or rejected. They wanted to be carefully listened to and respected. They all mentioned confidentiality. Finally, they also wanted to have fun. Their expectations and wishes for the group made up the group rules. When discipline problems cropped up, Mindy refered back to these rules that they all agreed upon.

Another way that Mindy established and maintained group rules was by her own modeling and by carefully monitoring the children's behavior. For example, when Ella became grouchy and complained about being improperly introduced, Mindy said: "Ella, it's now Nelly's turn to introduce you. You will have time to add whatever you want later." She also said, "I am now listening to Nelly, so I can't hear you."

The working stage, which started at the fifth session, was warm and open. The children presented such behaviors as self-disclosure, expression of negative emotions, and interpersonal exchange of feedback. Sasha started by expressing anger at his mother. During the activity, he selected a card of an older woman, which reminded him of his mother, and said, "All she cares about is my grades. I don't think she likes me because I am not good enough in school. She is always disappointed in me." After some of the other children shared similar experiences with their parents, Sasha went on, "It's not that I don't try, but I just can't concentrate for so many hours. So I just sit there, staring at my homework, and being angry." Most of the children felt he should involve his father and ask for his support. Mindy suggested that he talk to his mother. They did a role-play with his mother, and this convinced him that he may be able to try it out.

The next session started with a spontaneous self-disclosure. As she enters the room, Lily mentioned a Brazilian flag she saw on her way to the group. She rambled for a while, and Ella lost her patience, saying, "What does that have to do with us?" But the other children encourage her to talk.

Tom:	Take your time.
Lily:	I don't know where to start. It's many things.
Mindy:	Please start from wherever it is convenient.
Lily:	I am adopted, my mother brought me from Brazil.

The group fell into deep silence, then bombarded her with questions of "Why?" "When?" and so forth. Mindy suggested that they all just let her talk. Lily explained, "My mother could not give birth; she very much wanted a baby, so she went to Brazil to get me. I was just a baby." Lily went into detail and the group seemed very curious, throwing out even more questions. Only Ella continues to complain that this was boring. The kids trie to hush her, but Mindy instructed her to talk directly to Lily, hoping that direct communication would help Ella become more empathic.

Ella:	Yes, poor Lily. She does not have parents. (She is not able to talk directly to her.)
Lily:	But I do have a mother.
Ella:	But it's not the same.
Lily:	For me it's the same. She's always been my mother, she loves me and I love her.

But Ella continued to complain that it was boring, and the group became irritated at her. Someone said, "This is so exciting;" another said, "It's so interesting;" and a third child said, "It is sad." Lily replied, "I know that some people who have not had such an experience cannot understand it." Several children assure her that they do understand. Lily said, "That's all. I saw the flag and wanted to share this with you. I jut felt that we are a group and so it was important for me to share it with you." Angelina hugged her, saying "You are so nice." Mindy thanked Lily for trusting the group and thanked the group for being attentive and supportive.

When a group becomes cohesive and members start sharing private information, it becomes difficult to keep secrets from the group. I believe that this was Lily's primary motivation to share her big secret. Most of the group members were mature enough to handle the situation, the exception being Ella. However, the exchange of negative communication between the two may have been a powerful growth experience for both. Ella represented many possible other children who might respond with cruelty to Lily's story. In the group, Lily had an opportunity to face the challenge and practice some necessary skills. Indeed, she remained quite calm in the challenging exchange with Ella. She insisted that hers was not a sad story, that she loved her mother and her mother loved her. She also considered the possibility that some people just may not understand. For a withdrawn girl whose goal for the group was to feel less intimidated by others, this was a great lesson. At the same time, she was also supported by the other group members, and could conclude that not all people are nasty. Some are actually nice and supportive. This could help Lily cope with future nasty remarks as well.

Ella still had a long way to go. She needed to recognize that her reactions were different from the rest. She didn't yet understand how she contributed to her own rejection by her classmates. She needed help with this, but there were only a few sessions left.

In the next couple of sessions, Nelly talked about her difficulties in controlling her outbursts. Nelly had ADHD; she was restless and nervous. She presented her problem in a very unusual way—through a story of an exceptional boy that she chose to read to the group. In this way, she expressed her sense of being different. She said, "I am like the boy in the story. I am just different. I would like to relax, but I am kind of helpless." The other children acknowledged that she sometimes interrupts, but they also mentioned her kindness. They appreciated the way she responded to Ella when Ella accused her of not remembering everything she had said. They shared incidents in their own lives when they felt restless, as well as ideas for coping with stress. Nelly had been acutely aware of her difficulties, and she was thankful to the group for allowing her to be open rather than continue keeping it a secret. She said, "I thought I was the only one to be so stressed. It was helpful to hear that other children also have times when they are upset. I don't feel that exceptional any more."

Tom, the aggressive boy, followed Nelly's lead. He mainly talked about his feelings of guilt after he got into a fight and hurt someone.

Tom:	I knew I should not hurt him as soon as the fight was over. He was younger than me, and much weaker. I just did not think at the moment, I was so angry.
Nelly:	I've seen you fight more than once, but I didn't know you feel so bad afterwards. You are goodhearted.
Lily:	To me, you are mostly kind. You help me when some kids bully me.
Sasha:	But Tom, it does hurt people when you pick on them. I was intimidated by you more than once.
Angelina:	Yes, it does not help people if you are sorry afterwards. You need to control yourself before you get into a fight (she gives an example of a recent incident in which Tom was involved in a bad fight).

Some of the children felt empathy for Tom, while at the same time also challenging him. Although the challenges sometimes seemed quite harsh, they were apparently effective. This was the first time that Tom had been challenged by his peers rather than by authority figures, and this had occurred within a supportive climate.

At termination, Mindy conducted the Personal Award activity. She handed each group member a certificate and asked the child to give himself or herself the award for some kind of personal progress that had been made. She then asked the other group members to add feedback based on the progress they have noticed.

Lily wanted to go first. She gave herself an award for being creative. Angelina confirmed that she was, indeed, creative and that she helped them all during class time.

Nelly told her that she was brave. Ella, who complained of boredom during the session in which Lily told her secret, joined Nelly this time and expressed her appreciation of Lily's disclosure. "I don't think I would be able to be so open," she added. This was a turning point in Ella's mode of communication. Progress here was clear. The rest of the children appreciated her openness and honesty.

Sasha gave himself the award for being a good friend. He recalled how he supported many of the children in the group and that it felt good. He also believed that he was initiating more social interactions with others and felt less lonely. For Sasha, the group became the laboratory in which he could practice his new social skills. Lily confirmed that he was a supportive friend and mentioned the time that he gave her a piece of chocolate when she was upset. Nelly mentioned his success at playing an instrument and others join in to praise him.

Tom gave himself the award for getting into much fewer fights: "I feel I control myself much better now." Angelina added that Tom was also much better behaved in class. To support her opinion, she cited an example in which Tom gave up his turn to ride a car on a field trip. "He never did that before," she said. Lily added that he was less disruptive in class. And Mindy said that she had noticed his improvement in the group and that his teachers had also seen a change in him. Nelly, too, awarded herself for greater control over her behavior and was supported by the other children.

Angelina felt that she improved her communication skills. Children were less hurt by her remarks, because she had become aware of her behavior, she said.

Ella was unable to give herself an award. The others mentioned how she shared the story of her grandmother's death. They felt good and close to her when she did this, they said. However, although her interpersonal interaction with others improved (as witnessed by her feedback to Lily), Ella remained with a poor sense of self-esteem.

SUMMARY AND CONCLUSION

Overall, this was a growth experience for these young children. They experienced close relationships that permitted them to disclose some of their secrets and thus reduce their emotional burden. They also had an opportunity to identify and explore their difficulties and the consequent behavior, to develop some insights, and to take steps to change. Interestingly, just as in groups with older children, there was an exchange of both supportive and challenging feedback, which enhanced self-awareness through interpersonal learning. Most of the children made some evident progress. This process was not much different from groups of older children and adolescents, suggesting that even 8-year-olds can benefit from a therapeutic process in which self-expressiveness and group support are evident, and in which an exchange of interpersonal learning has been present. I am often asked as of what age children can participate in such process-oriented groups. Usually, work with young children is more structured and more teaching-oriented. This group is one example that young children do not necessarily need activity groups or educational training groups to change their behavior. They, too, can learn from reexperiencing positive relationships, from an honest and direct exchange of communication, and from peer support.

Appendix II
Group Activities with Children and Adolescents

INTRODUCTION

An important part of the work my colleagues and I do with children and adolescents is the use of therapeutic activities. Our research has shown that activities or games produced most of the participants' self-disclosure. Activities are triggers to elicit thoughts, emotions, and events that can help children in their growth experience. However, they should not replace processing of the issues that come up. Activities also need to be adjusted to the developmental ability of the children and to the developmental stage of the group.

In this Appendix, I illustrate some of the activities that we've found helpful in working with children, and that have not been illustrated previously in this book or were only briefly mentioned. Each activity starts with an outline of the goal, the procedure, and guidelines for processing. It is then followed by examples from our work with the children.

ACTIVITIES FOR THE INITIAL STAGE

The Circle of Emotions

Goal—To monitor feelings of the here-and-now.   There are several reasons to elicit participants' feelings about the group at the initial stage. First, such feelings, particularly when negative (e.g., fear, anger), provide important clinical material to work on. The children may not bring these feelings out unless they are invited to do so. Second, the feelings of group members are important indicators as to how to proceed with the group process. If participants feel relaxed and comfortable, the counselor can move more quickly to the working stage. When they feel anxious or intimidated, the counselor needs to slow down and work more on establishing a climate of trust and group cohesiveness. This is also an opportunity for the leader to identify those children that find the group situation difficult. The counselor may want to talk with a child who feels exceptionally threatened and decide together whether that child wants to continue being in the group. Third, working in an expressive–supportive modality, therapists want to stress the importance of the expression of feelings. This is one of the norms that my colleagues and I want to encourage in our groups. Finally, we want to work on the here-and-now so that the group becomes the agency of change.

Procedure.   Each participant receives a piece of paper and is instructed to draw a circle, divide it into four parts, and then write down in each quadrant a feeling they are presently having in the group. With younger children, we hand out a ready-made circle and provide a list of possible emotions that may help them identify their own feelings. The length of the list depends on the age of the participants.

Process.   The children are asked to share some of the feelings that they have written down. Processing relates to reasons they feel that way and how the group can help improve those feelings.

Example.   Sheila said that she felt anxious talking in a group. She was used to talking only with her close friend. She was assured that she would not be pressured to talk until she felt comfortable.

ACTIVITIES FOR THE INITIAL STAGE (CONTINUED)

Facial Expressions

Goal—To increase the language of feelings. Goals are similar to those in the previously described activity, except that this activity is not restricted to the here-and-now. It also has the advantage of allowing the children to move around, which they enjoy.

Procedure. The counselor hangs up a few posters with various facial expressions around the room: Happy, Sad, Anxious, Bored, etc. The children are asked to sit next to the facial expression that best suits them. They first share their reasons for selecting that expression with other children who made the same choice, which helps them find similarities in feelings. This in itself enhances the sense of universality and provides emotional support. Next, they share some of their feelings with the entire group.

Processing. The feelings that the children mention are connected to events or difficulties they face. Processing the feelings can help children identify and explore the difficulty. At this initial stage, insight and change are less expected, although they may be achieved as well.

Example

Ann:	I sat next to the happy face. All week, I was not involved in any fights with my friends. ...
	[She briefly reflected on her feelings, then added.] Lately, the girls in class pick on me. They blame me for things I didn't do and start fights with me. Today, nobody picked on me; instead they smiled at me, so I feel great.
Counselor:	How do you handle such situations?
Ann:	When I am wrong, I admit it, but when it's not true and they spread rumors about me, I am lost.
Counselor:	We have to remember your difficulty in coping with rumors. We will come back to this at a later stage in the group if you still find it a problem.

Note that at a beginning stage, the counselor stopped here and proceeded to another child. At a more advanced stage of the group process, the counselor and group would continue processing the issue.

ACTIVITIES FOR THE INITIAL STAGE (CONTINUED)

My Fantasy Group

Goal—To establish group rules based on children's needs.   Children in groups must have rules and regulations to prevent discipline problems. The transition from classroom discipline, based on the teacher's authority, to a small group seated in a circle is sometimes a sign that this is a place with no limits. So, most counselors who work with kids bring in some basic rules and instruct the children to follow them. In my opinion, rules established by the children themselves based on their declared needs have a better chance of being followed. There is, of course, more than one way to involve children in the establishment of group rules. This particular activity makes use of the children's imagination.

Procedure.   The children are invited to think about the group as their fantasy land, where they would feel really good. They are guided to think about the relationships they anticipate and the behavior they would want to see in that land. They can also mention types of relationships and behavior they do not want to let enter into their land. Younger children are invited to draw and color their fantasy land.

Based on the children's descriptions, the counselor generates the rules for the group and posts them conspicuously. The discussion then focuses on the ways each child can help keep the rules, so that fantasy land remains as nice as they wish. They may even sign a contract to keep the rules.

Processing.   Processing includes the cognitive and emotional exploration of the importance of each rule they have mentioned, the difficulties children sometimes have in keeping the rules, and ways they can help each other follow the rules.

Example.

Ann:	My fantasy land is a group of close friends who wish me only good. They respect me, listen to me, never interrupt. They greet me when I come in, invite me to sit next to them, and keep my secrets.
Counselor:	How can we help Ann stay in her fantasy land?
John:	I promise to listen carefully.
Rachel:	I promise to keep secrets.
Sue:	I will greet her when she comes to the group and in class.

ACTIVITIES FOR THE INITIAL STAGE (CONTINUED)

Ball Games

Goal—To increase interpersonal interaction.   Interpersonal interaction is a major mechanism in group counseling. But people, and especially kids, are used to communicating through an authority figure (such as the teacher). Talking to each other directly is a behavior they need to practice. The ball eases such communication.

Procedure.   The child who holds the ball chooses who to pass it to, and asks that person a question or makes a comment. The counselor starts, to provide modeling, then the children continue to throw the ball. The rule is that each child must receive the ball once, and only after everyone has had a chance to participate can they take a second turn. Each round is expected to be more meaningful in content. To achieve the goal, the counselor may ask the children to tie their questions to significant events that came up in the previous round. Children may, of course, pass the ball to the counselor.

Processing.   Processing involves exploring children's responses to the questions, as well as the reasons for having asked the question.

Example.   Ruth threw the ball to Larry and asked him why he had tears in his eyes when Dina spoke beforehand. Larry responded, "I, too, had a recent death in my family. I try to forget about it, but when she talked, the whole picture of the funeral and everything came back to me." The counselor invited him to share more, if he liked. Larry went on, "My parents' advice was just to forget it. But I was so close to him. I was the last one to see him." Larry continued to talk about his relationship with his dead relative. The counselor praised Ruth for being so sensitive and inquired why she asked the question. Ruth replied, "I assumed he would feel better after he got whatever it is off his chest." Larry confirmed that he, indeed, felt much better.

ACTIVITIES FOR THE INITIAL STAGE (CONTINUED)

The Accordion (A Compliments Game)

Goal—To increase positive feedback.   Interpersonal interaction must be positive if one wants honest and constructive feedback to follow. Most children are not familiar with direct positive feedback. This is just not the language that most kids speak nowadays. Therapists need to allow opportunities to provide positive feedback, train children in such feedback, and encourage its usage. There are many ways to achieve this goal described in this book; the Accordion Game is one of them.

Procedure.   Each child receives a sheet of paper and writes his or her name on top. The paper is then passed to each group member in turn, who writes something positive about that child. After each participant writes down the positive feedback, he or she folds the paper like an accordion, so the next child cannot see the previous statements. At the end, each child gets a sheet full of positive feedback. It is important to warn children about abusing the rules and to remind them about the group climate that they want to maintain.

Processing.   When the group is done with the written assignment, each child is invited to look at the sheet and explore his or her thoughts and feelings about how the other group members perceive him or her. The group also discusses the feelings and difficulties in providing the feedback.

Example.

Marina: (sharing the feedback she received)	It says I'm understanding and mature.
Counselor:	Do you see yourself as smart and mature?
Marina:	Not all subjects do I understand. Often I am not that good.
Counselor:	You are probably referring to academic success, but I think that the group is saying that you understand other people and are sensitive to what they say.
Marina:	Yes, I am like that with people, but I didn't know that the people here think that way about me.

ACTIVITIES FOR THE WORKING STAGE (CONTINUED)

My Personal Tree

Goal—To increase self-esteem and interpersonal empowerment skills.
Children and adolescents can best operate on a secure base, when they feel strong and accepted by group members. Participants need to develop skills to enhance each other's sense of confidence, showing each other their appreciation.

Procedure.   Each child is invited to draw a tree that has roots and branches. The roots represent the child's abilities and talents, and the branches represent his or her gains or achievements. The activity takes place in several phases. First, each child fills out his or her personal tree. Next, in pairs, they share their trees and expand on each other's tree. The contributions of each partner to the expansion of the tree are marked in color.

The activity may end in various ways. The children can express their feelings following the activity. They can share with the group the way in which they were enriched by their partner. One partner can report to the group positive impressions of the other partner. If the group is small, each child can present the tree to the whole group and the whole group can then contribute to the empowerment of that child.

Processing.   Children often have difficulty thinking positively about themselves. The counselor's help is often needed from the very start of the activity to provide examples of abilities and achievements. In the second stage, when the children work in pairs, the counselor's assistance may be needed in the empowerment process. Finally, when trees are shared by the whole group, the counselor should ensure that each child is empowered.

Example.   Alex recorded his "roots" as physical strength, a sense of humor, likes animals, good student, ambitious, and a loyal son. His (female) partner added good looking and popular in class. The group added sensitive and caring, good friend, smart, and gives good advice. Alex concluded, "I didn't know I am so highly appreciated."

ACTIVITIES FOR THE WORKING STAGE (CONTINUED)

My Life Continuum

Goal—To identify personal goals for working in the group.   Once   a group enters the working stage, my colleagues and I want participants to identify goals for their work in the group. However, we believe that identifying weaknesses is more effective when it is based on strengths. Therefore, we first identify strong points, then state one weak point or a goal for change.

Procedure.   The group participants are invited to mark their birthdays along a continuum. To the left of their birth date, they are asked to mark down some strengths, capabilities, talents, or achievements. On the right side of the date (the future), they are invited to write down one thing that they would like to improve.

Processing.   Each participant, in turn, shares with the group his or her strengths and the goal for improvement. When positive aspects of the self are shared, the group is invited to enhance the person's feelings by providing positive feedback. When he or she talks about the goal for improvement, the counselor and group often pose clarifying questions.

Example.

Alex:	I wrote that I am a good person, I am friendly, and I am a good student. Lately, though, I feel that I am too good. I give away everything I have and nothing is left for me. People have gotten so used to taking stuff from me that they feel free to take even without asking for permission.
Counselor:	Why do you think this happens?
Alex:	I am afraid to say no, because then I may lose friends.
Counselor:	So you want to be more assertive and be able to set some limits for others.
Alex:	Yes, but I don't succeed at it.
Counselor:	We will have to work on it at a later point. Right now we are only identifying goals. Thank you for being so honest with us.

ACTIVITIES FOR THE WORKING STAGE (CONTINUED)

The Echo Game

Goal—To enhance the expression of feelings.   As my colleges and I work in an expressive–supportive modality, the expression of feelings is the focus of our therapeutic work. However, this is not the language that children and adolescents commonly use. In fact, their vocabulary in this respect is quite limited. One way to help children express their deep emotions, which may eventually lead to insight and change, is through the Echo Game.

Procedure.   A child tells his or her story to the group. The group is helping explore as many emotions as possible. When the child needs help in emotional exploration, other children are invited to stand behind him or her, touch the child's shoulders, and express the feelings that he or she cannot express.

Processing.   Children express different emotions. Some are their own projections; others are those very feelings that the child is unable to express. It is important to ensure that the child listens to several emotions before selecting those that make sense to him or her. Usually, during this exercise it becomes clearer to the target child what he or she feels, making it possible to further explore the distinction between distorted and real feelings.

Example.   Joshua told the group that his father did not come for his weekly visit. He said he really didn't care because he wanted to go play with the kids on his block. He expanded on the experiences at the playground, mentioning a fight he got into and in which he was hurt. His best friend, Mike, called his own father for help, but Joshua rejected their kindness, because he did not like his friend anymore, or Mike's father. He did not respond to his mother's suggestion to take care of him and slammed the door.
Through the game, several emotions were echoed to Joshua:

Ann:	You were angry at your father for letting you down.
Dina:	You were frustrated because he did not come. You did want to see him; you are just pretending you do not care.
Gayle:	Maybe you were jealous of your friend and so you rejected him.
Dan:	You wanted your father to be there rather than your friend's father.

Bringing up the real emotions permitted Joshua to continue with the therapeutic work.

ACTIVITIES FOR THE WORKING STAGE (CONTINUED)

Our Group Pillow

Goal—To increase direct communication among group members.   A t the working stage the leader's intention should be to increase the power of the group through direct communication among members. This will allow interpersonal learning, one of the most important therapeutic factors.

Procedure.   One child holds the pillow and is invited to approach a group member of his or her choice and give him or her some feedback—something that the child has learned about him or her, something that he or she appreciates in this person, etc.

Processing.   The feedback provided must be carefully monitored to make sure that it is constructive and that the recipient has understood it. The leader should assist the recipient in using the feedback effectively.

Example.

Max: (gives the pillow to Seth)	Usually, you are a good friend, only sometimes you get angry and I don't understand why. It makes me feel rejected.
Seth:	I like to be your friend, but I keep inviting you to play with my new games and you hang up on me. I want you to know that it hurts me.
Max:	Oh, it really happened only once; I was in a bad mood.
Edie:	You can't do that to a friend; it hurts him.
Max: (after a long pause)	I did not mean to hang up the phone. I just was in a bad mood and I'm sorry. I don't think it was right.
Edie:	I agree that we should avoid hurting people. I would be insulted, too, if someone hung up on me. I would like people to explain themselves, to be gentle with me.
Max (to Seth):	I like to play with you, only you need to listen to the instructions and not pretend that you know.
Seth:	I didn't want you to think that I don't understand. I didn't know what irritates you. Now that I know, I will tell you when I don't understand.

ACTIVITIES FOR THE WORKING STAGE (CONTINUED)

The Damaged Paper

Goal—To take charge of one's behavior. Lack of self-control is one of the common characteristics of children and adolescents. They often say or do things that they eventually regret. This activity is aimed at improving their communication skills by examining the poor consequences of irresponsible communication.

Procedure. Children receive a sheet of paper and can do with it as they please. They can crumple it, cut it up, or tear it into tiny pieces. There is usually a lot of excitement in the room while they destroy the paper. Next, they are instructed to return the paper to its former state. The children realize this is impossible, and that the damage has been done.

Processing. The children express their thoughts and frustrations about the task, and then make the analogy to human relations. They explore the consequences of damaged communication, bring examples from their lives, and reach conclusions about their own behavior.

Example.

Jan:	I know that if I insult my friend and then ask for forgiveness, it will never be the same, because he hurts nevertheless.
Cristina:	I once had a fight with someone and I cursed him. Then I wanted to apologize but I didn't dare, as I didn't believe he would forgive me.
Counselor:	What did you do?
Cristina:	After a while I did try to apologize, but he became aggressive, so I was aggressive, too, and the fight only escalated. (Someone in the group disclosed that he, too, had a conflict with Cristina, but he did not respond aggressively.) It is true; I should apologize, as I hit him.
Counselor:	How do you feel now?
Cristina:	I am ashamed; I do apologize. You are a good person, a good friend.
Counselor:	What have you learned from this incident?
Cristina:	I need to think before I act, because I can never know how things will evolve and what price I will have to pay.

ACTIVITIES FOR TERMINATION

My Suitcase

Goal—To identify gains following the group experience.   Termination is not only the end of an experience; it is also a beginning or a continuance of a person's life. One of the goals of termination is to identify gains in the group process and see how these may serve a person in his or her life after the group ends. In other words, the therapist wants to help children identify their achievements following the group process and consider whether they can be transferred to real life.

Procedure.   Each child receives a drawing of a person carrying a suitcase. The children are invited to write on the suitcase what they take from the group experience into their real life: how the group helped them grow, in what way they have changed, what has improved in their lives following their participation. Outside of the suitcase, they are asked to write down those things that they would like to leave behind (get rid of).

Processing.   The children are invited to share with the group the gains that they noted on their suitcase. Gains are further explored, and their possible applications are discussed. The other group members are encouraged to add gains that they have observed but were not mentioned, or support those that were stated. They are also invited to share those things that they want to leave behind.

Example.

Emily:	I take from the group hope. The group gave me the hope to continue.
Counselor:	Hope for what?
Emily:	I don't know. I just feel stronger and more confident that I can achieve my aspirations.
Counselor:	In the group you talked about your conflictual relationships with your parents.
Emily:	Yes, and I feel that I am less angry at them and can communicate with them more effectively.
Counselor:	What do you leave behind?
Emily:	My anger, my loss of control.

ACTIVITIES FOR TERMINATION (CONTINUED)

Our Group, The Sun

Goal—To provide feedback on the group experience.   At termination it is important to receive feedback on the experiences in the group and understand how the group was helpful to its members.

Procedure.   Children are invited to draw the sun, which represents the group. Its rays represent the ways the group has sent its warmth to them—in other words, how the group made them feel good.

Processing.   When the children share their positive experiences with the group, expanding on their feedback may enhance their understanding of both the group and themselves. The leader can help them see what was meaningful to each of them.

Example.

Alex:	The group made me feel warm through the advice they gave me.
Counselor:	Can you give an example?
Alex:	When I talked about my test anxiety, the group gave me advice how to remain calm. They shared with me how they cope before an exam and it was helpful.
Counselor:	How was it helpful?
Alex:	I could see that they, too, are anxious. They did not pretend that they are smart. They wanted to help me.
Mark:	I actually remember that Alex was very good at helping others. He was very attentive when I talked. He had very good ideas; he even gave one good piece of advice to the counselor.

ACTIVITIES FOR TERMINATION (CONTINUED)

Catching the Last Train

Goal—To permit those who did not have a chance, to solve a problem.
Some group members wait for the last minute to share their concerns with the group, and sometimes they don't get to do it at all. My colleagues and I start termination a few sessions before the group actually ends to allow these children to "catch the last train."

Procedure.   The counselor brings in a toy train or a picture of a train and suggests that this is the train that the children can still catch, the last train leaving the group process. They are invited to bring up an issue that they had no chance to explore in the group.

Processing.   Processing involves cognitive and affective exploration of the shared difficulty. If time permits, the counselor can also seek some insight and possible actual change. The group helps by providing support, sharing similar experiences, giving feedback, and offering alternative ways of coping.

Example.

Karen:	I did not tell the group that I easily get insulted.
Counselor:	Would you like to do that now?
	Karen left the room crying. The group kept silent until she came back.
Karen:	I want to tell the group something, but I am afraid that it will leak out.

The group assured her that they kept secrets and that they, too, had already disclosed secrets and that they trusted each other. Karen, still crying, shared with them the poor relationships that she had with some girls in her class. These girls talked behind her back, gossiped, and were not loyal to her. The exploration process revealed that Karen was a good student, their teacher's favorite, and the girls in question were jealous. She understood that she needed to be more careful about picking her friends. She stopped crying and concluded:

I am responsible, I am a good student, I am smart; this is what the group said to me.... I want to thank all of you for listening and saying all those good things. I already feel stronger. I know I have you and that I am not dependent on them anymore.

ACTIVITIES FOR TERMINATION (CONTINUED)

In the Airport

Goal—To identify feelings about separation.   Termination can be a difficult experience for children who have had traumatic separations. It is important to identify the feelings attached to separation and check how the children feel about saying goodbye to the group. The more intimate the group, the more difficult it becomes to say goodbye. It is important to acknowledge such feelings to prevent a sense of abandonment.

Procedure.   The counselor invites the children to imagine that they are at an airport, saying goodbye to someone meaningful to them. Then they are to imagine that the rest of the group is on the plane and they remain alone in the airport. What do they want to say to the group?

Processing.   Processing involves exploring thoughts and feelings at times of separation in the past, as well as the messages they give to the group at separation.

Example.

Edie:	I am at the airport saying goodbye to my father, who remained behind in our previous country. I was 3 years old. My grandfather was also there. I cried a lot and I still miss them.
Counselor:	How did you feel?
Edie:	I was very frightened. I am still sad and I miss my dad.
Counselor:	What do you say to the group before they take off?
Edie:	Thanks to you guys, I have learned that if you treat people kindly, they respond with kindness. I have learned this in the group and now I use it also in class and during recess. I have more friends, thanks to you. Farewell.

ACTIVITIES FOR TERMINATION (CONTINUED)

The Group Rug

Goal—To strengthen ties among group members.   Group cohesiveness is the most important therapeutic factor in children's groups, throughout the group process. At the initial stage, it is the leader's most important role to establish it, as it serves as the basis for future work. During the working stage, it is important to maintain group cohesion to create trust and enhance self-disclosure. Cohesiveness at termination is the memory that stays in the children's minds and serves them during difficult times.

Procedure.   The counselor brings in a long piece of yarn and holds one end of it. He or she then approaches one group member, asking that person to hold onto the yarn and presents him or her with an imaginary gift that could help in the future. That child does the same for another participant, and so on, until all group members are holding onto the same piece of yarn. A group rug has been created by means of farewell wishes between all members.

Processing.   Sometimes it is necessary to help the children articulate the farewell wishes or to think of imaginary presents.

Example.

Counselor:	I am giving you a pair of tickets to a movie, so you can relax and forget for a while the many demands your mother makes.
Boris:	Yes, I would want that very much. (To Helen:) I give you rose-colored glasses to help you see the world in a more optimistic way.

Helen gave Jan a private tutor to help him with his homework, and so on.

Appendix III
Research Methods

INTRODUCTION

In this book, I refer to many empirical studies that tested the effectiveness and the processes of the groups my colleagues and I facilitate. Although the quantitative instruments that measure outcomes are quite well known, the instruments we used for the process analyses are less familiar. Moreover, as all of the instruments were borrowed from individual therapy research, some adjustments were made to fit group situations and to fit work with children. Therefore, a description of these tools and the information gathered on their psychometric properties may be helpful to researchers who would like to study group processes.

I discuss four tools that were most helpful in our research:

1. Rating Scale for Self-disclosure in Preadolescence (Vondracek & Vondracek, 1971)
2. Stages of Change (Prochaska, 1999)
3. Client Behavior System (Hill & O'Brien, 1999)
4. Helping Skills System (Hill & O'Brien, 1999).

RATING SCALE FOR SELF-DISCLOSURE IN PREADOLESCENCE (VONDRACEK & VONDRACEK, 1971)

This scale measures the frequency and level of self-disclosure. *Frequency* refers to the number of times a person discloses personal information and *level* refers to the depth of the disclosure (simple vs. intimate). Most of the disclosures obtained under both simple and intimate instructions can be grouped into eight categories: Family, Friends, Self, Activities, Evaluation of Performance, Transgressions, Tastes and Attitudes, and Expression of Feelings. My colleagues and I used only four of these categories in our studies. Therefore, I expand on these four categories (for a description of the entire scale, see Vondracek & Vondracek, 1971).

Categories of Self-Disclosure

Family (includes siblings, parents, relatives, and pets). Level 1: Statements incorporating routine data about family members and their tastes, interests, activities, and possessions (e.g., names, ages, school grades of siblings; description of family pets and their behavior; parents' occupations; location of home). Example: "I have one brother and two sisters."

Level 2: Statements yielding more personal data about family members, especially remarks about personality traits or physical appearance; description of incidents that reveal something meaningful; reports of antisocial behavior of parents or relatives; discussion of sibling's misbehavior; reports of personal problems of family members (e.g., discussion of father's heart attack, brother's quick temper, grandfather's loneliness, mother's disapproval of sister's boyfriend; reports of excessive drinking by parents or relatives; discussion of parents' difficulty with the law). Example: "When my father gets drunk, I am the first to suffer the consequences."

Friends. Level 1: Statements incorporating routine data about friends and significant adults and their tastes, interests, activities, and possessions. Example: "My best friend likes to play with computers."

Level 2: Statements yielding more personal data about friends and significant adults, especially remarks about personality traits or physical appearance; description of incidents that reveal such data; reports of their antisocial behavior; and reports of their personal problems. Example: "My friends like to abuse animals. They can be really cruel."

Self. Level 1: Statements incorporating routine data about the self, including descriptions of personal possessions, ambitions, desires, and plans of a public nature. Example: "I look forward to summer vacation because we are going to a resort."

Level 2: Statements dealing with own self-concept, personality traits, or physical appearance; descriptions of private fantasies and daydreams or personal wishes of an intimate nature; mention of health or personal problems; admission of difficulties in getting along with peers or family members. Example: "I would like to be a pilot but I doubt I can do it. My grades are not great and I don't seem to be able to resolve my learning difficulties on my own."

Expression of feelings. This category originally had three levels of disclosure: simple, medium, and high. To work with the same number of levels across categories, I eliminated level 1, which refers to simple expression of positive and negative feelings. Thus, level 2 became level 1 and level 3 became level 2.

Level 1: Reports of minor embarrassments that caused discomfort at the time, but do not appear to be the source of permanent psychological malaise; narration of minor worries that do not seem to preoccupy greatly and appear to be transient in nature; reports of minor disappointments, grief, or deprivation. Example: "I was embarrassed when my sister came out of the bathroom in front of my friends."

Level 2: Reports of major humiliations that do not appear to be transient and that appear to have made a permanent impression on oneself or caused considerable suffering; narration of deep grief, major disappointments, great unhappiness, or serious deprivation; admission of fears or worries that seem to preoccupy the self or be of sizeable proportions; reports of frightening experiences; expression of intensely positive or negative feelings. Example: "My mom died on my birthday, so I can never celebrate my birthday, because I am so terribly sad."

Psychometric properties.   The authors of the self-disclosure scale reported validity and reliability. Construct validity was established based on 73 subjects divided into three experimental conditions of self-disclosure. Instructions in each condition were as follows:

1. "Tell me things about yourself."
2. "Tell me things about yourself that you would usually tell only a few special people."
3. "Tell me something that you think people your age would tell only a few special people."

The disclosures obtained under these conditions formed the basis for the scoring system developed. Inspection of the disclosed statements by the 73 subjects revealed that instructional sets had indeed elicited disclosure of varying degrees of intimacy. The reported interrater agreement was satisfactory ($r = .96$). Test-retest reliability was high ($r = .92$; Vondracek & Vondracek, 1971).

My colleagues and I used the scale in several of our own studies. Internal consistency in our studies is similar to that reported by the authors. Kappa = .95 and .96 for simple and intimate self-disclosure, respectively, in one study (Shechtman et al., 2003); and .95 and .93, respectively, in another (Shechtman & Dvir, in press). Moreover, discriminant validity was found in two studies. In one, a significant difference between the experimental and control groups on the level of self-disclosure was revealed, with the former demonstrating a higher level of self-disclosure, as expected (Shechtman & Zaghon, 2004). In the other study, the scale differentiated between attitudes of Arab and Jewish adolescents in the expected direction (Shechtman et al., 2000).

Procedure

Analysis of the content of disclosure is based on audiotaped transcripts of sessions. The rating system involves several steps. First, the raters practice assigning the categories of self-disclosure on unrelated material. In case of disagreement, they consult with a senior researcher who is familiar with the scale. Second, they parse each transcript into units called speaking turns. A speaking turn is the main message a child delivers and can include one or more sentences (e.g., "In my neighborhood there are kids who abuse animals. I tried to explain to them that animals have feelings, too, but they would not listen."). Speaking turns are preferred to individual sentences because they contain one message.

The two raters work independently on the same transcripts and must first reach agreement of 95% on the speaking turns. Finally, each rater classifies the speaking turns into one of the four categories of self-disclosure and into one of the two levels of disclosure.

Usually, my colleagues and I use two raters to analyze all transcripts. However, with large samples and high interrater reliability, it is possible to continue with only one rater.

THE CHANGE PROCESS (PROCHASKA, 1999)

Stages of Change

The change process monitors peoples' process of change in the course of therapy and in life in general. Prochaska (1999) suggested six stages of change, as elaborated in the following.

Stage 1: Precontemplation. Individuals in this stage are unaware of their problem and have no intention to change. Example: "I am not aggressive. I only defend myself and so I have to hit back."

Stage 2: Contemplation. Individuals are aware of their problem behavior, but have not made a commitment to take action. Example: "I know I get easily irritated, but I actually like when people are afraid of me, as this way they have to respect me."

Stage 3: Preparation. Individuals acknowledge that they have a problem and intend to take action and some small steps. Example: "I would like to have more control over my actions, and I really try hard, but only rarely do I succeed."

Stage 4: Action. Individuals modify their behavior. Example: "Last week I managed to curb my reactions and had only a couple of fights."

Stage 5: Maintenance. Individuals work to retain their gains. Example: "It is a few months since we started working. I was in hardly any fights."

Stage 6: Termination. Individuals experience zero temptation and 100% self-efficacy in controlling their behavior. Example: "I know that no one can drag me into a fight anymore. I stopped being a bully."

Prochaska's (1999) research on the stages of change was based on questionnaires. My colleagues and I made two modifications. First, we applied the stages of change to our research on group counseling and psychotherapy. Second, we used content analysis of transcripts when applying the concept of the change process; as we did so mostly in work with aggressive boys, this observational data seemed more reliable that the available self-report questionnaires.

Psychometric Properties

My colleagues and I used Prochaska's (1999) scale in several studies. Interrater agreement was always high. In the first study (Shechtman & Ben David, 1999), kappa ranged from .70 to .88; in the second (Shechtman, 2003), it ranged from .91 to 1.00; and in the third study (Shechtman, in press), the range was .69 to .80.

Validity of the scale in its observational form was established based on the relation between the stage of change and progress in the course of treatment. At the beginning of treatment, most children were at the precontemplation and contemplation stages, unaware of their problems. At the final stages of the group (10th session), over 80% of the children reached at least the preparation stage, and about 45% reached the action stage.

The pattern of change across time was tested by Pearson correlation analysis; correlation coefficients (r) were calculated between session number and the percentage of talk in each stage of change. In Stage 1, $r = -.87$, $p < .001$; in Stage 4, $r = .86$, $p < .001$. These results indicate a significant relationship between the expected process of change and the course of treatment (Shechtman, & Ben David, 1999). In a later study (Shechtman, 2003), a hierarchical model was used to measure the slope of change during the time of treatment. A positive slope was found, $t(49) = 6.25$, $p < .001$), indicating an increase along time; that is, progress to an advanced stage of change is evident with time. Thus, Prochaska's (1999) change process appears to be a valid and reliable tool to measure children's and adolescents' progress in the course of counseling and psychotherapy.

Procedure

Two trained raters analyze transcripts of audiotaped sessions. There are several steps to the analysis. First, the raters are trained to understand the stages of the change process. Next, they practice on materials unrelated to the study until high interrater agreement (95%) is reached. Only then are they allowed to code the transcribed sessions of the study. Each of the trained raters independently classifies participant's statements for each analyzed session into one of the stages of change. There are two possible methods of classification: a child can be identified as being at particular stages several times within a single session, or the child can be classified once per session, based on the highest stage reached at that session. Coding is dichotomous: yes or no.

Illustration of the Coding System

Joseph was part of a group of five children. His progress (as of the third session) was coded as follows.

Session 3.
Response: "I choose to pair with John because I also fight very often."
Classification: Stage 2, contemplation.

Session 4.
Response: "Someone made me angry and I was just about to explode. I hit him, but now I regret it. I should have thought before I hit."
Classification: Stage 3, preparation.

Session 5.
Response: "On a scale of 1 to 10 of the level of aggression, I am a 7 right now. But I would like to move to 2 or 3, that is, only rarely do I want to be involved in aggressive acts."
Classification: Stage 3, preparation.

Session 6.
Response (this time the scale is of tolerance): "I am a 4, not very tolerant, but I would like to be an 8—tolerant most of the time."
Classification: Stage 3, preparation.

Session 7.
Response: "I am trying to stay away from fights during recess, but I don't seem to succeed."
Classification: Stage 3, preparation.

Session 8.
Response: "He jumped me and threw me on the floor. But I didn't put a hand on him, although I wanted to. I just talked and talked to him."
Classification: Stage 4, action.

Session 9.
Response: "I try to relax. I found that when I am busy I am less angry. I have learned to avoid a conflict, I simply move away."
Classification: Stage 4, action.

Session 10.
Response: "When they pick on me, I still want to hit back, but I don't, I control myself. I am my own commander now."
Classification: Stage 4, action.

CLIENT BEHAVIOR SYSTEM (CBS; HILL & O'BRIEN, 1999)

Based on a variety of theories, Hill and O'Brien (1999) has suggested eight behaviors that cover most possible client behaviors in individual therapy: Resistance, Agreement, Appropriate Request, Recounting, Cognitive Exploration, Affective Exploration, Insight, and Therapeutic Change. I have borrowed this scale to measure client behavior in group counseling and psychotherapy with children and adolescents. As the first four behaviors are considered less constructive than the latter four (Hill & O'Brien, 1999), I created one measure called Simple Response. This combined three of the four less constructive behaviors, leaving Resistance separate owing to its importance in the therapy process. Note that this CBS has been revised several times based on extensive research (see Hill, 2001); here I describe the latest version.

First, I present a short definition of each client behavior (for a more detailed definition, see Hill & O'Brien, 1999, pp. 384–385.). Each of these behaviors is followed by an example from actual group work with children and adolescents. Second, I provide a case illustration, as well as other research results, to validate the use of this scale for counseling and psychotherapy groups with young people.

Elaboration of Client Behaviors

These examples are drawn from one group of elementary-school children, for one female client.

Resistance.   Any behavior indicating that the client is unwilling to work therapeutically (for example, complaints, blame, defensiveness, sidetracking, abusiveness, or hostility). Example: "I can't talk to the group. They won't understand my situation."

Agreement.   Understanding or approval of what the client was told (by the counselor or a group member). Example: "Yes, I guess you are right. I am kind of shy."

Appropriate request.   An attempt to obtain clarification, information, or advice. Example: "Do you think the kids would listen to me?"

Recounting.   Small talk, answers to questions, or factual information about past events. Example: "My mother passed away on the way to Israel."

Cognitive exploration.   Statements indicating that the client is actively involved in the therapeutic process and is exploring significant thoughts or behavior. Example: "I am worried that the kids will not listen, and they will make fun of me later on."

Affective exploration.   Statements indicating that the client is involved and explores feelings about meaningful events in his or her life, or feelings in the here-and-now; the expression of feelings, verbally and nonverbally (e.g., crying), must be observed. Example: "I feel very sad on my birthdays, because my mother died on that same day. How can I be happy when everyone is so sad?"

Insight.   The client expresses an understanding of something about the self and understands reasons for thoughts, feelings, and behavior. Insight is evident when the client perceives something in the self or the world in a new way. Example: "In the role play that we had, I understood that my mom would want to see me happy once a year, as I do think of her all the time."

Therapeutic change.   The client expresses changes in behavior, thoughts, or feelings in therapeutically significant areas. Example: "This was the first birthday party I ever had and it was the best day in a long time. I look forward to my next birthday."

Case Illustration of One Group Session

Emily said, "I want to talk, but I can't" (*Resistance*). She turned to Sherri, the counselor, saying, "You know my problems. Can you tell them?" Sherri refused gently. She insisted that the group should hear it directly from Emily, but Emily was still silent. To help her, Sherri asked the group if anyone else had dealt with loss.

Joseph:	Two years ago my uncle was killed in a car accident. He was only 23. I was the last one to see him. I try not to think about him (*Cognitive Exploration*).
Sherri:	It sounds as if you were very close to him.
Joseph:	Yes, very much so. When he died, I didn't go to school for a whole week; I didn't go to tennis, which I love so much. I was afraid to be in a car for a long while (*Affective Exploration*).
Sherri:	How do you cope?
Joseph:	My mother said that I must forget him; I must not think about it. I have his pictures in my room, so sometimes I talk to him and tell him about myself (*Affective Exploration*).

The group continued to share events of loss.

In the next session the group used the story *The Soul Bird* (Snunit, 1999) to discuss their feelings. They opened drawers full with emotions.

Joseph:	I am the oldest at home, and I have no responsibilities. I get everything I want (*Recounting*).
Sherri:	You heard here from three girls who have a lot of responsibilities.
Joseph:	Yes, it is difficult to be a girl. I won't even baby-sit for my sister, because I prefer playing with my computer and listening to music (*Recounting*).
Maxine (cutting off the simple responses)	Didn't you ask to open a drawer?
Joseph:	I opened the drawer of anxiety. Now that I am 13, I am worried about many things of adult life: exams, school, bodily changes. Adolescence really worries me (*Cognitive Exploration*).
Sherri:	Tell us more.
Joseph:	Only now, after my Bar Mitzvah, did I start worrying about it. I am mostly worried about my body's changes, my health. It's as if I don't recognize myself anymore. It's frightening (*Affective Exploration*).

After a silence, some boys joined him and talked about the changes they had observed in themselves.

Sherri:	We have heard many worries of adolescents. What worries you most, Joseph?
Joseph:	I am most worried that I may end up like my uncle; I may not be strong enough, to be good at driving, and even army service frightens me (*Affective Exploration*).
Sherri:	So your uncle's accident is still very frightening to you.
Joseph:	Yes, I can see why I am so fearful, more than my friends (*Insight*).

The group helped Joseph by suggesting various coping mechanisms.

At termination, Joseph said about the group experience: "It was great. I would like to go on. It was so good to have someone to talk to. I am more relaxed now, and I don't worry that much anymore" (*Therapeutic Change*).

Psychometric Properties

The CBS scale has been widely investigated, showing good psychometric properties (see Hill, 2001). The reported reliability, tested in terms of agreement of four judges, indicated an average of 3.84 out of a maximum score of 4.00. In addition, kappa calculated for two judges was .92. Convergent validity was established on the basis of comparison of client responses in seven different therapist styles. Construct validity was based on comparison with client experiencing ratings (Hill, 2001), which indicated that Affective Exploration and Insight were significantly associated with higher levels of experiencing, as well as a comparison with client ratings of the helpfulness of counselor interventions.

My own work with the CBS scale supports the psychometric properties in several ways.

1. I found no difference in CBS responses between individual and group treatment (Shechtman, 2004a, 2004b), suggesting that the scale can be used to measure client behavior in groups. Moreover, in terms of frequency of responses, these appear to be in the same proportions as in adult individual therapy. Simple Response is the most frequent behavior, followed by Cognitive Exploration (Shechtman, 2004b) and then Affective Exploration (Shechtman, 2004a). Insight and Therapeutic Change are quite rare, as reported also in the literature on individual therapy (Hill, 2001). These results support the use of the scale when young people are involved.

2. Interrater reliability between different pairs of raters was consistently high. In the Shechtman and Pastor (2005) study, kappa ranged from .86 to .93; in the Shechtman (2004a) study, it ranged from .99 to 1.00.

3. Discriminant validity was shown based on a comparison of cognitive–behavioral and humanistic group therapy (Shechtman & Pastor, 2005). In humanistic therapy, children were engaged more in Affective Exploration and Insight; in cognitive–behavioral therapy they were engaged more in Cognitive Exploration and Resistance, as expected.

4. Construct validity was further supported based on the growth slope of each behavior. According to the Three Stage Model (Hill, 2005), the less constructive behaviors (e.g., Resistance and Simple Response) are expected to decrease with time, whereas the more constructive responses (Cognitive Exploration, Affective Exploration, Insight, and Therapeutic Change) are expected to increase. Results indicated that Resistance and Simple Response indeed decreased, and the other four client behaviors increased over time (Shechtman, 2004b; Shechtman & Pastor, 2005).

5. Predictive validity was not found in any of my studies with aggressive children. The CBS was unrelated to the reduction of aggression.

Procedure

My colleagues and I used audiotaped transcripts to analyze the group process. The analysis involved several steps. First, raters were trained to use the CBS on transcripts of sessions unrelated to the study. They were expected to reach 95% agreement on both the identification of speaking turns and the classification into categories of behavior. When in disagreement, they consulted an expert who had been trained in using the scale. Next, the two raters worked on the study transcripts independently. First, they had to agree on the units of analysis; only after high agreement (95%) was reached did they begin to categorize the client behaviors (for guidelines on analyzing transcripts, see Hill & O'Brien, 1999, Appendix C).

Once a large sample of behaviors had been accumulated, my colleagues and I measured kappa. With the high kappas we usually obtained, it was possible to continue with one rater, although we used two in most of our studies. Statistical analysis of the data was based on proportions rather than frequencies, as the eight client behaviors are expected to cover all the speaking turns. However, because we worked in groups and often used special tools (e.g., bibliotherapy), some of the speaking turns did not fit any of the eight behaviors identified in individual therapy. In those few cases, we either disregarded these speaking turns altogether (when we were only interested in the eight CBS behaviors) or we included our own categories. For example, in the Shechtman (2004a) study, two categories were added: Response to Another and Reference to the Literary Figure.

Overall, it appears that the CBS scale can be used with children and adolescents in studies of groups. Studies by my colleagues and I were limited to aggressive boys and children with LD. The lack of predictive validity calls for further exploration, using different populations and symptoms, as well as additional predictors that may be more appropriate for group studies.

THE HELPING SKILLS SYSTEM (HSS; HILL & O'BRIEN, 1999)

The HSS measures the skills of counselors in the course of individual counseling or psychotherapy. The authors suggest 12 skills that are assumed to cover all the verbal behaviors that counselors use. My colleagues and I borrowed the scale to measure counselors' behavior in group counseling and psychotherapy with children and adolescents. This scale, too, has been modified several times; here I describe the latest version, which we used in our research.

I begin by presenting a short definition of each behavior (for a more detailed definition, see Hill & O'Brien, 1999, pp. 366–371.). Each of these behaviors is followed by an example from group work with children and adolescents. I then provide results of our research to demonstrate the applicability of the scale to counseling and psychotherapy groups with youngsters.

Elaboration of the Helping Skills

The following examples are taken from an exchange of communication between a boy and his counselor during a specific group session. The boy is sharing an incident in which he saw a group of children abusing animals.

Approval and reassurance. Provides emotional support, encouragement, and reinforcement. *Example*: "It is so kind of you to try to help those abused animals."

Closed questions. A request for limited information or data. Example: "Did you try to stop them?"

Open questions. Asks client to clarify or to explore thoughts or feelings. Example: "How did you feel when that happened?"

Restatement. A simple repetition or rephrasing of the content or meaning of a client's statement. Example: "You are saying that it bothered you to see their cruel behavior."

Reflection of feelings. Repeating a client's statement, including an explicit identification of feelings. Example: "When you talked about these animals, you seemed so moved."

Challenges.
Pointing out discrepancies, contradictions, defensive behavior, and the like. *Example*: "It sounds like you can sense their pain, as if you yourself experienced such pain" (to this, the boy responded with a story about being beat up by a group of bullies).

Interpretation. Goes beyond what the client has overtly stated and gives a new meaning or explanation for behaviors. Example: "So you are sensitive to their sense of helplessness because you, too, experienced such helplessness, not long ago."

Self-disclosure. Reveals something personal (event, experience) about the counselor. *Example*: "I remember being bullied by a classmate. This happened long ago, and yet I am still afraid when I see him."

Immediacy. Reveals the helper's immediate feelings about the self, the client, or their relationship. Example: "I feel closer to you, now that you have shared with us the abusive experience."

Information.   Provision of data, facts, opinions, or resources. Example: "I hear that you are quite helpless when you are bullied. But you don't have to be alone in this situation. There are teachers, counselors, the school principal—you can ask for their help."

Guidance.   Provision of suggestions, instructions, or advice. Example: "I suggest that you start with your homeroom teacher. She will know what to do."

Other.   Helper's statements that cannot be categorized in the previously mentioned skills. Example: "Let's not talk in general terms, only about yourself."

Psychometric Properties

The authors reported good psychometric properties for the HSS scale. Validity was established on the basis of the relation between verbal skills, clients' immediate reactions, and client outcomes (Hill, 2001; Hill & O'Brien, 1999). Their reported rater agreement ranged from .55 to .94.

My own research contributes to the strength of the scale in several ways.

1. Studies comparing individual and group treatments have indicated that the helping skills are very similar in these two forms of counseling; only minimal differences were found between the two therapy formats (Shechtman, 2004b; Shechtman & Ben David, 1999). These results suggest that the scale is suited for use in group counseling and psychotherapy.

2. The frequency of each helping skill, as found in our groups, is highly consistent. Questions (open and closed), Guidance, and facilitative responses (i.e., Approval and Reassurance, Restatement, and Reflection of Feelings) were the most frequent, whereas Challenges, Interpretation and Self-disclosure were rare. This rank order was consistent across samples (Shechtman, 2004a, 2004b; Shechtman & Ben-David, 1999; Shechtman & Gat, 2006), and in many ways similar to the frequencies of skills reported in the literature (Hill & O'Brien, 1999). This suggests that the scale is suited for use with children.

3. Some support for the validity of the HSS scale was received from the correlations between some helping skills and client behavior. Facilitative responses and Challenges were positively related to Affective Exploration and Therapeutic Change, and Guidance was related to decreased Affective Exploration, as expected based on the literature.

4. Discriminant validity was observed in the comparative study of cognitive–behavioral and humanistic group therapy (Shechtman & Pastor, 2005). In this study, we selected only five counselor skills for which we expected to find differences, based on the unique characteristics of each treatment. Differences were found for all five: more Approval and Reassurance, Reflection of Feelings, and Interpretation were found in the humanistic groups and more Information and Guidance were present in the cognitive–behavioral groups. Moreover, whereas Reflection of Feelings continued growing in the humanistic groups, Guidance continued to increase in the cognitive groups.

5. Predictive validity was not revealed: No relation was found between helping skills and outcomes of aggressive children (Shechtman, 2004a).

6. Interrater agreement was high in all of our studies, using different pairs of raters. Kappa was .97, ranging from .88 to 1.00 in the Shechtman (2004b) study; and it ranged from .83 to .97 in a second study (Shechtman & Pastor, 2005).

Procedure

The procedure of analyzing the transcripts is similar to that previously described for CBS.

In sum, the results of studies by my colleagues and myself support the validity of the HSS as an instrument to be used with children and adolescents in counseling and psychotherapy groups. The frequency in which each helping skill is presented in the group process appears to be consistent across studies. The information we generated appears to be reliable. Further research is needed involving different populations of children with different symptoms, particularly to support the predictive validity of this instrument.

References

Achenbach, T. M. (1991a). *The Child Behavior Checklist (CBCL)*. Burlington: University of Vermont, Department of Psychiatry.

Achenbach, T. M. (1991b). *Teacher's Report Form (TRF)*. Burlington: University of Vermont, Department of Psychiatry.

Ackerson, J., Scogin, F., McKendree-Smith, N., & Lyman, R. (1998). Cognitive bibliotherapy for mild and moderate adolescent depressive symptomatology. *Journal of Consulting & Clinical Psychology, 66*, 685–690.

Ainsworth, M. D., Blehar, M. C., Waters, E., & Wall, S. (1978). *Patterns of attachment: A psychological study of the strange situation.* Hillsdale, NJ: Lawrence Erlbaum Associates, Inc.

Al-Kernawi, A. (1998). Family therapy with a multiparental/multispousal family. *Family Processes, 37*, 65–81.

Alpert, J. E., & Spillmann, M. K. (1997). Psychotherapeutic approaches to aggressive and violent patients. *Psychiatric Clinics of North America, 20*, 453–472.

Alyagon, M., & Bracha, I. (1996). *Shipur Hayecolot Hahevratit vramat hahistuglut.* [The enhancement of social skills and adjustment]. Tel Aviv, Israel: Ramot.

Amato, P. R. (2001). Children of divorce in the 1990s: An update of the Amato and Keith (1991) meta-analysis. *Journal of Family Psychology, 15*, 355–370.

American School Counseling Association. (1998). *Ethical standards for school counselors.* Alexandria, VA: Author.

American Psychiatric Association. (2000). *Diagnostic and statistical manual of mental disorders* (4th ed., rev. ed.). Washington, D.C.: Author.

Apodaca, T. R., & Miller, W. R. (2003). A meta-analysis of the effectiveness of bibliotherapy for alcohol problems. *Journal of Clinical Psychology, 58*, 288–304.

Aronowitz, M. (1992). Adjustment of immigrant children as a function of parental attitudes to change. *International Migration Review, 26*, 89–110.

Arrington, E. W. (1987). Managing children's conflict: A challenge for the school counselor. *The School Counselor, 30*, 188–194.

Aronson, S. (2005). A war that had come right to them: Group work with traumatized adolescents following September 11. *International Journal of Group Psychotherapy, 55*, 375–390.

Association of Specialists in Group Work. (1998). ASGW best practice guidelines. *Journal for Specialists in Group Work, 23,* 237–244.

Axline, V. (1947). *Play therapy.* Boston, MA: Houghton-Mifflin.

Bachelor, A., & Horvath, A. (1999). The therapeutic relationship. In M. A. Hubble, B. L. Duncan, & S. D. Miller (Eds.), *The heart and soul of change: What works in therapy* (pp. 133–178). Washington, DC: American Psychological Association.

Baker, S. B. (2000). *School counseling for the twenty-first century.* Englewood Cliffs, NJ: Prentice-Hall.

Barakat, H. (1993). *The Arab word.* Berkeley: University of California Press.

Barlow, S. H., Burlingame, G. M., & Fuhriman, A. (2000). Therapeutic application of groups: From Pratt's "thought control classes" to modern group psychotherapy. *Group Dynamics: Theory, Research, and Practice, 4,* 115–134.

Bauman, S., Siegel, J. T., Davis, A., Falco, L. D., Seabolt, K., & Szymanski, G. (2002). School counselors' interest in professional literature and research. *Professional School Counseling, 5,* 346–352.

Beelmann, A., Pfingsten, U., & Losel, F. (1994). Effects of training social competence in children: A meta-analysis of recent evaluation studies. *Journal of Clinical Child Psychology, 23,* 260–271.

Bender, W. N., & Wall, M. E. (1994). Social emotional development of students with learning disabilities. *Learning Disability Quarterly, 17,* 323–341.

Berkovitz, I. H. (1989). Applications of group therapy in secondary schools. In F. Cramer-Azima & L. H. Richmond (Eds.), *Adolescent group psychotherapy* (pp. 99–123). Madison, WI: International Universities Press.

Berg, R. C., Landreth, G. L., & Fall, K. A. (1998). *Group counseling: Concepts and procedures* (3rd ed.). Philadelphia: Accelerated Development.

Berman, L. (1993). *Beyond the smile: The therapeutic use of the photograph.* New York: Routledge.

Bernard, H. S., & MacKenzie, R. K. (1994). *Basics of group psychotherapy.* New York: Guilford.

Berndt, T. J. (2004). Children's friendships: Shifts over a half-century in perspectives on their development and their effects. *Merrill-Palmer Quarterly, 50,* 206–223.

Biran, Y. (1999). *Gader, kivsa, vyesh.im beaia.* [A fence, a sheep and a man with a problem] (5th ed.). Tel Aviv, Israel: Sa'ar.

Birani-Nasaraladin, D. (2004). *Tipul beimahot benosaf latipul beyeladim: hashvaa shel hesegin avur yeladim alimin.* [Mother treatment in addition to child treatment: A comparison of outcomes for aggressive boys]. MA thesis, Haifa University, Israel.

Bloch, S., & Crouch, E. (1985). *Therapeutic factors in group psychotherapy.* New York: Oxford University Press.

Bohart, A. C., O'Hara, M. M., Leitner, L. M., Wertz, F., Stern, E. M., Schneider, K., et al. (1997). Guidelines for the provision of humanistic psychological services. *The Humanistic Psychologist, 25,* 64–107.

Braaten, L. J. (1991). Group cohesion: A new multidimensional model. *Group, 15,* 39–55.

Buhrmester, D., & Furman, W. (1987). The development of companionship and intimacy. *Child Development, 58,* 1101–1113.

Burlingame, G. M., Fuhriman, A. J., & Johnson, J. (2004). Processes and outcomes in group counseling and psychotherapy: Research and practice. In J. L. DeLucia-Waack, D. A. Gerrity, C. R. Kalodner, & M. T. Riva (Eds.), *Handbook of counseling and psychotherapy* (pp. 49–61). Thousand Oaks, CA: Sage.

Burlingame, G. M., MacKenzie, R. K., & Strauss, B. (2004). Small-group treatments: Evidence for effectiveness and mechanisms of change. In M. J. Lambert (Ed.), *Bergin and*

Garfield's handbook of psychotherapy research and behavior change (pp. 647–696). New York: Wiley.

Buss, D. M. (2000). The evolution of happiness. *American Psychologist, 55,* 15–23.

Cain, D. J. (2001). Defining characteristics, history, and evaluation of humanistic psychotherapies. In D. J. Cain & J. Seeman (Eds.), *Humanistic psychotherapies: Handbook of research and practice* (pp. 34–54). Washington, DC: American Psychological Association.

Cassidy, J. (2001). Truth, lies, and intimacy: An attachment perspective. *Attachment & Human Development, 3,* 121–155.

Cheung, S., & Sun, S.Y. (2001). Helping processes in mutual aid organization for persons with emotional disturbance. *International Journal of Group Psychotherapy, 51,* 295–308.

Chi-Ying Chung, R. (2004). Group counseling with Asians. In J. DeLucia-Waack, D. Gerrity, C. R. Kalodner, & M. T. Riva (Eds.), *Handbook of group counseling and psychotherapy* (pp. 200–212). Thousand Oaks, CA: Sage.

Conyne, R. K. (1997). Developing a framework for processing experiences and events in group work. *Journal for Specialists in Group Work, 22,* 167–174.

Corder, B. F., Whiteside, L., Haizlip, T. M. (1981). A study of curative factors in group psychotherapy with adolescents. *International Journal of Group Psychotherapy, 31,* 345–354.

Corey, G. (1995). *Theory and practice of group counseling* (4th ed). Pacific Grove, CA: Brooks/Cole.

Corey, M. S., & Corey, G. (1992). *Groups: Process and practice* (4th ed.). Pacific Grove, CA: Brooks/Cole.

Corey, M. S. & Corey, G. (2006). *Groups: Process and practice* (7th ed.). Pacific Grove, CA: Brooks/Cole.

Cramer-Azima, F. (1989). Confrontation, empathy, and interpretation: Issues in adolescent group psychotherapy. In F. Cramer-Azima & L. H. Richmond (Eds.), *Adolescent group psychotherapy* (pp. 3–19). Madison, WI: International Universities Press.

Cramer-Azima, F. (2002). Group psychotherapy for children and adolescents. In M. Lewis (Ed.), *Child and adolescent psychiatry: A comprehensive textbook* (pp. 842–850). Baltimore: Williams & Williams.

Crouch, E. C., Bloch, S., & Wanlass, J. (1994). Therapeutic factors: Interpersonal and intrapersonal mechanisms. In A. Fuhriman & G. M. Burlingame (Ed.), *Handbook of group psychotherapy: An empirical and clinical synthesis* (pp. 269–318). New York: Wiley.

Dagley, J. C., Gazda, G. M., Eppinger, S. J., & Stewart, E. A. (1994). Group psychotherapy research with children, preadolescents, and adolescents. In A. Fuhriman & G. M. Burlingame (Eds.), *Handbook of group psychotherapy: An empirical and clinical synthesis* (pp. 340–370). New York: Wiley.

DeLucia-Waack, J. L. (1997). The importance of processing activities, exercises and events to group practitioners. *Journal for Specialists in Group Work, 22,* 82–84.

DeLucia-Waack, J. L., & Donigian, J. (2004). *The practice of multicultural group work.* Belmont, CA: Brooks/Cole.

Derlega, V. J., Wilson, J., & Margulis, S. T. (1993). *Self-disclosure.* Newbury Park, CA: Sage.

DiClemente, R. J., Hansen, W. B., & Ponton, E. E. (1996). *Handbook of adolescent health risk behavior.* New York: Plenum Press.

Dies, K. G. (2000). Adolescent development and a mode of group psychotherapy: Effective leadership in the new millennium. *Journal of Child and Adolescent Group Psychotherapy, 10,* 97–112.

Dies, R. R. (1994). Therapist variables in group psychology research. In A. Fuhriman & G. M. Burlingame (Eds.), *Handbook of group psychotherapy: An empirical and clinical synthesis* (pp. 114–154). New York: Wiley.

Dishion, T. J., McCord, J., & Poulin, F. (1999). When interventions harm: Peer groups and problem behavior. *American Psychologist, 54*, 755–764.

Dishion, T. J., & Patterson, G. R. (1997). The timing and severity of antisocial behavior: Three hypotheses within an ecological framework. In D. M. Stoff, J. Breiling, & J. D. Maser (Eds.), *Handbook of antisocial behavior* (pp. 205–217). New York: Wiley.

Dodge, K. A. (1991). The structure and function of reactive and proactive aggression. In D. J. Pepler & K. H. Rubin (Eds.), *The development and treatment of childhood aggression* (pp. 201–215). Hillsdale, NJ: Lawrence Erlbaum Associates, Inc.

Dodge, K. A. (2002). Mediation, moderation, and mechanisms in how parenting affects children's aggressive behavior. In J. G. Borkowski, S. Landesman-Ramey, & M. Bristol-Power (Eds.), *Parenting and the child's world: Intellectual and social development* (pp. 215–229). Hillsdale, NJ: Lawrence Erlbaum Associates, Inc.

Dohrn, E., & Bryan, T. (1994). Attribution instruction. *Teaching Exceptional Children, 26*, 61–63.

Duck, S. (1991). *Understanding relationships*. New York: Guilford.

Dwairy, M. (1998). *Cross-cultural counseling: The Arab-Palestinian case*. New York: Haworth.

Eisenberg, N., Fabes, R. A., & Murphy, B. C. (1996). Parents' reactions to children's negative emotions: Relations to children's social competence and comforting behavior. *Child Development, 67*, 2227–2247.

Elbaum, B., & Vaughn, S. (2001). School-based interventions to enhance the self-concept of students with learning disabilities: A meta-analysis. *The Elementary School Journal, 101*, 303–329.

Elliot, S. N., & Gresham, F. M. (1987). Children's social skills: Assessment and classification. *Journal of Counseling and Development, 66*, 96–99.

Epstein, S. (1994). Integration of the cognitive and psychodynamic unconscious. *American Psychologist, 49*, 709–724.

Erikson, E. H. (1974). *Identity: Youth and crisis*. Oxford, UK: Norton.

Eron, L. D. (1997). The development of antisocial behavior from a learning perspective. In D. Stoff, J. Breiling, & J. D. Maser (Eds.), *Handbook of antisocial behavior* (pp. 140–155). New York: Wiley.

Farrington, D. P. (1997). A critical analysis of research on the development of antisocial behavior from birth to adulthood. In D. M. Stoff, J. Breiling, & J. D. Maser (Eds.), *Handbook of antisocial behavior* (pp. 234–240). New York: Wiley.

Fisher, B. L., Allen, R., & Kose, G. (1996). The relationship between anxiety and problem-solving skills in children with and without learning disabilities. *Journal of Learning Disabilities, 29*, 439–446.

Fleckenstein, L. B., & Horne, A. M. (2004). Anger management groups. In J. L. DeLucia-Waack, D. A. Gerrity, C. R. Kalodner, & M. T. Riva (Eds.), *Handbook of group counseling and psychotherapy* (pp. 547–562). Thousand Oaks, CA: Sage.

Forman, S. G. (1993). *Coping skills interventions for children and adolescents*. San Francisco: Jossey-Bass.

Fuhriman, A., & Burlingame, G. M. (1990). Consistency of matters: A comparative analysis of individual and group process variables. *Counseling Psychologist, 18*, 6–63.

Fuhriman, A., Burlingame, G. M., Seaman, S. W., & Barlow, S. H. (1999, June). *Validating a behavioral measure of catharsis, cohesion, and insight, in group therapy*. Paper presented at the annual conference of the Society for Psychotherapy Research, Braga, Portugal.

Galea, S., Ahern, J., Resnick, H., Kilpatrick, D., Bucuvalas, M., Gold, J., & Vlahov, D. (2002). Psychological sequels of the September 11 terrorist attacks in New York City. *The New England Journal of Medicine, 346*, 982–987.

Gazda, G. M. (1989). *Group counseling: A developmental approach* (4th ed). Boston: Allyn & Bacon.

Gazda, G. M., Ginter, E. J., & Horne, A. M. (2001). *Group counseling and group psychotherapy: Theory and application.* Needham Heights, MA: Allyn & Bacon.

Ghirardelli, R. (2001). Silence and the use of objects brought to the session as a resistance in a group of adolescents. *Group Analysis: The Journal of Group Analytic Psychotherapy, 34,* 531–537.

Gilat, I. (2004). *hashpaat hatipul hakvuzati al regashot, metach, ushlita shel horim leyeladimim lekuyot lemida ubli lekuiot lemida.* [The effect of group counseling on parents' feelings, stress and control regarding their LD and their NLD child]. PhD dissertation, Haifa University, Israel.

Ginnott, H. (1961). *Group psychotherapy with children.* New York: McGraw-Hill.

Gladding, S. T. (2000). Group work practice ideas: The use of the creative arts in groups. *The Group Worker, 28,* 7–9.

Gladding, S. T. (2003). *Group work: A counseling specialty* (4th ed.). Upper Saddle River, NJ: Prentice-Hall.

Gladding, S. T. (2005). *Counseling as an art: The creative arts in counseling* (3rd ed.). Alexandria, VA: American Counseling Association..

Goldstein, A. P., & McGinnis, E. (1997). *Skillstreaming the adolescent: New strategies and perspectives for teaching prosocial slills.* Champaign, IL: Research Press.

Goodenow, C., & Epsin, O. (1993). Identity choices in immigrant adolescent females. *Adolescence, 28,* 183–184.

Goodheart, C. D. (2004, July). *Symposium: Plenary – Best psychotherapy based on the integration of research evidence, clinical judgment and patient values.* A paper presented at the 112th annual convention of the American Psychological Association, Honolulu, Hawaii.

Goodman, C., & Pickens, J. (2001). Self-blame and self-esteem in college-aged children from divorced families. *Journal of Divorce and Remarriage, 34,* 119–135.

Greenberg, K. R. (2003). *Group counseling in K–12 schools.* New York: Allyn & Bacon.

Greenberg, L. S. (2002). *Emotion-focused therapy.* Washington, DC: American Psychological Association.

Grolnik, W. S., & Ryan, R. M. (1990). Self-perceptions, motivation, and adjustment in children with learning disabilities: A multiple group comparison study. *Journal of Learning Disabilities, 23,* 177–183.

Grunebaum, H., & Solomon, L. (1987). Peer relationship, self-esteem and the self. *International Journal of Group Psychotherapy, 37,* 425–513.

Guerian, M. (1997). *The wonder of boys.* New York: Tarther/Putman.

Guldner, C. A. (1999). Children of separation/divorce. In S. C. Schaffer (Ed.), *Short-term group psychotherapy for children* (pp. 23–57). Mahwah, NJ: Aronson.

Guttman, J., & Rosenberg, M. (2003). Emotional intimacy and children's adjustment: A comparison between single-parent divorced and intact families. *Educational Psychology, 23,* 457–472.

Gysber, N. C., & Henderson, P. (2000). *Developing and managing your school guidance program.* Alexandria, VA: American Counseling Association.

Hage, S. M., & Nosanow, M. (2000). Becoming stronger at broken places: A model for group work with young adults from divorced families. *Journal for Specialists in Group Work, 25,* 50–66.

Ham, B. D. (2003). The effect of divorce on academic achievement of high school seniors. *Journal of Divorce and Remarriage, 38,* 167–185.

Hifstede, G. (1997). *Cultures in organizations: Software of the mind.* New York: McGraw-Hill.

Hill, C. E. (1986). An overview of the Hill Counselor and Client Verbal Response Modes Category Systems. In L. S. Greenberg & W. M. Pinof (Eds.), *The psychotherapeutic process: A research handbook* (pp. 131–160). New York: Guilford.

Hill, C. E. (1990). Is individual therapy process really different from group therapy process? The jury is still out. *Counseling Psychologist, 18,* 126–130.

Hill, C. E. (2001). *Helping skills: The empirical foundation.* Washington, DC: American Psychological Association.

Hill, C. E. (2005). *Helping skills: Facilitating exploration, insight, and action* (2nd ed.). Washington, D.C.: American Psychological Association.

Hill, C. E., & Kellems, I. S. (2002). Development and use of the helping skills measure to assess client perceptions of the effects of training and helping skills in session. *Journal of Counseling Psychology, 49,* 264–272.

Hill, C. E., & O'Brien, K. M. (1999). *Helping skills: Facilitating exploration, insight, and action.* Washington, DC: American Psychological Association.

Hilton, J. M., & Desrochers, S. (2002). Children's behavior problems in single-parent and married-parent families: Development of a predictive model. *Journal of Divorce and Remarriage, 37,* 13–36.

Hoag, M. J., & Burlingame, G. M. (1997a). Child and adolescent group psychotherapy: A narrative review of effectiveness and the case for meta-analysis. *Journal of Child and Adolescent Group Psychotherapy, 7,* 51–68.

Hoag, M. J., & Burlingame, G. M. (1997b). Evaluating the effectiveness of child and adolescent group treatment: A meta-analytic review. *Journal of Clinical Child Psychotherapy, 26,* 234–246.

Hoffman, M. A. (1997). The contribution of empathy to justice and moral judgement. In N. Eisenberg & J. Strayer (Eds.), *Empathy and development* (pp. 47–80). New York: Cambridge University Press.

Holmes, S. E., & Kivlighan, D. M. (2000). Comparison of therapeutic factors in group and individual treatment processes. *Journal of Counseling Psychology, 47,* 478–484.

Holmes, G. R., & Sprenkle, L. T. (1996). Group interventions in school. *Journal of Child and Adolescent Group Therapy, 6,* 203–223.

Hurley, D. J. (1984). Resistance and work in adolescent groups. *Social Work with Groups, 7,* 71–81.

Huth-Blocks, A., Schettini, A., & Shebroe, V. (2001). Group play therapy for preschoolers exposed to domestic violence. *Journal of Child and Adolescent Group Therapy, 11,* 19–34.

Ivey, A. E., & Ivey, M. B. (1999). *International interviewing and counseling: Its development in a multicultural society* (4th ed.). Pacific Grove, CA: Brooks/Cole.

Ivey, A. E., Pederson, P. B., & Ivey, M. (2001). *Intentional group counseling: A microskills approach.* Belmont, CA: Brooks/Cole.

Jackson, M. L. (1997). Counseling Arab Americans. In C. C. Lee (Ed.), *Multicultural issues in counseling: New approaches to diversity* (2nd ed., pp. 333–352). Alexandria, VA: American Counseling Association.

Jackson, S. A. (2001). Using bibliotherapy with clients. *Journal of Individual Psychology, 57,* 289–297.

Jones, K. D. (2002). Group play therapy with sexually abused preschool children. *Journal for Specialists in Group Work, 27,* 377–389.

Johnson, J. E., Burlingame, G. M., Davies, D. R., & Olsen, J. (2002, August). *Clarifying therapeutic relationships in group psychotherapy.* Paper presented at the American Psychological Association Annual Conference, Chicago.

Kazdin, A. E. (2003). Problem-solving skills training and parent management training for conduct disorder. In A. E. Kazdin & J. R. Weisz (Eds.), *Evidence-based psychotherapies for children and adolescents* (pp. 241–262). New York: Guilford Press.

Kazdin, A. E., & Johnson, B. (1994). Advances in psychotherapy for children and adolescents: Interrelations of adjustment, development, and intervention. *Journal of School Psychology, 32,* 217–246.

Kazdin, A. E., & Weisz, J. R. (2003). Context and background of evidence-based psychotherapies for children and adolescents. In A. E. Kazdin & J. R. Weisz (Eds.), *Evidence-based psychotherapies for children and adolescents* (pp. 3–20). New York: Guilford.

Kelly, J. B., & Emery, R. E. (2003). Children's adjustment following divorce: Risk and resilience perspectives. *Family Relations: Interdisciplinary Journal of Applied Family Studies, 54,* 352–362.

Kendall, P. C., Aschenbrand, S. G., & Hudson, J. L. (2003). Child-focused treatment of anxiety. In A. E. Kazdin & J. R. Weisz (Eds.), *Evidence-based psychotherapies for children and adolescents* (pp. 81–100). New York: Guilford.

Keymeulen, J. (Producer). (1987). *MADI.* Germany: Jekino Films/Barr Films.

Kirschenbaum, H. (1979). *On becoming Carl Rogers.* New York: Delacorte.

Kirschke, W. (1998). *Strawberries beyond my window.* Victoria, CA: Eos Interactive Cards.

Kivlighan, D. M., & Holmes, S. E. (2004). The importance of therapeutic factors. In J. L. DeLucia-Waack, D. A. Gerrity, C. R. Kalodner, & M. T. Riva (Eds.). *Handbook of counseling and psychotherapy* (pp. 23–36). Thousand Oaks, CA: Sage.

Kivlighan, D. M., Multon, K. D., & Brossat, D. F. (1996). Helpful impacts in group counseling: Development of multidimensional rating system. *Journal of Counseling Psychology, 43,* 347–355.

Kivlighan, D. M., & Tarrant, J. M. (2001). Does group climate mediate the group leadership-member outcome relationship? A test of Yalom's hypotheses about leadership priorities. *Group Dynamics: Theory, Research, and Practice, 5,* 220–234.

Kottler, J. A. (1986). *On becoming a therapist.* San Francisco: Jossey-Bass.

Kottler, J. A. (1994). Working with difficult group members. *Journal for Specialists in Group Work, 19,* 3–10.

Kulic, K. R., Dagley, J. C., & Horne, A. M. (2001). Prevention groups with children and adolescents. *Journal for Specialists in Group Work, 26,* 211–218.

Kymissis, P. (1996). Developmental approach to socialization and group formation. In P. Kymissis & D. A. Halperin (Eds.), *Group therapy with children and adolescents* (pp. 21–33). Washington, DC: American Psychiatric Press.

Ladd, G. D., & Troop-Gordon, W. (2003). The role of chronic peer difficulties in the development of children's psychological adjustment problems. *Child Development, 74,* 1344–1367.

Lazarowitz, Y. (1991). *Like fish in water.* Tel Aviv, Israel: Modan (Hebrew).

Lee, C. C. (1997). *Multicultural issues in counseling: New approaches to diversity* (2nd ed.). Alexandria, VA: American Counseling Association.

Leichtentritt, J., & Shechtman, Z. (1998). Therapists, trainees, and child verbal response modes in child group therapy. *Group Dynamics: Theory, Research, and Practice, 2,* 36–47.

Leon, K. (2003). Risk and protective factors in young children's adjustment in parental divorce: A review of the research. Family relations: interdisciplinary. *Journal of Applied Psychology, 52,* 258–270.

Lewinsohn, P. M., Solomon, A., Seeley, J. R., & Zeiss, A. (2000). Clinical implications of "subthreshold" depressive symptom. *Journal of Abnormal Psychology, 109,* 345–351.

Lieberman, M. A., & Golant, M. (2002). Leader behavior as perceived by cancer patients in professionally directed support groups and outcomes. *Group Dynamics: Theory, Research, and Practice, 6,* 267–276.

Lomonaco, S., Scheidlinger, S., & Aronson, S. (2000). Five decades of children's group treatment: An overview. *Journal of Child and Adolescent Group Psychotherapy, 10,* 77–96.

MacKenzie, K. R. (1987). Therapeutic factors in group psychotherapy: A contemporary view. *Groups, 11*, 26–34.

MacKenzie, K. R. (1990). *Time limited group psychotherapy*. Washington, DC: American Psychiatric Press.

MacLeanan, B. W. (2000). The future of adolescent psychotherapy in groups in the new millennium. *Journal of Child and Adolescent Group Therapy, 10*, 169–179.

MacLennan, B. W., & Dies, K. R. (1992). *Group counseling and psychotherapy with adolescents* (2nd ed.). New York: Columbia University Press.

Mahalik, J. (1994). Development of the Client Resistance Scale. *Journal of Counseling Psychology, 41*, 58–68.

Malekoff, A. (2004). *Group work with adolescents: Principles and practice* (2nd ed). New York: Guilford.

Margalit, M., & Al-Yagon, M. (2002). The loneliness experience of children with learning disabilities. In M. L. Donahue & B. Y. L. Wong (Eds.), *The social dimensions of learning disabilities: Essays in honor of Tanis Bryan* (pp. 53–75). Mahwah, NJ: Lawrence Erlbaum Associates, Inc.

Margalit, M., & Efrati, M. (1996). Loneliness, coherence and companionship among children with learning disorders. *Educational Psychology, 16*, 69–79.

Marziali, E., Munroe-Blum, H., & McCleary, L. (1997). The contribution of group cohesion and group alliance to the outcomes of group psychotherapy. *International Journal of Group Psychotherapy, 47*, 475–497.

Masalla, S. (1999). Psychodynamic psychotherapy as applied in an Arab village clinic. *Clinical Psychology Review, 19,* 987–997.

McCallum, M., Piper, W. E., Ogrodniczuk, J. S., & Joyce, A. S. (2002). Early process and dropping out from short-term group therapy for complicated grief. *Group Dynamics: Theory, Research, and Practice, 6,* 243–254.

McClure, B. A., Miller, G. A., & Russo, T. J. (1992). Conflict within a children's group: Suggestions for facilitating its expression and resolution strategies. *The School Counselor, 35,* 268–272.

McKay, M. (1992). Anger groups. In M. McKay & K. Peleg (Eds), *Focal group psychotherapy* (pp. 163–194). Oakland, CA: New Harbinger.

McKendree-Smith, N. L., Floyd, M., & Scogin, F. R. (2003). Self-administered treatments for depression: A review. *Journal of Clinical Psychology, 59*, 275–288.

McNally, R. J. (2003). *Remembering trauma*. Cambridge, MA: Harvard University Press.

Morganett, R. S. (1990). *Skills for living: Group counseling activities for young adolescents*. Champion, IL: Research Press.

Morran, K. D., Stockton, R., & Whittingham, M. H. (2004). Effective leader interventions for counseling and psychotherapy groups. In J. L. DeLucia-Waack, D. A. Gerrity, C. R. Kalodner, & M. T. Riva (Eds.), *Handbook of group counseling and psychotherapy* (pp. 91–103). Thousand Oaks, CA: Sage.

Myers, D. G. (2000). The funds, friends, and faith of happy people. *American Psychologist, 55*, 56–67.

Nichols-Goldstein, N. (2001). The essence of effective leadership with adolescent groups: Regression in the service of the ego. *Journal of Child and Adolescent Group Psychotherapy, 11*, 13–18.

Norcross, J. C., Beutler, L. E., & Levant, R. F. (2006). *Evidence-based practices in mental health*. Washington, DC: American Psychological Association.

Norris-Shortle, C., Parks, O. L., Walden, C., & Hayman-Hamilton, J. (1999). A photographic body life book. *Journal of Family Psychotherapy, 10*, 69–73.

Nuttman-Schwartz, O., Karniel-Lauer, E., & Offir, S. (2000). Group therapy with terror injured persons in Israel: Societal impediments to successful working through. *Groups, 26,* 49–59.

Ogrodniczuk, J. S., & Piper, W. E. (2003). The effect of group climate on outcome in two forms of short-term group therapy. *Group Dynamics: Theory, Research, and Practice, 7,* 64–76.

OH (2005). Cards developed by Ely Ramon and Joan Lawrence. Victoria, Australia: OH Publishing. Retrieved April 12, 2006 from www.oh=cards.com

Olweus, D. (2001). *Olweus's core program against bullying and antisocial behavior: A teacher handbook.* Bergen, Norway: Research Center for Health Promotion, University of Bergen.

Oppawsky, J. (2000). Parental bickering, screaming and fighting: Etiology of the most negative effects of divorce on children from the view of the children. *Journal of Divorce and Remarriage, 32,* 141–147.

O'Rourke, K., & Worzbyt, J. C. (1996). *Support groups for children.* Bristol, PA: Accelerated Development.

Ozawa, M. N., & Yoom, H. S. (2003). Economic impact of marital disruption on children. *Children and Youth Service Review, 25,* 611–632.

Page, R. C., Weiss, J. F., & Lietaer, G. (2001). Humanistic group psychotherapy. In D. J. Cain & J. Seeman (Eds.), *Humanistic psychotherapies: Handbook of research and practice* (pp. 339–368). Washington, DC: American Psychological Association.

Pederson, P. (2000). *A handbook for developing multicultural awareness* (3rd ed.). Alexandria, VA: American Counseling Association.

Pedro-Caroll, J. L., & Cowen, E. L. (1985). The children of divorce intervention program: An investigation of the efficacy of a school-based prevention program. *Journal of Consulting and Clinical Psychology, 53,* 603–611.

Pennebaker, J. W., & Seagal, J. D. (1999). Forming a story: The health benefits of narrative. *Journal of Clinical Psychology, 55,* 1243–1254.

Petrocelli, J. V. (2002). Effectiveness of group cognitive-behavioral therapy for general symptomatology: A meta-analysis. *Journal for Specialists in Group Work, 27,* 95–115.

Pettit, G. S., Laird, R. D., Dodge, K. A., Bates, J., & Criss, M. M. (2001). Antecedents and behavior–problem outcomes of parental monitoring and psychological control in early adolescents. *Child Development, 72,* 583–598.

Piaget, J. (1986). *The grasp of consciousness: Action and concept in young children.* Cambridge, MA: Harvard University Press.

Piper, W. E., Joyce, A. S., McCallum, M., Azim, H. E., & Ogrodniczuk, J. S. (2002). *Interpretive and supportive psychotherapies.* Washington, DC: American Psychological Association.

Pollack, K. M. (1998). *Real boys.* New York: Penguin

Pollack, K. M., & Kymissis, P. (2001). The future of adolescent group psychotherapy. *Journal of Child and Adolescent Group Therapy, 11,* 3–12.

Price, L. A., Johnson, J. M., & Evelo, S. (1994). When academic assistance is not enough: Addressing the mental health issue of adolescents and adults with learning disabilities. *Journal of Learning Disabilities, 27,* 82–90.

Prochaska, J. O. (1999). How do people change, and how can we change to help many more people? In M. A. Hubble, B. L. Duncan, & S. D. Miller (Eds.), *The heart and soul of change: What works in therapy* (pp. 227–257). Washington, DC: American Psychological Association.

Prout, S. M., & Prout, T. (1998). A meta-analysis of school-based studies of psychotherapy. *Journal of School Psychology, 24,* 285–292.

Redle, F. (1944). Diagnostic group work. *American Journal of Orthopsychiatry, 14,* 53–67.

Reis, H. T., & Shaver, P. (1988). Intimacy and interpersonal processes. In S. Duck, D. F. Hay, S. E. Hobfoll, W. Incks, & B. Montgomery (Eds.), *Handbook of personal relationships: Theory, research, and interventions* (pp. 367–389). New York: Wiley.

Richie, M., & Huss, S. (2000). Recruitment and screening of minors for group counseling. *Journal for Specialists in Group Work, 25,* 146–156.

Riva, M. T., & Haub, A. L. (2004). Group counseling in the schools. In J. L. DeLucia-Waack, D. A. Gerrity, C. R. Kalodner, & M. T. Riva (Eds.), *Handbook of group counseling and psychotherapy* (pp. 309–321). Thousand Oaks, CA: Sage.

Rivera, E. T., Garrett, M. T., & Brown-Crutchfield, L. (2004). Multicultural interventions in groups: The use of indigenous methods. In J. Delucia-Waack, D. Gerrity, C. R. Kalodner, & M. T. Riva (Eds.), *Handbook of group counseling and psychotherapy* (pp. 295–305). Thousand Oaks, CA: Sage.

Robbins, R. N. (2003). Developing cohesion in court-mandate group treatment of male spouse abusers. *International Journal of Group Psychotherapy, 53,* 261–285.

Rogers, C. (1980). *A way of being.* Boston: Houghton Mifflin.

Rose, S. R. (1998). *Group work with children and adolescents.* Thousand Oaks, CA: Sage.

Roth, B. E. (2002). Some diagnostic observations of post-September 11, 2001 crisis groups. *Groups, 26,* 155–161.

Sagi, I. (2000). *hashvaa shel kvuzot hinuc vkvuzot yeutz avur yeladim lemishpachot grushot.* [A comparison of an educational versus a counseling group for children of divorce]. Unpublished manuscript, University of Haifa, Israel.

Sason, V., & Razin, N. (2003). *nytuach tahalic kvutzati shel kvutzat mitbagrot.* [An analysis of the group process of one adolescent group of girls]. Unpublished manuscript, University of Haifa, Israel.

Savaya, R. (1998). The under-use of psychological services by Israeli Arabs: An examination of the roles of negative attitudes and the use of alternative sources of help. *International Social Work, 41,* 195–209.

Schaffer, C. E. (1999). *Short-term psychotherapy groups for children.* Northvale, NJ: Aronson.

Scheidlinger, S., & Kahn, G. B. (2005). In the aftermath of September 11: Group interventions with traumatized children revisited. *International Journal of Group Psychotherapy, 55,* 335–354.

Schiffer, M. (1969). *The therapeutic play group.* New York: Grume & Stratton.

Schneider, B. H. (1992). Didactic methods for enhancing children's peer relations: A quantitative review. *Clinical Psychology Review, 12,* 363–382.

Seligman, M. E., & Csikszentmihalyi, M. (2000). Positive psychology. *American Psychologist, 55,* 5–14.

Sharabany, R. (1994). Intimate friendship scale: Conceptual underpinnings, psychometric properties and construct validity. *Journal of Social and Personal Relationships, 11,* 449–469.

Shechtman, Z. (1991). Small group therapy and preadolescence same-sex friendship. *International Journal of Group Psychotherapy, 41,* 227–243.

Shechtman, Z. (1992). A group assessment procedure as a predictor of on-the-job teacher performance. *The Journal of Applied Psychology, 77,* 383–387.

Shechtman, Z. (1993). Group psychotherapy for the enhancement of intimate friendship and self-esteem among troubled elementary school children. *Journal of Social and Personal Relationships, 10,* 483–494.

Shechtman, Z. (1994). The effect of group psychotherapy on close same-gender friendships among boys and girls. *Sex Roles: A Research Journal, 30,* 829–834.

Shechtman, Z. (1999). Bibliotherapy: An indirect approach to treatment of childhood aggression. *Child Psychiatry and Human Development, 30,* 39–53.

Shechtman, Z. (2000). An innovative intervention for treatment of child and adolescent aggression: An outcome study. *Psychology in the Schools, 37,* 157–167.

Shechtman, Z. (2001). Prevention groups for angry and aggressive children. *Journal for Specialists in Group Work, 26,* 228–236.

Shechtman, Z. (2003). Therapeutic factors and outcomes in group and individual therapy of aggressive boys. *Group Dynamics: Theory, Research, and Practice, 7,* 225–237.

Shechtman, Z. (2004a). Client behavior and therapist helping skills in individual and group treatment of aggressive boys. *Journal of Counseling Psychology, 51,* 463–472.

Shechtman, Z. (2004b). The relation of client behavior and therapist helping skills to reduced aggression of boys in individual and group treatment. *International Journal of Group Psychotherapy, 54,* 435–454.

Shechtman, Z. (2006). The contribution of bibliotherapy to the treatment of aggressive boys. *Psychotherapy Research.*

Shechtman, Z., & Bar-El, O. (1994). Group guidance and group counseling to foster self-concept and social status in adolescence. *Journal for Specialists in Group Work, 19,* 188–197.

Shechtman, Z., Bar-El, O., & Hadar, E. (1997). Therapeutic factors in counseling and psycho-educational groups for adolescents: A comparison. *The Journal for Specialists in Group Work, 22,* 203–213.

Shechtman, Z., & Ben-David, M. (1999). Individual and group psychotherapy of childhood aggression: A comparison of outcomes and process. *Group Dynamics: Theory, Research, and Practice, 3,* 263–274.

Shechtman, Z., & Birani-Nasaraladin, D. (2006). Treating mothers of aggressive children: A research study. *International Journal of Group Psychotherapy, 56,* 93–112.

Shechtman, Z., & Dvir, V. (2006). Attachment style as a predictor of children's behavior in group psychotherapy. *Group Dynamics: Theory, Research and Practice, 10,* 29–42.

Shechtman, Z., Friedman, Y., Kashti, Y., & Sharabany, R. (2002). Group counseling to enhance adolescents' close friendships. *International Journal of Group Psychotherapy, 52,* 537–553.

Shectman, Z., & Gat, Y. (2006). *Predicting therapist behavior from one's own behavior as client and participant in a group.* (Unpublished Manuscript).

Shechtman, Z., & Gilat, I. (2005). The effect of group counseling on parents of a child with learning disabilities (LD) as compared with an NLD sibling. *Group Dynamics: Theory, Research, and Practice, 9,* 275–286.

Shechtman, Z., Gilat, I., Fos, L., & Flasher, A. (1996). Brief group therapy with low-achieving elementary school children. *Journal of Counseling Psychology, 43,* 376–382.

Shechtman, Z., & Gluk, O. (2005). Therapeutic factors in group psychotherapy with children. *Group Dynamics: Theory, Research, and Practice, 9,* 127–134.

Shechtman, Z., Haddad, L. & Nechas, L. (2000). *kavana-lehasifa atzmit bekvutza: hasvaa shel aravim vyehudim metbagrim.* [Intentions to self-disclose in a counseling group: A comparison of Arab and Jewish adolescents in Israel]. *Hayeuz Hahinuchi, 16,* 76–86.

Shechtman, Z., & Halevi, H. (2006). *Functioning in the group: Comparing Arab and Jewish trainees in a counseling program, 10.*

Shechtman, Z., Halevi, H., & Avraham, A. (2005). *A comparison of group processes for two populations: Children of divorce and children of intact families.* Unpublished manuscript, University of Haifa, Israel.

Shechtman, Z., Hiradin, A., & Zina, S. (2003). The impact of culture on group behavior: A comparison of three ethnic groups. *Journal of Counseling & Development, 81,* 208–216.

Shechtman, Z., & Nachshol, R. (1996). A school-based intervention to reduce aggressive behavior in maladjusted adolescents. *Journal of Applied Developmental Psychology, 17,* 535–552.

Shechtman, Z., & Pastor, R. (2005). Cognitive-behavioral and humanistic group treatment for children with learning disabilities: A comparison of outcomes and process. *Journal of Counseling Psychology, 52,* 322–336.

Shechtman, Z., & Pearl-Dekel, O. (2000). A comparison of therapeutic factors in two group treatment modalities: Verbal and art therapy. *Journal for Specialists in Group Work, 25,* 288–304.

Shechtman, Z., & Ribko, J. (2004). Attachment style and initial self-disclosure as predictors of group functioning. *Group Dynamics: Theory, Practice, and Research, 8,* 207–220.

Shechtman, Z., & Sender, E. (2006). *Process and outcomes in groups with LD students.* Unpublished manuscript, University of Haifa, Israel.

Shechtman, Z., & Vurembrand, N. (1996). Does self-disclosure in friendship increase following group counseling/therapy? A different case for boys and girls. *Sex Roles, 35,* 123–130.

Shechtman, Z., Vurembrand, N., & Hertz-Lazarowitz, R. (1994). A dyadic and gender-specific analysis of close friendships of preadolescents receiving group psychotherapy. *Journal of Social and Personal Relationships, 11,* 443–448.

Shechtman, Z., Vurembrand, N., & Malajek, N. (1993). Development of self-disclosure in a counseling and psychotherapy group for children. *Journal for Specialists in Group Work, 18,* 189–199.

Shechtman, Z., & Yanuv, H. (2001). Interpretive interventions: Feedback, confrontation, and interpretation. *Group Dynamics: Theory, Research, and Practice, 5,* 124–135.

Shechtman, Z., & Zaghon, I. (2004). PhotoTherapy to enhance self-disclosure and client-therapist alliance in an intake interview with Ethiopian immigrants to Israel. *Psychotherapy Research, 14,* 367–377.

Shure, M. (1992). *I can problem solve (ICPS): An interpersonal cognitive problem solving program for children.* Champaign, IL: Research Press.

Skitka, L. J., & Frazier, M. (1995). Ameliorating the effects of parental divorce: Do small group interventions work? *Journal of Divorce and Remarriage, 24,* 159–178.

Slavson, S. R. (1945/1986). Differential methods of group therapy in relation to age levels. In A. E. Reister & I. A. Kraft (Eds.), *Child group psychotherapy: Future tense* (pp. 9–28). Madison, WI: International Universities Press.

Slavson, S. R. (1943). *An introduction to group therapy.* New York: Grune & Stratton.

Smead, R. (1995). *Skills and techniques for group work with children and adolescents.* Champaign, IL: Research Press.

Smead-Morganett, R. (1994). *Skills for living: Group counseling activities for elementary students.* Champaign, IL: Research Press.

Smokowski, P. R., Rose, S. D., & Bacallo, M. L. (2001). Damaging experiences in therapeutic groups: How vulnerable consumers become group casualties. *Small Group Behavior, 32,* 223–251.

Snunit, M. (1999). *The soul bird.* New York: Hyperion.

Spiegel, D., & Classen, C. (2000). *Group therapy for cancer patients.* New York: Basic Books.

Stamko, C. A., & Taub, D. J. (2002). A counseling group for children of cancer patients. *Journal for Specialists in Group Work, 27,* 43–58.

Stockton, R., Morran, D. K., & Nitza, A. G. (2000). Processing group events: A conceptual map for leaders. *Journal for Specialists in Group Work, 25,* 343–355.

Stockton, R., Rohde, R. I., & Haughey, J. (1992). The effects of structured group exercises on cohesion, engagement, avoidance, and conflict. *Small Group Research, 23,* 1555–1568.

Sue, D. W., & Sue, D. (2003). *Counseling the culturally different: Theory and practice* (4th ed.). New York: Wiley-Interscience.

Sullivan, H. S. (1953). *The interpersonal theory of psychiatry.* New York: Norton.

Thompson, C. L., & Rudolph, L. B. (2000). *Counseling children* (5th ed.). Stamford, CT: Brooks/Cole.

Tolan, P. H. & Dodge, K. A. (2005). Children's mental health as a primary care and concern. *American Psychologist, 60,* 601–614.

Trotzer, J. P. (2004). Conducting a group: Guidelines for choosing and using activities. In J. L. DeLucia-Waack, D. A. Gerrity, C. R. Kalodner, & M. T. Riva (Eds.), *Handbook of group counseling and psychotherapy* (pp. 76–90). Thousand Oaks, CA: Sage.

Tschuschkle, V., & Dies, R. R. (1994). Intensive analysis of therapeutic factors and outcomes in long-term inpatient groups. *International Journal of Group Psychotherapy, 44*, 185–208.

Tuckman, B. W. (1965). Developmental sequences in small groups. *Psychological Bulletin, 63*, 384–399.

U.S. Bureau of the Census (1999). *Statistical abstract of the United States, 1999* (19th ed.). Washington, DC: U. S. Government Printing Office.

Van Dam-Baggen, R., & Kraaimaat, F. (2000). Group social skills training or cognitive group therapy as the clinical treatment of choice for generalized social phobia. *Journal of Anxiety Disorders, 14*, 437–451. Developmental sequences in small groups.

Vernberg, E. M. (2002). Intervention approaches following disasters. In A. M. LaGreca, W. K. Silverman, E. M. Vernberg, & M. C. Roberts (Eds.), *Helping children cope with disasters and terrorism* (pp. 55–72). Washington, D.C. : American Psychological Association.

Vondracek, I. V., & Vondracek, W. V. (1971). The manipulation and measurement of self-disclosure in preadolescence. *Merrill-Palmer Quarterly, 17*, 51–57.

Walker, H. (1976). *Walker problem identification checklist*. Los Angeles, CA: Western Psychological Services.

Wallerstein, J. S. (1983). Children of divorce: The psychological tasks of the child. *American Journal of Orthopsychiatry, 53*, 230–243.

Wallerstein, J. S., & Blakeslee, S. (1989). *Second chances: Men, women and children a decade after divorce*. New York: Ticknor & Fields.

Wallerstein, J. S., & Lewis, J. (1998). The long-term impact of divorce on children. *Family and Conciliation Court Review, 36*, 368–383.

Wallerstein, J. S., & Lewis, J. M. (2004). The unexpected legacy of divorce: Report of a 25-year study. *Psychoanalytic Psychology, 21*, 353–370.

Ward, D. E., & Litchy, M. (2004). The effective use of the processing in groups. In J. L. DeLucia-Waack, D. A. Gerrity, C. R. Kalodner, & M. T. Riva (Eds.), *Handbook of counseling and psychotherapy* (pp. 104–119). Thousand Oaks, CA: Sage.

Webb, N. B. (2005). Groups for children traumatically bereaved by the attack of September 11, 2001. *International Journal of Group Psychotherapy, 55*, 355–374.

Weiser, J. (1993). *PhotoTherapy techniques: Exploring the secrets of personal snapshots and family albums* ancisco: Jossey-Bass.

Weisz, J. R., Weiss, B., Alicke, M. D., & Kloz, M. L. (1987). Effectiveness of psychotherapy with children and adolescents: A meta-analysis for clinicians. *Journal of Consulting and Clinical Psychology, 55*, 542–549.

Whiston, S. C., & Sexton, T. L. (1998). A review of school counseling outcomes research: Implications for practice. *Journal of Counseling & Development, 76*, 412–426.

White, J. R. (2000). Introduction. In J. R. White & A. S. Freeman (Eds.), *Cognitive-behavioral group therapy for special problems and populations* (pp. 3–25). Washington, DC: American Psychological Association.

Wiener, J. (2002). Friendship and social adjustment of children with learning disabilities. In M. Donahue & B. Y. L. Wong (Eds.), *The social dimensions of learning disabilities: Essays in honor of Tanis Bryan* (pp. 93–114). Mahwah, NJ: Lawrence Erlbaum Associates, Inc.

Wiser, S., & Goldfried, M. R. (1998). Therapist interventions and client emotional experiencing in expert psychodynamic-interpersonal and cognitive-behavioral therapies. *Journal of Consulting and Clinical Psychology, 66*, 634–640.

World Health Organization. (2001). *The world health report, 2001—Mental health: New understanding, New hope*. Geneva, Switzerland: Author.

Yalom, I. D. (1985). *The theory and practice of group psychotherapy* (3rd ed.). New York: Basic Books.

Yalom, I. D. (1995). *The theory and practice of group psychotherapy* (4th ed.). New York: Basic Books.

Yalom, I. D. (1998). *The Yalom reader*. New York: Basic Books.

Yalom, I. D., & Leszcz, M. (2005). *The theory and practice of group psychotherapy* (5th ed.). New York: Basic Books.

Yasutake, D., & Bryan, T. (1995). The influence of affect on the achievement and behavior of students with learning disabilities. *Journal of Learning Disabilities, 28*, 329–334.

Zabatany, L., McDougall, P., & Hymel, S. (2000). Gender-differentiated experiences in peer culture: Links to intimacy in preadolescence. *Social Development, 9,* 62–79.

Zimmerman, B. J. (1995). Self-efficacy and educational development. In A. Bandura (Ed.), *Self-efficacy in changing societies* (pp. 202–231). New York: Cambridge University Press.

Author Index

Subject Index